OS-9 Insights

An Advanced Programmers Guide to OS-9

Second Edition

OS-9 Insights

An Advanced Programmers Guide to OS-9

Second Edition

By

Peter C. Dibble

MICROWARE SYSTEMS CORPORATION

Des Moines

OS-9 Insights An Advanced Programmers Guide to OS-9 Second Edition

Copyright © 1992 by Microware.

All Rights Reserved.

Printed in the United States of America.

No part of the publication may be reproduced, stored in retrieval system, or transmitted in any form or by any means, electronic, mechanical, photocopying, recording, or otherwise, without the prior permission of the publisher.

Microware Systems Corporation, 1900 NW 114th Street,
Des Moines, Iowa 50325–7077

This book reflects Version 2.4 of OS-9/68000. The information contained herein is believed to be accurate as of the date of publication; however, Microware will not be liable for any damages, including indirect or consequential, from use of the OS-9 operating system, Microware-provided software or reliance on the accuracy of this documentation. The information contained herein is subject to change without notice.

Publication Editor, and Author's Photo & Biography: David F. Davis
Technical Editors: Eileen Beck, Ellen Grant, and Debbie Baier
Cover Design: Tom West

OS-9 and Microware are registered trademarks of
Microware Systems Corporation.
OS-9/68000 is a trademark of Microware
UNIX is a trademark of AT&T Bell Laboratories.
TEX is a trademark of the American Mathematical Society.
HP and Laserjet Series II are trademarks of Hewlett Packard.
CP/M is a registered trademark of Digital Research Incorporated.
IBM is a registered trademark of International Business Machines Corporation.
PC-DOS is a trademark of International Business Machines Corporation.
GMX is a trademark of GMX Inc.
Motorola is a registered trademark of Motorola, Incorporated.
ProDrive is a trademark of Quantum Corporation.
All other names and product names are trademarks or registered trademarks of their respective holders.

Library of Congress Cataloging-in-Publication Data

Dibble, Peter.
    OS-9 insights : an advanced programmers guide to OS-9 / Peter C.
  Dibble. – 2nd ed.
      p.   cm.
    Includes index.
    ISBN 0–918035–03–1 :
    1. Operating systems (Computers)   2. OS-9 (Computer file)
I. Title.
QA76.76.063D53   1992
005.4'3–dc20   92–3488
                                                        CIP

ISBN: 0–918035–03–1

MSC Product Code INS 68 SE 68 MO

Foreword

The basis of this book is the latter part of *The Complete Rainbow Guide to OS-9* which Dale Puckett and I wrote for Falsoft several years ago. With the encouragement of Ken Kaplan, and the willing assistance of a large fraction of the Microware technical staff, I have brought this book near to the moving target of OS-9/68000.

First thanks go to Don Williams. He gave me my start as a writer for *68' Micro Journal.* Dale Puckett asked me to coauthor *The Complete Rainbow Guide to OS-9* and Lonnie Falk published the resulting book. It is with Lonnie's generous permission that I have used several sections of the Complete Guide that carry over to OS-9/68000.

At Microware, Ken Kaplan supplied encouragement (sometimes gentle prodding) and friendship. Warren Brown, Larry Crane, and Ken Kaplan read drafts and made extensive comments. The Microware technical writing group read the second edition carefully and made useful comments. Warren also spent hours worrying over device drivers with me. Robert Doggett and Larry Crane helped with file managers and general OS-9 internals.

Several people scattered around the world offered helpful comments about the first edition of this book. I appreciate this input very much and implemented as many as possible of the improvements they suggested.

My family and friends showed remarkable tolerance while I struggled with this.

OS-9 is both the subject and the source of this book. I wrote the book on my GMX Micro-20 using MicroEmacs (written largely by Daniel M. Lawrence) with some early editing by DynaStar. The typesetting was by Leslie Lamport's LaTeX macro package and the Web2C implementation (by Tomas Rokicki) of Donald Knuth's typesetting program, TeX. The draft output was on an HP Laserjet II using Tomas Rokicki's ***dvips*** dvi-to-PostScript filter also running under OS-9 and Adobe's PostScript cartridge running on the Laserjet. Final output was from a PostScript typesetter.

Contents

1	Introduction		1
2	**Modules**		**5**
	2.1	How Modules Are Identified	6
	2.2	The Header Check	6
	2.3	The Module CRC Bytes	7
	2.4	How the Module CRC Works	7
		2.4.1 CRC Algorithm in C	9
	2.5	Circumventing CRC Protection	10
	2.6	Module Types	10
	2.7	Module Security	12
	2.8	The Module Attribute Byte	13
		2.8.1 Reentrant Modules	13
	2.9	The Module Revision Number	14
	2.10	The Module Edition Number	14
	2.11	The Module Usage Field	15
	2.12	The Debugging Symbol Table	15
	2.13	The Module Directory	15
		2.13.1 Unlink Protection	16
	2.14	How Modules Are Generated	16
	2.15	SVC's that Deal with Modules	18
3	**Memory**		**23**
	3.1	Reentrant Modules	23
	3.2	Memory Fragmentation	24
	3.3	Careful Use of Memory	25
	3.4	Dynamic Memory Allocation	26

4 OS-9 Memory Management — 29
- 4.1 The Theoretical Base — 29
  - 4.1.1 Fixed Partitioned Memory — 29
  - 4.1.2 Dynamic Allocation — 30
  - 4.1.3 First-Fit Allocation — 31
  - 4.1.4 Best-Fit Allocation — 31
- 4.2 OS-9 Memory Management — 32
- 4.3 Memory Fragmentation — 35
- 4.4 Memory Protection — 38
- 4.5 Memory Management Service Requests — 38

5 Memory Management Internals — 41
- 5.1 The Process Memory Table — 41
- 5.2 Fragment Lists — 43
- 5.3 Colored Memory — 45
  - 5.3.1 Colored Memory and Fragment Lists — 47
  - 5.3.2 Case Studies — 48

6 Processes — 53
- 6.1 Starting Processes From the Shell — 53
- 6.2 Family Relationships — 54
- 6.3 A Program Named Alias — 54
- 6.4 Chaining New Processes — 55
- 6.5 Tuning Your Operation — 56
  - 6.5.1 Summary — 57

7 Signals — 59
- 7.1 An Undocumented Feature — 62
- 7.2 Masking Signals — 63
  - 7.2.1 Servicing Signals in the Mainline — 65
  - 7.2.2 Servicing Signals in the Intercept Routine — 68
  - 7.2.3 Async Safety — 72
  - 7.2.4 Horrible Example — 74
- 7.3 Broadcast — 75
- 7.4 Queued Signals — 76
  - 7.4.1 Performance — 78
  - 7.4.2 Fast RTE — 80
- 7.5 Special Signals — 82
  - 7.5.1 Wakeup — 82

CONTENTS

	7.5.2	Kill	84
	7.5.3	I/O Deadly Signals	84
7.6	Utility Programs		84

8 Alarms — 87
- 8.1 User-State Alarms ... 87
  - 8.1.1 Alarms as Guards ... 87
  - 8.1.2 Alarms as Tickers for Threads ... 93
  - 8.1.3 Alarms as Timers ... 96
- 8.2 System State Alarms ... 96
  - 8.2.1 Drivers ... 97
  - 8.2.2 File Managers ... 97
  - 8.2.3 System Calls ... 99
  - 8.2.4 System Processes ... 104
- 8.3 Programs ... 110

9 Process Scheduling — 115
- 9.1 A Low-Level View ... 115
- 9.2 Aging ... 116
- 9.3 Adjustments ... 117
- 9.4 Preemption ... 120
- 9.5 Tuning for Real-Time Applications ... 120

10 Events — 123
- 10.1 A Simple Analogue ... 123
- 10.2 Some Event-Handling Utilities ... 126
- 10.3 A Semaphore ... 129
  - 10.3.1 Fast Semaphores ... 134
- 10.4 Events as Selectors ... 139

11 Traps — 143
- 11.1 Linking to a Trap Handler ... 144
- 11.2 Writing a Trap Handler ... 149

12 OS-9 I/O — 159
- 12.1 The Unified File System ... 159
- 12.2 Paths ... 160
- 12.3 Path Options ... 160
- 12.4 Device Attributes ... 161

    12.5   Reading and Writing 161
    12.6   The Keyboard Signals 162
    12.7   Signal on Data Ready 163
    12.8   Modem Control Commands 164
    12.9   Adjusting the size of RBF Files 164
    12.10 Record Locking 165

13 The I/O Manager   169
    13.1   Attach/Detach 170
    13.2   Duping Paths 170

14 Pipes   173
    14.1   Unnamed Pipes 173
    14.2   Shell-Style Pipes 176
    14.3   Named Pipes 179

15 Interrupts   183
    15.1   Polling 184
    15.2   The Alternative 185
    15.3   Multitasking and the Clock 185
    15.4   The Polling Table 185
    15.5   Masking Interrupts 186

16 The RBF Disk Format   189
    16.1   The Identification Sector 190
    16.2   The Allocation Map 191
    16.3   The Root Directory 191
    16.4   The File Descriptor 192
    16.5   Raw Disks 193
    16.6   Disk Drive Incompatibilities 193
          16.6.1   The Universal Disk Format 194
          16.6.2   Foreign Disk Formats 194

17 Managing Disks   197
    17.1   Using Space Efficiently 197
    17.2   Disk Access Speed 198
          17.2.1   FDList 199
    17.3   Multi-Sector I/O 199
    17.4   Direct I/O 200

17.5	Sector Size	202
17.6	Allocation Units	203
	17.6.1 A Case Study	204
17.7	Disk Layout	206
17.8	Disk Caching	206
17.9	Repairing Damage	207
	17.9.1 Recover	208
17.10	Using Brute Force	210
17.11	How to Ignore a Bad Sector	211
17.12	Programs	211
	17.12.1 FDList	211
	17.12.2 DiskSpace	216
	17.12.3 Scavenge	219
	17.12.4 ForceCopy	222

18 Customizing OS-9 231
18.1 The Init Module 231
18.2 SysGo 231
18.3 The Customization Modules 232

19 Building a Device Descriptor 235
19.1 How OS-9 Uses the Descriptor 236
    19.1.1 The /dd Device 236
19.2 Managing Device Descriptors 237
19.3 Making and Modifying Descriptors 237
    19.3.1 Xmode 238
    19.3.2 Debug 239
    19.3.3 Module Permissions 240
    19.3.4 Moded 240
19.4 Building a Descriptor From Scratch 241
19.5 The Contents of a Device Descriptor 241
    19.5.1 SCF Initialization Table 243
    19.5.2 RBF Initialization Table 246
    19.5.3 RAM Disks 253

20 File Managers 255
20.1 Possibilities for New File Managers 256
20.2 Writing a File Manager 257

21 A Simple File Manager — 259
- 21.1 Using the C Language 259
- 21.2 A CStart for a File Manager 260
- 21.3 The Dummy File Manager 267
  - 21.3.1 Preprocessor Includes and Defines 267
  - 21.3.2 Open 268
  - 21.3.3 Seek 269
  - 21.3.4 Read 270
  - 21.3.5 Close 271
  - 21.3.6 MakDir 272
  - 21.3.7 Create 272
  - 21.3.8 ChdDir 272
  - 21.3.9 Delete 273
  - 21.3.10 Write 273
  - 21.3.11 ReadLn and WriteLn 274
  - 21.3.12 GetStat and SetStat 274
  - 21.3.13 Support Functions 275
  - 21.3.14 The Format.h Header File 277
  - 21.3.15 The Special PathDesc.h Header File 280

22 Adding a New Device Driver — 283
- 22.1 Why Create New Drivers? 284

23 Sample SCF Device Driver — 287
- 23.1 Module Header 287
- 23.2 Definitions 288
- 23.3 Static Storage 291
- 23.4 The Entry Vector Table 293
- 23.5 Init Routine 293
- 23.6 Read Routine 303
- 23.7 Sleep 305
- 23.8 Write Routine 306
- 23.9 GetStat Routine 308
- 23.10 PutStat Routine 310
- 23.11 Terminate Routine 315
- 23.12 Interrupt Handler 316

CONTENTS

24 An RBF Device Driver — **325**
  24.1 Hardware Overview 325
      24.1.1 The Quantum Disk Drive 327
  24.2 The Driver's Main Entries 329
      24.2.1 Init 329
      24.2.2 Term 331
      24.2.3 Read 332
      24.2.4 Write 336
      24.2.5 GetStat and PutStat 339
      24.2.6 PutStat 341
      24.2.7 IRQ Service 344
  24.3 Drive Management 345
      24.3.1 Read Sector 0 345
      24.3.2 Initialize a Drive 348
      24.3.3 Set Sector Size 352
  24.4 Miscellaneous 357
  24.5 SCSI Management 359
      24.5.1 Error Handling 365
  24.6 Direct Command Interface 370
  24.7 Assembly Language Glue 373
  24.8 Header Files 383
      24.8.1 drvr.h 383
      24.8.2 lowlevel.h 386
      24.8.3 dcmd.h 386
  24.9 Makefile 388
  24.10 Patchmod 389
  24.11 QuantumCache 390

25 The Philosophy of OS-9 — **409**
  25.1 Weaknesses 410
  25.2 Strengths 411
  25.3 Application of this Philosophy to User Code 411

A Recent History — **413**
  A.1 Version 1.2 413
  A.2 Version 2.0 413
  A.3 Version 2.1 414
  A.4 Version 2.2 415
  A.5 Version 2.3 415

	A.6 Version 2.4	416
B	**Technical Appendix**	**417**
	B.1 The Arithmetic of XOR	417
	B.2 Bootlist	418
C	**Building a File Manager**	**423**
	C.1 Interface to the C File Manager	424
	C.1.1 fmmain.a	424
	C.1.2 Makefile	431
	C.2 Main Entry Points	433
	C.2.1 Read.c	433
	C.2.2 ReadLn.c	435
	C.2.3 Write.c	437
	C.2.4 WriteLn.c	441
	C.2.5 MsOpen.c	443
	C.2.6 Create.c	449
	C.2.7 MakDir.c	450
	C.2.8 Close.c	452
	C.2.9 Delete.c	453
	C.2.10 Msfm.c	454
	C.3 Service Functions	459
	C.3.1 Dir	459
	C.3.2 Utils	467
	C.3.3 ReadSector	469
	C.3.4 WriteSector	471
	C.4 Artifacts of PC-DOS	472
	C.4.1 Drivetable.c	473
	C.4.2 GetFD.c	475
	C.4.3 TransDir	476
	C.4.4 FATSupport	480
	C.5 Special Header Files	489
	C.5.1 Format	489
	C.5.2 PathDesc	493
	C.6 The Device Descriptor	495
D	**Sample RBF Device Driver**	**499**
	D.1 Module Header	499
	D.2 Static Storage	500

CONTENTS

D.3 Definitions 501
D.4 The Vector Table 503
D.5 Device Initialization 504
D.6 Write Sector 506
D.7 Read Sector 507
D.8 Service Routines for Read and Write 508
D.9 Getstat and SetStat 523
D.10 Terminate 526
D.11 Interrupt Sevice Routine 527

List of Tables

1.1	Typographic Conventions	2
7.1	Summary of Signal Attributes	83
17.1	Supported Sector Sizes	202
17.2	Disk Space Efficiency	205
19.1	SCF Edit Control Characters	245
23.1	SC68681 Device Static Storage	292
24.1	SCSI Board Memory Map	326
A.1	Processor Support	416

List of Figures

2.1	C Code to Call _mkdata_module()	21
4.1	MDir of Modules Loaded at Startup	33
4.2	MFree at Startup	33
4.3	Displays while *Sleep*s are Active	35
4.4	Some *Sleep*s Done	36
4.5	Test for First-Fit Allocation	37
5.1	Colored Memory Structures	52
10.1	Sample Semaphore Experiment	134
10.2	Another Experiment with Semaphores	134
10.3	Sample Event Selector Experiment	141
12.1	Signal on Data Ready Protocol	164
16.1	Specified Fields in the Universal Disk Format	194
17.1	C Code to Change I/O Buffering	203
24.1	WD33C93A Device Registers	328
B.1	Two Bootlists	419
B.2	Two Init Modules	420
B.3	Directory of an Emergency Disk	421

Chapter 1

Introduction

This is the second edition of *OS-9 Insights*. It is a major update. The changes to *OS-9 Insights* were partly driven by changes to OS-9; colored memory, signal queuing and masking, disk caching, and variable sector size support have been added to OS-9 since the first edition of *OS-9 Insights*. Also, since I've been working at Microware, I've learned more about OS-9 users. You are an impressive group of people who need to know more about the advanced use of OS-9 than I had realized. This edition of *Insights* does not yet have *sufficient* information, but it has a great deal more to say about such topics as signals and scheduling.

I am pleased with the reaction to the PCFM file manager presented in the first edition. Since the publication of *Insights* several new file managers for OS-9 have been produced outside Microware. I like to think PCFM helped encourage file manager construction. This is good and proper exploitation of OS-9. I hope the device driver in C that I added to this edition will make device driver construction almost as casual as ordinary programming.

This book was written for programmers who would like to use the advanced features of OS-9. It explains and illustrates features of OS-9 ranging from memory management through file managers. The illustrations are examples, either programs or scripts of interactions with OS-9. They are intended to expose the details of the techniques under discussion and suggest interesting applications.

If you have never programmed for OS-9—particularly if you are experienced with another advanced operating system—you can survey the territory by skimming the entire book. Scanning the table of contents will give a faster overview.

Many programmers can use OS-9 very effectively without using *The OS-9 Technical Manual*. Those people will find part of this book useful. I suggest chapter 3, Managing Your Memory; chapter 12, OS-9 I/O; and chapter 17, Managing Disk Space.

Programmers who want to use the full power of OS-9 but don't want to adjust or extend the operating system should read everything up to chapter 21. The chapters on writing file managers and device drivers will serve as useful reference material on the details of I/O operations, but they are long and somewhat difficult... probably not worth studying unless you actually intend to write a driver or file manager.

The last few chapters concern operating system code. It is probably easier to add features to OS-9 than you expected (though not actually easy). Chapter 23 is a densely commented SCF device driver, and chapter 24 is a simple SCSI driver written mainly in C. A very simple RBF-like file manager is presented in chapter 21, and a much expanded version of the same file manager (capable of reading and writing PC-DOS disks) is presented in appendix C. The RBF device driver that was presented in the first edition has been moved to appendix D; it is out-of-date and comparatively hard to understand, but it was a production device driver. The C device driver that has taken its place in the main body of the book is easier to understand and probably a better starting point for a new driver, but it has not been tested to the level of production code. The details in *Rb765* are messy, but good reference material.

TeX makes it easy to let typography get out of control. It is easy to typeset text so it is almost impossible to read. Manuals of style suggest rather strongly that book designers restrain themselves. Text that keeps a consistent typestyle is easier to read than text that changes frequently. Typestyles are, however, a convenient way to mark special text. Table 1.1 shows the way fonts are used in this book.

Table 1.1: Typographic Conventions

Font	Used For
Typewriter	Output from a computer
Script	OS-9 system calls and CPU op codes
SMALL CAPS	CPU registers
Bold Italics	Program names
Italics	General emphasis
Roman	Everything else

The programs in this book are set in Roman type, slightly smaller than the surrounding text. I have departed from my typographical standard by setting comments for C programs in italic type. This practice has become a standard in the computer science community, and it makes the comments clearly visible.

The two-character C code -> has been replaced with → in all programs. Before I made the change, the leading hyphen was sometimes hard to see. The revised notation makes the operator easier to see, and I think the meaning of → is clear.

The cover of the first edition of *Insights* mentioned a book about CD-I. That book has never appeared, and probably never will. I wrote the book and tried for about six months to keep it current with the evolution of CD-RTOS. Then I gave up. Eric and Walden Miller have written a book on CD-I that should be available shortly before this book is ready. Since Eric is one of the world's leading experts on CD-RTOS, this should be a useful book.

I hope to write additional *Insights* volumes. I'd like to investigate some of the deeper possibilities for manipulating the OS-9 kernel, and discuss a number of "dirty tricks." I'd also like to write about real-time programming. I think these books are necessary, but I'm not sure I can write them. My expectations are high and the topics for discussion are controversial (the dirty tricks leave huge opportunities for mysterious and catastrophic bugs), but if everything goes perfectly, I should have another volume of *Insights* ready in early 1993.

Chapter 2

Modules

In this chapter we investigate OS-9 modules in considerable depth.

One of the first steps in the OS-9 boot procedure is a pass through memory checking for Read Only Memory (ROM), Random Access Memory (RAM) and, in some systems, defective memory. Good RAM is distinguished by its ability to store data. OS-9 tests memory by writing at least two different values into the memory and reading the memory after each write to make certain that the value can be recovered intact. ROM always contains the same data regardless of what is written into it. Unused addresses respond with a bus error when the bootstrap code attempts to read or write them.

The possible addressing ranges for a 68000-family processor extend from 16 megabytes to 4 gigabytes. A processor's range of addresses probably includes I/O devices that should not be touched during the memory search, and perhaps even multiple addresses that refer to the same memory. This would make a comprehensive search of all addresses for RAM and ROM slow and complicated. The bootstrap code avoids these problems by driving its memory initialization from a list of address ranges that are worth inspecting.

One problem that OS-9's designers faced was distinguishing modules in ROM and RAM from random junk. Their answer to this problem was structured memory modules. Module structure makes useful memory distinct from junk. That is the first use OS-9 makes of modules, but not the only use. Modules are central to the overall design of OS-9.

2.1 How Modules Are Identified

OS-9 must recognize modules accurately. It would be catastrophic if the kernel were inclined to find modules where there was only randomness. But since OS-9 is frequently called on to locate modules, the module-verification algorithm must detect non-modules quickly. The process OS-9 uses is something of a compromise between speed and accuracy. It verifies a module in stages. The first two stages quickly reject almost anything that isn't a module. The last stage is slow, but careful.

The beginning of a module is marked with a special two-byte code, hexadecimal $4AFC. It is possible that this code could occur somewhere other than the start of a module. To make certain that it has identified a module, and to learn more about the module (if that's what it is), OS-9 verifies that it fits a specified form.

The first 48 bytes in a module are called the module header. The header contains the sync bytes ($4AFC) and information about the module. There are twelve informational fields in the standard module header including the module's length, name, type, protection, and revision number. After these values is the second check on the validity of the module: the header parity word. This field contains the one's complement of the vertical parity of the preceding words (2-byte words) in the module header.

2.2 The Header Check

The header check is a simple form of Cyclic Redundancy Check (CRC). The vertical parity is taken by XOR'ing together the first 23 words (46 bytes) and the resulting 16-bit word is complemented. (See appendix B.)

When a number is XOR'ed with its one's complement the result is all one bits. This trick makes it easy to verify the header check value. All the words in the header, including the header parity, are exclusive or'ed together. If the result isn't %11111111 11111111, something is wrong. Actually, the easiest way to do this is to take the one's complement of the vertical parity (XOR) of all 24 words in the header. This is the same operation that was used to generate the header parity except that we include the header parity with the rest of the header in the calculation. If the result isn't 0, the check fails.

The type of CRC used to calculate the header parity is only able to catch one-bit errors in the header. If the header parity is being verified over random data, there is one chance in 65535 that it will accept the data as a valid header. If it is run on a damaged header, it can detect some problems, but if two words are damaged, verification of the header parity can miss the problem. If the third and fourth words in the header are %01111000 01111000 and %01010011 01010011, their exclusive or would be %00101011 00101011. There are many other pairs of binary numbers that

2.3. THE MODULE CRC BYTES

can be exclusive or'ed with each other to give the same result; %00000000 00000000 and %00101011 00101011 is a simple example. If only one word is changed, the header parity will not verify, but if two numbers are changed there is a chance the damage will go undetected.

2.3 The Module CRC Bytes

It isn't likely for the header parity and the sync bytes to be correct by chance, but, even if they are, one more check is made before a block of memory is considered a module. OS-9 keeps a much more sophisticated three-byte CRC check of the entire module. The CRC check is run starting from the sync bytes for the length given in the module header. OS-9's CRC algorithm detects any reasonable form of damage, and the chances of it checking out over random data are one in about sixteen million. Taken together with the chances of the header parity verifying on random data, the probability of mistaking junk for a module is only about one in four billion.

There is no need to know the CRC algorithm. It is always best to use the code in OS-9 to generate and check CRCs via the *F$CRC*, *F$SetCRC*, and *F$VModul* system service requests (SVC's.) However, the mark of a good systems programmer is curiosity about just this kind of trivia, so here are some details about CRC calculation. For those of you who are content to let OS-9 handle this stuff, it is perfectly safe to skip ahead.

2.4 How the Module CRC Works

Cyclic Redundancy Checking (CRC) is an algorithm for error detection in blocks of information. It detects errors more reliably than simple parity checking does, but it's substantially harder to do. In the CRC algorithm, the entire module to be checked is treated as one continuous stream of bits, a large binary number. First the number is shifted to the left enough to leave space for the CRC code at the low order end (in the case of OS-9 modules, a three byte left shift). The CRC code is the remainder after this number is divided by the "generating polynomial" using mod-2 division. (All operations are in base two, no borrowing or carrying.) The check bits are appended to the end of the module when the module is generated.

When the CRC algorithm is run on a bit stream including the CRC code, the resulting value is zero. Perhaps an example using standard decimal arithmetic would help (though, in fact, CRC is trickier in decimal).

If the generating polynomial is the number 13, the CRC code for the
number 275101712 is 5:

275101712 must be shifted left two decimal digits giving 27510171200.

Dividing by 13 gives 2116167015 remainder 5.

Subtracting 5 from the original number gives 27510171195.

Running the CRC algorithm on 27510171195 gives a CRC code of 0 because 2721017119500 is perfectly divisible by 13.

You probably noticed that the result of the CRC calculation in the decimal case wasn't the original number followed by the CRC code. When the operation is done in binary mod-2, everything works out smoothly. One important thing to notice about mod-2 arithmetic is that addition and subtraction give the same result. Since there are only the digits 0 and 1, and there is no carry or borrow:

$$1 + 1 = 0 \quad \text{and} \quad 1 - 1 = 0$$
$$1 + 0 = 1 \quad \text{and} \quad 1 - 0 = 1$$
$$0 + 0 = 0 \quad \text{and} \quad 0 - 0 = 0$$

Because of this peculiar behavior, subtraction is a useless operation in proper CRC calculation. Bearing this in mind, let's go a little deeper into the math.

Let the module be represented by the number M, let the generating polynomial be represented by G, let the number of bits in the CRC code be k, and X be M shifted left k bits, then:

$$X/G = Q + R/G$$

where Q is the quotient from the division and R is the remainder.

$$R = X - Q \times G$$

or, since addition and subtraction are the same

$$R = X + Q \times G$$

The module with the CRC code attached is $V = X + R$. Since $X + R = Q \times G$, V is evenly divisible by G.

The algorithm actually used in OS-9 is slightly different from the standard CRC algorithm. First, since division of large numbers is slow, OS-9 uses a special trick for finding the remainder of mod-2 division that uses mostly shift and XOR instructions. It also differs from the normal CRC algorithm in that the initial value for the CRC accumulator is $ffffff in OS-9 instead of the normal $000000, and the CRC code is complemented before it is used. The result of all the changes is that the CRC code for an intact module including CRC should be $800fe3, the CRC generating polynomial, instead of $000000.

2.4. HOW THE MODULE CRC WORKS

2.4.1 CRC Algorithm in C

A C-language implementation of the OS-9 CRC algorithm is shown below.

```c
crc(ptr,n,crcacc)
unsigned short *ptr;
long n;
unsigned long *crcacc;
{
    register unsigned long tmp,tmp1,accum = *crcacc & 0x00ffffff;
    register short tmp2;

    if(n & 1) {
        if(n == 1 && *(char*)ptr == '\0') {
            /* special case for one zero byte */
            tmp1 = tmp = (accum >> 16) & 0x0000ffff;
            accum <<= 8; tmp <<= 1;accum ^= tmp;
            tmp1 ^= tmp; tmp <<= 5; accum ^= tmp;
            tmp2 = tmp1; tmp2 <<= 2; tmp1 ^= tmp2;
            tmp2 = tmp1; tmp1 <<= 4; tmp2 ^= tmp1;
            if(tmp2 & 0x80) accum ^= 0x800021;
            accum &= 0x00ffffff; *crcacc = accum;
            return;
        } else exit(_errmsg(1, "odd count for crc"));
    } else n >>= 1;                              /*convert byte to word count */
    while(n-- > 0) {
        tmp = *ptr++;                            /* get (next) data word */
        tmp <<= 8;                               /* align data bit zero with CRC bit 0 */
        tmp ^= accum;                            /* get new data-CRC difference */
        tmp &= 0xffffff00;                       /* clear extraneous bits */
        accum <<= 16;                            /* shift current CRC; strip all but 23:16 */
        tmp >>= 2;                               /* shift */
        accum ^= tmp;                            /* add input bit 17 net effect (over 16 shifts) */
        tmp >>= 5;
        accum ^= tmp;                            /* add input bit 22 net effect */
        tmp2 = tmp;                              /* determine if even or odd number of bits */
        tmp >>= 1; tmp2 ^= tmp; tmp = tmp2;
        tmp <<= 2; tmp2 ^= tmp; tmp = tmp2;
        tmp <<= 4; tmp2 ^= tmp; tmp = tmp2;
        tmp <<= 8; tmp2 ^= tmp;
        if(tmp2 & 0x8000) accum ^= 0x800021;
        accum &= 0x00ffffff;                     /* clear extraneous bits */
    }
    *crcacc = accum;
}
```

2.5 Circumventing CRC Protection

Every module in memory is validated once before it is placed in the module directory. The validation takes place during bootstrap for ROMed modules, and while a module is being loaded for other modules. Fortunately, OS-9 doesn't reverify the validity of modules after they are in the module directory, because there are occasions when you will want to modify a module in memory, and generating a new CRC each time a modification is made might be slow work.

Debug may be used to modify a module in memory. It is commonly used to apply patches and make ad hoc modifications to various modules. Changes made by the debugger cause the CRC value for a module to change without actually altering the CRC bytes. If the CRC for modified modules were reverified, the changes would cause the module to be rejected because of its incorrect CRC value.

Since a module is safe once it is in the module directory, modules can be modified, either because of special circumstances (debugging), or as a matter of course, as is sometimes done with data modules.[1]

2.6 Module Types

The type byte in the module header can be used to specify any one of 256 module types, and the language byte specifies one of 256 languages. These values are used by the OS-9 kernel and the shell to place the module in the right place and do the right things with it.

Only seven of the available module languages have been defined. Of those seven, only three represent languages that are actually used; and of those three, only two have any real effect on the function of the module. The language specification doesn't necessarily reflect the programming language used to generate the module. It indicates the actual language in the module. If someone ever comes out with a C compiler that generates Microware Basic I-Code, the module will be tagged as I-Code, not CCode.

The primary use of the language specification is by the shell. When the shell prepares to execute a program, it checks the module's language. If the language is

---

[1] Modules may also be modified by defective programs. These problems are often subtle. They manifest as constants with strange values and other peculiar things. They are easy to find if you look for them. *Ident* reports that damaged modules have incorrect CRC. You can then save the damaged module and use *cmp* to compare the damaged module to the original. This reports the changes and their locations.

2.6. MODULE TYPES

object code it forks the module, but if it is Microware Basic I-Code it forks the *Basic* run time module, *runb*, to run the I-Code. This makes it appear that the I-Code file is being directly executed.

The type specification might be better named Usage. The type byte specifies the purpose of the module. Most non-system modules are programs, but not all. If you write a matrix algebra package as a module that programs can link to when they need matrix algebra services, the module would probably be of either the Subroutine or TrapLib type.

The subroutine module type is a feature of OS-9 that hasn't caught on as well as it deserves. They are modules that contain subroutines. Programs can link to and call whatever subroutine modules they need. Basic intermediate-code modules are excellent examples of subroutine modules.

The better programming languages permit a programmer to build a program a piece at a time. These pieces are combined by the language or a link editor to form one program which can be loaded and executed. The reasons for modular design have been exhaustively discussed in the Computer Science literature. Let's just say that most people agree that it is a good way to create software.

If the pieces (called modules) used to build a program are written generally enough, they can be collected until programs can be built largely from existing modules. Like any subroutine library, this saves time. If you run several programs at the same time, the subroutine modules that they share only need to be in memory once. That saves memory.

If a program is written in one large file, changes to that program require that the entire program be recompiled. If, however, the program is written using files that are bound into an executable module by a linker, then only the files containing changes need to be re-compiled. The linker will still need to consider all the files.

If the modules are bound while the program is executing, then only changed modules need be recompiled and linked. The old modules must be replaced with the new ones on disk or in memory, but that is the extent of the change. Sometimes modules in a running program can be replaced without stopping the program. I don't know of any way to rig a program so that modules actually being executed can be replaced, but with careful (slightly inefficient) programming a program can be designed so any module other than the one being executed can be replaced on the fly.

The TrapLib module type is another attempt by Microware to promote modular construction. They use the traplib mechanism heavily for I/O and floating point libraries. Traplib modules are much like subroutine modules. They serve as globally-accessible collections of services. Traplib modules are distinguished from subroutine modules by their access method. Trap handlers are easier to use (and less efficient) than subroutine modules.

Four special module types are used for OS-9 itself. The OS-9 kernel and the SSM module are examples of System modules. File managers like Pipeman, SCF, and RBF are File Manager Modules. Modules like rb1772 and sc68681 are device drivers, and device descriptors like term and D0 have their own type.

The system module types mark modules that belong in the system area and give an extra check on the identity of a module.

Three module type/language combinations are special in that they can't be executed. The device descriptors don't contain any executable instructions, just lots of information. The init module (there's only one) contains most of the constants that configure OS-9. There is a special provision for non-executable modules other than these. The data module type can be used for any module that you don't intend to have executed. Data modules are used to store global data and configuration information for user programs.

2.7 Module Security

Four values are used for module security. The file the module came from contributes the file owner and the file access permissions. The module header contributes the module's owner and the module access permissions. The module owner and access modes act somewhat like file access permissions. On systems without memory protection hardware, OS-9's ability to protect modules against invalid access once they are in memory is limited, but a careful programmer on a system with protected memory can make his modules about as secure as he wants.

The file the module came from is important when the *F$SUser* SVC is used. Processes start with the user number of the process that forked them, but OS-9 supplies a controlled way for a process to change its user number. Any process may use the *F$SUser* SVC to set the user number it is running under to the number in the owner field in its module header. Only processes running under the super user ID can reach arbitrary user IDs.

This protection should not be relied on to protect users from hostile programmers. A programmer can write a program that does a *F$SUser* to whatever number he wants by putting the desired value in the module-owner field when he constructs the module. There is a measure of protection against this trick. Modules that are owned by the super user must be loaded from files that are owned by the super user.

To further protect against malicious programmers, the kernel saves a value calculated as a function of the bytes in each module header in the module directory entry for that module. If this was not done, a programmer could load a module, then modify the user, type, and revision number of the module according to his requirements. Any module in a system without SSM or with the writable attribute can have its security attributes modified this way, but the module directory is a system data structure and, at least in systems with SSM, system data structures cannot be updated by user processes. The result is that module headers can be updated, but any module that has been modified in that way becomes unusable. It is impossible to link to a module with a modified header.

2.8 The Module Attribute Byte

Storage attributes of the module are coded in the module attribute byte. Three attributes are in common use.

ReEnt The high-order bit (bit 7) in the attribute byte denotes the reentrant attribute.

Ghost Bit 6 is used for the ghost module capability. Unless ghosting is disabled by setting the NoGhost bit in the M$Compat byte in the init module, modules with the ghost capability remain in memory when their link count goes to zero. They stay in memory until their link count goes to −1 or the memory is required for some other purpose.

Don't use the ghost attribute on programs that are under development. Ghosted (also called *sticky*) program modules remain in memory and later revisions have to be loaded explicitly. It is easy to forget that a module is ghosted and wonder why revisions don't seem to be taking effect.

SupStat Bit 5 indicates that the module must run in supervisor state.

Some systems may use another bit to indicate that the module is write protected.

2.8.1 Reentrant Modules

Most modules under OS-9 are reentrant. A typical system could run for years without executing a non-reentrant module. All the operating system modules are reentrant, and every compiler distributed by Microware generates reentrant code unless it is badly abused. A programmer can, of course, easily generate a non-reentrant module with the assembler. If a program is written so that it modifies constants that the compiler stores in the module, it will not be reentrant—and it will, very likely, fail on a system with memory protection.

A reentrant module can be used by several different processes at the same time without any of them knowing that they are sharing the module. The only requirement for this (under OS-9) is that the module must not alter itself.

Reentrant modules are a device which can save large amounts of memory, but only if they are well used. Some modules, like *umacs*, are frequently used by more than one process at a time. This saves about 42k for each process after the first because only one copy of *umacs* needs to be loaded for all the processes. Most modules aren't as widely used as *umacs*. Single-module programs are usually too specialized to be of general interest. These programs are probably full of code that would be useful to other programs, but there is no way to share it.

A well-designed modular program is built of a set of modules, each as independent of the others as possible and each performing one task or a closely related group of tasks. Modules that are part of a well-modularized program are very likely to be useful to other programs. If the modules are reentrant, only one copy of a module is stored in memory regardless of the number of programs using the module.

2.9 The Module Revision Number

The byte after the module attribute byte in the module header is the revision byte. The revision number has no influence on what is done with the module once it is loaded—revision two is treated like revision one. It is only important during the actual loading process. A module already in memory won't be replaced by another module loaded from disk unless the new module has a higher revision number.

Revision numbers aren't heavily used on disk-based systems. If a module is loaded with the *F$Load* SVC, it can be unlinked and replaced. ROM-based systems require revision numbers. A module that is stored in ROM can only be replaced by re-blasting the ROM or superseding the module with a module having a greater revision number. Revision numbers are also useful for development work on modules that must be included in the boot file. Boot modules cannot be removed from memory, so they can only be replaced by rebooting the system or loading a module with a higher revision number.

2.10 The Module Edition Number

The module edition number is stored in the word after the revision number. OS-9 ignores the module edition number, but it is good policy to increment the value in this field every time you finish an update to the module. Since it's a word, you can update the module many times before you run out of new edition numbers. The *ident* utility displays the edition number along with most of the other information in a module's header. *Ident*, in combination with conscientious use of the edition number field, is a good way to determine whether a module is the latest version.

2.11 The Module Usage Field

The module usage field has great promise, but its use isn't defined yet. We do know that the module usage is the offset from the beginning of the module to something that describes the usage of the program, but we can only speculate about what will describe the usage. It could be as simple as the string the system commands display when you invoke them with a "-?" argument. It could be as complicated as special code that explains the usage of each module in some elaborate way.

2.12 The Debugging Symbol Table

Modules are at the root of OS-9. Designing the module header was one of the first steps in Microware's design of OS-9. The debugger wasn't written until much later. There is a field in the module header that might have pointed at symbolic information for the debugger. When the debugger was written, they discovered that it was more efficient to put this information in a separate module. The M$Symbol field is used in the STB modules that contain symbol information used by debuggers, but otherwise the field is unused.

2.13 The Module Directory

OS-9 maintains a list of all the modules in memory called the module directory. There are only five fields in each module directory entry. Most of the information about a module is in the module header. A module directory entry contains the information about a module that is determined when the module is loaded (such as the module's address.)

The first field in a module directory entry is a pointer to the module header; it is followed by a pointer to the first module in the "module group" containing the module.

If a module is loaded by itself, its module pointer has the same value as the module group pointer. When you load a file with several modules in it, OS-9 combines them into a module group, and stores a pointer to the start of the group and the length of the group in the module directory entry for each module in the group. This feature is intended to conserve memory. When modules are loaded separately they must each start on a memory allocation boundary, but when they are combined in a file they are loaded into contiguous memory. With the standard memory allocation granularity of 16 bytes, the memory savings due to module groups are very small.[2] Incidental

---

[2]Systems with an MMU and SSM software often use a 4 kilobyte memory allocation granularity. This

advantages of module groups are usually more significant:

- The single large read used to read a module group is faster than multiple opens and reads that would be done for a collection of modules in separate files.

- A module group loads into one chunk of memory. Modules loaded separately use separate blocks of memory, potentially causing memory fragmentation.

- Modules in a module group stay in memory until all the modules in the group have a reference count of zero.

The next field in a module directory entry is a two-byte module link count. Each time a process gets a pointer to the module, the link count is incremented. Each time the module is unlinked or unloaded, the link count is decremented. No module is removed from memory unless its link count is zero (−1 for ghost modules). However, zeroing a module's link count isn't a sure way to remove it from memory. When modules are collected in a group, they must all be removed at once. If any module in a group has a non-zero link count, the group remains in memory.

A value computed from the values in the module header is also stored in the module directory. This makes it difficult for programs to modify the permissions and owner in their header and violate module security. The value is computed and recorded when the module is loaded and checked when the module is linked.

2.13.1 Unlink Protection

Prior to release 2.4.3, only a module's access protection protected it from being removed from memory by *F$UnLink*. The results were particularly unfortunate when someone would inadvertently unlink a trap handler like cio, or a program module that was in use at the time. In release 2.4.3, the unlink SVC became substantially more careful. It looks at each process descriptor checking the program module and trap handler modules for the process against the module that is being unlinked. If a module is referenced by a process descriptor, it cannot be fully unlinked.

2.14 How Modules Are Generated

The easiest and most common way to generate modules is with a compiler. The Microware Basic pack instruction turns Basic procedures into subroutine modules of Basic I-Code. Languages that compile to native code produce program modules

---

makes module groups a more useful memory-saving tool in systems with SSM.

2.14. HOW MODULES ARE GENERATED

of 68000 object-code. Assemblers are also used to produce program modules, but assemblers being what they are, you can produce any type of module with them.

The assembler doesn't actually build modules. It creates relocatable object files that the linker combines into a module. The constants and machine instructions are passed from the assembler through the linker to the final module without modification except that no promises are made about the order in which linker combines things. The only time you'll feel concerned about this is when you want to use a short *bsr* instruction between program sections (psects). The linker tends to combine code from different files in the order it gets to them, but that may change.

The assembler psect directive transmits information to the linker that it uses to construct the module header. The *psect* statement can have six or seven arguments:

1. The first argument is the psect name. The linker uses *psect* names in error messages to identify the source of errors.

2. The module type/language word. The module type must be shifted left by eight bits before it is combined with the language. This field actually has two purposes. If it is zero, the psect is not the main psect. If it is non-zero, the value is used to set the type and language bytes in the module header. Magic numbers work in the type/language field, but people who can't read OS-9 codes like English will understand you better if you use constant names from the sys.l and usr.l libraries like this:

   ```
   TypeLang  equ   (Prgrm<<8)+Objct
             psect Silly,TypeLang, ...
   ```

   The (Prgrm<<8) means that the assembler should take the value of the constant Prgrm and shift it eight bits to the left.

3. The module attribute/revision word. This trick of squeezing two one-byte fields into a word is left over from OS-9/6809. There, these two values shared a byte. Now they have a byte each, but the assembler hasn't caught up yet.

4. The module edition number is for documentation only. The ***ident*** command displays it, but other than that, a module's edition number is ignored by OS-9.

5. The stacksize field is your calculation of the amount of stack space that this psect might use. The linker adds the stacksize fields from the psects it combines into a module to get a value for the stacksize field in the module header. If a psect can use several different amounts of stack space depending on the data it gets, use the maximum.

6. The entry point field is the offset from the beginning of the psect to the entry point for the module. This field should only be non-zero for the main module.

7. The trapent field should never be zero. It should only be used on the main *psect*, and only if you have written code to deal with uninitialized trap exceptions. (See chapter 11). If you don't use this field, stop with six arguments for the *psect* directive.

The beginning of a file containing a program's main psect might look something like this:

```
            ttl    example program
            nam    example
            use    <oskdefs.d>
TypeLang    equ    (Prgrm<< 8)+Objct
AttrRev     equ    (ReEnt<< 8)+1
Edition     equ    1
StackMax    equ    249
            psect  example,TypeLang,AttrRev,Edition,StackMax,Entry
            ...
Entry
```

A subroutine *psect* is simpler:

```
            psect  sub1,0,0,0,273,0
```

Only the name and stacksize fields need to be filled in.

2.15   SVC's that Deal with Modules

The *F$Load* SVC reads modules from a file whose pathlist is passed to the SVC as a parameter. It loads all the modules in the specified file into memory and adds them to the module directory, but only the first module in the file has its link count incremented. The *F$Load* service request returns the same values in its registers that a *F$Link* on the first module in the file would have; that is, the module type/language word of the first module in the D0 register, the module attributes/revision word in D1, a pointer just past the path list in A0, the address of the module entry point in A1, and the address of the module header in A2.

The standard way to locate a module in memory is the *F$Link* SVC. It takes as input the address of a string containing the name of the module you want to find and the type/language of the module. The name of the module must start with a number or alphabetic character. It must be terminated with the OS-9 standard ending, a null byte. Use a C string "Modulename" or *dc.b* with an explicit zero to do this:

2.15. SVC'S THAT DEAL WITH MODULES

```
         dc.b     "Modulename",0
```

If a type/language is specified by loading its value into register D0 before calling *F$Link*, link will only find a module that matches both the requested name and the requested type/language. If you don't want to specify one of these values, use a zero. For example, the hex value $0100, the type/language code for program modules with no language specified, matches a program module in any language.

The type/language and attribute/revision bytes for a module found by the *F$Link* SVC are returned in the D0 and D1 registers. The A0 register is advanced past the module name it pointed at before the SVC. The address of the module's header is returned in A2 and the entry address in A1.

The *F$UnLink* SVC is used to decrement a module's link count. If all the modules in the module's group are ready to be released (link count of −1 for ghost modules, zero for other modules), *F$UnLink* releases the module group's memory and the module directory entries for the modules in the group. This SVC only requires the address of the module header for the module to be unlinked. Remember to save the address of the module header when the module is linked.

F$UnLoad has the same effect as *F$UnLink*, but it uses the module's name and language/type to locate it instead of a pointer to the module's header. This call is important when you want to remove a module that has extra links. If every program that has a link to a module remembers to unlink it, the module will disappear when no process is using it. If a process doesn't unlink a module as many times as it links the module (the link command is a program that does this) the *F$UnLink* SVC can't zero the module's link count without cheating.

When you unlink a module the module is mapped out of your address space. Your pointer to the module header isn't good any more. The only way to unlink it another time is to link it back into your address space then unlink it. You can't decrease the module's link count more than you increase it.[3]

The *F$UnLoad* SVC lets you decrease a module's link count without linking to it. Using this SVC, programs can zero a module's link count without hurting their portability to systems with memory protection.

F$CRC is used to calculate the CRC for a module, or, for that matter, anything else that needs a CRC. It uses the address of the block of data, and the length of the block. It leaves the CRC value for the data in D1. If it isn't convenient to calculate the CRC on an entire block of memory at once, *F$CRC* can be used on sections of the data provided that the sections are in order starting with the first part of the block. The D1 register is used to accumulate the CRC value, so it should be initialized to

---

[3]Since OS-9/68000 does not do address translation, the module's address is actually still correct, but if you play by the rules, you should treat it as invalid.

$ffffffff before the first call to *F$CRC* and then left alone until the entire block has been passed through *F$CRC*.

If you are using *F$CRC* to validate a module, accumulate the CRC through the entire module including its CRC bytes. The accumulator will contain the generating polynomial[4] if the CRC code checks out.

If you want to generate a CRC code for a block of memory, run *F$CRC* over the data, and complement[5] the generated CRC. The resulting value can be concatenated to the block of memory to give the block a valid CRC.

There is a special SVC just for updating the header parity and CRC for a module. The *F$SetCRC* SVC takes a pointer to a module in A0 and doesn't return anything unless it returns an error code.

The service request that verifies a module and places it in the module directory is *F$VModul*. It is a system mode request. It takes the address of the new module in A0, and the module's group id. It returns a pointer to the module's module directory entry.

The *F$DatMod* SVC builds data modules on the fly. You tell it the amount of data you want to store in the module, the name you want it to have, the desired attribute/revision word, and the access permission you want the module to have. The *F$DatMod* call builds the module in memory, registers it with the system, and returns the same values you would get from a *F$Link* SVC.

Data modules use the execution-offset field in the module header as the data offset. The field gives the offset from the beginning of the module to the first byte of the data area. The *F$DatMod*, and *F$Link* SVC's leave the A1 register pointing to the data area in the data module.

Creation of data modules is one of the areas where it is actually easier to use assembly language than C. You need a pointer to the beginning of the module so you can unlink it later. You also want a pointer to the data area. Since returning more than one value from a C function is a little clumsy and since you can calculate the location of the data from the module header, the _mkdata_module() function returns a pointer to the module header. Getting a pointer to the data requires some careful pointer arithmetic.

---

[4]The value of the CRC generating polynomial (CRC) is $00800fe3.
[5]Use the 68000 instruction *not* to complement the CRC code.

2.15. SVC'S THAT DEAL WITH MODULES

Figure 2.1: C Code to Call _mkdata_module()

```
#include <module.h>
typedef struct {
    struct modhcom _mh;                              /* Standard module header */
    long Data_Offset;
} mod _data;
/*
    This function creates a data module and returns a pointer to the data
    in the module. It also sets one of its arguments to point to the module.
*/
char *CreatDatMod(Module, Name, Size, Attr, Perm)
    char *Name;
    register mod_data **Module;                      /* A pointer to a pointer */
    unsigned Size;
    short Attr, Perm;
{
    if((*Module = (mod_data *)_mkdata_module(Name, Size, Attr, Perm))==-1)
        /* If _mkdata_module returns an error, pass it on to the caller. */
        return -1;
    /* Now calculate and return a pointer to the data area. */
    return((char *)*Module + (*Module)→Data_Offset);
}
```

Chapter 3

Memory

In this chapter we discuss prudent memory management.

OS-9 supervises the distribution of memory to programs. Sometimes it may seem that OS-9 has taken memory allocation completely out of your hands, but, in fact, there is a lot you can do about the way memory is used.

The memory chip manufacturers have cut the price of memory dramatically over the years. System designers have responded by designing each new generation of computer with a larger memory than the previous generation. Software designers have also noticed the availability of large memories and joyfully created software that requires at least as much memory as they expect to find. Perhaps because of this interaction between hardware and software, it is axiomatic that a computer will never have enough memory.

Since you will never have a computer with enough memory, it is always important to make the most of the memory you have. Under OS-9 that means using reentrant modules, using memory where it does the most good, and worrying about memory fragmentation.

3.1 Reentrant Modules

The most important step to take toward conserving memory is to use reentrant modules whenever possible. It is often worth considerable trouble to make a module reentrant, but reentrancy is seldom a difficult goal. The basic rules for reentrancy are simple:

- A reentrant program must base all its variables off address registers.

- PC-relative values and absolute addresses may only be used as constants.

- Programs that modify themselves are strictly out of the question.

The modules you are most likely to create will contain programs, either in intermediate code (like Microware Basic I-Code) or in 68000 object code. The Microware C compiler creates reentrant code by default, as do all high-level languages for OS-9.[1] If you write in assembler you can do whatever you want, including writing non-reentrant code.

The advantage of reentrant modules is that any number of processes can share them. Each process must have its own data storage, but many processes can share the module itself. Not having to store a separate copy of the program for each process can save significant amounts of memory. As an example, note that if the C compiler components weren't reentrant, each process using the compiler would start by requiring a large block of memory just for its copy of the compiler modules. As it is, even moderately small systems can run three or four compiles concurrently.

Making a module reentrant is easy. Making a module general enough that several processes might want to use it concurrently is harder. Important system programs like editors and shells have it easy. The designers knew those programs would be heavily used.

It isn't likely that most full-blown programs will be used by several processes unless the system is dedicated to the task performed by the program. However, there are some operations that many programs have in common: formatting output, math, validating input, formatting the screen, and handling database files are some examples. If all these functions are built into a single module, a program will have to incorporate the entire package if it wants any function from the module. If separate modules are built to do each of these operations, some of them might serve several different programs, and each program can get the services it needs without using memory for a whole class of services it does not need. OS-9 makes it easy for a program to collect a group of modules with the *F$Link* and *F$TLink* Service Calls (SVC's).[2]

3.2 Memory Fragmentation

Memory fragmentation is a problem that serious OS-9 users must learn to handle. OS-9 Level Two for the 6809 uses Dynamic Address Translation to make memory

---

[1]This isn't strictly true. You can write a non-reentrant program in C by modifying values that the compiler assumes are constant. The compiler permits this, but a system with memory protection may give bus errors when it attempts to run the program.

[2]Trap handlers are an easy way to share code. OS-9 comes with trap handler modules for mathematical functions and print formatting. Traps are not the best way to access shared resources, but they are easy to use.

3.3. CAREFUL USE OF MEMORY

fragmentation irrelevant, but there is no such facility for OS-9 on 68000-family processors. These systems can be configured with enough memory to solve the problem without address translation.

Memory fragmentation only becomes a problem when the available free memory is in so many little pieces that OS-9 can't find enough memory in one block to satisfy a program's request for memory. This is a serious problem, and is dealt with in more depth in chapters 4 and 5. The simple solution to memory fragmentation problems is to kill processes and unlink modules, starting with the ones you can spare most easily and continuing until there is enough contiguous free memory. The *mfree* command tells you how many blocks of free memory you have, and how big they are.

The OS-9 kernel and its satellite components (like file managers and device drivers) allocate memory as they required it. File managers and device drivers may allocate memory when a device is attached (initialized). Since this memory stays allocated until the device is detached, it can cause serious long-term fragmentation. Attaching every standard device when the system is booted is a good policy. A command line like:

```
$ iniz dd h0 d0 t1 t2 t3 r0
```

early in the startup file attaches the devices while there is free memory near the top of RAM. Devices that are attached later (by opening a file on a device that hasn't been used yet), are likely to allocate their memory near the middle of memory. This type of fragmentation is hard to control except by getting the system fully initialized while memory is mostly empty.

3.3 Careful Use of Memory

There are some ways to waste memory that (I think) can only be done intentionally. The best example is the *sleep* command. *Sleep* takes any memory it is given out of circulation for a specified interval. You can be certain sleep doesn't run any faster or better with more memory.

If you want to waste a little over 48 kilobytes of memory for some reason, use:

```
$ sleep 10000 #48&
```

The above command takes 57.75 kilobytes of memory[3] out of circulation for the duration of the sleep.

---

[3] *Sleep*'s requirement for 57.75 kilobytes is specific to edition 13 of *sleep* and the memory allocation parameters on my system. 48 kilobytes of it is governed by the shell command line, and 9.75 kilobytes of the memory is the normal requirement of *sleep*.

Programs can be given memory that they cannot use, or don't even notice. This is a subtle but effective way to waste memory. It is easy to allocate extra memory to a program with the # *shell* option, but many programs ignore extra stack space. Current-generation OS-9 software requests adequate stack space by default. The only time extra stack space should be required is for programs with recursive algorithms that will recurse more deeply than the programmer expected. Programs that don't allocate dynamic memory from the block of storage given to them by the shell may use kernel system memory requests for their dynamic memory requirements. The amount of space they allocate can usually be controlled with a –b command-line option.

In general, give a program extra memory only if you *know* it will help. The *copy* command is a good example. Everyone knows *copy* runs better if it is given extra memory. No question, it does. But how much better it runs depends on your disk controller, disk hardware, and what else is going on in your system. Extra memory usually makes a large difference in the performance of *copy*, but sometimes it will make almost no difference. It is worth experimentation. Text editors, however, usually have reliable memory requirements. They can only load as much of a file into memory as fits in the memory you give them. Even editors that can cleverly leave part of the file on disk when they can't fit the entire file in memory, run slowly or have difficulties with search and replace commands when part of the file remains on disk.

Some programs, like Microware Basic, make it very clear to you when they need more memory. They don't care how much memory they have available to them, provided it is enough. Programs like *backup* and *copy* run faster with extra memory, but how much faster depends your system. If you use the commands a lot and care about conservation of memory, it would be worth your time to make some tests to determine how the amount of memory allocated to a program affects the progam's speed in your environment.

3.4 Dynamic Memory Allocation

In one case wasting memory is necessary. If a program, running under OS-9/68000, wants to call for an enlarged data/stack allocation data memory, it should call for the memory in the module header even if it won't use the memory until late in the program execution. The stack and data memory cannot grow during program execution.

A program can request two kinds of memory:

- a contiguous extension of its data area,

- a new block of memory allocated wherever there is room.

3.4. DYNAMIC MEMORY ALLOCATION

However, only requests for new blocks of memory will succeed. The discontinuous blocks of memory are called system memory.

System memory may be allocated at any time. The only reason to allocate all your system memory when the program starts is that it prevents the program from terminating for lack of memory after running for a while.

Ghost modules can save time by keeping memory full of modules, but programs that use a large part of the system's memory can cause an interesting type of fragmentation when ghost modules are in the system.

Ghost modules remain in memory even when their link count goes to zero. They are available in memory for subsequent use, but OS-9 will remove them if a program needs their memory. If you run a program that allocates more than about half your system's memory for data, ghost modules can cause a program to make its own fragmentation.

- A program module is loaded. (Let's call it LaTeX.) There is room for it below the current batch of ghost modules, so OS-9 loads it without removing any ghost modules.

- Fork allocates memory for the stack, and later the program requests system memory.

- When it finds that there is insufficient memory to fill a memory request, OS-9 will remove ghost modules, but it won't help.

- The free memory is divided around the LaTeX program module. The module is located below the memory that was filled with ghost modules. It divides the available memory into two blocks.

The cure for a ghost-fragmentation problem is to delete the program module, LaTeX, and start over. By deleting the program module and loading it again, you move it up toward high memory and leave a large block of memory below it.

If you don't push your system, you probably won't have trouble with memory. Fragmentation seldom becomes an issue unless several processes are running simultaneously. Even if you run several processes, fragmentation is unlikely unless the processes are starting and stopping and allocating and freeing memory. Systems that set up a collection of processes, allocate memory, and run for a long time are fairly immune to fragmentation.

The final cure for memory fragmentation is plenty of RAM. I have never experienced fragmentation, even with a complex process environment and continuous memory allocation and deallocation, when the system had enough memory to always have twice as much free RAM as I needed. For a typical development system, 300 to 400 kilobytes of free memory is usually enough.[4]

---

[4]Three or four-hundred kilobytes of free memory not *always* enough. I have seen the source debugger use over a megabyte of memory to debug a large program.

Chapter 4

OS-9 Memory Management

> *This chapter discusses the mechanisms that support OS-9 memory management and the realization of those mechanisms in the OS-9 kernel.*

Any operating system that permits more than one program to run at the same time needs a way of dividing the system's memory between the programs. OS-9 uses a dynamic memory management scheme. Instead of jumping right into OS-9 memory management, we'll start with some simpler memory management schemes and work up to OS-9's techniques gradually.

4.1 The Theoretical Base

Managing a computer's memory is a lot like managing on-street parking. A system's memory, like curb space, must be divided among users. It is good to use memory (or curb space) as efficiently as possible, but keeping the amount of supervision required to a minimum is also important.

Of course, the simplest way to handle system memory is to ignore the problem. Operating systems that only deal with a single process don't need to concern themselves with memory. There are many examples of operating systems that don't provide any memory management facilities, including PC-DOS, CP/M, and FLEX.

4.1.1 Fixed Partitioned Memory

Another simple way to allocate memory is to divide it into several regions called partitions and allocate a partition to each process. The partitions are constructed when the computer is started and not changed except by restarting the operating system. Because of the permanent nature of the partitions, this method of memory management is called Fixed Partition memory allocation. This is analogous to the most common way of allocating parking space—marking off parking places with lines on the pavement and allowing one car in each place.

It is simplest if all partitions are the same size, but it may be better to make them different. If they are all the same size, a process can either fit in any partition, or none of them. Since all partitions are the same, the operating system can use any convenient rule to assign them.

Partitions of a variety of sizes accomodate processes that require lots of memory without requiring all the partitions to be big enough to hold them. The analogy in the parking world would be to have several different sized spaces. Some suitable for cars, others for trucks.

This enhancement to the partitioned memory system causes lots of trouble. If all the small partitions are full, can a process use a partition that's too large for it, or should it wait for a small partition to free up? How many different sizes of partition should be used to get the best possible use of memory? Think of the parking situation again. If all the car slots are full, should a car be permitted to use a truck place? Is it a good idea to have special motorcycle places? How about compact car parking spaces? Remember that small spaces are efficient ways to store small vehicles, but they are entirely wasted when small vehicles don't need to park.

An operating system that uses partitioned memory is easy to write, but it tends to waste memory. Attempting to fix the problem makes this method complicated without fixing anything.

There are some special cases where partitioned memory is fine. Many operating systems set aside a special area in memory for small utility programs. That is a trivial example of partitioned memory. It is wasted space much of the time, but it is a small partition so the waste is minimal. These small partitions are especially useful for running programs like print spoolers that are meant to be tucked out of the way.

4.1.2 Dynamic Allocation

If fixed partitions aren't good enough, memory can be allocated in suitable chunks as it is needed. This is a good idea, but it's not as easy as it might sound. Let's move right to the parking problem. This system is like having a parking attendant who directs vehicles to the right spot without any lines on the pavement. If there are a variety of different sized vehicles, the attendant should be able to use his freedom to pack them more efficiently than he could if he had to place them in pre-marked areas.

Things look very good as the first batch of cars and trucks are parked, but after a few leave and others arrive trouble starts to appear. Say the street is filled up end to end, then five small cars leave from five separate locations. Now a small truck arrives.

4.1. THE THEORETICAL BASE

It is small enough to fit in much less than the amount of space just vacated by the five cars, but, since the five empty slots are in five different places, they are useless to the truck. If a truck leaves and a car gets to the place first, it will take up some part of the space. Most of the space is still there, but it isn't any good for the next truck to come by.

There are two standard ways of managing memory when it is isn't partitioned in advance. They are called first-fit and best-fit.

4.1.3 First-Fit Allocation

First-fit allocation is the simplest method. The operating system chooses the first block of memory at least as big as the amount requested. It allocates as much of the block as required leaving the rest as a smaller unallocated block. Unfortunately this tends to use up big blocks of memory leaving lots of little chunks that can only be used to satisfy small requests.

4.1.4 Best-Fit Allocation

Best-fit requires the operating system to do more work, but it does a better job than first-fit of keeping large blocks of memory for programs that really need them. In best-fit allocation, the operating system scans through its available memory looking for the block that fits the request with the least memory left over. This method leaves slivers of unallocated memory around, but it preserves large blocks of memory by refusing to use them as long as any smaller blocks will do the job.

There are other methods. The oddest one I know of is worst-fit allocation. Worst-fit allocations are always made from the largest block of storage. The reasoning is that the fragment of the large block that is left over after the allocation is made will be larger, and therefore more useful, than it would be if the allocation were made out of a smaller block. This policy amounts to punishing large blocks of free memory. For typical sequences of memory allocation and free operations, the result is a lot of roughly equal-sized blocks of free memory.

Most people use first-fit to manage on-street parking when there is no attendant. Those whose parallel parking skills aren't so good lean toward a worst-fit method— perhaps that's why on-street parking is usually partitioned. If drivers park in the first space they see that is long enough for their car, they are using first-fit. Those who go out of their way to find a large space are using a modified worst-fit algorithm.

Best-fit probably wouldn't work without an attendant. It requires each driver to check all empty parking places and pick the spot that most precisely fits his car.

4.2 OS-9 Memory Management

To bring reality in for a moment, OS-9 uses first-fit allocation to manage its memory. Microware added a special twist by having module storage and system memory requests start from high memory, and data storage allocations start in low memory. You can watch it in action by starting several programs running in the background. The easiest program to use space with is *sleep*. *Mfree* reports on where free space is located, and *mdir* can list the addresses where modules reside. There is no standard command[1] in OS-9 that directly reports the data space associated with each process so this must be inferred from *mfree*'s output.

The following example is taken from a 2-Megabyte GMX Micro-20. It gives different numbers on other hardware or with a different software configuration, but it should have the same flavor on any configuration.

First set up a special startup file:

```
-np
-nt
load utils
link shell cio
setime -s
iniz d0 h0
```

Utils is a file containing *link*, *setime*, *date*, *mdir*, *mfree*, *sleep*, and *iniz*. This file contains all the modules we will use in this experiment. Loading them all from one file puts them in a contiguous block of memory and avoids extraneous memory fragmentation.

Now reboot the system to get a clean memory map, and use the *mdir −e* command. Examine the module addresses in the first column of its output. The modules that were loaded as part of the OS-9 bootstrap, from OS9Boot, probably appear all together, and probably at low addresses. Modules loaded from startup are at higher addresses. You should find all the modules loaded from Utils in a contiguous block of memory and the other modules used in startup, *shell cio* and *load*, nearby. *Load* is in memory as a ghost module. It was used by the startup script, and the memory has not been required for anything else yet.

After removing from the output of *mdir −e* all the modules loaded from the OS9Boot file, we are left with the modules shown in figure 4.1.

Now use *mfree −e* to get a better idea of the layout of memory. The output is shown in figure 4.2.

---

[1] The *maps* utility does show the memory associated with each process. It is included with any system that has SSM.

4.2. OS-9 MEMORY MANAGEMENT

Figure 4.1: MDir of Modules Loaded at Startup

```
Addr       Size       Owner      Perm Type Revs  Ed #  Lnk  Module name
--------   --------   ---------  ---- ---- ----  ----- ----- -----------
001f7530   20754      1.0        0555 Prog c001  52    2    shell
001f5720   3284       1.0        0555 Prog c001  16    0    load
001f07d0   17732      1.0        0555 Trap c009   6    2    cio
001e9210   3082       1.0        0555 Prog c001  15    1    link
001e9e1a   4702       1.0        0555 Prog c001  24    0    setime
001eb078   2824       1.0        0555 Prog c001  17    0    date
001ebb80   5214       1.0        0555 Prog c001  20    1    mdir
001ecfde   2736       1.0        0555 Prog c001  15    0    mfree
001eda8e   3312       1.0        0555 Prog c001  13    0    sleep
001ee77e   2426       1.0        0555 Prog c001  15    0    iniz
```

Figure 4.2: MFree at Startup

```
Minimum allocation size:       0.25 K-bytes
Total RAM at startup:       2044.00 K-bytes
Current total free RAM:     1859.00 K-bytes

Free memory map:

    Segment Address          Size of Segment
    -----------------        -------------------------
        $15700               $200            0.50 K-bytes
        $17700               $1D0600      1857.50 K-bytes
        $1F4E00              $100            0.25 K-bytes
        $1F6400              $100            0.25 K-bytes
        $1FC700              $200            0.50 K-bytes
```

Modules fill 121,350 bytes of memory plus an extra 12 bytes to bring the size of the boot file up to a multiple of 256 bytes and 238 bytes to bring the size of Utils up to a multiple of 256 bytes. Since there are 1859 kilobytes free, there are $2044k - 1859k - 118.75k = 66.25k$ bytes used to run *mdir* and for system data structures.

Now let's confuse issues by starting a bunch of *sleep*'s for different lengths of time with different memory requirements[2]. The best way to start several processes quickly is with a shell script. The following typescript records the process of creating a shell script with the *build* utility and executing it by giving its name to the shell:

```
$ build tmp
? sleep 1000 #460k&
? sleep 10000 #20k&
? sleep 1000 #350k&
? sleep 10000 #20k&
? sleep 1000 #480k&
? sleep 10000 #20k&
? <esc>
$ tmp
+5
+6
+7
+8
+9
+10
```

Immediately after all the *sleep*'s start, memory is in the state shown in figure 4.3.

When the three shorter *sleep*'s end, memory has changed to the state shown in figure 4.4.

There are 1761.50 kilobytes free, but if you try to run a program that needs more than 484.25 kilobytes, the program will not be able to find sufficient memory. Try it:

```
$ sleep 4 #500k
Error #000:237
```

Error number 237 is an "insufficient contiguous memory" error. It is telling us that OS-9 can't find enough memory in one block to satisfy our request. Since the problem took place while OS-9 was trying to allocate memory for a process it was forking, it gave a 237 error instead of the usual error 207.

We can use this setup to verify that OS-9 allocates memory using first-fit rules.

```
$ Sleep 600 #340k&
```

The memory for this *sleep* could fit in any of the four large blocks of free memory (see figure 4.4). If OS-9 is using best-fit, it will land in the 354.25 kilobyte slot. If

---

[2]The memory requirement of *sleep* can be specified by the # shell option.

4.3. MEMORY FRAGMENTATION

Figure 4.3: Displays while *Sleep*s are Active

```
Minimum allocation size:      0.25 K-bytes
Current total free RAM:     435.25 K-bytes

Free memory map:

    Segment Address         Size of Segment
    ----------------        ---------------------------
        $15700              $200            0.50 K-bytes
        $16700              $B00            2.75 K-bytes
        $170000             $6AB00        426.75 K-bytes
        $1E6D00             $800            2.00 K-bytes
        $1EF100             $400            1.00 K-bytes
        $1F0000             $500            1.25 K-bytes
        $1F4E00             $100            0.25 K-bytes
        $1F5400             $100            0.25 K-bytes
        $1F6400             $100            0.25 K-bytes
        $1FC700             $100            0.25 K-bytes
```

it is using first-fit, it will land in the 463 kilobyte slot or the 436.25 kilobyte slot depending on the direction from which it is searching. Using a worst-fit algorithm, OS-9 would pick the 484.25 kilobyte slot. Another *mfree* command gives the output in figure 4.5 This tells us that OS-9 used the memory from $17700 to $6d7ff for the memory needed by *sleep*. This demonstrates that OS-9 uses first-fit allocation.

4.3 Memory Fragmentation

Every method of allocating system memory on the fly can be pushed into a situation where there is plenty of memory available, but the memory is divided into so many small blocks that it is useless. If it were possible to shift the allocated blocks of memory around until all the free space between them was squeezed out to one end, fragmented memory could be made useful again. The process of rearranging memory to make large blocks of free space is called "garbage collection." Basic and lisp usually have built in garbage collection—they pause from time to time and organize their storage. OS-9 doesn't do garbage collection, but if you usually run just one or two processes at a time you probably won't have any trouble with memory fragmentation.

Memory fragmentation is caused by dynamic memory demands. When OS-9 only has to deal with one or two blocks of memory at a time, it can keep things in

Figure 4.4: Some *Sleep*s Done

```
Minimum allocation size:        0.25 K-bytes
Current total free RAM:      1761.50 K-bytes

Free memory map:

    Segment Address          Size of Segment
    ----------------         ----------------------
        $15700               $200         0.50 K-bytes
        $17700               $73C00     463.00 K-bytes
        $91400               $58900     354.25 K-bytes
        $EFE00               $79100     484.25 K-bytes
        $16F000              $6D100     436.25 K-bytes
        $1DDF00              $1600        5.50 K-bytes
        $1E0B00              $1E00        7.50 K-bytes
        $1E3100              $800         2.00 K-bytes
        $1E6D00              $1000        4.00 K-bytes
        $1EF100              $400         1.00 K-bytes
        $1EF700              $800         2.00 K-bytes
        $1F4E00              $100         0.25 K-bytes
        $1F5300              $200         0.50 K-bytes
        $1F6400              $100         0.25 K-bytes
        $1FC700              $100         0.25 K-bytes
```

good order. If you allocate and release large blocks of memory frequently, there is lots of potential for trouble.

One cause of fragmentation is hard to control. The first time a device is opened OS-9 allocates static memory for it out of system memory (high memory). If high memory is crowded when you open the device, the static storage could be located in an inconvenient spot. Killing processes and unlinking modules won't make the static storage go away. The best way to avoid the problem is to open your devices early even if you don't plan to use them until later. An *iniz* command in the startup file is the best way to get all the devices initialized early.

        $ iniz t1 t2 d0 d1 h1 r0

In the previous example, the fragmentation took place in data storage, but module storage can have the same trouble. If you use modules heavily—loading them when you need them and unlinking them when you don't—you can fragment memory.

4.3. MEMORY FRAGMENTATION

Figure 4.5: Test for First-Fit Allocation

```
Minimum allocation size:      0.25 K-bytes
Total RAM at startup:      2044.00 K-bytes
Current total free RAM:    1409.75 K-bytes

Free memory map:

    Segment Address        Size of Segment
    ----------------       ---------------------
        $15700           $200        0.50 K-bytes
        $6D800           $1DB00    118.75 K-bytes
        $91400           $58900    354.25 K-bytes
        $EFE00           $79100    484.25 K-bytes
        $16F000          $6D100    436.25 K-bytes
        $1DDF00          $1600       5.50 K-bytes
        $1E0B00          $800        2.00 K-bytes
        $1E3100          $800        2.00 K-bytes
        $1E6D00          $1000       4.00 K-bytes
        $1EF100          $400        1.00 K-bytes
        $1F4E00          $100        0.25 K-bytes
        $1F5300          $200        0.50 K-bytes
        $1F6400          $100        0.25 K-bytes
        $1FC700          $100        0.25 K-bytes
```

Starting lots of processes (as we did with *sleep*) exercises OS-9's memory-allocation system. Each process allocates some data space. If all processes retain their memory for about the same length of time, any fragmentation tends to heal eventually... at least it seems under control. The worst situation is caused by a long-running process that has a chunk of memory right in the middle.

There is only one way to de-fragment memory: kill some processes so they release their memory. Then restart them. The restarted processes will get memory at the far ends of memory and leave the prime locations in the middle free. In the previous example, the fragmentation situation would have been much improved if we had killed the second 20k sleep, process eight. If we had killed all of the sleeps with 20k of memory, free memory would have been nearly contiguous.

4.4 Memory Protection

Systems with memory protection hardware (an MMU[3]) can use OS-9 SSM support. This addition to the OS-9 kernel implements several protection boundaries.

- The kernel and other system code have unlimited access to memory.

- User-state processes have unlimited access to their data area and any memory they acquire with the *F$SRqMem* SVC. They also have access to modules that they find with the *F$Load* or *F$Link* SVCs. The main program module is linked for the process by the *F$Fork* that started it. Access to modules may be limited by the access permissions in the module header.

- A process has access to all the memory of processes that it spawns with the *F$DFork* call.

The limitations of the MMU constrain the values used for D_BlkSiz, the units of memory OS-9's memory management subsystem uses for allocation. Four kilobyte units of memory are common in systems with SSM because that block size is compatible with the MMU hardware Microware supports.

4.5 Memory Management Service Requests

There are only four system service requests that directly affect memory management: *F$Mem*, *F$SRqMem*, *F$SRqCMem*, and *F$SRtMem*. These requests are used to set the memory allocation of a process. The memory management SVCs control the allocation of two classes of memory: program data memory and system memory.

The program data area is for predictable memory requirements like a program's stack and static memory requirements. Each process is given one block of program data area when it is forked. The size may be decreased as the process runs, but a process can never have more than one data area.

System memory is for temporary or unpredictable memory requirements. A process can have many blocks of system memory, but the blocks can't be resized. Processes start with no system memory, but can request (and return) blocks of it as they run.

Program data area memory is located as near the bottom of memory as possible, and system memory is located high in memory. The different types of memory are allocated from areas that are as far apart as possible to work against fragmentation. It

---

[3]Microware supports several memory management units: the 68020 with the 68851 coprocessor, the 68030, the 68040, the 68451, and the P32. Other MMUs require new SSM modules.

4.5. MEMORY MANAGEMENT SERVICE REQUESTS

is particularly important to keep the operating system's tables (which tend to be small and long-lived) away from the process stacks (which tend to be large and short-lived). If system data structures were allocated from the same end of memory as process stacks, path buffers and similar system memory would quickly fragment memory by appearing directly above each stack allocation.

The *F$Mem* SVC controls the size of the program data area. When *F$Mem* is called, the D0 register must contain the number of bytes you would like the process to have in its data memory area. If the amount of memory requested is less than the current memory size, but not zero, OS-9 decreases the allocation to the amount requested and returns the new amount of memory in D0 and upper bound of the region in A1. If additional memory is required, OS-9 returns an E$NORAM error.[4] The actual size allocated is useful because OS-9 always allocates memory in pages of D_BlkSiz bytes. Your request will be rounded up to the nearest page. If the amount of memory requested is zero, OS-9 doesn't change the memory allocation. It only returns the size and high bound of the process' memory.

The *F$Mem* request has several possibilities for error. First, successful expansion is so unreliable that the kernel doesn't even try. Expansion requires free memory immediately above the current data memory. In a quiet system that might work, but if other processes are active, their data areas may be located directly in the expansion path. Even decreasing the memory allocation can cause trouble. If you try to release memory including the page containing the top of the stack (where the stack pointer, A7, is pointing), OS-9 will accuse you of a suicide attempt and return an error.

The data memory area is a contiguous block of memory that always contains the stack and the process' parameter area. Programming languages usually keep all variables in this area. The stack grows from the top of the data memory area down. Static variables are allocated from the bottom up. The following fragment of C code demonstrates this.

```
int array1[50];          /* Stored near the bottom of data memory  */
char *string="Test string";  /* The pointer, string, is near the    */
                         /* bottom of data memory. The string      */
                         /* itself is kept in the program module.  */
```

---

[4] I think OS-9 lost the ability to expand the stack with *F$Mem* when it gained colored memory. There is some sense to this new behavior. On OS-9/6809 Level Two the address translation hardware and software would let *F$Mem* succeed if there was free memory anywhere in the system. Without address translation, the chances of *F$Mem* finding free memory above the current data area are pretty good but not certain. Evidently the kernel implementors opted for speed, small size, and a reliable response even if the response is always no.

```
main()
{
    int test1;          /* These are automatic variables. They are */
    int test2;          /* stored on the stack.                    */
    static int test3;   /* This one's static. It is allocated      */
                        /* near the bottom of the data area.       */
    ...
}
```

The linker sets the size of the data area by adding up the stack-space and static data requirements of all the psects making up a program. You can increase this number with a linker option, or use the shell's "#" option to increase it when the program is started.

When a program needs memory in unpredictable amounts, it should use dynamic allocation. In C, the malloc() function is the usual way to dynamically allocate memory. Pascal programmers use NEW. These functions use the OS-9 *F$SRqMem* SVC to get blocks of memory from the system memory area. Once a block of memory is allocated by *F$SRqMem* its size is fixed, but a program can allocate up to 32 non-contiguous blocks of system memory. Each request for system memory is filled by a simple first-fit search of free memory. Programs routinely allocate and free system memory as they run.

The simple *F$SRqMem* system call is equivalent to the colored-memory system call *F$SRqCMem* with a memory type of 0. If a type other than zero is specified, the *F$SrqCMem* is constrained to return only the type of memory requested—or E$NoRAM.

System memory can be returned to the system one block at a time. The *F$SRtMem* SVC takes the address and size of the block of system memory and returns it to the pool of free memory. Even if a process fails to explicitly free memory that was allocated to it, OS-9 frees the memory when the process terminates.

Memory allocated to system code like device drivers, system-state processes, and SVC's is not automatically freed by the kernel. System state code that allocates memory *must* free the memory or it will remain allocated until the system is rebooted.

Chapter 5

Memory Management Internals

> *This chapter details some of the algorithms and data structures that the OS-9 kernel uses for memory management.*

5.1 The Process Memory Table

To insure that all memory allocated to a process is freed when that process exits, the kernel must keep track of the memory allocated to each user-state process. The process descriptor contains the location and size of the process' stack allocation and the locations and sizes of up to 32 other blocks of memory. Whenever the kernel allocates memory to a process via the *F$SRqMem* system call, it records the address and length of the memory block in the process' memory allocation table. In very early versions of OS-9, this literally meant that each process was allowed to do only a fixed number of *F$SRqMem* calls without freeing a block with *F$SRtMem*. Now, the number of *F$SRqMem* calls without a *F$SRtMem* varies. It will always be at least 32, but if the kernel is able to allocate memory that lies on either side of memory that is already in the process' memory table, the memory allocator will concatenate the new memory with the adjacent entry already in the table.

Processes very seldom run out of entries in the process memory table. If the table does overflow, the *F$SRqMem* will return a E$MemFul error. If the process is a C program that attempts to use the ibrk() function before it falls back on ebrk() or _srqmem() for memory allocation, it might be worth starting with a larger memory allocation, but increasing the size of malloc()'s minimum memory request with _mallocmin() is a more reliable technique.

Adding a call to _mallocmin() near the beginning of a C program—right after the declarations in main()—is the simplest and most effective way to prevent the process memory list from overflowing. The default minimum F$SRqMem size for the malloc family is the greater of 512 bytes or the value of D_BlkSiz from system globals.

For example, a program that attempts to use malloc() to allocate 124 kilobytes in little chunks and fails with E$MemFul, could be improved by adding

```
_mallocmin(124*1024);
```

to beginning of main(). This new minimum allocation value prevents the memory list from overflowing. It will also (sometimes quite importantly) usually prevent malloc() from making a system call: a potential major performance improvement.

Increasing the value of D_BlkSiz in system globals makes memory allocation table overflows less likely for all processes regardless of their language; see section 5.2. However, any changes to D_BlkSiz must be made before system initialization is complete. The best opportunity to change D_BlkSiz is in a P2 module's initialization code. Once the system is running, the kernel will object to any change to D_BLkSiz by crashing... probably for no obvious reason.

Changing the value of M$Mem to prevent fragmentation only rarely works, but it is easy and the technique can be used on modules for which the source code is not available. (Although changing M$Mem is not a reliable fix for process memory list overflows, it is very effective at curing stack overflows.) Before trying this approach, it is prudent to experiment by running the program with the process' initial memory allocation temporarily changed by the shell's # command line option. The process executed by

```
$ test #100k
```

will fork the program with 100 kilobytes more than its default allocation.

The default memory allocation for a module can be changed in the linker:

```
$ l68 -M=24k test.r
```

or in the C compiler executive:

```
$ cc -M=24k test.c
```

For modules that only exist in compiled and linked form, the default memory allocation can be changed with the debugger followed by *fixmod -u* to update the module's CRC and header checksum:

5.2. FRAGMENT LISTS

```
$ debug
dbg: l test                          Link to the module we want to change
dbg: cl .r7+38              Prepare to change the field at offset 38, M$Mem
0x0000003C+r7:00000C00 1000              Change it from 3k to 4k
0x00000040+r7:00005E42 .
dbg: q
$ save test                           Save the altered module to a file
$ fixmod -u test                              Fix the CRC in the file
Module:   test - Fixing module CRC
$
```

For OS-9 version 2.4, the memory allocation for program modules is the sum of the stack size and memory size from the module header, plus the size of parameters passed when the program is forked, plus any additional memory requested when the program is forked. From the kernel's point of view, it doesn't matter whether debug is used to change M$Mem or M$Stack.

5.2 Fragment Lists

SSM makes fragment lists necessary, but they are useful even when there is no memory protection hardware. They give excellent performance in one common special case, prevent performance from going completely bad in another common special case, and help prevent fragmentation.

Fragment lists form buffers between the kernel's main list of free memory and each process. The value of D_BlkSiz in system globals controls the minimum size of allocations from the system memory list; D_BlkSiz is generally set around 256.[1] D_MinBlk, in system globals, controls the minimum block size of memory allocated to processes; D_MinBlk is almost invariably set to 16 bytes.[2] Allocations from the system free memory list are rounded up to a multiple of D_BlkSiz bytes, and the amount of memory returned to the caller is rounded up to a multiple of D_MinBlk. When D_BlkSiz is not equal to D_MinBlk there may be a difference between the amount of memory taken from the system free memory list and the amount delivered to the caller. This extra memory is left in a fragment list.

Imagine a program that uses *F$SRqMem* calls to allocate memory for linked list nodes and *F$SRtMem* calls to release the memory from nodes that are not in use.

---

[1] 4096 for many systems with SSM.

[2] D_MinBlk must be set to a power of two, and since some processors only load full words (such as pointers) from full word boundaries, D_MinBlk must be at least 4 bytes. Sixteen-byte blocks of memory keep allocated memory aligned enough to make even the 68040 happy.

Pseudo-code for the insert and delete functions would look like this:

```
Insert(data, after)
    datatype data
    nodetype after                              Insert after this node
{
    newnode = F$SRqMem(nodesize)
    newnode→data = data
    newnode→next = after→next
    after→next = newnode
}

delete(after)
    nodetype after                              Delete the node after this one
{
    holdptr = after→next
    after→next = after→next→next
    F$SRtMem(holdptr)
}
```

If the kernel did not use fragment lists, these functions would run very slowly, and they would very likely cause such horrible fragmentation that no other process could allocate memory. With fragment lists in operation, these functions will not cause horrible fragmentation and their performance will be much better than they would be without fragment lists.

Without fragment lists, the best we could hope for would be for all the nodes to be allocated from contiguous memory. Then ten-thousand 64-byte nodes would use a bit more than half a megabyte and as further insertions and deletions took place, around ten-thousand nodes would continue to use around a half megabyte. If other processes had already fragmented memory somewhat, insertions would fill 32 empty spaces in memory. Then the process' memory list would fill and it would be unable to allocate more memory. The memory it had allocated would cause fragmentation until the process exited or freed the memory some other way.

With the fragment list, memory is drawn from the system list 256 bytes at a time. A *F$SRqMem* for 64 bytes gets 256 bytes from the system memory list, leaves 192 bytes in the process' fragment list and returns 64 bytes to the process. The next 3 *F$SRqMem* system calls are satisfied from the fragment list. *F$SRtMem* system calls for 64-byte chunks of memory are also caught in the fragment list, there the memory is used to satisfy further *F$SRqMem* calls until they can be coalesced with other memory in the fragment list into a 256-byte block that can be returned to the system memory list. After an initial allocation phase, the process will probably do almost all its memory operations in and out of its fragment list.

Since memory in the fragment list is already allocated to the process:

- Operations on the fragment list do not have to call the SSM functions to change memory's protection attributes.

- The process memory list does not need to be updated.

- Only the performance of the process owning the fragment list is hurt by the length of the free list caused by the tiny fragments.

- Since any contiguous block of D_BlkSiz or more bytes is returned to the system memory list, even the process owning the fragment list need not attempt to return freed memory to the fragment list when it frees more than D$BlkSiz bytes. This improves performance for all processes.

- When the process uses chiefly blocks of some particular small size (64-bytes here), the fragment list serves as a cache for those memory blocks. *F$SRqMem* system calls will almost always be satisfied from the first node in the fragment list.

Fragment lists generally improve performance and prevent process' memory allocation tables from filling as fast as they might. However, in a system without an MMU, the use of fragment lists removes memory from the general system pool and commits it to a process before the process requests the memory. For instance, with D_BlkSiz of 256 bytes and D_MinBlk of 16 bytes, a request for 32 bytes returns 32 bytes to the calling process and leaves $256 - 32 = 224$ bytes in the process' fragment list. If the process never requests another block of memory less than or equal to 224 bytes in size, that memory goes unused. If D_BlkSiz had been 16 bytes, no memory would have gone to the fragment list and those 224 bytes would have been available to other processes.

5.3 Colored Memory

All memory is not the same. Even a simple system usually contains RAM and ROM. More complicated systems have non-volatile RAM, fast RAM, slow RAM, video RAM, RAM that is available for DMA, and perhaps other classes of memory as well. The OS-9 colored memory structure lets the kernel recognize these distinctions and lets programs request specific types of memory when they have special requirements.

Colored memory might have been called typed memory or classified memory, but color is a nice attribute with hints of particle physics and graph theory. Any description that might actually make sense when applied to memory might constrain people's thinking about memory allocation. Nobody cares about the actual color of memory (if color applies at all), so we can use the adjective to mean whatever we like.

During initialization, the bootstrap code looks for a colored memory definition list in the init module. If it finds a colored memory list, it amends its builtin list of memory ranges using the colored memory list. This list itemizes each address range that might contain memory and the attributes of memory that might be found in that address range. The initialization code inserts each block of RAM into the system's list of free memory with the attributes given to that range of memory in the init module. Blocks of ROM identified by the colored memory definition are added to the list of ROM used by the boot code and are searched for memory at boot time.

Some of the information in the colored memory definition list is entirely for the convenience of the kernel:

- The range of local bus addresses for this memory. This is the high and low address the kernel should use when looking for this memory.

- The granularity of the boot-time search for memory in this address range. When the kernel is checking to see where memory exists in the address range, it probes for memory then skips ahead this many bytes. If the number is too small, booting will be slow. If the number is too large, the bootstrap might skip over some memory or fail to accurately find the end of a block of memory.

- The external bus translation address. On a multi-master system with dual-ported RAM this is the address of the beginning of the block when seen from another bus master's point of view. This value is used by the *F$Trans* SVC, which is mainly used by drivers and multi-CPU communication packages.

The other fields in the colored memory definition list directly affect the way memory is allocated.

- The memory type attribute is used when a system call requests a particular type of memory. The *F$SRqCMem*, *F$DatMod*, and *F$Load* system calls all take a memory type parameter. If the type is zero, the kernel ignores type when finding memory to satisfy this request. If the type is not zero, the kernel only considers memory of the requested type.

- The memory priority attribute is used for every system call that allocates memory. If the call does not specify a type, the call returns the highest priority memory

5.3. COLORED MEMORY

that it can find. If the call does specify a type, the search is performed in descending priority order constrained to colors of that type.

- The access permissions of the memory:

    B_USER Bit 0: This memory is available to user processes. In OS-9 release 2.4.3, the B_USER bit affects the memories *visibility* but does not affect its usability. B_USER should always be set for memory that should be available to user code. Future releases of OS-9 may (in my view, *should*) fully support the B_USER attribute such that only memory requests from system code can allocate memory without the B_USER attribute.

    B_PARITY Bit 1: The system initializes the parity in this range of memory at boot time. If parity checked memory is read before it is written for the first time, it has an even chance of returning a parity error; consequently, the boot code writes all parity checked memory as part of the bootstrap process.

    B_ROM Bit 2: This attribute is called ROM, but it should not be taken too literally. Only memory with this attribute is searched for modules at boot time. Setting this attribute for non-volatile RAM, or even ordinary RAM when the power is not turned off before the boot, causes the bootstrap to find any modules left in the RAM and register them in the module directory. Nevertheless, it is usually a bad thing to turn on the B_ROM attribute for memory that is not actually ROM. Parity checked RAM that is given the B_ROM attribute is not initialized—and consequently may have random parity after system initialization—even if it has the B_PARITY attribute, and memory with the B_ROM attribute is not included in the system free memory list, so it cannot be allocated by the kernel.

Memory with a priority of zero is a useful special case. It can only be allocated by a system call that specifically requests memory of that type.

When the kernel can satisfy a memory request from two areas with the same priority, it allocates the memory from the area with the most free memory.

5.3.1 Colored Memory and Fragment Lists

Memory retains its color information even after it has been moved from the system's main free memory list to a fragment list. Each process descriptor has pointers to a doubly-linked colored memory descriptor list that contains descriptors for every memory color that has ever been in that process' fragment list.

The following describes the colored memory data structures (see figure 5.1 for a picture).

- The memory list in the init module is used to build the kernel's master colored memory descriptor list. The colored memory descriptor list is a doubly-linked list of descriptors that contain information about the color and pointers to the free memory list and system fragment list for that color.

- The system fragment lists (one per color) are used for memory allocation services requested by operating system code.

- The free memory lists (one per color) are used for all memory allocation services that are not completed at the appropriate fragment list.

- Each process descriptor contains pointers, _cfrag[0] and _cfrag[1], that link it to a doubly-linked list of colored memory descriptors: one descriptor for each memory color that has ever been in that process' fragment list.

- The process colored memory descriptor lists use the same structures as the system colored memory descriptor lists, but they only have fragment lists attached to them; there are no process-specific free memory lists.

5.3.2 Case Studies

A system has fast memory and slow memory and we want to configure it to use the slow memory only when it runs out of fast memory. We give the fast memory a higher priority than the slow memory:

```
MemList
*               MemType  type,priority,attributes,blksiz,low-limit,high-limit,
*                        name,DMA-offset
                MemType  SYSRAM,136,B_USER,4096,0,$200000,Fast,0
                MemType  SYSRAM,120,B_USER,4096,$400000,$800000,Slow,0
                dc.l     0          end of list
Slow            dc.b     "Slow RAM",0
Fast            dc.b     "Fast RAM",0
```

With this memory list, all memory requests that can be satisfied from the memory with a priority of 136 use that block of memory. Other requests fall back on the memory with a priority of 120.

A system has fast memory and slow memory and we want to configure it so the fast memory is hard to get.

5.3. COLORED MEMORY

One approach is to make the fast memory available for all callers, but insist that they ask for it:

```
FSTRAM   equ       0x02
MemList
*        MemType   type,priority,attributes,blksiz,low-limit,high-limit,
*                  name,DMA-offset
         MemType   SYSRAM,128,B_USER,4096,$400000,$8000000,Slow,0
         MemType   FSTRAM,0,B_USER,4096,0,$200000,Fast,0
         dc.l      0         end of list
Slow     dc.b      "Slow RAM",0
Fast     dc.b      "Fast RAM",0
```

This use of priority zero memory forces callers to *ask* for fast memory. The kernel returns E$NoRAM to a caller rather than giving fast RAM to a process that asked for ordinary RAM.

Combining type and priority lets the system hand out fast or slow RAM preferentially but still allow callers to request the type they want. Here's the memory list that allocates slow memory first when the caller doesn't specify a type:

```
FSTRAM   equ       0x02
MemList
*        MemType   type,priority,attributes,blksiz,low-limit,high-limit,
*                  name,DMA-offset
         MemType   SYSRAM,136,B_USER,4096,$400000,$800000,Slow,0
         MemType   FSTRAM,120,B_USER,4096,0,$200000,Fast,0
         dc.l      0         end of list
Slow     dc.b      "Slow RAM",0
Fast     dc.b      "Fast RAM",0
```

A system has three types of RAM:

- 512 kilobytes of memory that can be used by video processor A,
- 512 kilobytes of memory that can be used by video processor B, and
- 1024 kilobytes of memory that neither video processor can reach.

Since data for the video processors tends to use large amounts of memory, we want to preserve the video memory for images when possible, but when no other memory is available, the kernel should allocate memory from the banks of memory accessible to the video processors. Programs call for memory that is accessible to one video processor or the other, but they generally ask for general-purpose memory without specifying a type. The memory list for such a system might look like:

```
MemList
*               MemType   type,priority,attributes,blksiz,low-limit,high-limit,
*                         name,DMA-offset
                MemType   SYSRAM,136,B_USER,4096,$100000,$200000,SysMem,0
                MemType   VIDEO1,120,B_USER,4096,0,$80000,Plane1,0
                MemType   VIDEO2,120,B_USER,4096,$80000,$100000,Plane2,0
                dc.l      0       end of list
SysMem          dc.b      "System memory",0
Plane1          dc.b      "Video Plane A memory",0
Plane2          dc.b      "Video Plane B memory",0
```

Since the two video planes have the same priority, the kernel satisfies requests that don't specify a memory type from the SYSRAM type, then, if there is insufficient RAM there, the request goes to the video plane with the most free memory. This keeps the memory load roughly evenly divided between the image planes.

Memory requests must be satisfied from one color of memory. This restriction can be used to create artificial barriers. This is generally a silly idea, but it could be useful in special cases. For instance, even a system with only one type of memory can use colored memory to set aside a block of memory for a special purpose:

```
MemList
RESRAM  equ       2
*               MemType   type,priority,attributes,blksiz,low-limit,high-limit,
*                         name,DMA-offset
                MemType   SYSRAM,128,B_USER,4096,0,$180000,SysRam,0
                MemType   RESRAM,0,B_USER,4096,$180000,$200000,Reserved,0
                dc.l      0       end of list
SysRam          dc.b      "System memory",0
Reserved        dc.b      "Reserved memory",0
```

There might also be some reason to reject requests for large quantities of memory:

```
MemList
*               MemType   type,priority,attributes,blksiz,low-limit,high-limit,
*                         name,DMA-offset
                MemType   SYSRAM,128,B_USER,4096,0,$200000,SysRam,0
                MemType   SYSRAM,128,B_USER,4096,$200000,$400000,OSRam,0
                dc.l      0       end of list
SysRam          dc.b      "System memory",0
OSRam           dc.b      "Reserved for OS",0
```

Even though these colors of memory have identical characteristics except for their address ranges, they are recognized as distinct colors and every memory request will

5.3. COLORED MEMORY

be satisfied from the color with the most free memory.[3] A system with this memory list will be unable to fill a request for more than two megabytes even if more than that much memory is free.

In some circumstances a memory list like the one shown above will control fragmentation, but colored memory offers potential for a better solution.

In OS-9 release 2.4.3, the following trick does not work, but it will be useful if Microware fully implements the B_USER attribute.

```
MemList
*              MemType  type,priority,attributes,blksiz,low-limit,high-limit,
*                       name,DMA-offset
               MemType  SYSRAM,128,B_USER,4096,0,$380000,SysRam,0
               MemType  SYSRAM,136,0,4096,$380000,$400000,SysRam,0
               dc.l     0          end of list
SysRam         dc.b     "System memory",0
```

Memory allocated by the kernel uses high RAM until it overflows. This prevents I/O buffers and other system data structures from appearing in the middle of memory. If the kernel expands the event table (or any other system data structure), and the memory allocator gives it memory in the middle of the main range of RAM, only a reboot or a sufficient increase in the number of events to call for another event table expansion will free that memory. Preventing that situation may be worth the small memory waste imposed by a reserved region for operating system memory.

---

[3]Though the other color will be tried if the first returns E$NoRAM. It is possible for the color with the most memory to be too fragmented to satisfy a request, while the color with less free memory could have a larger block of contiguous free memory.

Figure 5.1: Colored Memory Structures

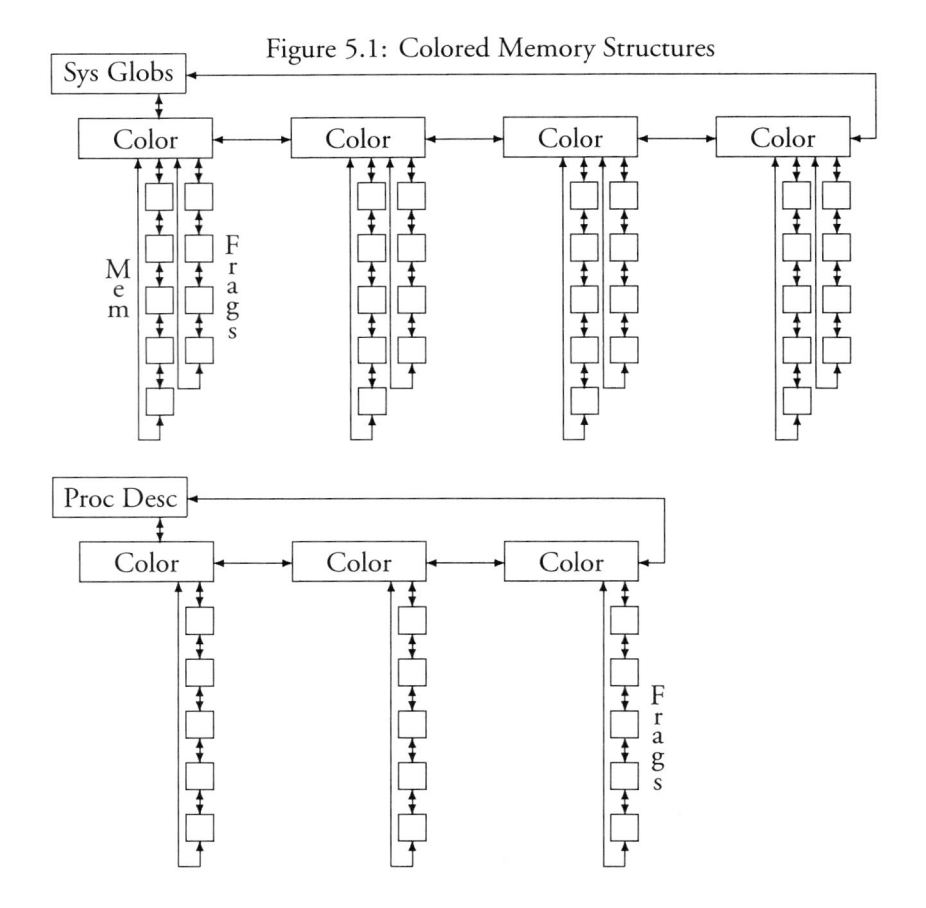

Chapter 6

Processes

In this chapter you will learn what processes are, how to create them, and how to control them. There is also a discussion of system tuning, the art of getting the best possible performance out of your computer.

Sometimes it seems that everything in OS-9 that isn't a module is a process. Modules hold information and processes do things. All programs involve at least one process while they are running. Frequently the words "process" and "program" are used interchangeably. All programs use CPU time, and processes are things that use CPU time. The difference is that a program is a higher-level entity. A program might involve several processes, but it certainly should do something. A process may sit around doing nothing most of the time. SysGo is a process that sits around waiting for the world to fall apart so it can rescue you. Even OS-9 itself is an odd sort of process.

6.1 Starting Processes From the Shell

When you run a program from the shell:

```
$ list /dd/defs/oskdefs.d
```

the shell "forks" a process to run the *list* program, then pauses until the new process completes. If you change the command:

```
$ list /dd/defs/oskdefs.d >/p
```

you have some options. You can just sit there and wait until the file has printed before you can start another command. If you hit control-C, the shell stops waiting. You get another prompt and can run another program (start another process). You can do this because the *list* program didn't do any I/O to your terminal. If it had, the control-C would have acted as it usually does to abort the listing.

If you know in advance that you want the listing to run in the "background," you can tell the shell not to pause after starting the process by putting an ampersand, &, after the command:

$ list /dd/defs/oskdefs.d >/p&

You get another shell prompt immediately and the listing proceeds without your attention. If you decide that cutting the list process loose was a mistake, you can change your mind with the "w" shell directive. Just type w on the command line:

$ w

The shell waits for a process it started (child process) to terminate before continuing.

6.2   Family Relationships

Processes are related by the same names as a family. There is a parent process and child processes. When a process creates a new process with the *F$Fork* SVC, it is said to have "spawned" a child. Two processes spawned by the same parent are called siblings.

6.3   A Program Named Alias

It is sometimes confusing to use several different operating systems on a daily basis, particularly when the operating systems are quite similar. It tempts one to make copies of programs and rename them to match the other operating system. Copying the files containing the programs, and editing them to change the module names, suffices to give multiple names for one program, but it uses extra memory as it results in two functionally equivalent modules with different names. Using a small program to translate the program name saves memory and adds some power as well. The *alias* program can be made to start any other program. It uses a small amount of memory, but it can set the priority or optional memory values for the program it forks. With a little extra work it can add command line options as well.

```
                    nam    alias
                    ttl    Alias Program to demonstrate F$Fork SVC
                    use    <oskdefs.d>
                    opt    -l
00000101  Type      set    (Prgrm<<8)+Objct
00008001  Revs      set    (ReEnt<<8)+1
```

6.4. CHAINING NEW PROCESSES

```
                      psect    alias,Type,Revs,1,256,Entry
00000101  AType       set      (Prgrm<<8)+Objct
00000014  AMem        set      20
0000 6469 AName       dc.b     "dir"
00000004              align
          Entry
          *
          *           This program always runs the program named dir.
          *           It will, however, appear that dir has aquired the new name, alias.
          *
          ****************
          *
          *           Prepare to fork AName
          *           Since AName gets the parms passed to alias,
          *           move a5 to a1 and d5.l to d2
          *           If AName should get alias' priority, move d2.w to d4,
          *           otherwise use a constant priority value.
          *           Dir (particularly) likes some extra memory, so give it some.
          *
0004 3802             move.w   D2,D4            move the priority to D4 for fork
0006 303c             move.w   #AType,D0        Type for forked module
000a 7214             moveq    #AMem,D1         Memory overide for forked process
000c 2405             move.l   D5,D2            Pass parameters (length)
000e 7603             moveq    #3,D3            number of paths to pass
0010 41fa             lea      AName(PCR),a0    name of module to fork
0014 224d             move.l   A5,A1            parm pointer
0016=4e40             os9      F$Fork
001a=4e40             os9      F$Wait
001e=4e40             os9      F$Exit
00000022              ends
```

To use *alias*, change the program name in the above psect (*ls* might be a good alias for *dir*) and set AName, AType, and AMem for the program you want to call. Although *alias* doesn't consider C-style environment variables, it *does* pass them through to the program it forks. Note that *alias* does not consider the path list. If *F$Fork* doesn't find the requested module (*dir*) in memory or in the default execution directory, *alias* will fail.

6.4 Chaining New Processes

The shell normally starts programs by forking them, but it can be made to chain to the program instead. The *F$Chain* service request eliminates the calling process and replaces it with the process requested by *F$Chain*. If you do this with the shell, you won't have a shell to return to. With other programs it is a way to save memory.

F$Fork followed by *F$Exit* acts almost like *F$Chain* except that between the Fork and the Exit memory is allocated for both the parent and the child process. Because of this, *F$Chain* is sometimes the only option when memory is tight.

There is also a small difference in the time required for the Fork and Chain requests. Chain is a little faster, but not enough to make a difference.

It is easy to change *alias* to use *F$Chain* instead of *F$Fork*. The result is more memory efficient and a little faster than *alias* with a *F$Fork*. Replace the three SVC calls at the end of *alias* with

```
        os9     F$Chain
```

6.5 Tuning Your Operation

One of OS-9's primary functions is to divide system resources among processes. It distributes memory and I/O devices on a first come, first served basis. Time on the microprocessor is distributed according to a combination of "demand" and "time-sliced" rules. Some things can't be delayed: keyboard input, for instance, has to be read before another character is typed. OS-9 itself provides time-critical services like I/O management. The OS-9 kernel can interrupt any process, or even itself, and take whatever time it needs.

Each process has a priority number. Processes with higher priority numbers run more frequently than processes with lower priorities. For most purposes the available range of priorities is absurdly large. A small difference between the priorities of two processes can make a large difference in their relative performance, and priority values are only important in their relation to other processes' priorities. A system running two processes at priority 50 runs exactly like the same system running those processes at a priority of 5000.

Careful adjustment of process priorities can increase the efficiency of your work. OS-9 doesn't know what each process is supposed to do, or how important it is to you. Without instructions it treats all processes the same.

All processes should not be scheduled the same way. Some processes don't need frequent access to the processor. A process that is running your printer is a good candidate for a low priority. You may think that 160 characters per second is fast; the computer doesn't. A process that has nothing to do except send 160 characters to the printer each second spends most of its time waiting. Even if it isn't right on the spot with a character to be written, it's no big deal if the printer has to wait a fraction of a second. Set the priority for this type of process low compared to other processes.[1]

---

[1] A small difference in priority numbers is enough to have a substantial effect. Giving a process a

6.5. TUNING YOUR OPERATION

It gets a crack at the processor every now and then. During its time slice the process feeds the device driver for the printer a buffer-full of characters. This buffer supplies the driver with output for the printer until the process's next turn.

A process that interacts with the world often needs high priority. It probably won't use most of its time slices because it will be waiting for input. (Actually, it won't get any CPU time at all if it's waiting for input.) When an event occurs in the world, the process waiting for that event should respond fast. Text editors usually sit around waiting for a keystroke, but it would be annoying if a key took half a second to register, or the screen updates took a few seconds. People, and other impatient real-world entities, need attention! Make sure your computer knows about your requirements by assigning a high priority to any programs that respond to impatient parts of the world.

Programs like *copy*, assemblers, and particularly the C compiler take all the resources they can get. If you want to run them with other processes, you need to protect the other processes by giving the hard-working processes a lower priority than the others.

As a rule, programs that do a lot of computation need to be interrupted by a timer and put at the back of the queue. Processes that do a lot of I/O, particularly SCF-style I/O, are already slowed by the device they are driving. They don't need to be controlled artificially. (Though they can tolerate low priorities with little degradation.)

6.5.1 Summary

Process priority has several uses. A low priority can tame CPU-intensive programs, or tuck a task that you aren't impatient about down where you won't notice its impact on the system. If you want alert responses to something you're doing, a text editor or maybe real-time graphics, a high priority insures it lots of attention from the CPU.

You won't speed anything up by assigning all your processes high priority. As the word priority implies, you have to rank processes. The difference between the priorities of processes in the system is the only aspect of priority that matters.

---

priority five or ten below other processes pushs it well into the background.

Chapter 7

Signals

In this chapter you will learn what signals are and how to control them.

Signals can be used for interprocess communication, for communication within OS-9, and for communication between the operating system and processes. In each case, signals act somewhat like hardware interrupts. When they are not masked, signals can interrupt a process after any instruction. Signals can be used to indicate exceptional conditions (like "time to clean up and exit") or as a fairly ordinary inter-process communication tool. With a handshaking protocol, signals can even be converted into a synchronous communication mechanism, but events or pipes are usually more suitable for synchronous communication.

OS-9 can send signals to processes. Some signals such as alarms and signal on data ready are requested by processes, but OS-9 sends other signals without special prompting: keyboard abort, keyboard interrupt, and a modem hangup signal. There is also a system abort signal that never gets to a process. It kills the process without warning. Keyboard abort, hangup, and keyboard interrupt kill unprepared processes, but a signal intercept can be set up to catch these signals and do whatever you like with them (including ignoring them).

A process can send most signals to any other process, but the *kill* signal is restricted. Every process carries the user and group number[1] of the process that started it. A process can only send a kill signal to processes with the same user and group. This prevents people from accidentally killing another user's processes. The super user (group 0) can kill any process; this allows the super user to kill out-of-control processes

---

[1] User and group numbers come from the password file. For each login the *login* utility starts a shell with user and group numbers drawn from the password file, and the numbers are passed through *F$Fork* to each new process that user starts.

and gives servers running under group 0 unrestricted communication with all processes.

Signals are a peep-hole that OS-9 leaves between processes. It is such a narrow communication channel that it takes ingenuity to use, but it is enough to build powerful systems of processes. The building blocks are the *F$Send* system service request, which sends a specified signal to a specified process; the *F$Icpt* request, which sets up a signal-intercept routine; *F$SigMask* which prevents signals from being delivered; and *F$Sleep*, which causes a process to wait for a signal.

Without an intercept routine, a process is killed by the first signal it receives. The intercept routine doesn't have to be very complicated. A simple *F$RTE* (return from exception) SVC is sufficient to prevent the process from being killed by any signal it receives.

A process need not sleep to receive signals, but frequently processes run of out of work while waiting for a signal. If no useful work is available, a process should sleep, wait for a child process to complete, or wait on an event. A sleeping or waiting process doesn't use any CPU time, and it responds immediately to signals.

The following example intercepts signals. It sets up an intercept routine, then waits until a signal arrives. When it receives a signal, **SigTrap** writes a brief message explaining the signal and calls *F$Exit*.

The A6 register only needs to be set before calling *F$Icpt* under exceptional circumstances. It is so painful to have offsets from A6 different in the main program and the intercept routine, that the small performance improvements that might come from adjusting A6 (smaller offsets from A6 in the intercept routine) are generally ignored. The only programs that adjust A6 before calling *F$Icpt* are those rare assembly language programs that don't use A6 as the base register for global storage.

Sleeping with D0 set to zero means sleep forever. A signal will wake a sleeping process, so this actually means sleep until a signal arrives.

The *F$PErr* service request prints an error message based on the number in D1. This service request formats the error number.

```
                    nam     SigTrap
                    ttl     Display signals
                    use     <oskdefs.d>
                    opt     -l
00000101  type      set     (Prgrm<<8)+Objct
00008001  Revs      set     (ReEnt<<8)+1
                    psect   SigTrap,type,Revs,1,200,Entry
0000 5369 Name      dc.b    "SigTrap"
0007 0d             dc.b    $0D
          ****************
          * Messages
          *
```

```
0008 0a      Int1       dc.b     $0A
0009 5761               dc.b     "Wake up"          we won't see this one
0010 0d                 dc.b     $0D
0011 0a      Int2       dc.b     $0A
0012 4b65               dc.b     "Keyboard Abort"
0020 0d                 dc.b     $0D
0021 0a      Int3       dc.b     $0A
0022 4b65               dc.b     "Keyboard interrupt"
0034 0d                 dc.b     $0D
0035 0a      Intx       dc.b     $0A
0036 4d69               dc.b     "Misc. Signal"
0042 0d                 dc.b     $0D

                        vsect
0000 0000 SigCode       dc.w     0                  Store intercepted signals here
00000002                ends

             Entry
0044 41fa               lea      Trap(PCR),A0       Address of intercept routine
0048=4e40               os9      F$Icpt             Set up intercept trap
 004c 6550              bcs.s    Error
004e 41fa               lea      Name(PC),A0        Prompt for a signal
0052 7207               moveq    #7,D1              Length of the prompt
0054 7001               moveq    #1,D0              Send it out std output
0056=4e40               os9      I$Write            Write the prompt
005a 6542               bcs.s    Error              Branch if error
005c 7000               moveq    #0,D0
005e=4e40               os9      F$Sleep            wait for a signal
0062 653a               bcs.s    Error              Possible E$NoClk
0064 302e               move.w   SigCode(A6),D0     check signal code
0068 b07c               cmp      #1,D0              if it was 1
006c 6606               bne.s    S2
006e 41fa               lea      Int1(PC),A0        write message Int1
0072 6020               bra.s    End
0074 b07c    S2         cmp      #2,D0              if signal was 2
0078 6606               bne.s    S3
007a 41fa               lea      Int2(PC),A0        write message Int2
007e 6014               bra.s    End
0080 b07c    S3         cmp      #3,D0              if signal was 3
0084 6606               bne.s    Sx
0086 41fa               lea      Int3(PC),A0        write message Int3
008a 6008               bra.s    End
008c 41fa    Sx         lea      Intx(PC),A0        Unknown signal
0090=4e40               os9      F$PErr
             End
0094 7250               moveq    #80,D1             Max length
0096 7001               moveq    #1,D0              std out
```

```
0098=4e40           os9     I$WritLn            Write signal description
009c 7200           moveq   #0,D1               Clean return
        Error
009e=4e40           os9     F$Exit
        Trap
00a2 3d41           move.w  D1,SigCode(A6)      save the signal code
00a6=4e40           os9     F$RTE
 000000aa           ends
```

7.1 An Undocumented Feature

The *OS-9 Technical Manual* states that the kernel sets the values of D1 and A6 before calling the intercept routine. It does not mention that D0 is also set to the number of queued signals for that process. Since it counts the signal being delivered as one of the queued signals, a value of one in D0 indicates that there are no waiting signals. The C interface to *F$Icpt* hides this value. The intercept() function buffers the intercept routine inside another function that hides the number of signals in the queue and issues an *F$RTE* when the catcher returns.

The following replacement for intercept() changes the rules for intercept routines. If a program uses OS9intercept(), the intercept routine receives two arguments and it must call *F$RTE* to return. If the intercept routine simply returns, bad things will happen.

```
                    nam     OS9intercept
                    ttl     OS9intercept
                    psect   OS9intercept,0,0,0,0,0
        * d0 points to the function to use as the intercept routine
0000 4e55 OS9intercept: link a5,#0
0004 2f08           move.l  a0,-(sp)
0006 2040           move.l  d0,a0
        * a0 and a6 are set
0008=4e40           os9     F$Icpt
 000c 7000          moveq.l #0,d0 Return value
000e 205f           move.l  (sp)+,a0
0010 4e5d           unlk    a5
0012 4e75           rts

        * This function knows it will be called from a C function,
        * so it does magic to unwind the stack.
        *
0014 4e5d rte:      unlk    a5
0016=4e40           os9     F$RTE

0000001a            ends
```

7.2. *MASKING SIGNALS*   63

A C program using OS9intercept() would follow this general form:

```
#include <stdio.h>
#define TRUE 1

Catcher(QLength, Signal)
int QLength;
short Signal;
{
    printf("Signal code: %d. Queue length: %d\n", Signal, QLength);
    fflush(stdout);
    rte();
}


main()
{
    printf("Ready\n");
    OS9intercept(Catcher);
    while(TRUE)
        sleep(0);
    exit(0);
}
```

7.2 Masking Signals

Ordinarily, a process can receive a signal any time it is not in its signal intercept routine. Both aspects of this rule can be inconvenient at times. A process may wish to delay returning from its intercept routine, but be unwilling to risk delaying a signal; such processes need to unmask signals without executing an *F$RTE*. Other processes may wish to share a complex data structure between the intercept routine and the mainline code. The mainline code can only safely update such shared data structures with atomic operations (e.g., *tas*), or by masking signals to create new atomic operations like:

```
sigmask(1);                                                         /* mask signals */
OldHead = QHead;
if(++QHead >= EndOfBuffer)
    QHead = 0;
if(QHead == QTail){                                                 /* Overflow */
    QHead = OldHead;
    Updated = FALSE;
```

```
} else {
   Array[QHead] = NewData;
   Updated = TRUE;
}
sigmask(−1);                                                    /* Unmask signals */
```

A process may also wish to mask signals to achieve slightly more deterministic performance during periods with exceptionally rigorous timing constraints.

sigmask(1);

/* A block of code that must execute with minimal interruptions */

sigmask(−1);
/* Service signals */
sigmask(1);

/* Another block of code that must execute with minimal interruptions */

sigmask(−1);

Of course, masking signals to prevent the signal intercept routine from running is futile if other processes steals the processor through timeslicing. A process with this kind of timing constraint will set D_MinPty to prevent any other process from running. Combining D_MinPty with sigmask(), the code protected by sigmask() can only be interrupted by hardware interrupts and the associated OS code.

The signal mask count, P$SigLvl in the process descriptor, is an unsigned byte value. When it is non-zero, the process' intercept routine will not be called.[2] The *F$SigMask* system call can operate on the value of P$SigLvl in three ways:

1. When *F$SigMask* is called with D1 equal to 1, the value of P$SigLvl in the calling process' process descriptor is incremented by one.

2. When *F$SigMask* is called with D1 equal to −1, the value of P$SigLvl in the calling process' process descriptor is decremented by one.

3. When *F$SigMask* is called with D1 equal to 0, P$SigLvl in the calling process' process descriptor is cleared to zero.

Any other value of D1 causes an illegal parameter error.

Attempts to increment the byte past 255 or decrement it below 0 are silently ignored.

---

[2]See section 7.5 for details on the special treatment of P$SigLvl for some signals.

7.2. MASKING SIGNALS

A function might include a sequence of operations that must be performed without interruption by the signal intercept routine. If the function is always called with signals masked, it can safely do nothing. But, if the function may be called with signals either masked or unmasked, it must mask signals. The function should unmask signals before returning, but must not use sigmask(0) to clear the signal mask; that would unmask signals even when returning to code that expected signals to be masked.

Unless a process definitely intends to unmask signals, it should use sigmask(−1). This returns the signal mask to the state before the most recent sigmask(1). Sigmask(0) is for those occasions when signals should be unmasked regardless of the process' past.

F$SigMask calls from intercept routines are treated like all other *F$SigMask* calls. The intercept routine can unmask signals by calling *F$SigMask* with D1 equal to −1, or it can cause signals to be masked even after the intercept routine returns by calling *F$SigMask* with a 1. This latter technique has potential for causing nearly impenetrable bugs, so don't do it unless there is no reasonable choice.

The sequence:

sigmask(1);
sleep(0);

seems like a sure way to lock up a process. It masks signals, then sleeps waiting for a signal. Not only does that kind of sequence work without locking the system, it's the trivial case of a common construct. Sleeping with signals masked works because *F$Sleep* unmasks interrupts. Without this feature of *F$Sleep*, some signal-driven code would be almost impossible to write.

7.2.1 Servicing Signals in the Mainline

The structure of a typical signal-driven program is:

```
sigmask(1);
while(TRUE){
   CallForSignals(a);
   CallForSignals(b);
   CallForSignals(c);
   sleep(0)
   while(SigCt[A]−− > 0)
      ServiceA();
   while(SigCt[B]−− > 0)
      ServiceB();
   while(SigCt[C]−− > 0)
      ServiceC();
   SigMask(1);
}
```

```
SigCatch(sig)
int sig;
{
   if(sig > FIRST_SIGNAL)                               /* Is this an interesting signal? */
      ++SigCt[sig];
}
```

1. The process masks signals.

2. Then the process requests signals from the I/O devices and other processes with which it interacts.

3. When the process sleeps, any signals that have been delivered since signals were masked are delivered. Since signals were masked before the process called for any signals, no signals will arrive before the sleep().

4. All waiting signals call the intercept routine, SigCatch(), as soon as sleep unmasks interrupts. If no signals are waiting, *F$Sleep* waits until a signal arrives.

5. SigCatch increments counters for each signal it receives.

6. When SigCatch() returns and finds no signals waiting, OS-9 resumes the mainline after the sleep() with signals unmasked.

7. Service all the signals that arrived during the sleep().

8. Mask signals, and repeat.

CallForSignals() should send a signal when it is called with work pending even if it has already signaled for that particular piece of work. If it doesn't do that, the driving loop must be restructured like:

```
sigmask(1);
while(TRUE){
   CallForSignals(a);
   CallForSignals(b);
   CallForSignals(c);
   sleep(0)
   SigMask(1);
   while(SigCt[A]-- > 0)
      ServiceA();
   while(SigCt[B]-- > 0)
      ServiceB();
   while(SigCt[C]-- > 0)
```

7.2. MASKING SIGNALS

```
        ServiceC();
}

SigCatch(sig)
int sig;
{
    if(sig > 255)
        ++SigCt[sig];
}
```

The new structure has sigmask() before all the service code instead of at the end of the main loop. This prevents a signal for serviceA() that arrives after SigCt[A] has been reduced to zero from being ignored until some other signal knocks the next iteration of the loop out of the sleep().

If each CallForSignals() calls for one signal and no other signals are sent until the next CallForSignals, the template can be simplified:

```
sigmask(1);
while(TRUE){
    CallForSignals(a);
    CallForSignals(b);
    CallForSignals(c);
    sleep(0)
    SigMask(1);
    if(SigCt[A]-- > 0){
        ServiceA();
        SigCt[A] = FALSE;
    }
    if(SigCt[B]-- > 0){
        ServiceB();
        SigCt[B] = FALSE;
    }
    if(SigCt[C]-- > 0){
        ServiceC();
        SigCt[C] = FALSE;
    }
}

SigCatch(sig)
int sig;
{
    if(sig > 255)
        SigCt[sig] = TRUE;
}
```

7.2.2 Servicing Signals in the Intercept Routine

A signal-driven process may choose to enclose all the signal-driven code in the signal intercept routine. Since signals are masked in the intercept routine, the code there can service a signal and set up for the next signal without worrying about a signal that might be missed between the time the process calls for the signal and the time it sleeps.

The following is a signal-driven program that runs entirely in the signal intercept routine after a minimal setup section. It is a program I wrote to kick off a contest on BIX. The object was to write a telecom program that would fit on one page. The result of the contest was a program that fit on a page with room for some comments. It was, however, even more cryptic than the following:

```
                      nam      j
                      ttl      Simplest communication program
            *
            * Attach stdin/out to the named device
            *
                      use      <oskdefs.d>
                      opt      −l
                      psect    j,(Prgrm<<8)+Objct,(ReEnt<<8)+0,1,256,Entry
00000400  BuffSize    equ      1024
000003ff  SizeMask    equ      $3ff
0000000f  EndChar     equ      $0f              control-O
                      vsect
00000000  Mpath       ds.w     1
00000002  Buffer:     ds.b     BuffSize
00000402  PathOpts:   ds.b     128
00000482  SPathOpts:  ds.b     128
00000000              ends
00000000              align
0000 204d Entry:      move.l   a5,a0            use parm ptr as path ptr
0002 7003             moveq    #3,d0            update mode
0004=4e40             os9      I$Open
* 0008 6528           bcs.b    Error
000a 3d40             move.w   d0,Mpath(a6)
000e 6166             bsr.b    CSetOpts         set options for Mpath
0010 760f             moveq    #EndChar,d3
0012 7000             moveq    #0,d0            stdin path number
0014 6162             bsr.b    SetOpts          set options for stdin
0016 41fa             lea      SigRtn(PC),a0    handler
001a=4e40             os9      F$Icpt           set up intercept routine
 001e 302e            move.w   Mpath(a6),d0
0022 6112             bsr.b    SetSig           for modem path
0024 7000             moveq    #0,d0
0026 610e             bsr.b    SetSig           for stdin
```

7.2. MASKING SIGNALS

```
0028 7000 Loop:     moveq   #0,d0
002a=4e40           os9     F$Sleep
002e 64f8           bcc.b   Loop
0030 7200 Done:     moveq   #0,d1              clear error code
0032=4e40 Error:    os9     F$Exit

0036=7200 SetSig:   moveq   #SS_SSig,d1        setstat code
0038 7408           moveq   #8,d2              Signal == 8
003a=4e40           os9     I$SetStt
003e 4e75           rts

0040 7000 SigRtn:   moveq   #0,d0
0042 362e           move.w  Mpath(a6),d3
0046 610a           bsr.b   IO
0048 2003           move.l  d3,d0              d3 is already Mpath
004a 7601           moveq   #1,d3
004c 6104           bsr.b   IO
004e=4e40           os9     F$RTE

0052=7200 IO:       moveq   #SS_Ready,d1
0054=4e40           os9     I$GetStt
0058 651a           bcs.b   IOX
005a 41ee           lea     Buffer(a6),a0
005e c27c           and.w   #SizeMask,d1
0062=4e40           os9     I$Read
0066 653e           bcs.b   SigDone
0068 2801           move.l  d1,d4
006a 61ca           bsr.b   SetSig
006c 2204           move.l  d4,d1              restore read size
006e 2003           move.l  d3,d0              choose write path
0070=4e40           os9     I$Write
0074 4e75 IOX:      rts

            * d0 is path, d3 is the end character
0076 7600 CSetOpts: moveq   #0,d3              set default end char (none)
0078 2f08 SetOpts:  move.l  a0,-(sp)
007a=7200           moveq   #SS_Opt,d1
007c 41ee           lea     SPathOpts(a6),a0
0080=4e40           os9     I$GetStt
0084 65ac           bcs.b   Error
0086 41ee           lea     PathOpts(a6),a0
008a=4e40           os9     I$GetStt
008e=74ff           moveq   #(PD_OVF-PD_UPC)-1,d2  number of bytes
0090 43e8           lea     1(a0),a1           point a1 at PD_UPC
0094 4219 InitOpt:  clr.b   (a1)+
0096 51ca           dbra    d2,InitOpt
009a=1d43           move.b  d3,PD_EOF-PD_DTP+PathOpts(a6)  set end char
009e=4e40           os9     I$SetStt
```

```
00a2 205f            move.l   (sp)+,a0
00a4 4e75            rts
00a6 7000  SigDone:  moveq    #0,d0
00a8=7200            moveq    #SS_Opt,d1
00aa 41ee            lea      SPathOpts(a6),a0   restore the old path options
00ae=4e40            os9      I$SetStt
00b2 6000            bra.w    Done
000000b6             ends
```

J opens the modem path and sets path options on its paths, then it calls for signal on data ready on its two input paths and sleeps. The main program just keeps going back to sleep every time it wakes up unless it wakes up with carry set... and that would be a big surprise since there is no error code returnable by an untimed sleep. All the real work is done from inside the intercept routine.

J relies on three characteristics of OS-9's signal handling:

- Send signal on data ready sends a signal immediately if there is data in the buffer when the setstat call is made.

- Signals are masked while *j* is in its intercept routine.

- Though the setstat call may return an error, it does no harm to call for a signal from a device that already has set send signal on data ready.

Assume that there is some data waiting in the modem device's input buffer when *j* starts. As soon as *j* executes the SS_SSig system call the driver sends a signal and *j* finds itself in the intercept routine. There it moves everything it finds in the modem to the terminal and resets SS_SSig on that device; then if there is data at the keyboard, it moves all of that data to the modem and resets SS_SSig on the keyboard device. This may generate more signals immediately, but they are masked because the process is in its intercept routine.

Eventually the mainline of the program reaches the sleep and loops there until *j* exits. The intercept routine awakens when there is work to do (and sometimes when there *was* input available that was handled by the previous iteration). It moves data from device to device and returns to the OS. The signal intercept routine acts like an interrupt service routine in that it responds quickly to input on either path. Like an interrupt service routine with multiple devices on one interrupt vector, the intercept routine must poll the devices to determine which sent the signal.

Even program termination is driven from the intercept routine. When the intercept routine calls *F$Exit* instead of *F$RTE*, OS-9 terminates the program.

7.2. MASKING SIGNALS

The *OS-9 Technical Manual* recommends keeping the signal intercept routines small and fast. Fast intercept routines are still a good idea, but support for queued signals and signal masking and unmasking makes "non-trivial" intercept routines an alternative worth consideration. Simply, signals are masked, with P$SigLvl set to 1, when a process enters its signal intercept routine. If the process doesn't unmask signals explicitly or with an F$RTE,[3] they will stay masked. That will keep other signals from being serviced. If the convenience of a long intercept routine is worth keeping signals masked for a long time, you can make that choice.

The most extreme cases of long intercept routines are ported from Unix. There, programmers habitually longjmp() out of the intercept routine back to the main program. They never *return* from the intercept routine. OS-9 supports that technique provided that the program is written with care:

- Unmask signals before or soon after longjmp'ing.

- If the program uses the C I/O library, realize that a signal may interrupt C I/O code in the middle of an operation. I/O data structures may be inconsistent. This can be solved by:

    – Using low-level I/O, or

    – Masking signals around each call to the C I/O library.

The following code fragment illustrates one way an intercept routine might correctly longjmp into mainline code.

```
    if(setjmp(buf1) != 0)
        sigmask(-1);                                     /* Unmask signals */
...
InterceptRtn(code)
int code;
{
    switch(code){
        case CODE1: longjmp(buf1, 0);
        case CODE2: longjmp(buf2, 0);
        case CODE3: longjmp(buf3, 0);
        default: /* ignore */
    }
}
```

---

[3] F$RTE does not unconditionally unmask signals. It decrements the signal mask counter. Just like SigMask(-1), F$RTE can leave signals masked.

By unmasking signals after the longjmp(), the code fragment prevents possible stack trouble. OS-9 places about 70 bytes of "stuff" on the stack when it calls an intercept routine. If signals are unmasked while the process is in the routine, another signal could add 70 more bytes to the stack. Enough signals could cause stack overflow. This is avoided by unmasking signals *after* the longjmp. When longjmp() resets the stack it removes the "stuff" OS-9 put there.

7.2.3 Async Safety

Signal intercept routines bring one of the trickiest aspects of kernel programming to user-state code. Unless you mask signals, a signal can occur after any machine instruction. This is invisible if the signal intercept routine doesn't touch any data structures used by the mainline, but since intercept routines usually need to communicate with the mainline, the mainline and the intercept routine generally need to share some data structures.

Few data structures can be updated in one machine instruction, and if an intercept routine gets control when a data structure is half-updated ("in an inconsistent state"), both the intercept routine and the mainline will be unhappy.

If your code manages its data structures so they work with intercept routines, the code and structures are called *async safe*. There are several ways to achieve async safety.

- You can use async =-safe algorithms. These are theoretically attractive, and sometimes there is no good alternative, but async-safe algorithms tend to be slow and complicated.

- You can mask signals whenever you update a shared data structure in the mainline code.

- You can use data structures that can be updated with a single machine instruction. The frequently-used instructions are:

    - *move* to memory or memory-to-memory
    - *addq* to memory
    - *subq* to memory
    - *bset*
    - *bclr*
    - *tas*

    The more sophisticated 68000-family processors support additional atomic instructions—*cas* for updating a singly-linked list, and *cas2* for doubly-linked

7.2. MASKING SIGNALS

lists—but these operations don't do the entire update in one instruction. They do the last part of the update after insuring that the update has not been interrupted. Here, for example, is the code to update a singly-linked stack:

```
* pointer to new node is in a0
          move.l   a0,d1            copy address to a data reg
retry     move.l   TOS(a6),d0       Get TOS
          move.l   d0,next(a0)      attach stack to new node
          cas      d0,d1,TOS(a6)
          bne.b    retry
```

The move before the *cas* points the new node to the node at the top of the stack. The *cas* checks to see whether the top of stack pointer has changed since it was saved in D0, and if it is unchanged, points TOS at the new node. If the TOS was changed, the algorithm knows it was interrupted and tries again.

In some cases you have no choice but to mask signals. C library routines don't mask signals, and they are not coded with consideration for async safety. In particular, it is unsafe to use standard I/O functions in the signal intercept routine unless you mask signals around each call to a standard I/O function in the mainline:

sigmask(1);
putchar('*');
sigmask(−1);

You can avoid this requirement by using low-level I/O throughout your program or by using distinct I/O paths in the intercept routine.

For paths that cannot seek, you can achieve async safety by using low-level I/O[4] in the intercept routine and standard I/O in the mainline. Using both standard I/O and low-level I/O produces bad results on RBF files even if intercept routines are not involved.

Flavors of *move* and the bit setting and clearing instructions safely manipulate data structures containing from 1 bit to 32 bits of data. You can use this to pass simple data between the intercept routine and the mainline.

Addq and *subq* update shared counters. With care, *addq* and *subq* are also enough to manage some types of shared array of data.

The intercept routine runs with signals masked, so it can run without fear of interruption. In most cases, this means that you can use data structures that are

---

[4]Low-level I/O is the set of C I/O functions that use the path number instead of a FILE pointer.

updated only by the intercept routine without much concern. The mainline has to realize that the data structure may change as it looks at it, but the mainline never sees the data structure half updated.

The general rules for async safety are:

- Minimize data structure sharing between the intercept routine and the mainline.

- Mask signals or use a single-instruction update whenever you update a shared data structure in the mainline.

- Unless you are ready to think hard about worst-case situations, also mask signals when you read shared data structures in the mainline code.

7.2.4 Horrible Example

Consider a simple, shared, singly-linked stack that is updated with the following algorithms:

```
                * pointer to new node is in a0
1       Push    move.l  TOS(a6),a1       Get TOS
2               move.l  a1,next(a0)      attach stack to new node
3               move.l  a0,TOS(a6)
4               rts
5       Pop     move.l  TOS(a6),a0
6               move.l  next(a0),TOS(a6)
7               move.l  a0,d0            return popped node ptr in d0
8               rts
```

The mainline is busy pushing node *x* onto the stack. The node at the top of the stack is node *a*. The mainline executes lines one and two, then it is interrupted by the intercept routine. The intercept routine pops *a* off the stack. When the mainline resumes, it points TOS at *x* and returns. The stack is now destroyed.

TOS points at *x* and *x* points at *a*. The node named *a* was at the top of the stack when the mainline started pushing *x* but now it has been popped by the intercept routine and is somewhere else. (For an extra horrible example, assume the intercept routine pushed it into a different stack.) The stack might have included hundreds of nodes, but after mainline finishes its push function, the stack contains only *x*. All the other nodes are lost. Nothing points to the node that used to be after *a*.

If the mainline had masked signals before running push or had used the *cas* protocol shown above, the integrity of the stack would have been preserved.

7.3 Broadcast

Signals sent to process zero are actually broadcast to all processes with the same user and group as the sending process. Broadcast carefully avoids sending a signal to the broadcasting process, so if *every* process belonging to the user should get the message, the sending process has to send an extra signal to itself.

The built-in shell command *kill* can be used to kill all the user's processes except the shell.

        $ kill 0

broadcasts a kill signal to all the user's processes except that shell. This is a good way to handle the processes belonging to a telecommunicating user who simply hangs up the phone instead of cleaning up and logging out. The telecom program will receive a S$Hangup from the modem port. It can then broadcast either the S$Hangup or S$Kill to all other processes belonging to the user.

It's also a convenient way for the super user to clean someone out of the system:

```
/* KillUser */
#include <stdio.h>
#include <errno.h>
#include <signal.h>

main(argc, argv)
int argc;
char **argv;
{
    int Usr, Grp;
    int GrpUsr;

    /*
        Get the grp.usr to kill from the command line.
    */
    if(sscanf(argv[1], "%d.%d", &Grp, &Usr) != 2)
        exit(_errmsg(1, "requires an argument of the form <usr>.<grp>\n"));

    /*
        Combine the group and user into one number.
    */
    GrpUsr = ((Grp << 16) & 0x0ffff0000) | (Usr & 0x0ffff);

    /*
        Don't let the caller kill the super group.
    */
```

```
    if(Grp == 0)
        exit(_errmsg(1, "Killing the super group is a bad idea\n"));

    /*
     * Make sure we're being called by the super user.
     */
    if(getuid() != 0)
        exit(_errmsg(1, "may only be run by the super user.\n"));

    /*
     * Change to the grp.usr we want to kill
     */
    if(setuid(GrpUsr) == -1)
        exit(_errmsg(errno, "Setuid to %d.%d failed.\n", Grp, Usr));

    /*
     * And kill all the processes except this one.
     */
    if(kill(0, SIGKILL) == -1)
        exit(_errmsg(errno, "kill(0, %d) failed with a %d\n",
            SIGKILL, errno));
    exit(0);
}
```

7.4 Queued Signals

OS-9 does not "throw signals on the floor" when signals are sent to a process that has a signal pending; it keeps pending signals in a queue and delivers them in the order they were sent. This is a powerful feature. It means that even processes that run at low priority or mask signals extensively see every signal that is sent to them.

Queuing signals can be quite expensive (depending the number of memory colors and the amount of memory fragmentation). It is best to assume that sending a signal to a signal queue can take ten times as long as sending an unqueued signal.[5] Signal queuing also causes OS-9 to mask interrupts for a comparatively long interval.

Signal queuing occurs when high-priority processes send rapid sequences of signals to low-priority processes or when any process masks signals for a long time compared to the interval at which signals are sent to it. To avoid these situations:

- Reduce the length of stretches of code that mask signals.

---
[5]It would be very hard to make a queued signal take 10 times as long to send as an unqueued signal. The point is that queued signals are a feature that should not be used lightly.

7.4. QUEUED SIGNALS

- If a low priority process is expected to service signals from a high priority process, raise its priority. Especially if the process is sleeping while it waits for signals, raising the priority is painless. A sleeping process doesn't use any cycles until it is awakened by a signal. The following code is a stub for the mainline of a signal handler:

```
#include <stdio.h>
#define TRUE 1
#define HIGH_PRIORITY 400
#define LOW_PRIORITY 50

main()
{
   int myid;
   myid = getpid();
   printf("Ready\n");
   OS9intercept(Catcher);
   while(TRUE){
      setpr(myid, HIGH_PRIORITY);
      sleep(0);
      setpr(myid, LOW_PRIORITY);
   }
   exit(0);
}
```

Depending on the desired result, the priority of the process could be set back to low priority in the mainline, as shown in the example, or in the intercept routine. The response of the signal handler can also be varied by setting the priority low before or after performing any computation motivated by the signal.

The code fragment:

```
while(TRUE){
   setpr(myid, HIGH_PRIORITY);
   sleep(0);
   DoHeavyComputation();
   setpr(myid, LOW_PRIORITY);
}
```

is unlikely to cause queued signals, but it steals processor time from other high-priority processes. The next code fragment:

```
while(TRUE){
    setpr(myid, HIGH_PRIORITY);
    sleep(0);
    setpr(myid, LOW_PRIORITY);
    DoHeavyComputation();
}
```

is more likely to cause queued signals, but has nearly no effect on high-priority processes. It will cause queued signals if LOW_PRIORITY is low enough to let several signals arrive between this process' time slices. The longer the computation and the lower the priority, the more likely signal queuing becomes. Generally, it is better to keep priorities high only around the sleep, and set the background priority of the process high enough to handle its work load with at least a few ticks of sleep time as padding.

A programmer can choose to view queued signals in any of three ways:

- They are too expensive and must be avoided.

- They are a nifty communication tool and the cost is fine.

- Signal queuing is a form of graceful degradation which lets designers cut timing tolerances much closer than they could without signal queuing.

The last point needs a little discussion. If the priority of a process like the one that calls DoHeavyComputation() is set high enough, signals will never queue, but other processes with even more crucial tasks might be degraded. If its priority is set low enough, the computation will take longer than the inter-signal time and the signal queue will grow until it uses all of memory. In the middle ground are a range of priorities that cause signals to queue occasionally. For instance, a priority of 200 might cause a queued signal every 10 minutes and a priority of 202 might cause a queued signal every 4 hours. The designer can balance the cost of a queued signal against the cost of various priority arrangements.

7.4.1 Performance

Here I need to emphasize that this book is not Microware documentation, and details of OS-9 in this book are not specifications. This section involves kernel implementation details of signal processing. These facts are important for the most demanding applications, but they are also subject to change as we find better ways to do things. If you don't find something in a manual, it isn't "official." Future releases of OS-9 might

7.4. QUEUED SIGNALS

make the tricks in this book official, or they might stop working. It would be good policy to look carefully at tricks after each kernel upgrade.

One trick is officially documented: OS-9 calls the intercept routine repeatedly until the end of the process' time slice or until the signal queue is empty. It has a high-performance path for this loop. Combining that with the undocumented fact that OS-9 passes the number of queued signals to the intercept routine gives a program enough information to throw signals on the floor when it chooses.

```
SigTrap(QueueL, signal)
int QueueL, signal;
{
   if(signal == VERYIMPORTANT)
      HandleIt(signal);
   else if(QueueL <= 1)
      HandleIt(signal);
   rts();
}
```

The above code uses some judgment. When there are queued signals, it only handles very important signals—all others it throws on the floor. When there is no queue, it handles all signals.[6]

The other trick is entirely undocumented: OS-9 allocates a small block of memory to store each queued signal.[7] For up to eight pending signals per process, it keeps the signal node after the signal is received and reuses it for future queued signals to that process. If there are more than eight empty signal slots, the surplus is freed after the the signal is delivered.

Allocating and freeing memory is by far the most undesirable aspect of queued signals. The time to send a queued signal varies according to the structure of free memory, and the memory allocation part of *F$Send* masks interrupts unless the memory is allocated from a process' fragment list. The other costs of queued signals are fairly trivial.[8] An eight-deep queue of signals is either a sign of very serious trouble, or a sign that the designer is using signal queues as a buffering mechanism and signal performance is secondary. For signal queues with fewer than eight pending signals, the first signal at each depth of queuing bears the startup cost for that level, and no

---

[6] A process could also raise its priority when it sees a signal queue and lower it when the queue length stays at one for a lengthy period.

[7] The process descriptor has room for one non-queued signal. That makes the discussion of queued signals a little confusing. A process with 8 pending signals has one in the process descriptor and another 7 in structures in a linked list attached to the process descriptor.

[8] Sending a signal that queues but does not require allocation of a new node takes about 10 instructions more than sending a signal to a process with an empty signal queue.

F$RTE from queue lengths up to eight does an *F$SRtMem*. A process can prime its signal queue and save other processes the cost of expensive *F$Sends*.

```c
#include <stdio.h>
#define TRUE     1
#define Q_DEPTH 8                        /* 7 queued plus one pending*/
#define JUNK_SIG 256

Catcher(QLength, Signal)
int QLength;
short Signal;
{
   /* Normally the program would throw out the priming signals. */
   printf("Signal code: %d.  Queue length: %d\n", Signal, QLength);
   fflush(stdout);
   rte();
}


main()
{
   int MyID;
   int i;

   MyID = getpid();

   OS9intercept(Catcher);
   sigmask(1);

   for(i=0; i<Q_DEPTH; ++i)
      kill(MyID, JUNK_SIG);              /* Send signals to self*/
   sigmask(-1);

   printf("Ready\n");
   while(TRUE)
      sleep(0);
   exit(0);
}
```

7.4.2 Fast RTE

The "stuff" on the stack when the kernel calls a signal intercept routine is the state of the mainline code when it was interrupted. A process should generally return through

7.4. QUEUED SIGNALS

the kernel with the *F$RTE* SVC, but

```
                * Shift sr, and pc down to sp we will return from
0000=4cef       movem.l R$sr(sp),d0-d1   Pick sr,pc,fmt off stack
0006=206f       move.l  R$a7(sp),a0      SP we want
000a 5d48       subq    #6,a0
000c=2f48       move.l  a0,R$a7(sp)
0010 20c0       move.l  d0,(a0)+
0012 4841       swap    d1               put half of pc in low-order half of d1
0014 3081       move.w  d1,(a0)
0016 4cdf       movem.l (sp)+,d0-d7/a0-a6
001a 2e57       move.l  (sp),sp
001c 4e77       rtr
```

returns to the mainline much more quickly.

This trick has five problems:

1. It does not restore the state of the FPU. Processes that use floating point instructions will generally break if they use a fast RTE. The only way around this is to alter the RTE return point so it acts like a long jump to a "clean point" for the FPU.

2. OS-9 may change the way the state is saved. This is not a very big problem. OS-9 usually makes old behavior available through a compatibility mode when it makes a major change.[9]

3. If other signals are queued, *F$RTE* calls the intercept routine again with the next signal. Returning directly doesn't give the kernel an opportunity to call the intercept routine again until an interrupt or system call activates the kernel.

4. *F$RTE* decrements the signal mask. Returning to the mainline without passing through the kernel leaves signals masked.

5. If the signal arrived while the process was in a system call, the mainline may not learn about the signal. Normally OS-9 would leave carry set and an error code in D1 telling the process that the system call was aborted by a signal.

These disadvantages are sometimes outweighed by the advantages.

---

[9]The only time the kernel will knowingly break code that follows the published rules is on a release with a new first digit; e.g., from 2.4 to 3.0. Even major updates will not break user-state code. (Microware has stuck with this rule even when the consequences are painful.) Tricks like the fast RTE presented here are not protected since they are not official behavior, but I would not expect them to become completely unsupported except at a first-digit release.

1. Returning directly is at least twice as fast as *F$RTE*... maybe much more than twice as fast.

2. Returning from an intercept routine without using a system call forces OS-9 to hold queued signals until next time the kernel takes control. Sometimes that's an advantage.

3. There is useful information in the stack. The intercept routine can discover where the mainline was when it was interrupted. It can also change the registers or PC in the stack before returning.[10]

4. Returning directly leaves signals masked until the process explicitly unmasks them.

7.5 Special Signals

Wakeup signals and kill signals get special treatment. For all other signals, any special significance of a signal number is a convention defined by the programmer or by non-kernel parts of OS-9. Keyboard abort and keyboard interrupt, for instance, are treated as ordinary signals by the kernel.

7.5.1 Wakeup

A wakeup signal does not store a value in P$Signal and it is never queued. Wakeup signals do not call the intercept routine and they do not kill processes that have no intercept routine. Since wakeup signals do not queue, sending them is always fast. If there is already a signal pending for a process, a wakeup signal does nothing.

Wakeup has different effects on *F$Sleep*, *F$Wait* and *Ev$Wait* issued from system state and the same system calls issued from user state. The system-state requests return immediately after clearing B_WAKEUP if the bit is set, while the user-state requests only return immediately if there is a non-zero value in P$Signal. This means that a wakeup signal causes the next system-state wait or sleep to return quickly, but is be silently cleared by the user-state SVCs.

This special treatment of wakeup signals by system state requests that move processes out of the active queue is important to device drivers. The persistence of wakeup makes the following sequence work:

---

[10] Changes to the process state in the intercept routine's stack will be passed back through the kernel if a process returns with *F$RTE*.

7.5. SPECIAL SIGNALS

Table 7.1: Summary of Signal Attributes

- Signals are queued and delivered in first-in-first-out order.

- Delivery of a signal is complete after the process is placed in the active queue and the intercept routine is called.

- If the target process is active or current, signals consider the process activated.

- If a signal intercept routine is not defined, a signal will kill the recipient process.

- If signals are masked, the call to the intercept routine is deferred. Activation is not deferred.

- If signals are unmasked, the intercept routine is called before the target program is resumed.

- *F$Send* sets the B_WAKEUP bit in P$SigFlg and stores the signal number in P$Signal in the process' process descriptor.

- B_WAKEUP is cleared by a call to a process' intercept routine or before the process returns from a sleep or wait.

- P$Signal is updated to the next queued signal (or 0) before each call to a process' intercept routine.

```
do
    Is input ready?
        return it
    else
        wait for a signal
forever
```

A signal can arrive any time after input is tested. In particular, it can arrive between the test and the wait. Since even a wakeup signal in that interval causes the wait to return, the driver doesn't need to worry about signals that arrive before the wait.

7.5.2 Kill

A kill signal is not queued, it cannot be ignored, and masking signals has no effect on it. It can only be sent between processes with the same owner or from the super group, group zero, to any process. OS-9 sends kill signals as as it does other signals, except that the S$Kill signal value is replaced with E$PrcAbt in P$Signal, and the recipient process is condemned when the signal is sent. Next time it is scheduled the process will terminate with E$PrcAbt as its return code.

7.5.3 I/O Deadly Signals

Signals between 2 and 31 are given special treatment by the I/O system. Only those signals will interrupt pending I/O; other signals are ignored by I/O code. Deadly signals are a new development which is mainly an extension to SCF's special SIGINT and SIGQUIT signals. The handling of deadly signals is not (and probably will never be) uniform. SCF device drivers look for deadly signals and abort when they are received. RBF and SBF device drivers ignore deadly signals, but the RBF file manager looks for deadly signals at convenient moments. SBF seems to ignore deadly signals entirely.

7.6 Utility Programs

The following program is useful for experimenting with signals. On the command line, you give it a destination process id and a signal. It attempts to send the signal to the process

7.6. UTILITY PROGRAMS

```
/* send <pid> <signal> */
#include <stdio.h>

main(argc, argv)
int argc;
char **argv;
{
    int sig, pid;

    if(argc < 3)
        exit(_errmsg(1, "needs two args <pid> and <sig>\n"));
    pid = atoi(argv[1]);
    sig = atoi(argv[2]);
    if(pid <= 1)
        exit(_errmsg(1, "Invalid <pid>: %d\n", pid));
    kill(pid, sig);
    exit(0);
}
```

It is mostly good for playing with demonstration programs, but it can also send stuck processes a wakeup signal...which sometimes helps.

Chapter 8

Alarms

This chapter discusses the use of alarms for time- or interval-dependent processing.

Alarms initiated from user-state cause OS-9 to send specified signals to processes at a selected time or interval. Alarms from system state cause the OS-9 system process to execute specified routines at the indicated times or intervals. System-state alarms do not simply send signals to the system process because the system process is not sensitive to signals, but the action of system-state alarms parallels the user-state execution of signal intercept routines.

8.1 User-State Alarms

Probably the two most important applications of user-state alarms are to provide timeouts for operations that aren't guaranteed to complete in bounded time and to schedule time-dependent activities.

8.1.1 Alarms as Guards

The standard OS-9 file managers do not support I/O operations with time-outs. A read() with the option to return either with *n* bytes of data or after *t* seconds, whichever comes first, is crucial for applications like data transfer protocols.[1] Before alarms were available, we coded reads with timeouts like this:

```
for(time = 0 ; time < TIMEOUT / POLL_INTERVAL; ++time){
    if(_gs_rdy(InPath) >= Size)
        if(read(InPath, buffer, Size) == −1)
```

---

[1] ZModem and kermit are two examples of data transfer protocols that use timed reads.

```
        /* Handle error */
    else
        goto ReadOK;
   sleep(POLL_INTERVAL);
}
/* Deal with timeout */
ReadOK:
```

These polled timeouts forced programmers to balance quick response against wasted processor time. If there was no other process active in the system, polling with no sleep at all was acceptable, but if other activity was likely, polling without delay was too wasteful of CPU resources. Longer sleep intervals make polling less wasteful but increase the time it takes to recognize and read input.

With alarms, polling is no longer necessary. An I/O operation will return to the caller for any of three reasons:

1. The operation completes.

2. An error or end of file condition arises.

3. The process receives a deadly signal.

An alarm can be used to "protect" each operation that might wait in the file system by sending a signal after the maximum time the operation can be permitted to wait. Any deadly signal sent by the alarm signal aborts the process out of an I/O wait or sleep.

A timed fgets() is included in the following demonstration program:

```
#include <stdio.h>
#include <signal.h>
#include <errno.h>

#define TIME(t)              (0x80000000 | (int)(t * 256))

#define INTERVAL             5
#define STRINGLEN            256
#define ALARMSIG             SIGINT
char *Timedfgets();

void IgnoreSig(sig)
{
   return;
}
```

8.1. USER-STATE ALARMS

```
main()
{
    char string[STRINGLEN];

    *string = '\0';
    intercept(IgnoreSig);

    printf("%d second timed read. Type something: ", INTERVAL);
    fflush(stdout);

    Timedfgets(string, STRINGLEN, stdin, INTERVAL);
    exit(0);
}


char *Timedfgets(string, len, file, seconds)
char *string;
int len;
FILE *file;
int seconds;
{
    int AlarmID;
    char *RVal;

    if((AlarmID = alm_set(ALARMSIG, TIME(seconds))) == -1)
        exit(_errmsg(errno, "Error %d setting alarm\n", errno));

    RVal = fgets(string, len, file);
    if(*string == '\0')
        printf("\nNo input\n");
    else
        alm_delete(AlarmID);
    return RVal;
}
```

Timed open(), close(), wait(), _ev_wait(), write(), and so forth are simple modifications of the timed fgets().

Properly, alarms should use some signal greater than SIGHUP and less than SIGDEADLY. The signal numbers through SIGHUP should be avoided because they already have meanings. The signals from SIGHUP + 1 through SIGDEADLY are (currently) undefined and should all abort an I/O operation.

The Timedfgets() example uses SIGINT as the alarm signal. This is an inelegant choice, but drivers that support the range of deadly signals are not yet widespread, so

I chose SIGINT to insure that Timedfgets() works with slightly out-of-date drivers. Fully-conforming device drivers make all signals less than SIGDEADLY suitable for aborting an I/O operation. Overloading SIGINT by making it mean keyboard interrupt or time-out is not good practice, but it works even with device drivers that don't yet support the *sigdeadly* convention.

A fairly general timed function mechanism can be implemented with this header file (named timed.h):

```
#include <setjmp.h>
#include <signal.h>
#include <errno.h>

#define ALARMSIG            SIGINT
#define TIME(t)             (0x80000000 | (int)(t * 256))
#define TIMED_FUNCTION(timeout)  {int AlarmID; jmp_buf jmp_buffer;\
                            if(setjmp(jmp_buffer) == 0){ \
                            AlarmID = SetAlarm(jmp_buffer, timeout);

#define IF_TIMEOUT          ClearAlarm();}else{
#define END_TIMED_FUNCTION  ClearAlarm();}}
```

The header file defines three macros: TIMED_FUNCTION, IF_TIMEOUT, and END_TIMED_FUNCTION, that can be used somewhat like the C-language if-then-else. The macros use the following library of C code:

```
#include <stdio.h>
#include "timed.h"

typedef struct CN {
    struct CN *Next;
    int AlarmID;
    void *jmpbuf;
} CatchNode;


static CatchNode *TOS = NULL;

SigCatch(sig)
{
    if((void *)TOS != NULL && sig == ALARMSIG){
        int Alarm;
        Alarm = TOS→AlarmID;                    /*Hang onto alarm handle */
```

8.1. USER-STATE ALARMS

```
            TOS→AlarmID = −1;              /*Alarm doesn't need deleting */
            longjmp(TOS→jmpbuf, Alarm);
        }
}

SetAlarm(buffer, Time)
void *buffer;
int Time;
{
    int Alarm;
    CatchNode *NewNode;

    if((Alarm = alm_set(ALARMSIG, 0x080000000 | Time)) == −1)
        exit(_errmsg(errno, "Error %d setting alarm \n", errno));

    if((NewNode = (CatchNode *)malloc(sizeof(CatchNode))) == NULL)
        exit(_errmsg(errno, "Out of memory in SetAlarm \n"));
    NewNode→Next = TOS;
    NewNode→AlarmID = Alarm;
    NewNode→jmpbuf = buffer;
    TOS = NewNode;
    return Alarm;
}

void ClearAlarm()
{
    CatchNode *ptr;
    if(TOS == NULL) return;
    if(TOS→AlarmID != −1)
        alm_delete(TOS→AlarmID);
    ptr = TOS;
    TOS = ptr→Next;
    free(ptr);
}
```

The following tiny program illustrates use of the timed-code macro package. It uses the timed-code macros to build a timed fgets() function call.

```
#include "timed.h"
main()
{
    char string[16];
    void *RVal;
```

```
    intercept(SigCatch);
    printf("ready for timed input: ");
    fflush(stdout);

    TIMED_FUNCTION(256*5)
        RVal = fgets(string, 16, stdin);
    IF_TIMEOUT
        printf("No input\n");
        fflush(stdout);
        RVal = 0;
    END_TIMED_FUNCTION
    exit(RVal);
}
```

A problem with the preceding set of macros and library functions is that the macros define variables. Since C doesn't let macros define a scope for names, the names in the macro must be unique in each function that calls them. This restriction prevents nested timeouts and only permits one block of code per function to be guarded with a timeout. Passing the variable names, or even a prefix for variable names, to the macros would make them more flexible but a little harder to use.

The general timeout mechanism suggests an unusual application of timed functions. Operations that interact with other processes or with hardware are expected to need timeout protection, but strictly computational problems also may have widely variable response depending on their input data.

A real-time designer might be willing to budget up to 500 milliseconds to compute an exact value to control some physical process. The designer calculates that the computation may take as little as 100 milliseconds or as much as 1000 milliseconds depending on the input data. One option is to instrument the computation so it notices when its allotted time expires and returns some sort of error. This technique, however, adds overhead to the function as it constantly checks for timeout. More typical is to look for a less accurate computation that was guaranteed to complete on time. A timed computation offers a third alternative.

```
TIMED_FUNCTION(timeout)
    HeavyComputation();
IF_TIMEOUT
    UseQuickSolution();
END_TIMED_FUNCTION
```

8.1. USER-STATE ALARMS

8.1.2 Alarms as Tickers for Threads

Yet another application of alarms is a primitive version of time-sliced threads within a process that can be implemented with simple C code.

```
/* Threads */
/* compile cc threads.c */
/* Run: threads */
#include <stdio.h>
#include <errno.h>
#define TICKRATE        (0x080000000 | 20)      /* about .1 seconds */
#define TICKSIG         256

typedef struct TN {
    struct TN *Next;
    void (*ThreadCode)();
} ThreadNode;


static ThreadNode First = {&First, NULL};
static ThreadNode *Head = &First;
static int TickAlarm;

/*
    This function calls the threads in the ThreadNode list in rotation. The
    threads are represented by pointers to functions.
*/

Dispatcher(sig)
{
    if(Head→Next != Head && sig == TICKSIG){
        ThreadNode *This;
        This = Head;
        Head = This→Next;                       /* next thread */
        if(Head→ThreadCode == NULL)             /* pre-select for next time */
        Head = Head→Next;                       /* bump over dummy node */
        sigmask(-1);                            /* unmask signals */
        (*This→ThreadCode)();                   /* run a thread */
    }
}

/*
    Add a node to the ThreadNode list.
    If it is the only node in the list start the ticker alarm.
*/
```

```
void *MakeThread(ptr)
void (*ptr)();
{
    ThreadNode *NewNode;

    if(Head→Next == Head)                                              /*first thread */
        if((TickAlarm = alm_cycle(TICKSIG, TICKRATE)) == -1)
            exit(_errmsg(errno, "cannot setup thread ticker alarm\n"));

    if((NewNode = (ThreadNode *)malloc(sizeof(ThreadNode))) == NULL)
        exit(_errmsg(errno, "Out of memory in MakeThread\n"));

    /*Make this the next thread */
    NewNode→Next = Head→Next;
    NewNode→ThreadCode = ptr;
    Head→Next = NewNode;
    Head = NewNode;
    return NewNode;
}




/*
    Remove a node from the ThreadNode list.
    If there are no threads left in the list, delete the
    ticker alarm.
*/
void KillThread(id)
register ThreadNode *id;
{
    register ThreadNode *ptr, *trailer;
    for(trailer = &First, ptr = First.Next; ptr != &First;
            trailer = ptr, ptr = ptr→Next)
        if(ptr == id){
            trailer→Next = ptr→Next;
            if(Head == ptr)
                Head = ptr→Next;
            free(ptr);
            if(trailer→Next == trailer)                                /*if no threads are left */
                alm_delete(TickAlarm);                                 /*turn off the tick */
        }
}
```

8.1. USER-STATE ALARMS

```
/*
    The thread functions. This program uses separate code for each thread,
    but they could share code.
    Since the threads could theoretically interrupt each other, they are coded
    async-safe.
*/

Thread1()
{
    write(1,"1",1);
}


Thread2()
{
    write(1,"2",1);
}


Thread3()
{
    write(1,"3",1);
}


main()
{
    void *T1, *T2, *T3;
    int ticks;

    intercept(Dispatcher);
    T1 = MakeThread(Thread1);                         /*start a thread */
    T2 = MakeThread(Thread2);                         /*start a thread */
    T3 = MakeThread(Thread3);                         /*start a thread */
    for(ticks = 0 ; ticks < 200 ; ++ticks)            /*let the threads run a while */
        sleep(0);
    KillThread(T1);                                   /*kill one thread */
    for(ticks = 0 ; ticks < 100 ; ++ticks)            /*see what happens */
        sleep(0);
    KillThread(T2);                                   /*kill another thread */
    for(ticks = 0 ; ticks < 100 ; ++ticks)
        sleep(0);
    KillThread(T3);                                   /*now all the threads are dead */
    sleep(10);
```

```
    T1 = MakeThread(Thread1);                    /*start up again */
    for(ticks = 0 ; ticks < 20 ; ++ticks)
        sleep(0);                                /*and shut down */
    KillThread(T1);
    sleep(10);
    exit(0);
}
```

With much extra work, similar techniques can be used to implement a fully-functional multithreaded environment. One difference between the primitive threads implemented here and "real" threads is that real threads require the run time library to support multiple stacks. The above example uses one stack for all the threads. Consequently, it gets into serious trouble unless the threads use only a fraction of the available processor time.

8.1.3 Alarms as Timers

The most conventional use of alarms is to trigger activities at set times or intervals. A text editor might protect its users against serious data loss caused by power failure or other crashes, by using an alarm to write its buffer to disk every minute. Other programs with long expected running times can similarly checkpoint their data to disk. This was a standard trick for super-computer programs that often ran longer than the computer would stay up. Embedded programs often run, approximately, forever. Like those old super computer programs, they should expect the computer to go down for some reason before they complete. Embedded programs with some form of non-volatile storage could use a timer to cause their latest data to be saved into the non-volatile storage.

The classic demonstration function for alarms is the clock program. The clock program calls for an alarm every minute and sleeps. Each time it is awakened the clock program updates the clock's hands and sleeps again. The clock program could become an alarm clock by setting an additional alarm that causes the program to beep.

Alarms set for a particular date and time can do things like initiate backup operations, turn on lights, adjust thermostats, activate security systems, activate a VCR, or switch a computer into or out of daylight savings time.

8.2 System State Alarms

Programmers who dig around in OS-9 writing drivers, file managers and kernel enhancements have long and enthusiastically wished to add code to the clock driver.

8.2. SYSTEM STATE ALARMS

There are many nifty things you could do if you could execute time dependent operations without sleeping or polling the tick counter. Microware recommended against hooking things to the clock interrupt or adding to the clock driver; they saw problems with the context for user code attached to the clock (like how much stack space was available), but that didn't stop everyone.

System-state alarms constitute an official, "front door" way to write time-dependent system code.

8.2.1 Drivers

Drivers sometimes need to turn disk drive motors off. They want to do that after the drive has been inactive for 15 seconds or so. But, when a drive has been inactive for 15 seconds, control is not in the driver. If it was, the device would no longer be inactive. If the the driver sets a system-state alarm to go off 15 seconds after each operation finishes and clears the alarm before each operation, the alarm's target routine will be called after 15 seconds of inactivity.

From a device driver, alarms can protect low-level I/O requests. The normal form for the request launches an I/O operation and then waits for an interrupt. With alarm protection the driver can launch the operation without concern that the device might not respond.

To insure that it notices when a disk is replaced with a different disk RBF reads sector zero each time it opens a file. Drivers can improve performance by keeping sector zero in a special buffer and returning that buffer each time the sector is read, but this makes RBF's checking ineffective for drives with removable media. If the driver invalidates its sector-zero buffer every half second, it stands a good chance of catching disk changes, and might save a few reads. Longer intervals give better performance, but might miss disk changes. Invalidating the sector zero buffer after a second of disk inactivity would only miss a disk change that took less than a second. Since head-unload time is generally more than half a second, that technique should be safe and give good performance when the disk is busy.

8.2.2 File Managers

It would be interesting, and probably good, to add system-state alarms to all disk file managers (i.e., RBF and PCF). It would definately make PCF safer, and it might make RBF faster. Consider PCF, which is descended from the *pcfm* file manager found in appendix C. PCF keeps the disk's allocation map (the FAT) in a buffer and only writes it to disk during open and close operations. As files are created and extended, the copy of the FAT in RAM is updated. If the system were to crash, the FAT might not match the data written on the disk and additions to files that were open when the system crashed would be lost. The PCF directory entries, which contain the equivalent of RBF file descriptors, are also kept in RAM until the file is closed. This keeps them from indicating a file longer than the FAT can find, but it is another chunk of data that is lost if the system crashes.

The reliability of PCF could be improved by adding a system-state alarm to each path. The alarm would be initialized as part of the *I$Open* processing for each path with write capability, and deleted as part of *I$Close*. It would attach to a routine that would write the directory entry for the file and the FAT to disk.

This would give PCF the disconcerting tendency to flash the disk light every 15 seconds or so, but it would decrease the data loss in case of a system crash.

PCF's open function would call an assembly language function to set up the alarms. The function would go something like this:

```
              *
              * SetupAlarm(pd, ProcDesc)
              * called from Open and Create when a path is opened for write.
              SetupAlarm:
01c4 48e7         movem.l  d1-d3/a0,-(sp)
              * sysglobs will be a6
              * the alarm routine will actually only get d0-d7/a0-a3,
              * and it doesn't need nearly that much.
01c8=4fef         lea.l    -R$Size(sp),sp   make space for register image
01cc 48d7         movem.l  d0-d1,(sp)
01d0 41fa         lea.l    DoAlarm(pc),a0
01d4 2f48         move.l   a0,R$pc(sp)
01d8 204f         move.l   sp,a0            a0 for call to a$cycle
01da 4280         clr.l    d0
01dc=323c         move.w   #A$Cycle,d1
01e0 4282         clr.l    d2
01e2 263c         move.l   #$80000000+(256*15),d3 Alarm interval 15 sec
01e8=4e40         os9      F$Alarm          Ignore errors
 01ec=4fef        lea.l    R$Size(sp),sp    Clear stack
01f0 4cdf         movem.l  (sp)+,d1-d3/a0
01f4 4e75         rts

              * DoAlarm
              * Called with d0 = pathd
              *             d1 = procd
              *             a4 = system procd
              *             a5 = register image
              *             a6 = sysglobs
              * Calls C function AlarmFlush()
              DoAlarm:
```

8.2. SYSTEM STATE ALARMS

```
01f6 48e7        movem.l a4/a5,-(sp) save the registers we have to preserve
01fa 48e7        movem.l d1/a4/a6,-(sp) set up for call
01fe 220d        move.l   a5,d1 regs
0200=6100        bsr      AlarmFlush (pd, regs, ProcDesc, SysProcDesc, SysGlobs)
0204 508f        addq.l   #12,sp
0206 4cdf        movem.l  (sp)+,a4/a5
020a 4e75        rts
```

There is an important inconsistency in register handling by system-state alarms. The system calls that start alarms want a complete 48-byte register packet, but they only use the data registers, the first four address registers, and the PC. A pointer to the entire register structure is passed to the alarm service routine, but the values are not placed in registers. Furthermore, the alarm service routine must return with the values in registers A4 through A6 unchanged.

The code executed by system state alarms must not do anything that could cause the system process to wait, so we cannot initiate a disk-write operation to flush the FAT and the FD from AlarmFlush(). We could use a system-state process to do the writes and release it with a signal or event from AlarmFlush(), or we could set a bit in the path descriptor instructing the next operation on the path to clean the FAT and FD.

PCF uses a write-through scheme for writes of less than a sector. This means that each *I$Write* of one byte results in a write of one sector to the disk. It would be much faster to write the sector just before reading another sector to take its place in the path buffer or when the path is closed, but that would leave PCF with another type of lost data if the power goes off. Like the FAT and FD, the path buffer could be flushed periodically under the control of an alarm.

8.2.3 System Calls

The most obvious reason to use alarms in system calls is to provide new SVCs that do for events what alarms do for signals. They probably aren't part of OS-9 because events are so much more flexible than signals that timed events would be too complex. Furthermore, it is easy to implement specific timed event functions using alarms.

Here is a new system call that pulses an event:

F$EvTick

Input d0.l event ID number
d1.l Pulse interval in seconds/256
d2.l event pulse value

Output The alarm id in D0.

Errors The *F$Alarm* error set.

Function *F$EvTick* pulses an event under the control of an alarm. It functions like *Ev$Pulse* except that it does not have the option to activate all processes waiting for the pulsed value.

```
                nam     evtick
                ttl     Test version of OS9P2
                use     <oskdefs.d>
                opt     −l
                psect   os9p2,(Systm<<8)+Objct,((ReEnt+SupStat)<<8)+1,1,256,Entry

000000f0 F$EvTick equ   $f0

                *
                * Startup for os9p2 called during system coldstart
                * a3 Global data pointer for os9p2
                * a6 System global data pointer
                *
                * Return:
                * with carry clear. Otherwise startup will abort
                *
                Entry
0000 43fa       lea     SvcTbl(pc),a1
0004=4e40       os9     F$SSvc
 0008 4e75      rts                             return (carry as set from F$SSvc)

                SvcTbl
000a 00f0       dc.w    F$EvTick
000c 0002       dc.w    EvTickCod−∗−2           offset to code
000e ffff       dc.w    −1                      end of table


                * Input
                *       d0.l Event ID number
                *       d1.l Pulse interval
                *       d2.l Event pulse value
                * Output d0.l Alarm ID
                * Error: A$Cycle errors
                *       d1 Error code
                EvTickCod
                *
                * Make stack image
                *
0010=4fef       lea.l   −R$Size(sp),sp   Make space for register image
```

8.2. SYSTEM STATE ALARMS

```
                *
                * prepare register image for EvPulse system call
                *
0014=2f40       move.l    d0,R$d0(sp)      Save event ID number
0018=7000       moveq.l   #Ev$Pulse,d0
001a=2f40       move.l    d0,R$d1(sp)      Set Ev$Pulse function code
001e=2f42       move.l    d2,R$d2(sp)      Save event pulse value
0022 41fa       lea.l     Pulser(pc),a0    Address of alarm action
0026=2f48       move.l    a0,R$pc(sp)
                *
                * Setup for A$Cycle call
                *
002a 2601       move.l    d1,d3            Move timer interval from d1 to d3
002c 7000       moveq.l   #0,d0
002e=323c       move.w    #A$Cycle,d1
0032 2400       move.l    d0,d2
0034 08c3       bset      #31,d3           Turn on high bit to indicate sec/256
0038 204f       move.l    sp,a0            Point a0 at register image
003a=4e40       os9       F$Alarm
 003e=48ed      movem.l   d0,R$d0(a5)      Don't change cc
0044=4fef       lea.l     R$Size(sp),sp    Clear stack
0048 4e75       rts                        Return with carry from F$Alarm
                *
                * Called by the system state alarm.
                *
                Pulser
004a=4e40       os9       F$Event
 004e 4e75      rts
00000050        ends
```

To test the new *F$EvTick* system call from a C program we need new function to provide a C binding for the SVC:

```
                nam       TstTick
                ttl       Test EvTick system call
                use       <oskdefs.d>
                opt       −l
000000f0 F$EvTick equ     $f0
                psect     TstTick,0,0,0,200,0

                *
                * EvTick(event, interval, pulse_value)
                *
                EvTick:
0000 2f02       move.l    d2,−(sp)
0002 242f       move.l    8(sp),d2
0006 4e40       os9       F$EvTick
```

```
    000a 6504              bcs.b     EvErr
            EvXt
    000c 241f              move.l    (sp)+,d2
    000e 4e75              rts
            EvErr
    0010 7000              moveq     #0,d0
    0012=2d41              move.l    d1,errno(a6)
    0016 60f4              bra.b     EvXt
    00000018               ends
```

The following C program tests and demonstrates the new *F$EvTick* SVC. It sets up a ticking event and waits for the event 40 times. For each tick the program prints a dot. After 40 ticks it cleans up and exits.

```
#include <stdio.h>
#include <events.h>
#include <ctype.h>
#include <errno.h>

#define TRUE 1
#define FALSE 0
#define PULSE 10
/*
    testtick:
        Usage: testtick wait_event

    This program links to one event: Wait_Event, and starts the event ticker for that
    event. After a few dozen ticks it deletes the alarm.
*/

char *Wait_EName=NULL;

int Wait_Event;
int Wait_val=PULSE;

main(argc, argv)
int argc;
char **argv;
{
    int ct;
    int AlarmID;

    stdout->_flag |= _UNBUF;                            /* Unbuffered output */
    Process_Parms(argc, argv);
```

8.2. SYSTEM STATE ALARMS

```
    Link_To_Event();
    if((AlarmID = EvTick(Wait_Event, 350, PULSE)) == 0)
        exit(_errmsg(errno, "EvTick failed with error %d\n", errno));

    for(ct=0 ; ct < 40; ++ct){
        if(_ev_wait(Wait_Event, Wait_val, Wait_val) == −1){          /*Error */
            fprintf(stderr, "Failure in _ev_wait. Errno %d\n",
                errno);
            exit(errno);
        }
        putchar('.');
    }
    if(alm_delete(AlarmID) == −1)
        _errmsg(0, "alm_delete failed with error %d\n", errno);
    EvUnlink();

    exit(0);
}
Process_Parms(argc, argv)
int argc;
char **argv;
{
    register int ptr;

    if(argc != 2)
        exit(_errmsg(1,"needs an event name\n"));

    Wait_EName = argv[1];
}


Link_To_Event()
{
    if((Wait_Event = _ev_link(Wait_EName)) == −1)
        exit(_errmsg(errno, "Failure in ev_link to %s. Error %d\n",
            Wait_EName, errno));
}


EvUnlink()
{
    _ev_unlink(Wait_Event);
}
```

To test the new system call, compile and assemble the programs:

    r68 evtick.a –o=os9p2.r
    l68 os9p2.r –l=/h0/lib/sys.l –f=os9p2
    r68 tsttick.a –o=tsttick.r
    r68 evwait.a –o=evwait.r
    cc testtick.c tsttick.r evwait.r –f=testtick

then create a new boot file on a floppy:

- copy your bootlist.d0 file into bootlist.d0.test.
- Add os9p2 to the customization module list.
- run "os9gen –z=bootlist.d0.test –e /d0" (replacing d0 with some other mountable disk drive name if your usual floppy boot is not on /d0).
- Reboot your system from /d0.

You can now create a new event with *evcreate*,

    $ evcreate test

and test the ticker:

    $ testtick test

Testtick writes a period to the screen a bit less than once per second for a while, then it removes the alarm and goes away.

8.2.4 System Processes

In many cases, a system process can execute periodically either by using timed sleeps or with alarms. If a system process is *only* concerned with periodic execution, timed sleeps are generally a better tool than alarms. If the process wants to execute non time-driven code *and* time-driven code at the same time, or wait for either a time interval or some other event, alarms are the best tool.

The following example of a system-state process using alarms stretches the point a little. It uses a wait() to pause until its child process terminates, and alarms make it run periodically while it waits. It could be redesigned to use some other method than wait() to detect termination of its child, but wait() plus alarms was easy to do and it makes a good example program.

8.2. SYSTEM STATE ALARMS

The following system-state process is called *profiler*. It runs another process and creates a module that gives some sort of statistical notion of the execution profile of the child process.[2]

Profiler creates a data module twice the size of the executable part of the primary module of the monitored process. A system-state alarm hits every clock tick. The code executed by the alarm uses the offset of the child process' PC in its module as an array subscript into an array of 32-bit counters in the data module and increments the counter.

When *profiler* terminates, the data module can be saved or analyzed in memory. *Dump* is an adequate analysis tool, but *Analyse* is slightly better. Much more useful analysis programs should be easy to write. The nicest tools would use the .stb module for the monitored module to relate PC values to symbolic names.

```
#include <types.h>
#include <stdio.h>
#include <module.h>
#include <errno.h>
#include <signal.h>
#include <machine/reg.h>
/*
    Usage:
        profiler <module> <args> <redirection>
Creates a datamodule named profiler.data twice the size of the main module of
the monitored process. The data module is treated as an array of unsigned longs.
Profiler uses system state alm_cycle to cause its monitor routine to be called on each
tick. Then it forks the module with args and waits for it to complete. Each time
the monitor routine is awakened, it increments the array entry corresponding to
its offset from the beginning of the main module.

    The module to monitor must already be in memory.
*/
#define TRUE            1
#define HEADER_SIZE     72
#define CRC_SIZE        3

unsigned long *counters;
unsigned char *progcode;
unsigned ProgSize;

mod_exec *datamodule;
mod_exec *progModule;
```

---

[2] Like any system-state process, *profiler* must be run by the super user.

```c
extern char **environ;
int os9fork();
void *procDesc=NULL;


int Monitor();

InitRegs(regs, pid)
REGISTERS *regs;
int pid;
{
    regs→d[0] = pid;
    regs→d[1] = progcode;
    regs→d[3] = ProgSize;
    regs→a[2] = counters;
    regs→a[3] = &procDesc;
    regs→pc = Monitor;
}

main(argc, argv)
int argc;
char **argv;
{
    int pid;
    int AlarmID;
    unsigned *status;
    REGISTERS RegSet;

    if(argc < 2)
    exit(1);

    Init(argv[1]);
    /*
        keep the pid in d0
        the primary module body pointer in d1
        the program size in d3
        the counters pointer in a2
        the proc desc pointer pointer in a3

        The alarm service routine:
            compares current proc to d0
            if != it returns
            Gets proc→pc into d2
```

8.2. SYSTEM STATE ALARMS

```
            Calculates d2 = (d2− (a3)) The answer will be even.
            Doubles d2
            increments 0(d2,a2)
            returns
     */
     if((pid = os9exec(os9fork, argv[1], argv + 1, environ, 0, 0)) == −1)
        exit(_errmsg(errno, "Fork of %s failed with error %d\n",
            argv[1], errno));

     InitRegs(&RegSet, pid);
     if((AlarmID = CyclicAlarm(&RegSet)) == 0){
        kill(pid, SIGKILL);
        exit(_errmsg(errno, "Error %d initializing the alarm\n", errno));
     }

     while(wait(&status) != pid);                /* Keep waiting 'till child exits */
     if(status != 0)
        fprintf(stderr, "%s terminated with status %d\n",
            argv[1], status);
     alm_delete(AlarmID);
     exit(0);
}


/*
   Init links to ModName and creates a data module with a data area
   twice the size of the the non-header area of modName.
   Initialize progModule, counters, progcode, and ProgSize.
*/
Init(ModName)
{
   char dmName[64];

   if((progModule = modlink(ModName,0)) == −1)
      exit(_errmsg(errno, "Link to %s failed with error %d\n",
          ModName, errno));
   progcode = (unsigned long)progModule + HEADER_SIZE;
   ProgSize = progModule→_mh._msize − (HEADER_SIZE + CRC_SIZE);
   strcpy(dmName, ModName);
   strcat(dmName, "_prof");
   if(MakeDM(dmName, ProgSize * 2) != 0)
      exit(_errmsg(errno,
          "Make data module for %s failed with error %d\n",
          dmName, errno));
```

}


```
/*
MakeDM(Name, Size)
return 0 if OK. Error number if bad.
Also set errno.
*/
#asm
            use      <oskdefs.d>
_sysattr:   equ      ((ReEnt|SupStat)<< 8)|1
DMAttr      equ      (ReEnt<<8)+1
DMTyLn      equ      (Data<<8)+0
MakeDM:     movem.l  d1-d4/a0-a2,-(sp)
            link     a5,#0
            move.l   d0,a0              Module name string
            move.l   d1,d0              Module size
            move.w   #DMAttr,d1         Attr/rev
            move.w   #Updat_+PRead_,d2  Permissions
            move.w   #DMTyLn,d3         Type/Lang
            moveq.l  #0,d4              Any color
            os9      F$DatMod
            bcs.b    MakeDMEr
            move.l   a2,datamodule(a6)  Data module pointer
            move.l   a1,counters(a6)    Counter's array
            moveq.l  #0,d0              Good return
MakDMX      unlk     a5
            movem.l  (sp)+,d1-d4/a0-a2
            rts
MakeDMEr    moveq    #0,d0              Sweep register
            move.w   d1,d0              Error code
            move.l   d0,errno(a6)
            bra.b    MakDMX

* CyclicAlarm(regs)
CyclicAlarm: movem.l d1-d4/a0,-(sp)
            link     a5,#0
            move.l   d0,a0              Register image
            moveq.l  #0,d0
            move.w   #A$Cycle,d1        Function code
            move.l   d0,d2              Must be zero
            moveq.l  #1,d3              Time interval
            os9      F$Alarm
            bcs.b    CAErr
* alarm id is in d0
CAEx        unlk     a5
            movem.l  (sp)+,d1-d4/a0
            rts
```

8.2. SYSTEM STATE ALARMS

```
         CAErr     moveq    #0,d0              Sweep register
                   move.w   d1,d0              Move error code
                   move.l   d0,errno(a6)
                   moveq.l  #0,d0
                   bra.b    CAEx

*
*          d0 = pid
*          d1 = program code start
*          d3 = program code size
*          a2 = address of counters
*          a3 = pointer to pointer to process desc (or pointer to 0)
*
         Monitor:  tst.l    (a3)               Is proc desc ptr set yet?
                   bne.b    MProcOK            Yes: use it
                   move.l   D_PrcDBT(a6),a0
                   os9      F$FindPD           Get pointer to proc desc in a1
                   move.l   a1,(a3)
         MProcOK
                   move.l   (a3),a1
* now process desc ptr is in a1
                   move.l   P$sp(a1),a0        Proc's stack pointer
                   move.l   R$pc(a0),d2        Process's PC
                   sub.l    d1,d2              PC − prog_start
                   bcs.b    MonX               Before the prog area
                   cmp.l    d2,d3              Out of range?
                   bls.b    MonX               Yes; ignore
                   lsl.l    #1,d2              Multiply offset by two
                   addq.l   #1,(a2,d2)         Increment counter[word_number]
         MonX      rts
#endasm
```

I chose to write large parts of *profiler* in assembly language because I find it easier to understand the exact behavior of assembly language than C for some of the manipulation done in *profiler*. I think the entire program, except the actual call to F$Alarm (which is slightly different from user-state alarms), could have been written in C.

You might notice that InitRegs() passes a pointer to the global variable procDesc to the alarm code. This seems odd, but it is not as peculiar as it seems.

I could have calculated the pointer to the process descriptor before starting the alarm and passed the address of the process' descriptor instead of the address of a variable where the alarm code could store a pointer to the process descriptor. I didn't do that because the program needs a pointer to system global data to get the address of the process descriptor. The address of global data is easy to calculate, but the technique is hardware dependent.

I thought I could have the monitor routine (which is given a pointer to system globals) save a pointer to the process descriptor of the monitored process in the register packet it is given. Unfortunately, OS-9 tries to help by giving the alarm code a copy of the register packet. Only by digging through the alarm list can the alarm routine alter the register packet in a way that will be visible to the next execution of the alarm routine.

Since I couldn't precalculate a pointer to the process descriptor and could not update the register packet, my options were to determine the pointer each time the alarm routine was executed or to calculate it once and cache it at an address known to the alarm routine. I chose to cache the pointer. The code would have been a little easier to read if it recalculated the process descriptor on each entry to Monitor, but the time to call *F$FindPD* would have been much more than the rest of the Monitor routine.

The alarm routine, Monitor, takes advantage of OS-9's careful treatment of registers. Monitor saves no registers; this feels dangerous, but in this case it is correct.

8.3 Programs

The following program is a trivial analysis program for the data module produced by *profiler*.

```
#include <stdio.h>
#include <module.h>
#include <errno.h>

#define HEADER_SIZE     72      /* Same value profiler uses */
#define CRC_SIZE        3

/*
    Analysis should be called with the name of the data module
    it should analyse.
*/
main(argc, argv)
int argc;
char **argv;
{
    register unsigned long *array;
    register int i;
    register unsigned long ArraySize;
    register unsigned long MaxVal=0;
```

8.3. PROGRAMS

```
    register int MaxIdx;
    register mod_exec *modPtr;

    if((modPtr = modlink(argv[1], 0)) == -1)
        exit(_errmsg(errno, "Cannot link to data module\n"));

    (unsigned long)array = (unsigned long)modPtr +
            modPtr→_mexec;
    ArraySize = ((modPtr→_mh._msize - HEADER_SIZE) - CRC_SIZE -
        (strlen(argv[1]) + 1)) / sizeof(unsigned long);
    printf("Visit Table\n");
    printf("%10s\t%10s\n", "Offset", "Count");
    for(i = 0; i < ArraySize; ++i)
        if(array[i] > 0){
            printf("%10x %10u\n", (i * 2) + HEADER_SIZE,
                array[i]);
            if(array[i] > MaxVal){
                MaxVal = array[i];
                MaxIdx = i;
            }
        }
    printf("Max count %d at %x\n", MaxVal, (MaxIdx*2) + HEADER_SIZE);

    munlink(modPtr);
    exit(0);
}
```

When I run *profiler* on a tiny program named *eatmpu*,

    $ analysis eatmpu_prof

generates the following output:

```
Visit Table
    Offset         Count
       2aa          1710
       2ac           489
       2b0          9838
       2b2           308
       2b4           409
       2ba          1299
Max count 9838 at 2b0
```

These numbers are more meaningful when I use *debug* or *srcdbg* to give them a symbolic interpretation:

```
$ debug eatmpu
default symbols belong to 'eatmpu'
dbg: l eatmpu
dbg: di .r7+2aa
main+0x1A      >2004              move.l d4,d0
main+0x1C      >4C060000          mulu.l d6,d0
main+0x20      >2A00              move.l d0,d5
main+0x22      >5284              addq.l #1,d4
main+0x24      >0C8402625A00      cmpi.l #40000000,d4
main+0x2A      >6D00FFEE          blt.w main+0x1A
main+0x2E      >4CED0070FFF4      movem.l -12(a5),d4-d6
main+0x34      >4E5D              unlk a5
main+0x36      >4E75              rts
```

It's not a surprise that the *mulu* in the loop is the most popular instruction.[3]

Srcdbg gives a C interpretation of *analysis* output:

```
1.$srcdbg eatmpu
Reading symbol file "eatmpu.dbg".
eatmpu.c
Reading symbol file "eatmpu.stb".
Context: eatmpu\_cstart
SrcDbg: li eatmpu
SrcDbg: dil .r7+0x2aa
    6:         k = i * j;
                   ^
main+0x1a      >2004              move.l d4,d0
main+0x1c      >4C060000          mulu.l d6,d0
main+0x20      >2A00              move.l d0,d5
    5:    for(i = 0 ; i < 40000000; ++i)
                          ^
main+0x22      >5284              addq.l #1,d4
    5:    for(i = 0 ; i < 40000000; ++i)
                      ^
main+0x24      >0C8402625A00      cmpi.l #40000000,d4
main+0x2a      >6D00FFEE          blt.w main+0x1a
main+0x2e      >4CED0070FFF4      movem.l -12(a5),d4-d6
```

---

[3]When the clock ticks during an instruction, the PC points at the *next* instruction.

8.3. PROGRAMS

```
main+0x34      >4E5D          unlk a5
main+0x36      >4E75          rts
SrcDbg(DILIST):
```

Chapter 9

Process Scheduling

> OS-9 was originally designed as an operating system for real-time applications, and it hasn't moved far from that heritage. Real-time work required that OS-9 offer fast response. It didn't require a whole range of options for adjusting each process' performance, but Microware included them anyhow. In this chapter we will discuss the way that OS-9 distributes processor time and the control that you have over it.

9.1 A Low-Level View

If you get too close to the machine, processes disappear. Everything looks like one big program. The microprocessor doesn't know that it is executing several processes. It hums along executing instructions; gets an interrupt and branches to the vector for that interrupt; executes more instructions.... Sometimes it moves the stack pointer around.

If we move a little bit back from the processor's view of the system, we can see that the processor is running a process for a while, then it runs OS-9 itself, then it either returns to the same process, or moves to a different one. The processes are distinguished by the values in the machine registers (the MPU's registers, the FPU's registers, and the state of any memory management hardware that's in use).

When the system clock ticks, it asserts a hardware interrupt. This interrupt causes control to be vectored through the OS-9 kernel to the part of OS-9 responsible for the management of the process queues. The action of this code can be divided into three steps:

1. The kernel checks the queue of sleeping processes. Any processes that are ready to wake up are moved to the active queue.

2. Then it checks the number of ticks during which the current process has been active. If the current process has used its time slice, the process descriptor is inserted in the active queue and the process at the front of the active queue is made the current process.

Each time OS-9 is called on to add a new process to the active queue (for instance, when the current process reaches the end of its time slice), it ages all eligible processes. This aging doesn't actually involve running through the active queue and changing the age of each process. Process age is recorded as an offset from a counter associated with the active queue. The entire queue is aged by incrementing the counter. When the 32-bit counter overflows, the kernel must adjust all the process descriptors in the active queue to reflect the counter's change from $ffffffff to $00000000, but that problem only occurs rarely. It takes more than 10,000 hours of continuous operation to cause the counter to roll.

The current process is the one that OS-9 runs next. There is a pointer to the current process' process descriptor in system global data. A process is made "current" by removing its descriptor from the active queue and putting a pointer to the descriptor in the current process field.

9.2 Aging

Aging eligible processes is the crux of the OS-9 scheduling algorithm. In the simplest case, the scheduler increments the base age of the active queue. This increases the age of each process in the queue that hasn't reached some maximum age. It doesn't change the positions of the processes in the queue relative to one another, but it does alter the position at which a new process will be inserted. When a process is placed in the active queue, its priority is used as its age and the queue is searched for a place to insert the new process so the queue remains sorted by age.

Imagine that there are only two active processes; one with a priority of ten, the other with a priority of one. The high-priority process is inserted at the front of the queue and run until its time slice is up, say four ticks. When the high-priority process returns to the active queue the scheduler increases the age of the other processes in the queue. The low-priority process now has an age of one. The high-priority process with its priority of ten is inserted at the front of the queue and run again immediately. After another time slice of four ticks, the age of the low-priority process becomes two. The high-priority process is inserted before it and run for a third time slice. After the high-priority process has used nine time slices, it enters the queue with the same age as the low-priority process. The high-priority process is inserted at the end of the queue, and the low-priority process runs. It only runs for one time slice because the other process will age to 11 and the low-priority process will go to the end of the queue with an age of one.

There are some important things to note about this time-slicing scheme. High-priority processes run for longer stretches and they run frequently. Low-priority processes don't run long or often, but they do get a share of the processor no matter how busy it is. If all the processes have the same priority, each process runs for one time slice then drops to the end of the queue behind all the aged processes.

Think of the processor as a merry-go-round. You can pay almost any amount you like for a ticket. The more you pay, the more priority you have. Priority works for you in two ways. It helps you get a good position in line. The attendant finds you a place in line where there are no people with lower priorities ahead of you. It may also let you ride longer. You are allowed to stay on the ride until the first person in line has more priority than you.

Now, the merry-go-round operator has a notion of fairness. He hates to see people wait in line, so every time he lets someone onto the ride he goes through the line and increases the priority on each person's ticket. Even if you purchased the least expensive ticket, eventually it will be worth enough to get you to the front of the line. Once you get on the ride, the priority of your ticket reverts to what you paid for it. The length of your wait in line (your age) no longer counts. If you bought a cheap ticket you probably won't ride for long.

9.3 Adjustments

The aging algorithm, adjusted with priorities, works well for most situations, but special problems need different solutions. There is no way to deactivate OS-9's normal aging algorithm, but some priorities can be made special.

If you want to run a program with the least possible impact on other programs, OS-9 gives you a special trick that prevents the program from running when *any* other process wants the processor. You can't do that by simply assigning the process a low priority—eventually it will age until it reaches the front of the active queue—but you can designate a range of priorities for a low-priority class by adjusting the D_MaxAge field. The D_MaxAge field defines all priorities less than its value as low priority. Processes with priorities less than D_MaxAge never age to a position in the active queue ahead of a process with a priority greater than D_MaxAge.

Normally D_MaxAge is zero. That's a special value that means "don't use

D_MaxAge." It doesn't mean that no process may age beyond zero. All processes on the active queue will be aged. If you write a program (which must be run in superuser mode) that resets D_MaxAge to some other value, D_MaxAge takes effect.

The following code is a skeleton for a program that, for a while, shuts out all processes with lower priorities.

```
#include <setsys.h>
main()
{
   short OldMaxAge, Priority;
   /*... */
   OldMaxAge = _getsys(D_MaxAge, 2);
   _setsys(D_MaxAge, 2, GetPty());
   /* We should check for a -1 return in case the user isn't */
   /* super user. */

   /* Code to be run with processes at lower priorities locked out */
   /*... */

   /* Now restore D_MaxAge to its original value. */
   _setsys(D_MaxAge, 2, OldMaxAge);
   exit(0);
}


#asm
GetPty    move.l    d1,-(sp)    save d1 and d2
          move.l    d2,-(sp)
          os9       F$ID
          move.w    d2,d0       move priority to d0
          ext.l     d0          extend it to an integer
          move.l    (sp)+,d2    restore d1 and d2
          move.l    (sp)+,d1
          rts
#endasm
```

Since the range of priorities is from 0 to 65535, let's start by dividing the range at 32767. With D_MaxAge equal to 32767, no process will age past that value. If you tend to run most of your work with a priority of 100 or so, your processes will probably never reach D_MaxAge. Your system will run exactly as it did before you altered the value.

If you run a job with a priority of 40000, it will enter the queue with a priority greater than D_MaxAge. None of the processes with priorities less than D_MaxAge run unless the high-priority process signifies that it doesn't want the processor time by

9.3. ADJUSTMENTS

waiting or sleeping; i.e., *F$Sleep*, *F$Wait*, *Ev$Wait*, or any of several ways to wait in an I/O operation.

The barrier formed in the range of priority values by D_MaxAge is an effective way to separate processes into low and high priority classes, but it doesn't give high-priority processes exclusive use of the processor. OS-9 continues to schedule processes with priority below D_MaxAge when no process above D_MaxAge is ready to run. When a waiting high-priority process is activated, it immediately replaces any low-priority process as the current process provided that the current process is not in system state. No process can be replaced as the current process when it is in system state, so a high-priority process may have to wait for a low-priority process in system state to return to user state or explicitly relinquish control.

There is another tool for adjusting process scheduling. The D_MinPty field divides processes into classes much more strictly than D_MaxAge. The D_MaxAge value is used to give OS-9 a strong preference for a group of processes. D_MinPty causes OS-9 to completely ignore a group of processes.

All processes with a priority less than D_MinPty are not considered for aging or execution. The scheduler stops scanning the active queue when it gets to a process with a priority lower than D_MinPty, and the dispatcher refuses to run them even if they are at the front of the queue. Processes below D_MinPty continue to hold any system resources (memory, open files, links to modules) that they acquired when they were running, but they don't have access to the processor. Processes with priorities above D_MinPty are aged and run as usual.

D_MinPty is normally set to zero. Since zero is the lowest possible priority, all processes are eligible for aging and execution. If you (a super user) reset D_MinPty to a higher value, any processes below that priority lose their right to run until you set D_MinPty back down again.

You can cause serious trouble by being careless with D_MinPty. If a process set the value of D_MinPty higher than its own priority, the process will finish its time slice and be placed in the active queue *below* D_MinPty. Unless a high-priority program that can set D_MinPty back down or a high-priority shell is running, the system is stuck. D_MinPty remains high and the system is useless until it is rebooted.

D_MaxAge is used to divide processes into high and low-priority classes. D_MinPty is used to give a process (or group of processes) exclusive use of the processor. Normal applications don't need either of these facilities. Programs that deal with humans need good response time, but they can afford to give up a time slice once in a while. Programs that do real-time control, however, often handle hardware that cares about hundredths or even thousandths of seconds. D_MinPty and D_MaxAge give the programmer tight control over process scheduling that is useful when a time slice interval is not negligible time.

9.4 Preemption

If D_MinPty and D_MaxAge are not set, aging eventually brings every process to the head of the active queue. There, they are given at least a few cycles of processor time, but they are not guaranteed a full time slice, or even a full clock tick of processor time. A process that is placed in the active queue either because it is freshly forked or because it has been moved from a sleep, wait, ev_wait, or I/O queue, causes any lower-priority current process to be bumped back into the active queue.

If process x with priority 50 has aged itself to the front of the active queue and been activated, it might get a full time slice. However, if a process with priority 51 is activated by an interrupt service routine or by inter-process communication from process x, process x will dumped back into the active queue immediately. The bumped process is treated exactly as if it had used its entire time slice. This is called preemption.

The process that bumped the current process is not automatically made current. It is inserted in the active queue according to its priority and the age of the other processes in the queue. It will be ahead of the preempted process, but it may be behind other processes.

Preemption has interesting applications to inter-process communcations. If process x releases process y from a sleep or wait, the effect depends on their relative priorities.

- If the priority of process x is greater than or equal to the priority of process y, process x will probably return from the system call that released process y. The system call moves process y to the active queue, but it has no effect on process x.

- If the priority of process x is less than the priority of process y, process x will give up its time slice just before returning from the system call. It is returned to the active queue and allowed to age back to the front.

9.5 Tuning for Real-Time Applications

The easy way to handle real-time applications is to use one processor per process. It works. If there is only one active process, you can be certain that no time sharing will take place. Insisting on only one active process at a time isn't as strict a requirement as it seems. A single-user system probably has at most one active process most of the time. If you check the state of the processes in a simple workstation with procs, you will find that most of them are waiting or sleeping.

Restricting a real-time system to one active process per processor may be a sad waste of OS-9's power. As soon as a real-time controller has to handle at least two independent ports, it has to use multiprocessing or simulate multiple processors. A

9.5. TUNING FOR REAL-TIME APPLICATIONS

simple example is a system that controls the water level in fifty tanks by reading the level in each tank and adjusting its input valve. Checking and adjusting each tank about once every two seconds is easy for a 68000. The neatest way to program the solution is to use fifty processes, one for each tank. Each process sleeps for two seconds, adjusts the valve, and sleeps again. If all the processes woke up and wanted to adjust their tanks at the same time, they would queue up in the active queue. If the delay were too long, a tank might overflow or go dry, but let's assume there is plenty of extra time.

To complicate the problem, let's say that once the computer reads the water level in a tank it must adjust the valve within a very short time. Delaying as much as a hundredth of a second could cause deep trouble. If OS-9's process scheduler is left alone, a process could reach the end of its time slice between the time it reads the level and the time it sends instructions for a valve adjustment. Returning the process to the active queue and leaving it there while other processes run would cause the process to miss the deadline for adjusting the valve. The solution is careful use of MaxAge.

Each process must lock all others out of the processor before it reads the water level and unlock the system after it sends the valve adjustment instructions. If processes tended to have a priority around 256, the sequence might go like this:

1. Set D_MaxAge to 1000
2. Sleep for 2 seconds
3. Do setup
4. Set priority to 2000
5. Read level
6. Set valve
7. Reset priority
8. Repeat from 2

Note that the priority is set high at step four. From that step until step seven, the process can not be interrupted by another process.

The only protection on the interval between step one and step four is the duration of a time slice. The definition of the problem allows variable intervals between level checks, so this is not a problem.

OS-9's standard process scheduling algorithm almost always works best if you leave it alone. Under some circumstances you will want to mark off classes of special processes, and in those cases the D_MaxAge and D_MinPty fields alone or in combination can modify OS-9's scheduling behavior. A non-zero value for D_MaxAge gives you two classes of process, both runable. D_MinPty gives you two classes with only the high-priority class runable.

Chapter 10

Events

Events are the primary synchronization tool OS-9 offers programmers. Events are wonderfully versatile. In this chapter, we'll investigate the reasons for events and some of the things that can be done with them.

10.1 A Simple Analogue

Let's start with a parking analogy. This time we'll avoid on-street parking and go to regulated parking lots.

Parking lots sometimes have flimsy little gates on them. Cars approach the gate and follow some protocol, the gate opens, they go through, and the gate closes. I know of a parking lot (in front of the Yale CoOp) where the gates keep track of the number of cars in the lot. If the lot is below capacity, the entry gates open immediately. If the lot is full, they don't open until a car leaves.

I imagine that there is a small computer somewhere in that system. It keeps the number of cars in the parking lot in mind. While the number is below the lot's capacity things are simple. When it reaches capacity things get interesting. The lot is full because many people want to shop. Naturally there are lines of cars waiting at each entry gate—not patiently. The computer would be vehemently despised if it were incorrect or unfair in its handling of the gates.

When a car leaves, the variable that counts the cars in the lot is decremented. Since the number is now below the capacity of the lot, the computer opens an entry gate and lets a car in. When the car passes the gate, the counter is incremented. Now the lot is at capacity again and the entry gates stay closed until another car leaves.

Let me phrase the parking-lot-regulation problem as an algorithm with events.

Initialize: Create an event called Car_Count with a value of zero, a signal increment of -1 and a wait increment of 1	
Entry Gate Algorithm: Link to the Car_Count event When a car arrives Ev$Wait on Car_Count for Min value of 0 and Max value of Capacity -1 Let the car in	**Exit Gate Algorithm:** Link to the Car_Count event When a car leaves Let the car out Ev$Signl Car_Count

Until the lot is full, *Ev$Signl* and *Ev$Wait* just increment and decrement *Car_Count*. When *Car_Count* passes *Capacity* − 1, *Ev$Wait* blocks. All the entry gates get to an *Ev$Wait* and stop. *Ev$Signl* never blocks, so cars can always get out of the lot. When a car leaves, the exit gate algorithm does an *Ev$Signl* which decreases *Car_Count* to *Capacity* − 1. One of the waiting entry gates is selected and its *Ev$Wait* is unblocked. The first thing *Ev$Wait* does after unblocking is to increment *Car_Count* by one.

If the parking lot system uses events, the entry and exit algorithms are pretty simple. Without the help of events, some nasty problems appear. Actually, they probably won't appear ... not immediately. They stay hidden until the worst possible moment, then savage the programmer. The event functions allowed us to confidently say, "One of the waiting entry gates is selected ...". It also permits us to increment and decrement *Car_Count* without elaborate precautions.

Picking a gate doesn't seem difficult, nor does arithmetic on *Car_Count*. It's easy to write the entire control algorithm without appealing to system events. The resulting program might go something like this:

	Initialize: Create a data module called Car_Count Set the integer variable in Car_Count to 0	
	Entry Gate Algorithm	**Exit Gate Algorithm**
1	Link to the Car_Count module	Link to the Car_Count module
2	Call the integer in Car_Count n	Call the integer in Car_Count n
3	When a car arrives	When a car leaves
4	While n > Capacity − 1 wait	Let the car out
5	n := n + 1	n := n − 1
6	Let the car in	

First let's look at statement 5 in the entry algorithm. To understand how this

10.1. A SIMPLE ANALOGUE

statement can cause trouble, you have to imagine what the compiler will do with it. It might do the operation with one instruction:

    addi.l   #1,n(A6)

This is safe provided that all the processes are running on the same processor (reasonable). However, the compiler might generate these instructions instead:

    move.l n(A6),D0
    addq.l   #1,D0
    move.l D0,n(A6)

Since the operating system could catch an interrupt and give control to another process in the middle of this string of instructions, we have to see what happens when two processes try to update *n* at the same time.

Entry Gate One	Entry Gate Two
move.l n,D0 addq.l #1,D0	
... The clock ticks ... and the process for Entry Gate Two starts running	
	... move.l n,D0 addq.l #1,D0 move.l D0,n
... Time passes ... and the process for Entry Gate One runs again	
move.l D0,n	

    The process for Entry Gate One just wiped out the change Entry Gate Two made to *n* and any other changes to *n* made during the interval marked "Time passes."

    This problem with altering shared variables (like *n*) can cause the program to lose count of the number of cars in the lot.

    The other problem with the naive parking lot algorithm is that all the entry gates might open at the same time, each thinking it is the only one opening. Imagine that the lot is full and there are lines waiting at five entry gates. A car leaves and *Car_Count*'s counter is decreased to *Capacity* − 1. All the entry gates have been busily watching *Car_Count* for that change so they all leave their loops and let a happy driver into the lot. Then they each increment the counter and discover, too late, that there are four cars too many in the lot.

There are ways to avoid these problems. The easiest way is to use events. OS-9 takes care that only one process updates an event's variable at a time: it protects the event's shared variable. It also lets you decide whether to let all the processes waiting on an event go at once or select just one; it can force waiting processes into a queue. The event system in OS-9 takes those two features, a protected shared variable and process queuing, and elaborates on them.

10.2 Some Event-Handling Utilities

It is useful have a list of all the events in your system. The *Ev$Info* function of the event system is meant for exactly that purpose. The following program uses *Ev$Info* to produce a directory of active events.

```
/*
    EvDir
    List all events defined to OS-9 together with their properties
*/
#include <stdio.h>
#include <events.h>
#define TRUE 1

main()
{
    event Buffer;
    int i;

    /* Print a header line for the event directory */
    printf("Event Directory\n ID Name Value W S Links\n");
    /*
        For each defined event, use Ev$Info to get its name and
        attributes, then print a line with all the info.
    */
    for(i=0;TRUE;++i){
        if(_ev_info(i, &Buffer) == −1)
            break; /* end of events */
        printf("%5d %11s %5d %2d %2d %2d\n",
            Buffer._ev_eid,
            Buffer._ev_name,
            Buffer._ev_value,
            Buffer._ev_winc,
            Buffer._ev_sinc,
            Buffer._ev_link);
```

        }
        exit(0);
}

It's also nice to be able to dispose of an event that is left around in the system.

```
/*
    EvDel
    There isn't a utility command to delete events (yet). This fills that role. Use the
    command: evdel Wait1 to delete the event Wait1. Ev$Delete won't delete
    an event with a non-zero link count, so, if Ev$Delete fails, unlink the event
    until it can be deleted. This a little dangerous. Somewhat like an unlink utility
    that would always unlink a module until it was removed from memory.
*/
#include <stdio.h>
#include <events.h>

main(argc, argv)
int argc;
char **argv;
{
    int Event_id;
    char *Event_Name;

    if(argc < 2){
        printf("%s usage is:\n %s EventName\n", *argv, *argv);
        exit(1);
    }
    Event_Name = argv[1];
    /*
        If the event is defined, get its event ID. If it isn't,
        we can't delete it, so exit with an error code.
    */
     if((Event_id = _ev_link(Event_Name)) == −1)
        exit(errno);
    /*
        Keep doing Ev$Unlink/Ev$Delete until the event is gone.
        We use a loop with unlink because an event with a non-zero
        link count can't be deleted.
    */
    do
        _ev_unlink(Event_id);
    while(_ev_delete(Event_Name) == −1);
```

```
    exit(0);
}
```

Events are normally created by the programs that use them, but experimenting with events is easier if you can create them to specification without modifying a program each time you want a new event. The following program takes all the parameters for *Ev$Creat* on its command line and issues the *Ev$Creat* for you.

```
/*
    EvCreate
    Create an event. The usage of this command is:
    EvCreate Event_Name Wait_increment Signal_increment Initial_value
    If it is only given an event name, EvCreate will make an event that can be used
    as a semaphore (with Ev$Wait triggering on 0).
*/
#include <stdio.h>
#include <events.h>

#define WAIT 0
#define SIGNAL 1
#define INITIAL 2

main(argc, argv)
int argc;
char **argv;
{
    register char *Event_Name;
    int Values[3];
    register int ID, i;

    if(argc < 2){
        fprintf(stderr, "%s Usage:\n %s %s\n",
            *argv, *argv,
            "Event_Name [wait_inc signal_inc [initial_value]]");
        exit(1);
    }
    /*
        Set default values
    */
    Values[WAIT] = −1;
    Values[SIGNAL] = 1;
    Values[INITIAL] = −1;
    Event_Name = argv[1];
```

10.3. A SEMAPHORE 129

```
        for(i=2;i<argc;++i)
            Values[i-2] = atoi(argv[i]);

        ID = _ev_creat( Values[INITIAL],
            Values[WAIT],
            Values[SIGNAL],
            Event_Name);
        if(ID == -1){
            fprintf(stderr, "Ev_Create(%d, %d, %d, %s) gave error %d\n",
                Values[INITIAL], Values[WAIT],
                Values[SIGNAL], Event_Name, errno);
            exit(errno);
        }
        /*
            Unlink the event before exiting to keep the event's
            link count accurate.
        */
        _ev_unlink(ID);
        exit(0);
}
```

10.3   A Semaphore

Limiting the event variable to two values and only releasing one waiting process at a time reduces events to the basic process synchronization operation. It comes in several similar flavors, and is usually called a semaphore or (on IBM mainframes) an event.

A semaphore needs two values, to represent *open* and *closed*. When the semaphore is open, an *Ev$Wait* doesn't block but closes the semaphore. An *Ev$Signl* opens the semaphore. You can pick any values for open and closed that please you, but if you choose 0 for open and 1 for closed a semaphore works like this:

Ev$Creat
   initial value: 0 or 1 *depending on whether you want the semaphore to be initially open or closed.*
   auto-increment for *Ev$Wait*: 1
   auto-increment for *Ev$Signl*: −1
Ev$Signl:
   only activate one process

With a semaphore set up like this, you have to make certain that a process doesn't signal a semaphore with a value of −1. Giving *Ev$Wait* a very negative minimum activation value (e.g., −10000) avoids this problem—mostly—but might not be just what you want. The following two programs let you experiment with a semaphore set up either way.

/*
> SyncWait
> This program is a general-purpose tool for experimenting with events. It can use either a Wait/Signal or a simple Wait protocol. Its usage is:
> Syncwait Wait_Event [Signal_Event] low [high]
> In its simplest form: SyncWait WaitEvent low, it uses a loop with an Ev$Wait in it. Each time it gets through the wait it prints a message with its process number and the low bound for the Ev$Wait. Leaving out the high bound for the Ev$Wait on the command line tells the program to use the same number for low and high bounds.
> If a Signal-event name is given on the command line (with a wait-event name), SyncWait uses a Wait/Signal protocol. It adds an Ev$Signl to the loop, which now goes:
>> Wait
>> Print a message
>> Signal
> This lets the driving process coordinate with this one better than the simple Wait loop does.

*/
```
#include <stdio.h>
#include <events.h>
#include <ctype.h>

#define TRUE 1
#define FALSE 0
#define FOREVER TRUE

char *Wait_EName=NULL,
     *Signal_EName=NULL;

int Wait_Event, Signal_Event;
int Wait_Min, Wait_Max;

main(argc, argv)
int argc;
char **argv;
{
    Process_Parms(argc, argv);
    Link_To_Events();
```

10.3. A SEMAPHORE

```
        while(FOREVER){
            if(_ev_wait(Wait_Event, Wait_Min, Wait_Max) == -1){    /* error */
                fprintf(stderr, "Failure in ev_wait. Errno %d\n",
                    errno);
                exit(errno);
            }
            printf("%d:%d\n", getpid(), Wait_Max);
            if(Signal_EName == NULL)
                continue;
            if(_ev_signal(Signal_Event, 0) == -1){
                fprintf(stderr, "Failure in ev_signal. Errno %d\n",
                    errno);
                EvUnlink();
                exit(errno);
            }
        }
        EvUnlink();
        exit(0);
}
Process_Parms(argc, argv)
int argc;
char **argv;
{
    register int ptr;

    if(argc < 3){
        printf("%s needs at least three parameters. Usage:\n%s %s\n",
            *argv, *argv,
            "Wait_Event [Signal_Event] Activation_Max Activation_Min");
        exit(1);
    }
    Wait_EName = argv[1];
    if((!isdigit(*argv[2])) && (*argv[2] != '-')){                        /* Signal_EName */
        Signal_EName = argv[2];
        ptr = 3;
    }else
        ptr = 2;
    Wait_Min = atoi(argv[ptr]);
    if(argc <= ptr+1)
        Wait_Max = Wait_Min;
    else
        Wait_Max = atoi(argv[ptr+1]);
```

```
        return;
}

Link_To_Events()
{
    if((Wait_Event = _ev_link(Wait_EName)) == −1){
        fprintf(stderr, "Failure in ev_link to %s. Error %d\n",
            Wait_EName, errno);
         exit(errno);
    }
    if(Signal_EName)
        if((Signal_Event = _ev_link(Signal_EName)) == −1){
            fprintf(stderr, "Failure in ev_link to %s. Error %d\n",
                Signal_EName, errno);
            exit(errno);
        }
    return;
}

EvUnlink()
{
    _ev_unlink(Wait_Event);
    if(Signal_EName)
        _ev_unlink(Signal_Event);
    return;
}
```

The next program is the driver for the semaphore experiments. It can be used for both the simple (Wait), and the synchronized (Signal/Wait), protocols.

```
/*
    Semaphore
    This is the driver for the semaphore experiments. It is used:
    Semaphore Event1 [Event2]
    Event1 is the event which this process will signal and SyncWait will wait for. If
    Event2 is given, this process will wait for that event after it signals Event1.
*/
#include <stdio.h>
#define LOOPS 100
```

10.3. A SEMAPHORE

```
main(argc, argv)
int argc;
char **argv;
{
    char *WaitEvent=NULL;
    char *SignalEvent=NULL;
    int WEvent, SEvent;
    int i;

    if(argc < 2){
        printf("%s Usage:\n %s SignalEvent WaitEvent\n", *argv, *argv);
        exit(1);
    }
    SignalEvent = argv[1];
    if((SEvent = _ev_link(SignalEvent)) == -1){
        fprintf(stderr, "Error %d in ev_link for %s\n",
            errno, SignalEvent);
        exit(errno);
    }
    if(argc > 2){
        WaitEvent = argv[2];
        if((WEvent = _ev_link(WaitEvent)) == -1){
            fprintf(stderr, "Error %d in ev_link for %s/n",
                errno, WaitEvent);
            exit(errno);
        }
    }
    for(i=0;i<LOOPS;++i){
        _ev_signal(SEvent, 0);
        if(WaitEvent)
            _ev_wait(WEvent, 0, 0);
        else
            tsleep(20);
    }
    exit(0);
}
```

The following steps should make two different number pairs alternate on the screen. Stop the display for a while (causing the *semaphore* to get ahead of the *syncwaits*), and note what happens when you let it go.

Stop the experiment with a control-C, then kill the remaining *syncwait* and *semaphore* processes.

Figure 10.1: **Sample Semaphore Experiment**
$ evcreate Wait 1 −1 1
$ syncwait Wait −100 0&
$ syncwait Wait −100 0&
$ semaphore Wait&
$ w

Delete the event with *EvDel*.

The experiment in figure 10.2 uses a hand-shaking protocol. You will find that the numbers fly by much faster. If you stop the display, *semaphore* will wait, so stopping the display only has the obvious effect (the display pauses).

Figure 10.2: **Another Experiment with Semaphores**
$ evcreate Wait 1 −1 1
$ evcreate Sig 1 −1 1
$ syncwait Wait Sig 0 0
$ syncwait Wait Sig 0 0
$ semaphore Wait Sig

Stop the experiment and clean up as before.

10.3.1 Fast Semaphores

The simplest possible semaphore is only two instructions long:

```
waitloop    tas     flag(a0)
            bne.b   waitloop

signal      clr.b   flag(a0)
```

The wait code loops until flag becomes zero, then it sets a bit in the flag byte to claim the semaphore. To release the semaphore the signal code clears the flag byte. This technique is called **busy waiting**. There is no faster way to claim a free lock, but it wastes CPU time looping if it has to wait. Busy waiting sometimes makes sense as a locking mechanism in a multiprocessor system, but busy waiting works better if the main wait loop doesn't include the elaborate *tas* instruction:

10.3. A SEMAPHORE

```
waitloop    tst.b    flag(a0)
            bne.b    waitloop
            tas      flag(a0)
            bne.b    waitloop

signal      clr.b    flag(a0)
```

This code doesn't use a *tas* until it has good reason to believe the flag will be zero.

Often a semaphore is used to protect a resource that will almost never experience contention. If the protection wasn't there, the application would crash every few hours, but it seems foolish to call for the full power of events and almost never use it. A *tas* is hundreds of times faster than an *Ev$Wait* and it is enough to lock a resource.

The processor load imposed by the busy wait loop can be reduced by inserting a *F$Sleep*:

```
waitloop    tas      flag(a0)
            beq.b    Gotit
            move.w   #1,d0
            os9      F$Sleep
            bra.b    waitloop
Gotit

signal      clr.b    flag(a0)
```

The sleep may introduce at least a one-tick delay between the time the semaphore is released and the time a waiting process claims it, but it is simple. When contention[1] for a semaphore is rare, busy waiting with a sleep in the loop is often adequate.

Events can be combined with a *tas* to give the best of both worlds. The code is a little more complicated than busy waiting, but the result uses the scheduling power of events when it is required, and has the speed of *tas* when the semaphore need not wait.

```
            nam      Semaphore
            ttl      Fast Semaphore
            use      <oskdefs.d>
            opt      -l
            psect    FSem,0,0,0,200,0
*
* FWait
*
```

---

[1]Contention is competition. When processes almost never have to wait for a semaphore, contention is light.

```
*       d0 Is the event ID number for the semaphore's event
*               The event must have
*                       an initial value of 0,
*                       a wait increment of −1,
*                       a signal increment of 0.
*               d1 Is a pointer to the event byte.
*                       The high order bit of the byte is controlled by a tas.
*                       The other bits are a count of waiting processes (in the range 0 to 127)
*       returns 0 for success or −1 for an error (and stores the error code in errno)
*
0000 2f08  FWait:    move.l    a0,−(sp)
0002 2041            move.l    d1,a0
0004 5210            addq.b    #1,(a0)              Request a signal
0006 4ad0  loop      tas       (a0)
0008 6a24            bpl.b     GotIt
000a 48e7            movem.l   d2−d3,−(sp)
       * d0 is already the event ID number
000e=7200            moveq     #Ev$Wait,d1
0010 7401            moveq     #1,d2                Minimum activation value
0012 2602            move.l    d2,d3                Maximum activation value
0014=4e40            os9       F$Event
 0018 6506           bcs.b     WError
001a 4cdf            movem.l   (sp)+,d2−d3
001e 60e6            bra.b     loop
           WError
0020 48c1            ext.l     d1
0022=2d41            move.l    d1,errno(a6)
0026 70ff            moveq     #−1,d0
0028 4cdf            movem.l   (sp)+,d2−d3/a0
002c 4e75            rts
           GotIt
002e 7000            moveq     #0,d0
0030 205f            move.l    (sp)+,a0
0032 4e75            rts


           *
           * FSignal
           *       d0 is the event ID number for the semaphore event
           *       d1 is a pointer to the event byte
           *
0034 2f08  FSignal:  move.l    a0,−(sp)
0036 2041            move.l    d1,a0                Make byte pointer useful
0038 0890            bclr      #7,(a0)              Clear the flag bit
003c 5310            subq.b    #1,(a0)              Uncount this process
003e 6712            beq.b     SigDone
0040 2f02            move.l    d2,−(sp)
0042 243c            move.l    #1,d2                Signal waiter
```

10.3. A SEMAPHORE

```
0048=7200              moveq    #Ev$Set,d1
004a=4e40              os9      F$Event          Signal a process
 004e 6508             bcs.b    SError
0050 241f              move.l   (sp)+,d2
0052 205f  SigDone     move.l   (sp)+,a0
0054 7000              moveq    #0,d0            Good return
0056 4e75              rts
0058 48c1  SError      ext.l    d1
005a=2d41              move.l   d1,errno(a6)
005e 70ff              moveq    #-1,d0           Error return
0060 4cdf              movem.l  (sp)+,d2/a0
0064 4e75              rts
00000066               ends
```

The counter for waiting processes is only 7 bits long. It could easily be expanded to 15 or 31 bits by changing the size of the *addq* and *subq* instructions, but 127 is a large number of waiting processes, especially for a semaphore with light contention.

Although *tas* is a multi-processor instruction, *addq* and *subq* are not. Multi-processor fast semaphores use more complicated strategies to count waiting processes.

This implementation of a fast semaphore is not *fair*. A process waiting in the event is not guaranteed to get out of FWait() before a process that arrives later. This is not a problem if fast semaphores are used when contention for the semaphore is light. When contention is heavy, a more elaborate version of FSignal() could solve the problem, but these fast signals only have an advantage when contention is light, so a *fair* FSignal() is difficult to justify.

The code to call fast semaphores looks like:

```
#include <stdio.h>
#include <module.h>
#include <errno.h>
#define TRUE 1
#define FALSE 0
/*
    FSemTst EventName

    The event must already be created with an initial value of 0
    a signal increment of 0, and a wait increment of -1.
    evcreate fsem -1 0 0
    fsemtst fsem & fsemtst fsem & fsemtst fsem&
*/

void *ModPtr;
void *GetDMPtr();
```

```
main(argc, argv)
int argc;
char **argv;
{
    int SemID;
    void *SemPtr;
    /*
        Find or create a data module for the event.
        The data module has the same name as the event.
    */
    SemID = _ev_link(argv[1]);
    SemPtr = GetDMPtr(argv[1]);
    while(TRUE){
        FWait(SemID, SemPtr);
        printf("%d ", getpid());
        fflush(stdout);
        FSignal(SemID, SemPtr);
    }
    _ev_unlink(SemID);
    ReleaseDM();
}




void *GetDMPtr(name)
{
    mod_exec *ptr;

    if((ptr = (mod_exec *)modlink(name, 0)) == (void *)-1)
        if((ptr = (mod_exec *)_mkdata_module(name, 1, (MA_REENT*256)+1,
            0x07777)) == (mod_exec *)-1)
            exit(_errmsg(errno, "mkdata module for %s failed\n",
                name));
    ModPtr = ptr; /*save pointer value */
    return ((char *)ptr + ptr->_mexec);
}

ReleaseDM()
{
    munlink(ModPtr);
}
```

10.4 Events as Selectors

OS-9 events can do much more than semaphores. Instead of behaving like on/off switches, they can act like elaborate selector switches. First let's build a selector that just turns clockwise through 10 selections. It turns on 1, then 2, then 3, ..., then 10, then 1 and around again. This is done by setting the *Ev$Wait* increment to zero. Making *Ev$Signl* increment the variable is easy. Finding a way to set it from 10 back down to 1 is trickier.

If the selector corresponds to some physical mechanism like the sectors on a disk track or the scan lines on a CRT display, an arrangement for events is:

Ev$Creat
   initial value −10 (initially off-scale)
   auto-increment for *Ev$Wait*: −10
   auto-increment for *Ev$Signl*: 0
Ev$Wait
   min = max = trigger selection for this process (1..10)
Ev$Signl
   not used
Ev$Set
   event value from the hardware (scan line or whatever)

The auto-increments must be large enough that each *Ev$Wait* throws the event's value entirely out of the range of selections. If it doesn't do that, it can cause another *Ev$Wait* to unblock. If the *Ev$Wait* increment is 0, a process will stay unblocked until the event is set or signaled. You can try it with the next example program. Set the auto-increment for *Ev$Wait* to 0, and the auto-increment for *Ev$Signl* to 1. Everything will work fine except that each time a process is selected, it executes at least a dozen times.

If the selector is not controlled by hardware and there is more than one process setting the event, we need a subsidiary semaphore to protect a *Ev$Read/Ev$Set* pair. If there is only one process setting the event, the following arrangement will work:

Ev$Creat
   initial value −10 (initially off scale)
   auto-increment for *Ev$Wait*: −10
   auto-increment for *Ev$Signl*: 11
Ev$Wait
   min = max = trigger selection for this process
Ev$Signl
   start only one process
Ev$Set

used every tenth time to set the event variable to 1

The following example implements a 10-position selector-event to drive tasks that wait on the values 1 through 10. For this kind of event, we don't usually worry about synchronization. The processes waiting for the event are supposed to complete before the event comes around to them again, or at least not fail if they miss a turn. A tsleep() in the driver makes the demonstration easier to watch. It slows down the rotation of the selector until the numbers can easily be displayed in the time between *Ev$Signls*.

```
/*
    Selector:
    This program is used to experiment with events as selectors.
    Usage:
    Selector Event_Name
    The event name should be the same name that a bunch (10) of syncwaits are
    waiting for.
*/
#include <stdio.h>
#define LOOPS 100
#define FALSE 0

main(argc, argv)
int argc;
char **argv;
{
    char *SignalEvent=NULL;
    int SEvent;
    int i, j;

    if(argc < 2){printf("%s Usage:\n %s SignalEvent\n", *argv, *argv);
        exit(1);
    }
    SignalEvent = argv[1];
    if((SEvent = _ev_link(SignalEvent)) == −1){
        fprintf(stderr, "Error %d in ev_link for %s\n",
            errno, SignalEvent);
        exit(errno);
    }
    for(i=0;i<LOOPS;i++){
        for(j=1;j<10;j++){
            tsleep(50);
            _ev_signal(SEvent, 0);
        }
```

10.4. EVENTS AS SELECTORS

```
            tsleep(50);
            _ev_set(SEvent, 1, FALSE);
        }
        _ev_unlink(SEvent);
        exit(0);
    }
```

The example in figure 10.3 produces pairs of numbers containing 1..10 again and again. You may need ten control-C's to stop it, or you may be able to kill *selector* and the *syncwaits* with a *kill* command.

> Figure 10.3: **Sample Event Selector Experiment**
> $ evcreate Wait −10 11 −10
> $ syncwait Wait 1&
> $ syncwait Wait 2&
> $ syncwait Wait 3&
> $ syncwait Wait 4&
> $ syncwait Wait 5&
> $ syncwait Wait 6&
> $ syncwait Wait 7&
> $ syncwait Wait 8&
> $ syncwait Wait 9&
> $ syncwait Wait 10&
> $ selector Wait&
> $ w

It's interesting to watch what happens if you kill a few *syncwait*'s and leave *selector* running.

Probably the simplest application of events is selecting numbers on demand. The *Ev$Pulse* call jumps to a value out of sequence and back. The *Ev$Set* call sets the variable to a particular value, and *Ev$SetR* sets the variable up or down by the specified amount. These three operations allow the programmer plenty of flexibility in twisting the selector knob.

Processes doing *Ev$Wait*s can be more flexible than those in the above examples. They don't need to wait on one value. They can wait for any value in a range. You can set an *Ev$Wait* to unblock for any of a number of consecutive values.

A computer monitoring a house's security system can have many processes in *Ev$Wait*s blocked for each event. When a door opens, it could unblock a process for that particular door, and another process that was waiting for any door on the ground floor, and two other processes that comfort the motion detectors on either side of the door.

Chapter 11

Traps

Trap handler support is a tool for late binding and modular programming. Trap handlers are similar in flavor to SVCs and subroutine modules.

A trap handler is rather like a subroutine module. To use trap handlers, a program selects the trap handler modules it wants to use and uses *trap* instructions to call functions in the trap handlers. Trap handlers are called with the same protocol that is used for SVCs except that while SVCs use *trap 0*, trap handlers are reached through the other fifteen traps. This chapter first illustrates access to the trap handlers supplied with OS-9. Then it discusses the construction of a small but complete trap handler module.

The standard trap handlers are mainly a memory conservation tool. The *cio* module handles all the C printf() and scanf() functions. Without cio, a C program with just one printf() in it includes five or ten kilobytes of printf() support code. The next printf() only adds a few bytes, but the cost of the first one is important for small programs. With the *cio* trap handler, a program has to initialize a trap for *cio* (which takes about four instructions) and use a *trap* to call *cio* for each I/O function. Using *cio*, the first printf() adds a few dozen bytes to a program instead of several kilobytes.

It is faster to call I/O functions from the C library than the *cio* trap handler. On a 20 Mhz 68020, calling and returning from a null trap handler takes about 22 microseconds, versus from 2.0 μs to 3.8 μs for a C function call depending on whether stack checking and floating-point coprocessor support are active. This is about an order of magnitude performance difference, but even this major difference is only noticeable for fast functions. Even just placing

```
register int x, y;
x = (25 * x + y);
```

inside the null C function increased the benchmark time to between 15.2 μs and 17.0 μs for a function call and around $35\mu s$ for the equivalent trap call.

The linker attaches library functions to the programs that use them. The program modules are bigger than they would be if they used traps to access the functions, but they can get at each function with a single *bsr* or *jsr* instruction. Traps are also accessed with a single instruction, a *trap* instruction. The *trap* invokes OS-9 which uses a string of instructions to transfer control to the trap handler.

The *cio* trap handler is a part of every OS-9 system. The utility programs use it and your programs can use it too, but unless you use C, it requires hard work. Probably more work than it is worth. *cio* isn't documented in the *OS-9 Technical Manual,* so you have to figure it out from the source that comes with the C compiler.

The math trap handler (and the corresponding library) may be even more useful than *cio*, and it *is* documented. It supports 57 functions related to numbers. It deals with 32-bit integers, 32-bit unsigned integers, single precision floating point numbers, double precision floating point numbers, and ASCII (printable) numbers. There's one function, *T$DNrm* (denormalize) that produces a 64-bit integer. Think about the amount of code you'd have to include in a program just to calculate the square root of two and reformat the floating point result into ascii (easily a thousand bytes), and you'll understand the motivation for the math trap handler.

11.1 Linking to a Trap Handler

Low-level *trap* instructions refer to a trap handler by number, but since the trap hander is a module, it is known to the system by an alphanumeric name. Before a process can invoke a trap handler, it must associate a number with the trap handler module. A program can select up to fifteen trap handlers and assign them trap numbers 1 through 15. It makes the selections with *F$TLink* SVC's. An *F$TLink* takes the name of a trap handler and the trap number you have chosen for it, and arranges things so next time you issue the selected trap, you reach that handler.

Trap handler modules can have static data associated with them. Each process that TLink's to the handler sets up a special block of static storage for that link. Each process descriptor has pointers to all the trap-handler static storage allocated by that process' *F$TLink*'s.

Systematic programmers do all their *F$TLink* SVC's right at the beginning of their program—certainly before they use any traps. There is, however, an alternative. If you use an uninitialized trap (a trap without a trap handler TLinked to it), OS-9 will generate a special error. If there is an uninitialized trap exception vector, M$Excpt, in

11.1. LINKING TO A TRAP HANDLER

your program's module header, OS-9 will call some of your code instead of returning an error. It works something like a signal intercept.

Postponing making links to trap handlers isn't necessarily just procrastination. The *F$TLink* SVC takes some time. If you probably won't use a trap handler, you can save a little time by not linking to it. The exception handler can patch things up for you if you do use the trap. Another reason for making links to trap handlers only when you use them is that you can delay determining which handler to use until you actually need it. The exception routine gets the address of the unbound *trap* instruction, the trap number, the function code, and the contents of all the caller's registers. A program can use different trap handlers depending on where the trap is first used. That's not elegant, but it could be useful.

A simple use for deferred trap linkage is run-time support for high-level languages. It would be possible to have several versions of the code that sets up the run time environment for programs (e.g., cstart), but it is easier to have one version that sets up an uninitialized trap handler but initializes no traps. When a trap is used, the run-time support code does the required *F$TLink*. If no traps are used, no *F$TLink*'s are done.

The following example sets up a link to the math trap handler, then quits. In a real program, this code would come before any traps were used.

```
                    nam      InitTraps
                    ttl      Initialize math trap before it is called
00000001 Edition    equ      1
00000101 Typ_Lang   equ      (Prgrm<<8)+Objct
00008000 Attr_Rev   equ      (ReEnt<<8)+0
00000100 StackSiz   equ      256
0000000d CR         equ      13             ASCII for carriage return
00000001 StdOut     equ      1              Standard Output path number
                    psect    InitTraps,Typ_Lang,Attr_Rev,Edition,
                             StackSiz,Entry
         * Collected strings and constants
         *
0000 6d61 MathName  dc.b     "math",0
0005 556e BadMthL   dc.b     "Unsuccessful link to math",CR
0000001a BadMthLL   equ      *-BadMthL
00000000 T$Math     equ      T$Math1        Use The Math1 code for math
00000020            align
         Entry
         *
         *                   Do TLink for Math
         * Put the standard trap number for math, T$Math (15), in D0,
         * and point to the trap handler module name, MathName (math), with
         * A0. We don't want to give math more static memory than its
         * default so we load D1 with 0.
         *
```

```
0020=7000              moveq     #T$Math,D0      Chosen trap number for math
0022 7200              moveq     #0,D1           No extra static storage
0024 41fa              lea       MathName(pc),A0 Point A0 at the name
0028=4e40              os9       F$TLink         Link to math as trap T$Math
002c 6410              bcc.s     Math_OK         Carry Clear: Continue
002e 3f01              move.w    D1,-(A7)        save error code
0030 7001              moveq     #StdOut,D0      Output path
0032 721a              moveq     #BadMthLL,D1    Length to write
0034 41fa              lea       BadMthL(pc),A0
0038=4e40              os9       I$WritLn        Write the message
003c 321f              move.w    (A7)+,D1
            Math_OK
            Exit
003e=4e40              os9       F$Exit
00000042               ends
```

The next program uses deferred TLink's and does something only a little less trivial than nothing at all. It converts the integers 10000 and 3 to double precision floating point and divides one by the other to get 3333.3333333. It converts that floating point number to a printable format and thrashes around inserting the decimal point where it belongs. Finally it prints the resulting string.

It demonstrates a way to handle several trap numbers with the same routine by checking for math2 traps as well as math1 traps. Math2 was a separate trap handler for transcendental functions that has been phased out. If the routine gets a math2 trap it will generate an error (216, invalid path) because the trap handler "oldstuf" doesn't exist.

```
                       nam       InitTraps
                       ttl       Initialize math trap after it is called
00000001 Edition       equ       1
00000101 Typ_Lang      equ       (Prgrm<<8)+Objct
00008000 Attr_Rev      equ       (ReEnt<<8)+0
00000100 StackSiz      equ       256
0000000d CR            equ       13              ASCII for carriage return
00000001 StdOut        equ       1               Standard Output path number
                       psect     PatchTraps,Typ_Lang,Attr_Rev,Edition,StackSiz,
                                 Entry,TInit
                       vsect
00000000 DAccum        ds.l      2               Accumulator for doubles
00000008 Buffer        ds.b      15              Buffer for formatted output
00000000               ends
            *
            * Collected strings and constants
            *
```

11.1. LINKING TO A TRAP HANDLER

```
0000 6d61  MathName dc.b    "math",0
0005 6f6c  Math2Nam dc.b    "oldstuf",0
0000000e           align
           Entry
000e 203c          move.l   #3,D0
0014=4e40          tcall    T$Math1,T$LtoD Convert int to float
0018 2d40          move.l   D0,DAccum(A6) Save the result (3)
001c 2d41          move.l   D1,DAccum+4(A6) more saving
0020 203c          move.l   #10000,D0
0026=4e40          tcall    T$Math1,T$LtoD Convert int to float
 002a 242e         move.l   DAccum(A6),D2 Recover the 3 we saved
002e 262e          move.l   DAccum+4(A6),D3 Move the 3
0032=4e40          tcall    T$Math1,T$DDiv Figure 10000/3
0036 243c          move.l   #$0006000C,D2 12-digit #. 6 after '.'
003c 41ee          lea      Buffer(A6),A0
0040=4e40          tcall    T$Math1,T$DtoA Convert to printable form
           *
           * First find the closing null on the string
           *
0044 41ee          lea      Buffer(A6),A0       Beginning of string
0048 700b          moveq    #12-1,D0            Maximum possible length (minus 1)
           Search
004a 4a18          tst.b    (A0)+
004c 57c8          dbeq     D0,Search
           * Now A0 is pointing one past the null
           * We want to shift the last 6 digits of the number
           * right one byte to make room for a decimal point.
           * A0 already points to the end of the shift.
0050 43e8          lea      -1(A0),A1           Source
0054 7005          moveq    #6-1,D0             Set up to shift 6 times
           Shift
0056 1121          move.b   -(A1),-(A0)         Shift Buffer right one
0058 51c8          dbf      D0,Shift            Loop
005c 12bc          move.b   #'.',(A1)           Place decimal point
0060 137c          move.b   #CR,7(A1)           Close string with a CR
0066 7001          moveq    #StdOut,D0          Set output path
0068 720e          moveq    #14,D1              Length of buffer
006a 41ee          lea      Buffer(A6),A0       →String to output
006e=4e40          os9      I$WritLn
0072 7200          moveq    #0,D1               Return with no error
           Exit
0074=4e40          os9      F$Exit              and end
```

```
*
* Deal with uninitialized trap
* First check the trap vector to discover whether it is for Math1
* or Math2. Do the TLink for whichever it is.
* Math2 is an antique—left over from old versions of OS-9—
* but we use it anyway.
*
* To set up for a TLink:
* Put the required trap number in D0, and point to the trap
* handler module name with A0. We don't want to request memory
* for the trap handlers beyond their defaults so we load D1 with 0.
*
   TInit
*
* The stack has the following information on it:
*         8(SP)   caller's return address (4-byte)
*         6(SP)   trap vector number (2-byte)
*         4(SP)   function code (2-byte)
*         0(SP)   caller's A6 register (4-byte)
*
* Except for SP (A7), which points to the stack frame above, the
* registers are the caller's registers.
*
* We have no need for the caller's A6 register or the function code
* so clear them off the stack.
*
```

```
0078 5c8f               addq.l    #6,SP              Toss some of the stack frame
007a 48e7               movem.l   D0–D1/A0,–(SP)     Save registers
0000000c  TVector  set       (3*4)              Offset from SP to vector
007e 302f               move.w    TVector(SP),D0     Get the vector
```

```
*
* The vector is an offset into a table of 4-byte entries.
* The first user trap vector is at an offset of $80 from the
* beginning of the table.
* To get a trap number from the vector we subtract $80 from it
* and shift the result right by two (dividing by four).
```

```
0082 907c               sub.w     #$80,D0            convert it to a trap #
0086 e440               asr.w     #2,D0
0088=b07c               cmp.w     #T$Math1,D0        Is this Math1?
008c 6608               bne.s     TryMath2
008e 41fa               lea       MathName(pc),A0    Address of handler name
0092 7200               moveq     #0,D1              No extra memory
0094 600c               bra.s     SetTrap
          TryMath2
0096=b07c               cmp.w     #T$Math2,D0        Is this Math2?
009a 6616               bne.s     TError
009c 41fa               lea       Math2Nam(pc),A0    Address of handler name
```

11.2. WRITING A TRAP HANDLER

```
         00a0 7200              moveq      #0,D1              no extra memory
              SetTrap
         00a2=4e40              os9        F$TLink
         00a6 65cc              bcs.s      Exit               Quit if error
         00a8 4cdf              movem.l(SP)+,D0–D1/A0
         00ac 548f              addq.l     #2,SP              Pop the vector off the stack
                        *
                        * Subtract four from the the return address so it will
                        * return to the trap instruction that caused the error and re-execute it.
                        *
         00ae 5997              subq.l     #4,(SP)            Back the return address up
         00b0 4e75              rts
              TError
         00b2=7200              moveq      #E$ITrap,D1        set invalid trap # error
         00b4 60be              bra.s      Exit
         000000b6               ends
```

11.2 Writing a Trap Handler

Writing a trap handler isn't quite like writing a program. A trap handler's module header is more elaborate than a program's, and the trap handler's initial register values don't have the same meanings as a program's.

The module header for a trap handler contains all the fields from a program module's header, plus an initialization execution offset and a termination execution offset. A special rule in the linker causes the constants defined after the trap handler's main *psect* to be kept after the module header. Putting the two extra fields after the *psect* directive for the trap handler has the effect of adding them to the module header.

The following trap handler illustrates trap handler construction with most of the bells and whistles. It uses static storage and offers several different functions. It doesn't use the termination entry (which isn't supported by OS-9 yet).

This trap handler is called *Silly*—which describes its functions. It enhances the F$Time SVC by returning a string that comments on the time as well as the time in printable format. If you don't like the present time, it will format and add a comment to any time you give it.

It also provides random-number services in two forms. It can return the same type of text strings as the oracle (from the chapter on pipes), or simple random numbers.

Formatted time is returned by function code 1. It takes one argument, a pointer to a 25-byte space for the string, in A0.

Function code 2 formats a given time. It takes the time in D0 and a pointer to a 25-byte space in A0. It stores its result at A0.

Function code 3 returns an oracle response. It needs a pointer, in A0, to a 10-byte buffer for its answer.

Function code 4 returns a random integer in D0. It doesn't take any arguments.

```
                    nam     Silly
                    ttl     Entertaining Trap Handler
            mod     macro
                    divu    #\2,\1
                    lsr.l   #8,\1
                    lsr.l   #8,\1
                    endm

00000001  Ed        equ     1
00000b01  TypeLan   equ     (TrapLib<<8)+Objct
00008000  Attr_Rev  equ     (ReEnt<<8)+0
00000100  Stack     equ     256

00000001  SeedType  equ     1                   Julian without ticks
00000000  Gregorian equ     0                   Gregorian without ticks

          *
          * psect to define module header
          *
                    psect   Silly,TypeLan,Attr_Rev,Ed,Stack,Entry
0000 0000           dc.l    Init                Initialization entry point
0004 0000           dc.l    Term                Termination entry point

          *
          * Define the Trap handler's static storage
          *
                    vsect
00000000  Seed      ds.l    1                   Seed for random number generator
00000000            ends
          *
          * Trap init initializes the seed for the random number generator.
          * It is passed:
          *       d0:     The user trap number (2-byte)                    ignored
          *       d1:     Addition storage allocated (4-byte)              ignored
          *       d2-d7:  Caller's registers                               ignored
          *       a0:     End of trap handler module name ptr              ignored
          *       a1:     Trap handler execution entry point               ignored
          *       a2:     Trap handler module                              ignored
          *       a3-a5:  Caller's registers                               ignored
          *       a6:     Trap static storage base address
          *       a7:     Trap initialization stack frame
          * The stack frame contains:
          *       8(sp)   Caller's return PC (4-byte)
```

11.2. WRITING A TRAP HANDLER

```
             *              4(sp)
             *      0(sp)   Caller's A6 register (4-byte)
             *
             Init
0008 48e7    movem.l  D0–D3,–(SP)      save registers
000c 7001    moveq    #SeedType,D0     type of time to use as seed
000e=4e40    os9      F$Time           get the current time
0012 652a    bcs.s    Error
0014 2d40    move.l   D0,Seed(A6)      Save the time as a random seed
             *
             * The following movem restores registers including the caller's
             * A6 register. It also clears the 4 bytes of nothing off the stack.
             * Popping the stack pointer only moves the stack pointer.
             * It doesn't actually load it from the stack. Including it in the
             * list of registers to be popped only causes the stack pointer to
             * move 4 more than it would have.
             *
0018 4cdf          movem.l  (sp)+,D0–D3/A6–SP  Restore registers
0000001c Term  equ      *                      Just return
001c 4e75          rts


             *
             * The main entry point for Silly is a dispatch routine that notes
             * the function code and calls the appropriate routine to service it.
             *
             * It is passed:
             *      D0–D7 and A0–A5: Caller's registers
             *      A6:     Trap handler's static data pointer
             *      SP:     Stack frame
             * The stack frame is:
             *      8(SP):  Caller's return address (4-byte)
             *      6(SP):  Vector number (2-byte)             ignored
             *      4(SP):  Function code (2-byte)
             *      0(SP):  Caller's A6 register (4-byte)      ignored
             *
             * This trap handler deals with functions:
             *      1:      Return current time, formatted
             *      2:      Return given time, formatted
             *      3:      Return oracle's answer
             *      4:      Return a random number
             *
             *
             * Define stack offsets for convenience
             *
00000000           org      0
00000000 C.D0     do.l     1               Caller's D0
00000004 C.ORegs  do.l     6               Other registers
```

```
0000001c  C.A6      ds.l   1            Caller's A6
00000020  FuncCode  ds.w   1
00000022  Vector    ds.w   1
00000024  RetAddr   ds.l   1

          Entry
001e 48e7           movem.l  D0–D3/A0–A2,–(SP)  Save registers
0022 322f           move.w   FuncCode(SP),D1    Get the function code
         * The function code must be 1, 2, 3, or 4.
0026 6f14           ble.s    FInvalid           Function le 0 is invalid
0028 b27c           cmp.w    #4,D1              Another range check
002c 6e0e           bgt.s    FInvalid           Function > 4 is invalid
         * Set function code up as an offset for a branch table
002e 927c           sub.w    #1,D1
0032 e541           asl.w    #2,D1              Multiply by 4 (length of bra)
0034 43fa           lea      BranchT(PC),A1
0038 4ef1           jmp      (A1,D1)

003c=7000 FInvalid  moveq    #E$IllFnc,D0       Illegal Function code error
003e=4e40 Error     os9      F$Exit             Quit

 0042 6000 BranchT  bra      CTime              Format current time
 0046 6000          bra      FTime              Format any time
 004a 6000          bra      Oracle             Return oracle's words
 004e 6000          bra      Random             Return random number

         *
         * CTime takes a pointer to a 25-byte buffer in A0.
         * It puts a formatted version of the current time with a suitable
         * comment in the buffer.
         *
          CTime
0052 7000           moveq    #Gregorian,D0      Set the code for Gregorian time
0054=4e40           os9      F$Time             Get the current time
         * And drop through to FTime which will format it
         *
         * Format the time given in D0 into a buffer at A0
         *
         *
         * Describe the layout of the caller's buffer.
         * These offsets are used as offsets from A0 to define the
         * parts of the buffer that should receive various values.
         *
00000000            org      0
00000000  Hours     ds.b     2
00000002  Colon1    ds.b     1
00000003  Min       ds.b     2
```

11.2. WRITING A TRAP HANDLER

```
00000005  Colon2    do.b   1
00000006  Sec       do.b   2
00000008  Space1    do.b   1
00000009  AMPM      do.b   2
0000000b  Space2    do.b   2
0000000d  Comment   do.b   12

          FTime
0058 1200           move.b  D0,D1           Move seconds from D0 to D1
005a 43e8           lea     Sec(A0),A1      A1→ place to put sec
005e 6176           bsr.s   bindec          Convert byte in D1 to decimal at A1
0060 e080           asr.l   #8,D0           Shift seconds out of D0
0062 1200           move.b  D0,D1           Move minutes from D0 to D1
0064 3400           move.w  D0,D2           Save hours/minutes for later
0066 43e8           lea     Min(A0),A1      A1→ place to put min
006a 616a           bsr.s   bindec
006c e080           asr.l   #8,D0           Shift minutes out of D0
006e 1200           move.b  D0,D1           Move hours from D0 to D1
          *
          * Fill in AM or PM according to whether it is before or after noon
          *
0070 117c           move.b  #'M',AMPM+1(A0) AM and PM both have M
0076 b23c           cmp.b   #12,D1          AM or PM?
007a 6c08           bge.s   PM
007c 117c           move.b  #'A',AMPM(A0)
0082 600a           bra.s   AMPMSet
          PM
0084 117c           move.b  #'P',AMPM(A0)
008a 923c           sub.b   #12,D1          Adjust to 12-hour clock
          AMPMSet
008e 43e8           lea     Hours(A0),A1
0092 6142           bsr.s   bindec
          *
          * Fill in constants
          *
0094 117c           move.b  #':',Colon1(A0)
009a 117c           move.b  #':',Colon2(A0)
00a0 117c           move.b  #32,Space1(A0)
00a6 117c           move.b  #32,Space2(A0)
          *
          * Find a suitable comment for the time.
          * Use the hours/minutes word that is saved in D2
          *
00ac 43fa           lea     CmtTabl(PC),A1  Address of Comment table
00b0 93fc           sub.l   #CTESize,A1     Back up to starting place
00b6 7008           moveq   #CTSize−1,D0
```

```
00b8 d3fc   FCmtLoop  add.l   #CTESize,A1       Point to next Comment
00be b451             cmp.w   (A1),D2           Check bound
00c0 5fc8             dble    D0,FCmtLoop

00c4 43e9             lea     2(A1),A1          Source for move
00c8 41e8             lea     Comment(A0),A0    Destination
00cc 700b             moveq   #12−1,D0          Size

00ce 10d9   MCmtLoop  move.b  (A1)+,(A0)+       Move comment to caller's buffer
00d0 51c8             dbf     D0,MCmtLoop

00d4 605a             bra.s   Return

        *
        * One-byte binary number is in D1
        * Convert it to a two digit decimal number at A1
        *
            bindec
00d6 4881             ext.w   D1
00d8 48c1             ext.l   D1                Make the byte into a long
00da 83fc             divs    #10,D1            This gives us both digits
00de 1281             move.b  D1,(A1)
00e0 0619             addi.b  #$30,(A1)+        Decimal adjust
00e4 4841             swap    D1                Swap words
00e6 1281             move.b  D1,(A1)
00e8 0611             addi.b  #$30,(A1)         Decimal adjust
00ec 4e75             rts


            Oracle
00ee 6124             bsr.s   NewRand           Get a random number
                      mod     D0,OTabSiz        MACRO
00f8 c0fc             mulu    #10,D0            Offset in table of 10-byte entries
00fc 43fa             lea     OTable(PC),A1     Point A1 at table
0100 d3c0             add.l   D0,A1             Bump A1 to the right entry
0102 7009             moveq   #10−1,D0          Number of bytes to move

0104 10d9   OLoop     move.b  (A1)+,(A0)+       Move wise words to caller's buffer
0106 51c8             dbf     D0,OLoop          Loop 10 times

010a 6024             bra.s   Return

            Random
010c 6106             bsr.s   NewRand
010e 2140             move.l  D0,C.D0(A0)       Zap caller's D0 with rand #
0112 601c             bra.s   Return
```

11.2. WRITING A TRAP HANDLER

```
              NewRand
0114 202e              move.l  Seed(A6),D0
0118 c0fc              mulu    #39709,D0
011c d0bc              add.l   #13,D0
                       mod     D0,65401
012a 2d40              move.l  D0,Seed(A6)
012e 4e75              rts

              Return
              *
              * Use the same trick as Init to clear an
              * extra long word off the stack.
              *
0130 4cdf              movem.l (sp)+,D0–D3/A0–A2/A6/SP
0134 4e75              rts
              *
              * Strings for time comments.
              * The layout is ending hour, ending minute, comment.
              *
              CmtTabl
0136 0400              dc.b    4,0              Midnight to 4 AM
0138 5570              dc.b    "Up late! ",0
0000000e CTESize       equ     *–CmtTabl
0144 0800              dc.b    8,0              4:01 AM to 8:00 AM
0146 496e              dc.b    "In early ",0
0152 0b2d              dc.b    11,45            8:01 AM till 11:45 AM
0154 2020              dc.b    " ",0            Nothing to say
0160 0d00              dc.b    13,0             11:46 AM till 1 PM
0162 4c75              dc.b    "Lunchtime! ",0
016e 0f00              dc.b    15,0             1:01 PM till 3:00 PM
0170 2020              dc.b    " ",0            Nothing to say
017c 101e              dc.b    16,30            3:01 PM till 4:30 PM
017e 5465              dc.b    "Tea time? ",0
018a 1200              dc.b    18,00            4:31 till 6:00
018c 5469              dc.b    "Time to go ",0
0198 1400              dc.b    20,00            6:01 PM till 8 PM
019a 476f              dc.b    "Go Home ",0
01a6 183b              dc.b    24,59            8:01 PM till midnight
01a8 2020              dc.b    " ",0            Nothing to say
00000009 CTSize        equ     (*–CmtTabl)/CTESize

01b4 5965 OTable       dc.b    "Yes "
01be 4e6f              dc.b    "No "
01c8 4d61              dc.b    "Maybe "
01d2 4465              dc.b    "Definitely"
01dc 476f              dc.b    "Go Away "
01e6 5768              dc.b    "Why Not? "
```

```
00000006 OTabSiz    equ     (*−OTable)/10
000001f0            ends
```

The following program tests *Silly*. It links to the *Silly* trap handler and calls each of its functions.

```
                    ttl     Exercise the Silly trap handler
00000001 Edition    equ     1
00000101 Typ_Lang   equ     (Prgrm<<8)+Objct
00008000 Attr_Rev   equ     (ReEnt<<8)+0
00000100 StackSiz   equ     256

0000000d CR         equ     13              ASCII code for carriage return
00000001 StdOut     equ     1               Standard Output path number
                    psect   Test,Typ_Lang,Attr_Rev,Edition,StackSiz,Entry
                    vsect
00000000 Buffer     ds.b    26
00000000            ends
         *
         * Collected strings and constants
         *
0000 5369 SillyName dc.b    "Silly",0
00000001 T$Silly    equ     1
00000006            align
         Entry
         *
         * Do TLink for Silly
         *
0006 7001           moveq   #T$Silly,D0     Chosen trap number for math
0008 7200           moveq   #0,D1           No extra static storage
000a 41fa           lea     SillyName(pc),A0 Point A0 at the name
 000e=4e40          os9     F$TLink         Link to Silly as trap T$Silly
0012 6540           bcs.s   Exit


         *
         * Use the "Silly" functions
         *

0014 41ee           lea     Buffer(A6),A0
0018 4e41           tcall   T$Silly,1        Get formatted current time
001c 1d7c           move.b  #CR,Buffer+25(A6) Seal with a CR
0022 7001           moveq   #StdOut,D0
0024 721a           moveq   #26,D1
 0026=4e40          os9     I$WritLn

002a 203c           move.l  #$000D1620,D0 A time, 1:22:32 PM
```

11.2. WRITING A TRAP HANDLER

```
0030 4e41          tcall    T$Silly,2          Format a given time
0034 1d7c          move.b   #CR,Buffer+25(A6)  Seal with a CR
003a 7001          moveq    #StdOut,D0
003c 721a          moveq    #26,D1
003e=4e40          os9      I$WritLn

0042 4e41          tcall    T$Silly,3          Get words of oracle
0046 7001          moveq    #StdOut,D0
0048 720a          moveq    #10,D1
004a=4e40          os9      I$WritLn

004e 4e41          tcall    T$Silly,4          Just get a random number

0052 7200          moveq    #0,D1              Clean return

          Exit
0054=4e40          os9      F$Exit
00000058           ends
```

Chapter 12

OS-9 I/O

> *Unless you write operating-system-level code, you'll never deal with input/output (I/O) hardware. The I/O manager-file manager-device driver hierarchy isolates you from the hardware by presenting you with an abstract view of files. High-level languages may pile on yet another layer of abstraction. Other chapters consider I/O from various points within OS-9. This chapter views files from a program's viewpoint.*

12.1 The Unified File System

Different devices have different characteristics, but OS-9 protects user programs from device peculiarities as much as it can. This doesn't mean that OS-9 ignores the special qualities of each device class. Random access is an important feature of RBF files. OS-9 doesn't hide the random access capability of disks in order to make disk files compatible with SCF files. What a unified file system does mean is that a reasonable number of I/O operations work predictably across all the file types and devices. These operations are: *I$Create, I$Open, I$Close, I$Read, I$ReadLn, I$Write,* and *I$Writeln*.

All the OS-9 utilities and most other programs limit their operations on the three standard paths to this group of SVC's (actually, they leave out *I$Open* and *I$Close* because the standard paths are open when a program starts). Because of this policy and the uniformity of the OS-9 file systems, you can redirect the input and output of programs without considering the types of the files. It is entirely normal for a person to redirect the output of a program from his terminal to a printer, a pipe, or a disk file.

12.2 Paths

A program sees files as paths. OS-9 keeps a path descriptor for each path and gives programs numbers that identify them. When a program reads from standard input, it is reading from path 0. When it writes a message to the standard error path, it is writing to path 2. When it opens a file, *I$Open* returns a new path number (say, 3) for the program to us for subsequent operations on that file.

Each process can have up to 32 paths open at any time. All the OS-9 I/O services use a path number to find a path descriptor which defines the environment for the operation. The path number leads to a system path number which in turn leads to a path descriptor. The path descriptor holds everything that distinguishes the path.

From a program's point of view, a path number is a name for an open file, but it is also a name for a path descriptor. A program can get several paths (and several path descriptors) to a file by opening the file several times. Each path has a distinct path number and path descriptor. A program can also get several paths that lead to the same file *and have the same path descriptor.*

The *I$Dup* system call is passed a path number. It returns a new path number that shares the same path descriptor. Since duped paths share a common path descriptor, they share the path options. If you want to open several paths to one device with the same options, the *I$Dup* SVC is the easiest way to do it.

12.3 Path Options

You can see the effect of duped paths when you use the tmode command. Changes you make to one of the standard paths almost always affect all three. This is because *sysgo* and *tsmon* start the shell with a path to the terminal duped into all three standard paths.

If you want to open a path with fresh options, just open it. The I/O system builds you a fresh path descriptor from the device descriptor. Things can get tricky here. A device is initialized whenever the number of paths using the device goes from zero to one. The second path to the device doesn't cause it to be reinitialized. This caused a problem since programs could not adjust device behavior such as baud rate, XOn/XOff, and disk stepping rate. Now, well-behaved device drivers respond to SS_Opt setstat calls by updating popular parameters as requested. SCF drivers usually do a good job with options. RBF drivers are not so uniformly good with options. The main RBF hardware option a program might change with a setstat is disk stepping rate, and the drivers that specify the stepping rate for each command generally respect the value in options while those drivers that set the stepping rate when a driver is initialized sometimes fail to notice the change.

12.4 Device Attributes

You can also change device initialization parameters by altering the device descriptor, but only if you subsequently initialize the device.

Devices all have attributes. They are stored in the device descriptor and used whenever a path to the device is opened. The attributes determine what operations are valid on the device. A printer, for example, is writable, but reading or executing from the printer would probably be forbidden. Printers are also usually not sharable. A shared printer might mix printouts together. It is better to be told that the printer is busy than to have your listing combined with someone else's.

12.5 Reading and Writing

The *I$Read* and *I$Write* SVC's underlie all unformatted I/O. They move data directly between your program and the file. There is, however, an exception: if you have software handshaking active on an SCF path, the protocol is treated as a property of the device. The flow-control characters are not included with data that is read.

When you do I/O to SCF devices you may want to use the extra power of the *I$ReadLn* and *I$WritLn* SVC's. These calls use the parameters in the path descriptor's option section to do line editing.

For the *I$WriteLn* SVC, line editing amounts to adjusting the output to fit the peculiarities of the output device.[1]

OS-9 terminates each line with a carriage return, but some SCF devices need a line feed after the return. There is an "auto linefeed" option to allow SCF to adjust to this. Some devices (especially old mechanical devices) need to be fed a stream of nulls while they do time-consuming operations. The "end of line null count" option tells SCF to send the specified number of nulls to cover each return. These days very few devices can't handle lower case letters, but if you use one of the few, there is an option that makes all letters upper case.

The pause option is for human consumption. If you list a file to a terminal with the pause option off, it will fly by at whatever rate the terminal can handle. There are two options that can help. One option, "end of page pause," causes output to stop

---

[1] It used to be possible to trick SCF into writing several lines with one *I$WriteLn* SVC. The operation only writes characters up to the first carriage return. The trick was that it processed carriage returns or line feeds as new lines, but only a carriage return would end the writeln. If you wanted to write several lines with one *I$WriteLn*, separating them with line feeds would cause the output to look like the output from a set of *I$WriteLn*'s. This "bug" is now fixed, and it is time to fix old programs.

after each page is displayed and instructs SCF to wait for a character (any character) to be typed before proceeding. The other option, "pause character," names a character that you can type to pause output.

The "end-of-page pause" option uses the "page-length" option. In addition to being used by SCF for page pausing, the page length stored in the path descriptor and device descriptor is a convenient place for user programs to discover the number of lines on a page for a device.

The *I$ReadLn* SVC does input line editing. Many of the path options affect the amount or type of line editing it does. By including the line editing function in SCF, OS-9 makes it possible for individual programs to ignore the problem. It also makes a standard interface available.

To a program, the most important part of line editing is that it handles backspaces (though backspace processing is not the only form of input editing delivered by SCF). Unless backspace processing is disabled, the buffer returned from an *I$ReadLn* looks just the way the line looked on the screen. Backspaces, and the characters before them, are eliminated by SCF.

The *I$ReadLn* and *I$WritLn* operations may not be as fast as the simpler *I$Read* and *I$Write* SVC's. They shouldn't be used unless their line-editing capability is required.

The most efficient way to read or write is to use big blocks. A large part of the cost of each I/O operation is constant overhead. You spend the overhead for each SVC, so stretch it as far as you can by transferring lots of data.

12.6 The Keyboard Signals

Two signals can be sent to a process with single keystrokes: the keyboard interrupt and the keyboard abort. These signals are sent to the process that last used the device—not to the last process to gain access to the device. This distinction is important. A process is not vulnerable to the keyboard signals until it "uses" the keyboard device. Reading or writing constitutes using a device... inheriting a path to it or checking its status does not.

If you fork a process and wait for it to complete, you should be ready for a keyboard signal. Even though the child process has dups of your paths, the devices for the paths send any signals to you until your child is recognized as the last user of the device. It is an interesting question what you should do with a signal that wasn't meant for you.

The shell demonstrates misdirected signal handling nicely. The signal releases it from a wait. If the signal was a keyboard kill (signal 2), the shell forwards the signal to its child and prints `abort`. If the signal was a keyboard interrupt (signal 3), the shell continues as if the forked process had finished. The reaction to the signal is simple (though not immediately obvious) and useful. You can use this trick to push a process into the background after you start it. Start a process that doesn't use the terminal:

$ cc HugeProgram.c >>>Prog.Out

then realize, too late, that you should have used an ampersand on the command line. You can bail yourself out with a control-C. Type control-C and the shell will respond with `interrupt` and give you a new prompt. The compile continues undisturbed.

12.7 Signal on Data Ready

Reading data from a path is simple: you do the read, and it returns to you when it has collected the data. So what do you do if you can't wait for the data to arrive? If you are expecting data on any of several paths, you can't let yourself get stuck in a read for one of them. Every telecommunication program is plagued by this problem. It needs to wait for input from the keyboard and the modem, and can't let itself get stuck waiting for either of them.

One solution is to poll the paths. Put your program in a loop where it does *I$GetStt* SVC's testing for data ready on each path of interest. When some data appears, read it. This works, but it uses large amounts of CPU time doing almost nothing. It doesn't respond to input very fast either.

The cleanest way to handle this problem is to use the "send signal on data ready" *I$SetStt* option on each SCF path you want to read. This instructs OS-9 to send you a signal when data is ready on any of the paths. Even better, you can ask it to send you a different signal for each path (provide the paths are to separate devices). You set up an intercept routine with the *F$Icpt* SVC, and plant one of these signal trip wires on each path from which you expect data. Then you sleep. When there is data to read, a signal wakes the process and tells it where to look for data.

This system is not perfect. A few timing problems can catch you if you aren't careful.

- The wakeup signal can be lost if it arrives when the process is not sleeping.

- Even if multiple signals are queued, the process will only be awakened once. The intercept routine is called once for each queued signal, then the sleep will end. A program that does not account for this possibility can fail to notice that several paths may have data when it is awakened.

If input is already buffered when the process starts, the request for a signal on data ready will send a signal immediately. It will be serviced by the intercept routine, and

Figure 12.1: Signal on Data Ready Protocol

Empty IntQueue
Set up an signal trap that enqueues the signal number on IntQueue.
Set a trip wire for signal x on path x.
Set a trip wire for signal y on path y
Loop:
  Sleep
  for each path in IntQueue
    Dequeue the path number.
    Use an I$GetStt for data ready to determine how much data is ready.
    Read all the data that's ready from the path.
    Set a new trip wire on the path.
  goto Loop

will leave a wakeup in the process descriptor that will cause the next sleep to return immediately.

Waiting for signals from paths has a subtle useful feature when compared to simply waiting in *I$Read*. Although a device with a "set signal" pending is considered too busy for any path to read, writes to the device can proceed while you wait for input.

12.8 Modem Control Commands

Some SCF drivers are able to send signals when they detect or lose data carrier. This can be used to initiate special processing when a modem connects or disconnects. The SS_DCOn and SS_DCOff *I$SetStt* calls assign signal number to transitions of the DCD line.

Other setstats control the request to send (RTS) handshake line. SS_EnRTS enables RTS and SS_DsRTS disables the line. Some modems come off hook when they detect RTS and hang up when RTS drops.

12.9 Adjusting the size of RBF Files

OS-9 uses a simple rule to determine the length of a file. Every point in the file that you write to or even point to with an *I$Seek* while the file is open for writing is in the file. You can increase the size of a file by seeking to the new end of the file.

Shortening a file is another problem. OS-9 won't shorten a file unless it is explicitly asked. The *I$SetStt* set-filesize option can be used to shorten or lengthen a file.

As you write to a file or seek beyond its end, OS-9 allocates disk space to you in chunks that may be more than a sector long. The idea is that the bigger the chunks it gives to you, the less fragmented a large file will be. Normally, the unused space is returned to the system when you close the file, but if you don't leave the current location pointing at the end of the file when you close it, OS-9 will leave the unused space attached to the file. If you expect to expand a file later, you can help prevent it from being fragmented by rewinding the file before you close it. You must do this every time you close the file after opening it for writing or updating. The first time you close a writable file with the current location pointer at the end of the file, OS-9 reclaims the unused space.

12.10 Record Locking

If you only run one process at a time, you will never have to worry about contention for disk files, but you would be a most unusual member of the OS-9 community. Since OS-9 is a multitasking operating system, it includes tools to help you manage shared files. If you have an RBF file open for update, OS-9 gives you ownership of the last block of data you read. Until you read or write that file again no other process can touch the data you have claimed. This prevents lots of nasty timing-dependent problems.

The best way to see what record locking does is to watch what can happen without it. Lets say we have two processes, one and two, both updating file A.

- Process one reads the first 100 bytes of A.

- Process two reads the first 100 bytes of A.

- Process one updates what it read with lots of important data and writes it back to A.

- Process two makes a trivial change to what it read and writes it back to A.

The changes made by process one are overwritten by process two. Process one might as well have never existed. For a full appreciation of the trouble this can cause, imagine that the two programs pace one another through the file, alternating the order in which they write their updates. Both programs believe that they successfully updated the file, but the actual result is a mess with half of the records reflecting process one's changes and the other half updated by process two.

With record locking in place, process one would have locked the first 100 bytes of the file when it read them. When process two went to read the same data, it would be locked out. It would wait for process one to read or write before it continued. The result is that process one updates the record, then process two updates it.

In one case, a path that is only open for writing (not updating) can lock a record. Reading or writing data at the end of a file asserts an end-of-file lock. This lock keeps things straight if several processes want to extend a file. It also lets a process follow along behind another process that is extending a file. If you redirect the standard output of a program to a disk file, then list the file to a printer. You will see the end-of-file lock in action. The *list* program won't read what is written to the file and reach the end before the program writing the file has finished. The end-of-file lock that the writer keeps on the file keeps *list* from reaching the end of the file until the writer is done.

Record locking for RBF files prevents many problems, but it creates some new ones. Holding a lock you don't need is not good behavior. Imagine how frustrating it would be if someone read and locked a record, then went out for lunch. That record might not be available to anyone else for hours! A program that doesn't plan to update a record that it reads can release the record by using the *I$SetStt*/SS_Lock SVC for a length of zero.

Deadlock and lockout[2] are other problems that only occur when resources can be locked. You'd have to struggle to get OS-9 to let you into a lockout situation, so we'll ignore that problem except to define it. You have lockout when a process can get to a resource (e.g., part of a file), but other processes conspire to keep it out. Lockout is mostly a problem for theorists to worry about. Deadlock is easier to get and more serious than lockout.

Deadlock takes place when two or more processes each are holding resources that the other processes require. Let's say you and a friend are ready to make an ice cream cone. You grab the cones and go for the ice cream. He grabs the ice cream and goes for the cones. You both stand there waiting for the other to put down what he has. If your algorithms don't allow for this kind of problem you are both stuck—deadlock.

The same problem can happen with record locks. To make the example more interesting, let's use three processes: one, two, and three. Each process wants to execute the following steps:

- Read a byte from one file

- Read a byte from another file

- Update the first file

---

[2]Deadlock is sometimes called Deadly Embrace and Lockout is also known as Starvation.

12.10. RECORD LOCKING

- Update the second file

If the three processes are not arranged correctly, we can get into trouble.

- Process one reads the first byte of file A
- Process two reads the first byte of file B
- Process three reads the first byte of file C
- Process one tries to read the first byte of B and sleeps for a record lock
- Process two tries to read the first byte of C and sleeps for a record lock
- Process three tries to read the first byte of A and sleeps for a record lock

We have a three-way deadlock. Those three process sit there locking up the three files until they are killed.

The first rule for avoiding deadlock is that all processes that lock more than one resource should request resources in the same order, say alphabetically. In the example, process three read the files in reverse alphabetical order. If it read them in order it would have tried to read file A before file C. It wouldn't have locked A until process one was done, so it wouldn't have locked C. Since C wasn't locked, process two could read it and update B and C. When process two updated B, it would release process one. Eventually all the processes would complete. By having all the processes lock the files in the same order we avoided deadlock.

Remember that files aren't the only resources that can be locked. Any non-sharable resource is locked when you have access to it; i.e., files with the non-sharable attribute and devices that are not sharable. When you open a path to a non-sharable printer, you lock that device.

If you can't count on all processes to follow a simple rule, like requesting resources in alphabetical order, you may have to write programs that deal with deadlock. If OS-9 detects a deadlock, it will return an error from the operation that caused it to detect the deadlock. That process can try to deal with it. It could just retry the operation, or it could free everything it has a lock on, sleep for a short time and start locking again. Either trick might work.

If you don't trust OS-9's deadlock detection algorithm, or if you don't want to wait for a long time for some part of a file even if it isn't held by a deadlock, you can specify the number of ticks that you will wait for a locked-out operation to complete with *I$SetStt*/Ticks. If that interval expires, the operation will return to you with an error, E$Lock.

Chapter 13

The I/O Manager

> *OS-9 used to include a separate module called IOMan. This module contained the operating system code responsible for managing I/O paths. IOMan has been moved into the OS-9 kernel, but it still exists as an OS-9 function. In this chapter I will cover the philosophical role of IOMan and many of its practical duties.*

The Input/Output Manager, IOMan, does just the things you would think a manager should do. IOMan catches each call for I/O services, collects the necessary resources, and passes the request to the appropriate file manager. It was once a separate system module, but it has moved into the OS-9 kernel. It is still, however, a functional entity responsible for all the I/O system calls.

IOMan sits at the top of the I/O hierarchy. It processes every I/O system service request. For open and create requests, it creates and initializes a path descriptor and forwards the request to the proper file manager. For SVC's that pass a path number, IOMan finds the corresponding path descriptor and passes it to the file manager. Some requests, such as make directory and delete file, don't explicitly use a path descriptor; for these SVC's IOMan creates and initializes a path descriptor, then destroys it when the file manager returns to it. IOMan takes responsibility for the security of read and write requests. It uses the *F$ChkMem* SVC to check the pointer and length values that the process passes as arguments to I/O SVCs. If SSM is installed, it uses MMU hardware to check the process's right to access the memory. If SSM is not installed, *F$ChkMem* only ensures that the memory is accessible to the kernel.

13.1 Attach/Detach

The attach request is unusual. It is seldom used except by the I/O Manager itself. It places a new device in the device table and calls the device driver to initialize it. The device table is a quick reference table used by the I/O Manager to determine whether a device has already been attached. Knowing whether a device has been attached prevents IOMan from wasting time attaching it again. It also prevents IOMan from having the driver reinitialize the device. All the facts that Attach collects about a new device are contained in the device table; these facts can then be taken from the table each subsequent time the device is opened.

Detach is the inverse operation for Attach. It decrements a device's use count. If the use count becomes zero, IOMan removes the device from the device table and calls the termination routine for the device.

Users seldom attach a device; however, they often open files. When a file is opened, IOMan attaches the device if necessary. It also creates a path descriptor for the new path, and calls the file manager to do anything it might need to do about a new file; e.g., find the location of an RBF file on disk.

13.2 Duping Paths

When a path number needs to be changed, the Dup call is used. IOMan is responsible for Dup. It assigns an additional path number to a path descriptor and increments the use count of the path descriptor. This sounds like a trivial operation, but it is the only way to save the path descriptor for a path if you have to close it.

A program might need to open a path to the printer as standard output without losing the current standard output file. This can be done by:

dup path 1 *standard output*
save the new path number x
close path 1

open the printer

The printer appears as path 1 because IOMan always assigns the lowest available path number and path 0 is already taken by standard input.

To restore the original standard output file:

close path 1
dup path x

Path x is the dup of the original standard output. It is duped to the lowest available path number. Since we just closed path 1, releasing that path number, this dup is to path 1.

13.2. DUPING PATHS

```
close path x
...
```

Close is another operation on which IOMan may act. If the use count of the path descriptor for the path being closed is greater than one, the I/O Manager just decreases it by one. If the use count is one, there aren't any other paths using the descriptor so IOMan returns the memory for the descriptor. If there are no other paths using the device, IOMan will also detach the device.

The real working I/O operations are passed right through the I/O Manager to the file manager. IOMan passes read and write requests through to a file manager as fast as possible, and wouldn't know a directory or a carriage return if it bit "him" on the nose. Its only involvement with the bulk of commands is to get the address of the path descriptor and pass it along to a file manager.

The I/O Manager takes requests for services, arranges the paper work, and gets the right team of modules together. Its main direct involvement is at the start and end of a project (Open and Close). The noun, "manager," fits IOMan exceptionally well.

Chapter 14

Pipes

In this chapter we will cover pipes. You will learn how to create named and unnamed pipes, and some of the things for which they can be used.

Pipes are sequential files that never leave your system's RAM memory. They can be made large if you are willing to dedicate a lot of memory to them, but usually a pipe uses only a small amount of RAM. It is possible to store bulk data in a pipe, but in most cases, data only stays in the pipe briefly as it passes between two processes. Even a one-byte buffer would suffice.

14.1 Unnamed Pipes

Unnamed pipes are only known by their path numbers to the process that created them. Like any path they can be inherited by a process' children. That's what makes unnamed pipes useful. First let's consider creating a pipe that is only known to the process that created it.

If you write enough data into a pipe to fill it, the write will block until enough data is emptied from the pipe to allow the write to complete. If only one process has access to a pipe, a blocked write is trouble. Since the only process that can read from the pipe is the writer—the one that is blocked—the process waits here until it is killed. If you are careful never to write enough data to the pipe to fill it, a pipe that is known to only one process has some limited use as a storage place for a queue.

If you fork a process while you have a pipe open, you can pass the pipe's path number to the new process. Now two processes have access to the pipe and it can be used as a communication device between those processes. In the following example, a process starts a child that feeds it the square roots of the integers one through ten.

Piping the standard output path of a child process back to its parent is a good trick. The most common use is to get the output from a system utility command.

```c
#include <stdio.h>
#include <modes.h>
/*
    This program starts Sqrts, a program that generates the square roots of the
    numbers one through ten. It fixes it so the standard output of Sqrts is a pipe that
    leads to a path here. We don't do anything reasonable with the numbers; just
    add them up and print out the total.
*/

extern char **environ;
extern int os9fork();

main()
{
    int SaveStdout;
    int PipePath;
    double x, Total;

    /* Dup the stdout path so we can mess with it.          */
    SaveStdout = dup(1);                    /* 1 is the stdout path number */
    /*
        Now close stdout to make room for the pipe Don't bother to
        tell stdio about this. We'll put it back before he notices.
    */
    close(1);
    /*
        Open a pipe. It will go into path one because that is the
        lowest-numbered free path number.
    */
    open("/PIPE", S_IREAD+S_IWRITE);
    /* The pipe's all set. Let's start sqrts.               */
    if(os9exec(os9fork, "Sqrts", NULL, environ, 0, 0) <=0){
        fprintf(stderr, "Can't fork Sqrts\n");
        exit(errno);
    }
    /*
        We need stdout back, but don't want to lose the pipe file. So
        dup the pipe, close the original pipe, and put the original
        stdout back where it belongs.
    */
    PipePath = dup(1);
    close(1);                               /* Close original pipe          */
```

14.1. UNNAMED PIPES

```
    dup(SaveStdout);              /* Will go into path 1        */
    close(SaveStdout);            /* We're through with this    */
    /*
        We're ready to roll. The paths are now:
            0 Standard input
            1 Standard output
            2 Standard error
            4 The pipe path
        For Sqrts, path 1 is the other end of the pipe.
    */
    Total = 0;
    while(read(PipePath, &x, sizeof x) != 0)
        Total += x;
    printf("Total of Square roots is %lg\n", Total);
    exit(0);
}
```

The next program is the one that is forked by the previous program. There is nothing about it (except the comments) that would let you know that it will write to a pipe.

```
#include <math.h>
#include <stdio.h>
/*
    This program simply writes the square roots of the first ten integers out its
    standard output path. The output will be real numbers. We have a choice of
    two ways to write the data. We can format the output for human consumption
    and terminate each number with a return, or we can write them in internal
    form (as doubles). Just to show that pipes can handle non-printable data, we'll
    send the data in its internal representation.
*/
main() /* Called Sqrts */
{
    register int Counter;
    double Square_Root;

    for(Counter=1;Counter<=10;++Counter){
        Square_Root = sqrt((double)Counter);
        fwrite(&Square_Root,
            sizeof Square_Root,
            1,
            stdout);
    }
}
```

```
        exit(0);
}
```

14.2   Shell-Style Pipes

The shell uses pipes to let you hook processes together stdout-to-stdin. It takes a little playing with path numbers, but you can do the same trick yourself. The following example pipes the output of *procs* to *qsort*, and reads the output of *qsort* from another pipe.

```
#include <stdio.h>
#include <modes.h>
#define BUFFERSIZE 133

/*
    This program demonstrates pipes between sibling processes.  Since the previous
    example covered basic pipes carefully, this one will hurry through most of the
    duping and concentrate on the sibling bit.
*/

extern int os9fork();
extern char **environ;

char *Procs_Arglist[ ] = {
   "procs",
   0
};

char *Qsort_Arglist[ ] = {
   "qsort",
   "-f=2",
   0
};

main()
{
   int SaveStdin, SaveStdout;
   int PipePath;
   char buffer[BUFFERSIZE];
```

14.2. SHELL-STYLE PIPES

```
/*
    Build a pipe for stdout
*/
SaveStdout = dup(1);
close(1);
open("/PIPE", S_IREAD+S_IWRITE);

/*
    Start procs with its output going to a pipe
*/
os9exec(os9fork, "procs", Procs_Arglist, environ, 0,0);
/*
    Move the pipe to stdin
*/
SaveStdin = dup(0);
close(0);
dup(1);                         /* Dup the pipe (in stdout) to path 0      */
/*
    Open a NEW pipe for stdout
*/
close(1);
open("/PIPE", S_IREAD+S_IWRITE);
/*
    Now start qsort with both stdin and stdout
    going to pipes.
*/
os9exec(os9fork, "qsort", Qsort_Arglist, environ, 0, 0);
/*
    We don't need the pipe between procs and qsort any more. They can take care of
    it. Close that pipe and move the other to a special path so we can read from it
    and use the original stdout.
*/
close(0);                       /* close one of the pipes                  */
/*
    We don't plan to use stdin again, but lets put it back where it belongs just to keep
    everything neat.
*/
dup(SaveStdin);
close(SaveStdin);

PipePath = dup(1);              /* move the stdout pipe                    */
close(1);
dup(SaveStdout);
close(SaveStdout);
```

```
    /*
        Now we're all set. The paths open now are:
            0 The original stdin
            1 The original stdout
            2 The original stderr
            4 A pipe leading to qsort's stdout
        We could use fdopen to turn the pipe path
        into a full C file, but for the simple
        reading we mean to do a plain path will do.
    */
    printf("(Process ID, Parent ID) sorted by parent ID\n");
    while(readln(PipePath, buffer, BUFFERSIZE) > 0){
        /* pick the first 7 chars of line */
        buffer[7] = '\0';
        /* If it isn't the header line print it */
        if(buffer[1] != 'I')
            printf("(%s) ", buffer);
    }
    printf("\n");
    exit(0);
}
```

Pipes are almost always used with one process at each end, but that is not a restriction. If you have several readers and several writers on a pipe, the pipe file manager will do the best it can for you. It ensures that data which is written in one write arrives in one piece provided that the process that reads it issues a read for the right amount of data.

Once a process does a read or write to a pipe, it has control of that end of the pipe until the operation completes. If the pipe can't hold the entire amount you want to write, it will block the write until some data is read from the pipe. When it is empty enough to permit more writing, it lets the blocked process continue. In the same way, if a pipe doesn't hold enough data to satisfy a read, it gives the reader all it can, then blocks until more data is written to it. Other processes waiting to read or write wait until the current processes have finished.

In general, OS-9 tries to prevent a resource from being monopolized by any process. However, if pipeman didn't use the locking algorithm it does, any message longer than one byte could be scrambled by other messages. A process might write, say, ten bytes of a five-hundred byte message into the pipe. Another process might then get the pipe and write fifty bytes into it. The first process might get back in and finish its write. Meanwhile one process could read the first fifty bytes, and another process empty the pipe. Both readers would receive garbled messages.

14.3 Named Pipes

Sending and receiving fixed-length messages on a shared pipe isn't too hard. If the messages must be variable length, you must use readln and writeln. Tricks like coding the length of the message into its first two bytes would only work if you could read the first two bytes of a message, then read the rest. Given the way pipes are shared, you couldn't count on the rest of the message being there when you went back to read it.

14.3 Named Pipes

Unnamed pipes can be passed among closely related processes, but they can't get out of the immediate family. Named pipes are accessible to any process that knows the pipe's name. *I$Create* is all that is required to create a named pipe, which will exist as long as any paths lead to it or there is any data in the pipe. A pipe name is the name of a pipe device (/PIPE is the default descriptor) followed by up to 28 characters that follow the usual OS-9 file naming conventions.

Examples that use Pipe Names

```
$ copy test.file /pipe/test.pipe
$ list /pipe/test.pipe
```

PipeFile = fopen("/pipe/x", "w");

You should choose a pipe's name carefully. It must be unique, and, somehow, the programs that want to use the pipe have to know its name. Still, a pipe with a well-known name can be used by any process in the system. It's an elegant way to get at a shared resource.

You can begin to get a feel for named pipes without writing any code. Try listing a file into a named pipe:

```
$ list /dd/defs/oskdefs.d >/pipe/test&
```

You'll see the program start up, then nothing will happen. It filled the pipe and is waiting for someone to read from it. You can see the named pipe with the *dir* command. Try:

```
$ dir /pipe
```

You'll see `test` in the directory listing.

You can read from the pipe as if were a normal file:

```
$ list /pipe/test
```

and you'll see the contents of /dd/defs/oskdefs.d.

There are some differences between named and un-named pipes. (There's the name, of course.) A named pipe is meant to be opened from one end; then wait for someone to open the other end. You can write to a named pipe with no readers; try that on an un-named pipe and you'll get an error. You can also leave a named pipe around with no processes attached to it provided you leave some data in it.

Named pipes are best used with servers. Here's a program that I call an *oracle*. It pumps answers into a pipe. Any other process can get an answer from the *oracle* by reading the pipe.

```
#include <stdio.h>

#define PIPENAME "/PIPE/Oracle"
#define FOREVER 1

#define ANSWERCT 8
char *Answer[ANSWERCT]={
    "Yes",
    "No",
    "Of course",
    "Absolutely not",
    "Why not",
    "Huh?",
    "Maybe",
    "The Oracle is sleeping"
};

main() /* Named Oracle */
{
    FILE *Pipe;

    /* Open the named pipe just like any file */
    if((Pipe = fopen(PIPENAME, "w")) == NULL){
        fprintf(stderr, "Can't open %s. Error %d\n",
            PIPENAME, errno);
        exit(errno);
    }
    /* Execute the next statement until the world ends. */
    while(FOREVER)
        fprintf(Pipe, "%s\n", Answer[Rand()]);
}
```

14.3. NAMED PIPES

```
static long seed=0L;

Rand() /* return a random number */
{
    int time, date, tick;
    short day;

    if(seed == 0L){
        _sysdate(3, &time, &date, &day, &tick);
        seed = (long)(date + (tick & 0xffff));
    }
    seed = (long)abs((seed * 39709L + 13L) % 65537L);
    return (int(seed % (long)ANSWERCT));
}
```

The next program, called *consult*, consults the oracle. It opens the pipe for reading and reads one line from it. It uses raw OS-9 I/O because it needs to be sure of using a readln in order to get just one line from the pipe.

```
#include <stdio.h>
#include <modes.h>

#define ANSWERLENGTH    100
#define ORACLENAME      "/pipe/oracle"

main()
{
    char Answer[ANSWERLENGTH];
    int PipePath;
    int ReadLength;

    /*
        Don't open a full C file. We don't want the pipe buffered.
        (We only want to read one line from it.)
    */
    if((PipePath = open(ORACLENAME, S_IREAD+S_IWRITE)) < 0){
        fprintf(stderr, "The oracle doesn't answer\n");
        exit(errno);
    }

    if((ReadLength = readln(PipePath, Answer, ANSWERLENGTH)) < 0){
        fprintf(stderr, "The oracle curses\n");
        exit(errno);
```

```
    }
    /*
        The string from Readln isn't terminated with
        a \0. Stick one on the end.
    */
    Answer[ReadLength] = '\0';
    printf("%s\n", Answer);
     exit(0);
}
```

To use the oracle, you first start it running in the background:

    $ oracle&

The oracle should just keep running. It only uses time when it has to refill the pipe. To consult the oracle, run *consult*:

    $ consult

Consult will read a line from the oracle's pipe and print it on your terminal.

Chapter 15

Interrupts

> *In this chapter you will learn what interrupts are and what they have to do with I/O and multitasking.*

Interrupts are requests for the attention of the processor chip. When a 68000-family processor accepts an interrupt, it stops what it is doing, enters system state, and executes some code to "service" the interrupt. In a sense, an interrupt is a switch that the hardware outside the microprocessor can use to cause the microprocessor to execute special subroutine calls. Interrupts are usually serviced as soon as they are raised (caused), but the processor can ignore interrupts by masking them.

The 68000 family of microprocessors can deal with external interrupts at seven priority levels. The first thing the processor does when it services an interrupt is to mask all interrupts except those at higher priorities than the interrupt it is servicing. The interrupt mask can be adjusted by altering the system byte in the status register.

The processor can also generate numerous internal interrupts, called exceptions. Some exceptions are friendly, like the *trap* interrupts which call trap handlers and OS-9 SVCs. Other exceptions indicate unfortunate occurrences like addressing non-existent memory or trying to divide by zero.

All interrupts (including software exceptions) do about the same things. They push the processor's context on the system stack, find a "vector," and jump to that address. Each type of interrupt gets the address it jumps to from a different place. This makes it easy to handle each type of interrupt with a different routine.

Most interrupts get their vectors directly from a vector table. The VBR register points to the vector table on the more advanced members of the 68000 family. On early processors—the 68000, 68008, and 68070—the vector table is fixed at addresses 0 through 1024. The division-by-zero exception, for example, causes a branch to the address at offset 20 ($14) in the vector table.

Hardware interrupts can select any vector from the vector table by vector number, or they can use the default vector assigned to each interrupt level. Interrupts that specify a vector number are called vectored interrupts, and interrupts that only provide an interrupt level are called autovectored interrupts. A pin on the processor indicates to the chip whether an interrupt is vectored or autovectored.

Interrupt level seven cannot be masked by software. Since software cannot protect itself against interruption by level seven interrupts, that level must be used carefully. The safest rule is to avoid level seven interrupts entirely, but level seven interrupts are tempting. The only latency for level seven interrupts is whatever delay is built into the hardware. Sometimes level seven interrupts may be the best way to guarantee very fast and repeatable interrupt response time. But since level seven interrupts can interrupt the kernel at any time, *don't make system calls or touch system data structures from level seven interrupt service routines.* Any data structures shared between level seven interrupt service routines and other code should be treated with extreme care. Queues managed with *cas2* instructions are useful for communication between non-maskable interrupt service routines and other code.

If devices must share interrupt priority levels, vectored interrupts can give them separate vectors. When the processor receives a vectored interrupt, it asks the device which vector number it should use. The hardware that caused the interrupt responds with an 8-bit number which is interpreted as a vector number. The vector selected by the device is picked out of the vector table. There are 192 vectors in the table just for vectored interrupts (they can also use the 64 vectors that have other purposes).

Vectored interrupts require more sophisticated hardware than autovectored interrupts, but they can give faster response. If several devices share a priority level and use autovectored interrupts, each time there is an interrupt OS-9 will have to determine which device caused it. If there are enough devices in a system, even vectored interrupts will eventually leave two devices on the same vector, but 192 vectors leave more room than 7 vectors.

15.1 Polling

Some operating systems (e.g., CP/M) use a technique called polling, or force user programs to poll for themselves. In this type of system, each piece of hardware that might need attention is polled (or checked) at frequent intervals. In a system with a printer on a parallel port and a terminal on a serial port, the overhead involved in polling the I/O devices isn't too much. The serial port needs to be checked a few thousand times per second; the printer (being a slow output device) can be polled much less frequently—two hundred times per second should be enough for an ordinary dot-matrix printer. When a program is running, it must take responsibility for any polling. There is no automatic way for the operating system to take over at intervals.

15.2 The Alternative

Under OS-9, interrupts are precisely a way for the operating system to take over when it is required. I/O ports are programmed to produce an interrupt every time they need attention. When the interrupt is received, OS-9 is given control of the machine to service the interrupt. Since an interrupt is only generated when something actually needs doing, there is no constant need to watch for devices that need service. Neither user programs nor OS-9 need poll constantly.

The most important result of the use of interrupts is that I/O is simplified for users. OS-9 deals with all I/O hardware. If a program isn't ready for input when a byte arrives, OS-9 holds it in a buffer until the program requests it. Similarly, OS-9 maintains a buffer of characters ready for output if a program is producing output faster than the output device can take it.

15.3 Multitasking and the Clock

OS-9 multitasking capability is also based on interrupts. I/O hardware may produce frequent interrupts in an OS-9 system, but they can't be relied on. Minutes might pass without a single I/O operation. To insure that OS-9 gets control at frequent intervals, every OS-9 system has a special device that produces interrupts. These interrupts, called timer interrupts, come ten to a hundred times per second, depending on the system.[1] OS-9 uses the timer interrupt as a trigger for its housekeeping operations. When several processes are running, OS-9 switches the current process off and starts another every few clock ticks (different numbers of ticks for different systems).

Switching from one process to another several times per second makes it possible for OS-9 to appear to run several programs at the same time. If you were a very fast-moving house painter, you could work on all four walls, moving quickly around the house. If you moved fast enough, a spectator might think that four painters were working slowly, one on each wall.

15.4 The Polling Table

When an interrupt comes in, OS-9 only knows that something on that vector needs attention. It has a list, called the polling table, of every device that might cause an

---

[1] Timer interrupts are almost always generated at 100 interrupts per second.

interrupt. For each interrupt, OS-9 runs through the table checking all the devices on that vector to see if they sent the interrupt. This is classical polling and involves overhead in that it doesn't go directly to the source of the interrupt. The advantage OS-9 has over other operating systems that use polling without interrupts is that OS-9 only needs to poll when something needs attention.

The first entries in the table get slightly faster service than later entries. Devices that need extra fast service can force themselves to the beginning of the table by requesting a high priority[2] when they enter themselves in the table. The *F$IRQ* service request is used to update the table. Check the example device drivers in chapters 23 and 24, and appendix D for samples of the *F$IRQ* SVC in action.

15.5 Masking Interrupts

Sometimes a block of instructions must be executed without interruption. This is almost never a concern for regular programs, but for parts of OS-9 it is crucial. When a device driver is in the middle of updating a queue, it can't tolerate anything writing to the same queue. This is an example of a *critical section*: a block of code that must have exclusive access to some resource.

The most elegant way to protect a sequence of instructions is with the 68000 instructions that read, modify, and write memory all in one instruction. These instructions can't be interrupted even by a separate processor or DMA hardware. They are *tas* on all the processors in the 68000 family, and *cas* and *cas2* on the 68020, 68030, 68040, and other related processors. None of these instructions mask interrupts, but they do modify memory without leaving an opening for an interrupt or even access by another processor that shares the same memory. *Tas* is usually used for synchronization, *cas* for singly-linked lists, and *cas2* for doubly linked lists. These special instructions are the easiest way to handle memory that can be written by more than one processor.

If only one processor can access memory, every instruction is indivisible, but often no single instruction is enough. masking interrupts is an easy way to protect instruction sequences. (Only system code can mask interrupts.) The system byte in the status register contains a 3-bit interrupt mask. This mask can be used to mask out all interrupts whose priority level is not greater than the mask's value. For example, if the interrupt mask has the value binary-101, interrupts at priority level 5 and down will wait. Setting the interrupt mask to 111-binary will block all but non-maskable interrupts. Since non-maskable interrupts should only be generated in case of an emergency, code protected by an interrupt mask of %111 can be considered non-interruptible most of the time.

---

[2] A high priority in the polling table is signified by a *low* number.

15.5. MASKING INTERRUPTS

The sequence is:

```
move.w  SR,-(SP)        Save SR
ori     #$700,SR        Set interrupt mask
...
move.w  (SP)+,SR        Restore SR from the stack
```

The ellipses (...) represent instructions that can't be interrupted except by a non-maskable interrupt (NMI) or reset (this section of code is a Critical Section). If you must use this trick, keep the number of protected instructions to a minimum. Don't use any OS-9 service requests; they may unmask interrupts for you. When interrupts are masked, OS-9 can't service interrupts. I/O comes to a halt. In some systems, even the clock falls behind.

Device drivers mask interrupts to the interrupt level of their device when they access data structures that are shared between their interrupt service routine and their mainline. The kernel masks interrupts all the way to level seven when it executes code that must not be interrupted by any interrupt service routine. Masked interrupts are a necessary evil. The kernel masks interrupts as seldom as possible and device drivers should be similarly careful. Masked interrupts add to interrupt response time, and excessive interrupt masking ultimately causes poor I/O performance.

Chapter 16

The RBF Disk Format

In this chapter we discuss the way OS-9 structures data on disks. We take a low-level look at file allocation and directory structures.

Formatting a disk changes it from a piece of iron-oxide-coated mylar or metal into a carefully organized empty file structure. There are some features of formatted disks that are common across all hardware and operating systems.

Information is recorded on the surface of a disk. Some drives only use one side of the disk, others have a read/write head on each side of the disk so they can use both surfaces. Hard disks may be built of two or more platters turning on the same spindle. Hard disks, and some mutated versions of floppy disks, may have more than two sides. Three platters offer six sides (though only five are usually used for data).

A disk's surface is divided into tracks, which are concentric circular paths around the disk reminiscent of the grooves in a phonograph record. The number of tracks depends on the quality of the disk drive. The more tracks, the more data can be stored on the disk, and the more precision the disk drive must have to position the head over a track. Low-performance floppy disk drives can only handle 35 tracks on a disk. High-performance hard disk drives may support more than 1000 tracks.

Each track is divided into sectors. These sections of the track are the pigeon holes where data is stored. The data part of each sector is surrounded by timing and identifying bytes. These bytes help the disk controller find a sector for which it is searching. The timing bytes around each sector leave the controller time to recognize a sector and respond.

The number of sectors on a track varies widely depending on the sector size, the size of the disk, and the recording density that is used. The smallest number of sectors per track currently being used is ten 256-byte sectors for single density five-and-a-quarter inch and three-and-a-half inch disks. Eight inch double density disks have twenty-eight 256-byte sectors per track. Hard disks may have thirty-two (or more) sectors per track depending on the controller you use and the sector size.

16.1 The Identification Sector

After we get above the level of the physical disk, all OS-9 disks have the same characteristics. Information about the disk as a whole is stored in its first sector, that is, the first sector on the first track. The sector containing this information is called the "identification sector." The information in the identification sector includes the specifications for the way the rest of the disk is written, the location and size of the bootstrap (if it's there), the name and creation date of the disk, the user and group of the owner of the disk, and a pointer to the root directory.

One of the fields in the identification sector is DD_BIT. This field indicates the number of sectors in a cluster. For most systems this will be one, but if your disk is exceptionally large, DD_BIT can be made greater than one. (DD_BIT can take any power of two that will fit in a 16-bit word.) A cluster is the unit of allocation for disk space. Cluster size must be considered when a large-capacity disk is formatted. It can also be used for some subtle performance optimization.

An OS-9 disk can be formatted with as many as 524,288 clusters. When a disk is formatted, the number of sectors per cluster must be chosen such that the number of sectors on the disk divided by the number of sectors per cluster is no greater than 524,288.

As a general rule, clusters should be no larger than necessary. Files seldom exactly fill the clusters that are allocated to them, and the empty space at the end of the last cluster is wasted. The smaller the clusters, the less space is lost at the end of each file. For example, one-hundred hundred-byte files actually contain 10,000 bytes of information. With 256-byte sectors and one-sector clusters the files consume a total of 25,600 bytes on disk plus another 25,600 bytes for file descriptors (see section 17.2). With four-sector clusters the files consume 102,400 bytes for the files (RBF will squeeze the file descriptors in with the files). Sixty-five percent of those 102,400 bytes are unused.

Large clusters are not all bad. First, many files on a typical hard disk are a thousand bytes or more in size. The wasted space from large clusters is not so bad with reasonably large files. Large clusters can also improve disk performance. A cluster represents a group of contiguous sectors on the disk. These sectors are placed so they can be read one after the other as quickly as possible. The cluster size sets a maximum on the disk fragmentation. If you are willing to trade some disk space for performance, larger

16.2 The Allocation Map

clusters are worth trying.[1] (See section 17.6 for more discussion of cluster size and performance.)

16.2 The Allocation Map

The sector right after the identification sector contains the beginning of the disk allocation map. This is an array of bits which indicate whether each cluster on the disk is allocated or free. If the bit corresponding to a cluster is one, the cluster is allocated; if it is zero, the cluster is free.

Disks with bad sectors will show allocated clusters that are not contained in any file. RBF does not have any special way to mark bad sectors, so they are just marked "allocated" in the disk allocation map. *Dcheck* will complain about these clusters, saying that they are allocated but not in any file. In this case, that is fine. Don't let *dcheck* "fix" those clusters.

The disk allocation map is used whenever a file is created or deleted, or when the size of a file is changed. In each of these operations disk space is used or freed. The disk allocation map contains the location of each free cluster on the disk.

16.3 The Root Directory

One of the fields in the identification sector is a pointer to the root directory. Every RBF disk, even those on which you never create a directory, has a root directory which is named after the device holding the disk; i.e., if you do a directory command on /d0 the result will be a list of the files in the root directory for /d0, and if you move the disk into drive one, the same directory will appear as *dir* /d1. The directory linked to the identification sector is called the root directory because if you view the directories on a disk as forming a tree, the root directory is at the base (or root) of the tree.

The root directory, like every other OS-9 directory, is a file of directory entries, each entry consisting of a 28-byte file name, one empty byte for alignment, and the 3-byte logical sector number of the file descriptor for the file. The first directory entry has a file name of . (that's a single dot) and points to the file descriptor for the directory itself. The second directory entry has a file name of . . (two dots) and points to the file descriptor for the parent of the directory. The root directory has no parent, so the . . entry in the root directory points to the root's file descriptor. Because of this, a command like "chd . . . ." doesn't fail if you use too many dots. It just reaches the root directory and stays there.

---

[1] After considerable research, the BSD development team decided that 4k was the best cluster size for the Berkeley fast file system, but they have a trick that allows a file to use part of a cluster.

A directory may contain empty directory entries. When a file is deleted, the directory entry is marked "empty" by writing a $00 as the first byte of the file name. The directory file is never shortened, so after many files are deleted from a directory, a dump of the directory file will show a long list of empty entries.

A directory file has a special purpose, but it can be read or even written much like any other file. RBF only insists that the program must know it is accessing a directory. The open-mode parameter must specify directory access mode whenever a program attempts to open a directory file, otherwise the open will return an error.

Directory files should only be written to with great caution, but reading them is harmless. A directory file can be examined with *dump*.

```
$ dump .
```

The result is a dump-format listing of the working directory.

16.4 The File Descriptor

Directory entries don't point directly at files. They point at file descriptor sectors which give all the information about a file except its name and the directory it's in. The most interesting result of keeping most of the information about a file out of the directory is that a file can be renamed, moved about, and even given aliases (alternate names) without special effort.

Think about what would happen if two directories had entries pointing to the same file descriptor. The file could be accessed under two names from two separate directories. This kind of trickery upsets some OS-9 commands, notably *dcheck* and *dsave*, but in most cases OS-9 handles it smoothly. There is even a field in the file descriptor that can be used to give the number of directory entries pointing to it. A file's space allocation won't be returned until this counter is zero.

Microware currently doesn't support multiple links to files at the utility-program level because multiple links make it difficult to keep the disk structure consistent. It is possible to support multiple links to files and ensure file system integrity, but that cannot be done to RBF without undesirable side effects. The usual compromise that permits multiple links is to accept that there will be occasional disk problems, and patch the problems when they show up. So far Microware has chosen not to do this under OS-9.[2]

---

[2]There are numerous utility programs circulating in the OS-9 community that take advantage of multiple links. RBF seems to deal with multiply linked files correctly.

16.5 Raw Disks

The super user can skip around all the structure that RBF imposes on a disk, and access the entire disk as a simple array of bytes. Any process can open a *raw* device and see the disk as a single unstructured file, but only the super user can read beyond the allocation bit map, and only the super user can write to the raw device.

A raw device can be addressed by name:

- /d0@ names the raw disk in device /d0.

- /h0@ names the raw disk in device /h0.

Raw devices can also be allowed to default. Opening the file named @ for read or write opens whatever device holds the default data directory. Opening @ for execution opens the device that holds the execution directory.

Careful access to the raw device is useful. It is the best way to access a corrupted disk and make repairs. It is a good way to quickly copy one disk to another (e.g., the *backup* utility), or to create a file that will be an image of the raw disk. And it is the only way to get away from RBF's careful control of writes to FD sectors, or to directly read and write sector zero or the disk allocation map from a program.

Programs should access a raw device carefully. Although the raw device overlaps every file on the disk, RBF ignores that fact. It treats the raw device as a separate file for purposes of record locking. Nor does RBF take note when an application writes FD or directory information on a raw device.

One other useful application of raw device access is benchmarking. A program that reads a raw disk pays little RBF overhead. Consequently, reading several hundred kilobytes from a raw device is a good measurement of hardware and driver speed.

16.6 Disk Drive Incompatibilities

Once, all OS-9 disks were readable with standard device descriptors and any drive that was physically capable of reading the data. That time is past.

All OS-9 disks had track zero formatted single density. Thus, a disk driver could configure itself for single density and read sector zero on track zero. Sector zero gave it the disk's disk ID sector, which contains enough information about the disk format that the driver could initialize the driver's drive table entry and configure itself to read or write the rest of the disk.

Two hardware problems were enough to end the old universally usable format. Some disk controllers were unable to deal with disks that numbered sectors starting at zero, and some disk controllers could were unable to read track zero at single density.

Figure 16.1: Specified Fields in the Universal Disk Format

Device Descriptor Option	Value
PD_TotCyls	80
PD_CYL	79
PD_SCT	16
PD_DNS	MFM and 96 tpi (135 tpi on 3in disks)
PD_SOffs	1
PD_TOffs	1

16.6.1 The Universal Disk Format

The sector base offset field instructs drivers to convert the zero-based logical sector numbers used by RBF into physical sector numbers offset such that they start at one (or some other number noted in the sector base offset field). The universal disk format avoids special cases by not using any part of the disk that may be unreachable or has special meaning to any known controller. The universal format jumps over the first track on the disk and numbers sectors starting at one. The universal disk format also specifies the recording format on the other tracks (see table 16.1).

If you use floppy disks primarily to exchange data with other systems, you should default to universal format. Every OS-9 system with at least an 80-track floppy drive should be able to communicate with you. Any floppy controller can handle universal format disks, and more capable disk drives can degrade themselves by tricks like double-stepping to read and write universal format.[3]

16.6.2 Foreign Disk Formats

Universal format is not yet a widely-enough used standard. It is a prudent disk format to use if you plan to send a disk to someone with a system unlike your own, but the restriction on tracks and density may be uncomfortable if you have a disk drive that can use much higher densities.

RBF and the RBF drivers automatically adjust to many disk configurations. The disk ID information in sector zero lets the driver adjust its understanding of the disk format invisibly. This only fails when the driver encounters a disk outside the range of variation it expects.

If you receive a disk that you cannot read, investigate the following:

- Do you have a file manager that is compatible with the disk? There are many

---

[3]If you have only a 40-track drive, or a controller or drive that only accepts single density, you are out of universal format's space.

16.6. DISK DRIVE INCOMPATIBILITIES

more disk formats than RBF's and PCF's. If you don't have the right file manager you may be able to dump the raw disk and sort what you need out of the resulting mess, but it is generally enough reason to look for someone with the right file manager.

- Can your hardware handle the disk? The disk might be higher density than your drive can read. The disk could also be recorded with constant linear velocity (like a CD-I disk) instead of the more traditional constant angular velocity. That's a good reason to search for someone with compatible hardware.

If your hardware and file manager are ready for the disk, the next step is to create an experimental device descriptor based on your existing descriptor for the device you mean to use to read the foreign disk. If you can talk to the person who formatted the disk the descriptor-generation job is easy: build a new descriptor whose options section matches as nearly as possible the options section of the disk creator's descriptor.

For experimentation purposes start by attempting to dump the disk in "raw" format:

```
$ dump /d0@
```

The most likely error while reading foreign OS-9 disks is invalid sector number. Try using a different value of sector base offset or track base offset.

If you can dump the disk, examine sector zero. That sector contains enough information to construct a good device options section.

Once you have the descriptor configured well enough to read sector zero (which is usually a matter of getting the track zero density and the sector base offset set correctly), you should be able to read the rest of the disk.

Remaining problems often fall into one of the following classes:

- Specifying too many sectors per track gives bad sector number errors.

- Specifying too few sectors per track can cause the driver to skip the sectors that are "not supposed to be on the track."

- Getting the number of sectors per track right for track zero is not enough. The rest of the tracks may need a different value. The wrong number of sectors on track one can cause data skipping or bad sector numbers further out in the disk.

- Specifying double stepping for a single-stepped disk, or specifying single-sided for a double-sided disk will attempt to skip half the data on the disk.

- Creating a modified version of a device descriptor only works if the old descriptor is removed from memory by *deiniz*'ing it until *devs* no longer shows that device. After the old device descriptor is removed, the new descriptor may be loaded and *iniz*'ed. Failing to completely remove the old descriptor will cause the new descriptor to have no effect.

It may take up to a half hour to fiddle with a device descriptor until it can read an unknown disk, and occasionally the disk will be beyond what you can accommodate. If you send a disk to someone, it is friendly to send enough information with the disk to build a descriptor for it. It is even more friendly to use universal format.

Chapter 17

Managing Disks

Disk space is another kind of memory the OS-9 programmer might need to help OS-9 manage. In this chapter we'll discuss how to use disk space efficiently—or at least know when you're using it inefficiently. We'll also discuss things that can slow down access to disk files and some tricks for recovering damaged or deleted files.

Two types of files make inefficient use of disk space: small files and unexpectedly large files.

17.1 Using Space Efficiently

Small files carry a heavy overhead burden compared to their size. The directory entry is a barely noticeable 32 bytes. The file descriptor takes a sector (often 256 bytes). The data takes at least a sector. A file with just one byte in it uses 544 bytes of disk space. Often it is easier to have a few small files than one large one, but balance easy programming against wasted disk space. If you have a choice of many small files or fewer large ones, choose larger files when efficient use of disk space is your first priority. Don't, for instance, use a directory as a telephone directory for a large organization. Letting the file name be the person's name and the contents of the file be the telephone number is easy. The entire system can be constructed from OS-9 utilities. But, at 544 bytes per member, about 1,200 entries fill an 80-track floppy.

A program can accidentally increase the size of an RBF file without any ill effects other than wasted disk space. All it has to do is write a byte at a position beyond the end of a file and the file will be lengthened to include that byte. If you aren't careful, that trick can cause you to allocate more space for a file than it needs. If a file seems remarkably large, check the programs that update it for seek errors.

17.2 Disk Access Speed

The speed of RBF is chiefly influenced by the speed of the I/O hardware, the amount of multi-sector I/O that is done, the number of times data must be copied, the effectiveness of disk caching, and the appropriate choice of the sector interleaving factor.

The speed of the hardware is not a software issue, but it is a limiting factor. Ultimately, it is impossible to move data to and from a disk faster than the speed of connection from memory through the controller and the drive's electronics and mechanism.

OS-9 isn't known for its high-speed disk access, though access to a file is seldom significantly slower than for any other operating system on the same hardware.[1] The most common cause for slow access to files is the environment; that is, what other files are being accessed and what processes are running. After a disk has been in use for a long time, disk fragmentation breaks files into pieces scattered over the drive. Fragmentation can cause serious disk performance problems when a disk is nearly full and has been used heavily with a typical work load (editing, compiling, downloading files, and other activities that create and delete files).

It takes time to move a disk drive's read/write head from track to track on a disk. Because of this, it is fastest to access a file with the minimum movement of the heads. The disk organization that OS-9 uses is flexible and safe, but it can generate extra head movement.

Before reading a file, OS-9 must read the directory to find the address of its file descriptor. Then it must read the file descriptor. The file descriptor contains a list of address/length pairs that describe the location of the file on the disk. The file descriptor for an open file is stored in memory attached to the path descriptor. If a file's directory entry is located near the beginning of the directory, the file can be read with only two extra reads: one for the directory entry, the other for the file descriptor.

Since RBF expands the segment list to fill an FD sector, a file on a disk with 256-byte sectors has room in each file descriptor for 48 segment descriptors, and 512-byte FD sectors can reference up to 99 segments. Each segment is described by a starting logical sector number and a length stored in the file descriptor. A file may use more than one segment because it is too long to fit in one segment (more than thirty-two

---

[1] OS-9 actually has rather fast disk I/O when compared to other operating systems running with similar I/O hardware. There is an important extra cost when disks are written in that OS-9 always updates the disk immediately. Great care is taken to protect the integrity of the disk.

megabytes). It may also use multiple segments because the file grew each time it was written, and RBF found that its last segment was blocked by another file, or because there were not contiguous blocks of disk space long enough to hold the entire file. Files that use more segments than the minimum number required for their size are a signal that the file system is becoming fragmented. Fragmented files require extra seeks to move the head from one segment to another.

The only utility Microware provides to deal with fragmentation is *copy*. Copying the contents of a disk file by file from one disk to another or from place to place on a single disk leaves the file in one piece if the disk has enough contiguous free space to hold the file. Using *backup* doesn't help because *backup* makes a mirror image of the disk; each fragmented file is just the same on the new disk as on the old.

17.2.1 FDList

Running *fdlist* (see section 17.12.1) against the file containing the text for this chapter gives the following output:

```
Owner Grp.User: 1.1
File Size: 38080 bytes (37.19k)
Attributes: ------wr
Creation Date: 91/9/23
Last modified: 91/10/6 16:57
(start: $212cd, len: 1)   (start: $2183c, len: 74)
```

This shows that the file is not badly fragmented. It has a segment containing one sector, and another segment containing the rest of the file. The output of
$ dir -e disk.tex

```
 Owner    Last modified    Attributes  Sector  Bytecount  Name
 -------  ---------------  ----------  ------  ---------  ----
   1.1    91/10/06 1657    ------wr    212CC       38080  disk.tex
```

shows that the FD sector for disk.tex is located in the sector before the first data sector for the file. This indicates that they are sharing a cluster.

17.3 Multi-Sector I/O

For ordinary I/O, control passes from RBF, down through the device driver, and back into RBF for each sector. That trip is slow in any case and if it causes the sector interleaving factor to change, it can seriously hurt performance. If it *should* cause the interleaving factor to change but does not, performance will really turn to mush.

Many disk drivers now support multi-sector I/O. This facility lets RBF request a contiguous sequence of disk sectors in one request to the driver. For instance, RBF might request 32 sectors starting at sector 1368, and the driver would deliver them all without further direction from RBF.

17.4 Direct I/O

Buffered I/O is staged through the file manager and the device driver. For instance, a buffered read copies a sector of data from the disk to the buffer attached to the path descriptor. Then the data is copied from the path descriptor buffer to the user's buffer. If the requested data spans more than one sector, the driver is then called to read another sector into the path descriptor buffer, and that is copied and the iteration continues until the requested number of bytes has been copied.

RBF runs much more quickly when it can avoid buffering data in the path descriptor and let the driver access the calling process' buffer directly. It can do that provided the following two conditions are met:

- Direct I/O only works for full sectors of data. This does not mean that the I/O operation must start on a sector boundary and copy an integral number of sectors. RBF buffers partial sectors at the beginning and end of a read or write and lets direct I/O operate on the sectors in the middle.

- The user's buffer must be word aligned. This is a conservative restriction on RBF's part. Some DMA controllers cannot handle unaligned memory. The buffer attached to the path descriptor is always at least 16-byte aligned, so all DMA devices can read or write that buffer, but there is no rule that forces user buffers onto a word boundary, so some DMA hardware fails for some user buffers. In practice, unaligned buffers are rare so RBF and PCF simply check the alignment of addresses passed to them, and buffer I/O to unaligned addresses. RBF and PCF do not have special code to take advantage of the rare DMA controllers that can handle odd addresses.

Direct I/O to the user's buffer is a big performance boost. By itself, it can provide nearly a factor of two improvement. Together with multi-sector I/O, it may improve performance by around a factor of eight for some hardware.

Direct I/O and multisector I/O have the strongest effect when large blocks of data are read or written. If there is sufficient RAM, programs can get an excellent performance boost by reading and writing entire files in one operation:

17.4. DIRECT I/O

```
int readit(name, buffer)
char *name;
char **buffer; {
    int size, n;
    int path;

    if((path = open(name, S_IREAD)) == -1)
        return -1;
    if((size = _gs_size(path)) == -1){
        close(path);
        return -1;
    }
    if((*buffer = malloc(size)) == 0) {
        close(path);
        return -1;
    }
    if((n = read(path, *buffer, size)) != size){
        free(*buffer);
        close(path);
        return -1;
    }
    close(path);
    return size;
}


char *writeit(name, buffer, size, perm)
char *name, *buffer;
int size;
uchar perm;
{
    int n;
    int path;

    if((path = create(name, S_ISIZE + S_IWRITE, perm, size)) == -1)
        if((path = open(name, S_IWRITE)) == -1)
            return -1;
        else
            if(_ss_size(path, size) == -1){
                close(path);
                return(-1);
            }
```

Table 17.1: Supported Sector Sizes

RBF	Hardware
256	256
512	512
1024	1024
2048	2048
4096	4096
8192	
16384	
32768	

```
    if((n = write(path, buffer, size)) != size){
        close(path);
        return −1;
    }
    close(path);
    return buffer;
}
```

17.5 Sector Size

RBF supports several sector sizes (see table 17.1). If the disk driver and hardware also support a variety of sector sizes, you can choose a sector size that tunes your disk performance to your needs.

Sector size is a tradeoff between disk space and speed. In general, I/O speed increases with sector size, but two sectors (one sector for the file descriptor and one for data) is the minimum allocation for a file, and 1000 50-byte files in 4096-byte sectors waste about 8 megabytes of disk space. This kind of profligate waste of disk space may also hurt performance. Disks work fastest when they don't need to seek, and seeks are minimized when as much data as possible is placed on each cylinder. Large amounts of empty space push data onto other cylinders.

Choice of the optimum sector size requires tests with the specific set of files and applications that should be optimized, but there are some useful rules of thumb:

- If you use large files and read and write large buffers, the best sector size is generally the one that fits the most data on the disk. This transfers the most data per rotation of the disk.

- It is fairly easy to use the output of *dir -er* to calculate the amount of disk space a

17.6. ALLOCATION UNITS

Figure 17.1: C Code to Change I/O Buffering

```
Resize(file, size)
FILE *file;
short size;
{
    /* Call this function after the file is opened but before any */
    /* other operation is performed on the file */
    if(size < 0)
        exit(_errmsg(1, "Resize called with size less than 0 (%d)\n",
            size));
    file→_bufsiz = size;
}
```

particular set of files will waste with a particular sector size. (See section 17.12.2.)

- If most of your programs are in C (as are most of the important Microware utilities, like the C compiler) reads and writes use 512-byte buffers. You can change the I/O buffer size for C's I/O library (see figure 17.1), but unless the buffer size is changed only 512- and 256-byte sectors give good performance. Larger sector sizes cannot use direct I/O.

- Large sectors are an easy cure for error 217 (segment list full). A 256-byte sector holds a file descriptor with room for 48 segments, but 512-byte sectors give each file descriptor room for 99 segments. The more segments a file descriptor can describe, the less likely error 217's are.

- Large sectors also increase the maximum possible file size. Since increased sector size increases both the number of segment descriptors in the FD and the maximum number of bytes in each segment, doubling the sector size quadruples the maximum file size.

The easiest rule of thumb is "use 512-byte sectors for hard disks."

17.6 Allocation Units

The number of sectors per cluster is set when a disk is formatted. The command

```
$ format −c=4 /h0fmt
```

formats /h0fmt with 4 sectors per cluster. Cluster size does not affect direct I/O, but it does affect disk fragmentation and may limit the use of multi-sector I/O. Like large sectors, however, large clusters probably waste disk space.

Clusters containing 1024 bytes are a good size for general use on large hard disks. This guarantees that multi-sector I/O can always transfer at least one kilobyte per operation (more if the file isn't fragmented) and it doesn't waste much disk space with a collection of files typical for programming and word processing work. With 512-byte sectors, and two sectors per cluster, the two-sector minimum allocation[2] for a file fits neatly in a cluster.

Segment allocation size is specified by the PD_SAS field in the path descriptor. Large values of PD_SAS are good for performance. They improve multi-sector I/O by decreasing file fragmentation, and large values of PD_SAS do not generally cause wasted disk space. If you have plenty of disk space, set PD_SAS to at least a track... perhaps as much as a cylinder, but in most cases a track is a good value for PD_SAS.

A non-obvious use of PD_SAS is to set the minimum directory allocation. Sectors allocated to directory files are not released until the directory is deleted, consequently directory files are allocated some multiple of PD_SAS sectors.

Programs that have trouble with error 217 (segment list full), should set the file size when the file is created—if they can. If that isn't an option, set the value of PD_SAS for that file very large. A file is given the initial allocation specified in PD_SAS and keeps that allocation until it either grows beyond it, or the file is closed with the file position at the end of the file. If a file is closed with the file position at the end of the file (the normal state after a file is written sequentially), any unused clusters at the end of the file will be freed.

17.6.1 A Case Study

The program *diskspace* (found in section 17.12.2) accepts the output of *dir –ear* (filtered through several instances of *grep*) as input and generates an estimate of the disk space used by the particular files it encounters under various combinations of sector size and cluster size.

On my main hard disk, this program yielded table 17.2. I chose 512-byte sectors and two sectors per cluster. That uses 106% of the space I would have used with 256-byte sectors at one sector per cluster. On my hard disk that is trivial space overhead. Even four 512-byte sectors per cluster would have been quite reasonable, but it would be hard to convince me to use eight sectors per cluster.

Sectors bigger than 512-bytes use too much space for their FD sectors. The 99 segments provided by 512-byte FDs are sufficient for all but exceptionally-fragmented

---

[2]A file descriptor sector and a sector for data.

17.6. ALLOCATION UNITS

Table 17.2: Disk Space Efficiency
The disk contains 98910320 bytes of data or directory storage.
There are 9323 files and directories on the disk.

Sect Size	Sect/ Clus	Data Space	FD Space	Overhead
256	1	97755.5k	2330.8k	100.00%
256	2	98838.2k	2330.8k	101.08%
256	4	101278.3k	2330.8k	103.52%
256	8	106737.3k	2330.8k	108.97%
512	1	99003.5k	4661.5k	103.58%
512	2	101076.5k	4661.5k	105.65%
512	4	106010.5k	4661.5k	110.58%
512	8	117810.5k	4661.5k	122.37%
1024	1	101592.0k	9323.0k	110.82%
1024	2	105261.0k	9323.0k	114.49%
1024	4	115845.0k	9323.0k	125.06%
1024	8	141813.0k	9323.0k	151.01%
2048	1	107246.0k	18646.0k	125.78%
2048	2	113258.0k	18646.0k	131.79%
2048	4	137242.0k	18646.0k	155.75%
4096	1	119880.0k	37292.0k	157.04%
4096	2	129996.0k	37292.0k	167.14%

disks. Taking that view, sectors greater than 512 bytes waste a great deal of space on FDs. For instance, 4096-byte sectors would "waste" about 32 megabytes on my disk.

Throughout the table, going from one-sector clusters to two-sector clusters has a comparatively small penalty. The minimum allocation of one cluster per file, or one sector for data and one sector for the FD causes this. Since every small file (with no more than one sector full of data) uses two sectors in any case, they don't bear any additional cost from a two-sector cluster size.

17.7 Disk Layout

If optimization is very important, the directory entries for the most critical files should be placed early in the directory; otherwise several sectors of directory may have to be read before the right entry is found. This trick is most useful in the execution directory. There are many entries in that directory, and most of the files are small enough that a few extra reads to search through the directory increase the time required to read the file by a noticeable proportion.

For maximum speed, put your most-used files near the beginning of the directory.[3] The best way to do this is to start with an empty directory and copy files into the directory in the order you wish them to appear.

17.8 Disk Caching

RBF disk caching is very useful with floppy disk drives and other slow devices. Its benefits are most obvious with programs that use directories heavily like *dir*, *make*, and *dsave*. It has little influence on programs that chiefly use large reads and writes.

The size of the cache is set when the cache is enabled, but it is always at least 10 kilobytes. The cache is basically a write-through cache with least-recently-used aging. It has two special features that adjust it to RBF: directory data is aged half as fast as other data, and read requests for more than two sectors do not use the cache. Long reads work well from disk. Furthermore, reading a single moderate-size file would flush everything else out of the cache if long reads did not bypass the cache.

The cache's write-through design does not perform as well as a more aggressive caching strategy would, but it is robust. Disk caching can be turned on and off at any time without special ceremonies (like *sync sync sync*).

---

[3]The *dir* command can be deceptive. It normally sorts the directory entries. The result is a list of file names that has no relation to the actual order in the directory file. Use *dir −s* to see the true order of a directory.

A small cache accelerates directory operations nicely on a slow disk drive. A large cache dramatically decreases disk access during typical program development. A disk cache is most effective when combined with defs and libs on a RAM disk.

In systems with light disk contention, high-performance disk drives are barely slower than the disk cache and they use no system RAM. Disk caching offers comparatively small performance improvement with high-performance disk drives, but this is balanced by the comparatively heavy use that high-performance disks get. Even very fast disks in active use on a multi-user system will respond well to a fairly large disk cache.

Time spent searching a very large cache can cause the cache to hurt I/O performance. Like many tuning decisions, the best approach is experimentation. Some interesting configurations are:

- No disk cache and a RAM disk big enough for temporary files.

- The smallest supported disk cache, 10 kilobytes, and a RAM disk big enough for temporary files.

- A 10 kilobyte disk cache and a RAM disk big enough for defs and libraries. This configuration is good when the size of temporary files cannot be predicted.

- A disk cache of up to a megabyte and a RAM disk big enough for temporary files, defs, libraries, spool, and sys.

The first configuration is most memory economical. Configurations further down the list use more memory with diminishing returns.

17.9 Repairing Damage

To recover a damaged or deleted file on disk, you must have a way of reading and modifying selected sectors on disk. Several programs are available to do this, including a program from the OS-9 Users Group and a sample Basic program in the Microware Basic Manual.

If a small file has been erased and you catch it before any files are created or extended, you can recover it. The requirement that the file system remain unchanged from the time the file is deleted until the recovery is complete makes this technique unlikely to work on a multi-user system, or even a system with several active processes. If nothing has happened since the file was deleted, you can probably recover it.

This method for recovering a deleted file depends on internal details of the release 2.4.3 RBF. It does not work with versions of RBF before release 2.2, and it is not absolutely guaranteed to work with future versions.

1. First inspect the directory from which the file came. You should find a directory entry that has the file name of the deleted file in it minus the first and last letters. The first letter was changed to a $00 to indicate that the file was deleted. The last letter isn't a standard ASCII character because the high order bit was set on to mark the last byte in the file name.

2. When you have found the right directory entry, change its first byte back to the first character in the file name.

3. Now the file appears in the directory and is readable. Don't write anything on this disk yet! The sectors that made up the deleted file are still marked as free for use. The next file that gets written to the disk may well use an important part of the file you are trying to rescue.

4. Change your default directory to another disk (perhaps a RAM disk) and run *dcheck −r* on the disk containing the file you wish to recover. *Dcheck* should give error messages about clusters that are allocated to your file but not in the bitmap. Let *dcheck* mark the sectors as allocated.

5. If the previous step doesn't work, a file was probably created or extended before you ran *dcheck*. Give up unless you want to search through all the sectors on your disk pulling out those that contain parts of the file.

6. The disk is now usable.

17.9.1 Recover

The following code recovers a freshly deleted file in the current data directory. It assists with the steps up to 4.

```
#include <stdio.h>
 #include <direct.h>
#include <modes.h>
#include <errno.h>
#include <ctype.h>

#define FALSE 0
#define TRUE 1

main()
{
   int dirpath;                              /* I/O path for directory update */
   struct dirent Entry;
```

17.9. REPAIRING DAMAGE

```
    int ct;                                              /* Count of bytes read per read */
    int location;                                        /* Location in directory */

    stdin→_flag |= _UNBUF;                               /* Request unbuffered input */

    if((dirpath = open(".", S_IFDIR + S_IREAD + S_IWRITE + S_ISHARE)) == -1)
        exit(_errmsg(errno, "Error %d attempting to open . directory\n", errno));
    ct = read(dirpath, &Entry, sizeof(Entry));           /* Priming read */
    location = 0;
    while(ct == sizeof(Entry)){
        /* Is this a deleted file name ?*/
        if(Entry.dir_name[0] == '\0' && (isalnum(Entry.dir_name[1]) ||
               Entry.dir_name[1] == '.' ||
               Entry.dir_name[1] == '-' ||
               Entry.dir_name[1] == '$'))
            if(QRecover(&Entry)){                        /* Yes: do we want to recover it? */
                if(lseek(dirpath, location, 0) == -1)
                    exit(_errmsg(errno,
                        "Error %d seeking to %d in '.'\n",
                        errno, location));
                write(dirpath, &Entry, 1);               /* Write updated part of file name */
                lseek(dirpath, location, 0);             /* Restore file location */
            }
            ct = read(dirpath, &Entry, sizeof(Entry));
            location += sizeof(Entry);
    }
}


QRecover(Entry)
struct dirent *Entry;
{
    int c;

    printf("Erased file name \"?%-.27s\"\n", Entry→dir_name + 1);
    printf("Type <CR> to skip or a valid first character for the recovered file name: ");
    fflush(stdout);
    c = getchar();
    putchar('\n');
    if(c == '\n')
        return FALSE;
    Entry→dir_name[0] = c;                               /* Update file name */
    return TRUE;
}
```

17.10 Using Brute Force

If the consequences of losing a file are so dreadful that it's worth hours of your time to recover it, you can retrieve the data the hard way. This requires two disk drives and takes a lot of time and effort.

This isn't really a trick. It's just a brute force approach to the problem. In essence we're about to treat the entire disk with the deleted file as a single file that includes all the sectors on the disk. You look through all the sectors selecting ones that look like part of the file you want to recover and build a file including all those sectors. Then, using an editor, you put those sectors into the right order.

It's difficult to recognize a chunk out of the middle of an object module, so this approach is mainly useful when the deleted file contained text. The C program *scavenge* (found in section 17.12.3) runs through each sector on the disk named in its command line:

    $ scavenge /d1@

It displays the sector number and the contents of the sector on the screen with the question `Keep this?  (yn)`. If you reply, `Y`, it will copy the sector to a file named recover in your data directory. If you reply `N`, the program goes to the next sector.

It is easy to reject the last sector in a file by mistake. The last sector in a file contains the file's last characters, but the rest of the sector is filled with junk. To prevent the junk from deceiving you, keep your eye on the beginning of each sector.

If you are certain you have retrieved all you want of a file before *scavenge* has worked through the entire disk, abort the program with a keyboard interrupt. You'll spend long enough running *scavenge* without extending the pain!

You won't find a damaged file very often. If you use high-quality diskettes and take good care of them, you may never see a damaged file. The only disks I have had any trouble with are those I received in the mail. The Post Office is the great destroyer of diskettes. Diskettes can only stand so much heat, cold, and folding. Even when a diskette makes it though the Postal filter intact there is a chance for disaster. Your drives may have trouble reading disks created on someone else's drives. Don't give up at the first #244 error. If you can read part of a file, there is a good chance you can get at most of it.

If there is a bad sector somewhere in the file, your best bet is to try to read it several times. If that doesn't work, you'll have to give up on that sector and try to rescue the rest of the file.

17.11 How to Ignore a Bad Sector

You can eliminate a bad sector from a file by fussing with the file descriptor or by copying the file with a program that ignores bad sectors.

The file descriptor describes the location of every sector in a file. A bad sector can be removed from a file by removing the reference to the sector from the file's file descriptor. This leaves the bad sector marked as allocated in the disk's allocation map and will prevent another file from using the sector. The segment of the file that contains the bad sector must be split into two sections with neither containing the bad sector.

Editing a file descriptor sounds (and often *is*) complicated. A special copy program that handles bad sectors as it copies the file is less error-prone than editing an FD's segment list. A robust copy program's only major cost is that it has to copy the file; this is a concern with huge files or when there is insufficient disk space for a second copy of the file.

A sample robust copy program, named *ForceCopy*, can be found in section 17.12.4.

17.12 Programs

Unlike most of the chapters in this book, this chapter uses several programs which generate interesting results but have little educational value in themselves. So instead of interrupting the text, most of the programs for this chapter are collected here.

17.12.1 FDList

The *fdlist* program displays the information from a file's FD sector. In particular, it displays a list of the segments allocated for the file.

```
/*
    FDList
    Usage: fdlist <filename>
*/
#include <stdio.h>
#include <direct.h>
#include <sgstat.h>
#include <errno.h>
#include <modes.h>

#define SEGSPERLINE     3

void *malloc();
```

```c
static short GetSectSize();
static struct fildes * GetFD();
static void OutputFD();
static void OutputAttributes();
static void OutputSegList();

/*
    direct.h does not define a type for segment list entries
    so we have to include one here.
*/
typedef struct {
    unsigned char addr[3];
    unsigned char size[2];
} FDArray;


main(argc, argv)
int argc;
char **argv;
{
    register struct fildes * FDPtr;
    int FilePath;
    unsigned long FileLength;
    short SectSize;


    if(argc != 2)
    exit(_errmsg(1, "needs a file name to select an FD\n"));

    /*
        Open for neither read nor write so we cannot be refused access based
        on file protection. The only chance for an access violation is directory
        files. They are handled separately.
    */
    if((FilePath = open(argv[1], 0)) == -1)
    /*Handle directory files */
    /*Error != E_FNA means opening with dir-mode won't help */
    if(errno != E_FNA ||
    (FilePath = open(argv[1], S_IFDIR)) == -1)
    exit(_errmsg(errno, "error %d opening %s\n",
    errno, argv[1]));

    SectSize = GetSectSize(FilePath, argv[1]);
```

17.12. PROGRAMS

213

```
    FDPtr = GetFD(FilePath, SectSize, argv[1]);


    FileLength = (unsigned char)FDPtr→fd_fsize[3] +
    256 * ((unsigned char)FDPtr→fd_fsize[2] +
    256 * ((unsigned char)FDPtr→fd_fsize[1] +
    256 * (unsigned char)FDPtr→fd_fsize[0]));


    OutputFD(FDPtr, (SectSize − 16) / 5, FileLength);

    free(FDPtr);
    close(FilePath);
    exit(0);
}


static short GetSectSize(FilePath, FileName)
int FilePath;
char *FileName;

{
    struct sgbuf PathOptions;

    if(_gs_opt(FilePath, &PathOptions) == −1)
    exit(_errmsg(errno, "error %d getting options for %s\n",
    errno, FileName));
    return PathOptions.sg_sctsiz;
}


static struct fildes * GetFD(FilePath, SectSize, FileName)
int FilePath;
short SectSize;
char *FileName;
{
    struct fildes *FDPtr;

    if((FDPtr = malloc(SectSize)) == NULL)
    exit(_errmsg(errno, "cannot allocate a sector buffer\n"));
    if((_gs_gfd(FilePath, FDPtr, SectSize)) == −1)
    exit(_errmsg(errno, "cannot get FD sector for %s. Error %d\n",
    FileName, errno));
```

```
       return FDPtr;
}


static void OutputFD(FDPtr, segs, FileLength)
register struct fildes *FDPtr;
int segs;
unsigned long FileLength;
{
   char K[16];

   /*Link count is almost always 1, so only output it if it's not 1  */
   if(FDPtr→fd_link != 1)
   printf("Link count: %u\n", (unsigned char)FDPtr→fd_link);

   printf("Owner Grp.User: %d.%d\n", FDPtr→fd_own[0], FDPtr→fd_own[1]);

   if(FileLength > 1024)
   sprintf(K, " (%.2fk)", (double)FileLength/1024.0);
   else
   K[0] = '\0';
   printf("File Size: %u bytes%s\n", FileLength, K);

   OutputAttributes(FDPtr→fd_att);

   printf("Creation Date: %d/%d/%d\n",
   FDPtr→fd_dcr[0],
   FDPtr→fd_dcr[1],
   FDPtr→fd_dcr[2]);

   printf("Last modified: %d/%d/%d %d:%2d\n",
   FDPtr→fd_date[0], FDPtr→fd_date[1],
   FDPtr→fd_date[2], FDPtr→fd_date[3],
   FDPtr→fd_date[4]);

   OutputSegList(segs, FDPtr→fdseg);
}


static void OutputAttributes(Test)
unsigned char Test;
{
   char *bits = "dsewrewr";
   unsigned char mask;
```

17.12. PROGRAMS

```
        printf("Attributes: ");
        for(mask = 0x080; *bits; mask >>= 1, ++bits)
        if((Test & mask) == 0)
        putchar('-');
        else
        putchar(*bits);
        putchar('\n');
}

static void OutputSegList(segs, SegPtr)
register FDArray *SegPtr;
int segs; /*Number of segments in array */
{
    int segment;
    unsigned short Length;
    unsigned long FirstSector;
    int SegsOnLine;
    char outstr[64];

    for(segment=0; segment < segs; ++segment){
        FirstSector = SegPtr[segment].addr[2] +
        256 * (SegPtr[segment].addr[1] +
        256 * SegPtr[segment].addr[0]);

        Length = SegPtr[segment].size[1] +
        256 * SegPtr[segment].size[0];
        if(Length == 0)
        break;

        sprintf(outstr, "(start: $%x, len: %u)",
        FirstSector, Length);

        if(++SegsOnLine == 4){
            SegsOnLine = 0;
            printf("%s\n", outstr);
        } else
        printf("%-25s", outstr);
    }
    if(SegsOnLine != 0)
    putchar('\n');
}
```

17.12.2 DiskSpace

```c
#include <stdio.h>
/*
    Diskspace

    Pipe the output of
        dir -ear ! grep -v "-eDirectory of" ! grep -v "-e- -" ! grep -v "-et m"
    to this filter.
    The pipe of grep filters will leave only lines with information
    about files and blank lines.

    Diskspace ignores two factors that use disk space:
        Format overhead: sector 0, the allocation map,
        and the root directory.

        Pre-extended files, particularly directories.
        (directories are all at least <segment allocation size>
        sectors in size.)

*/

#define PROPOSALS 17

struct {
    short SectorSize;
    short ClusterSize;
} Proposal[PROPOSALS] = {
    256, 1, /*Must be here */
    256, 2, 256, 4,
    256, 8, 512, 1,
    512, 2, 512, 4,
    512, 8, 1024, 1,
    1024, 2, 1024, 4,
    1024, 8, 2048, 1,
    2048, 2, 2048, 4,
4096, 1, 4096, 2};

unsigned long FileCt = 0;
unsigned long ByteCt = 0;
unsigned long DataSpace[PROPOSALS];
unsigned long FDSpace[PROPOSALS];

unsigned long GetSize();
```

17.12. PROGRAMS

```
main(argc, argv)
int argc;
char **argv;
{
    char line[256];
    unsigned long Size;

    stdout→_flag |= _UNBUF;

    ParseArgs(argc, argv);

    Initialize();

    while(gets(line) != NULL){
        if(*line == '\0') /*a blank line */
            continue;
        Size = GetSize(line);
        AccumulateSize(Size);
        /*
            This program might run for a long time.
            Make a reassuring "exclamation point."
        */
        if((FileCt % 50) == 0)
            putchar('.');
    }

    PrintResults();
    exit(0);
}


ParseArgs(argc, argv)
int argc;
char **argv;
{
}


Initialize()
{
    register int i;

    for(i=0; i<PROPOSALS; ++i){
        DataSpace[i] = 0;
```

```
         FDSpace[i] = 0;
   }
}


unsigned long GetSize(line)
char *line;
{
   int n;
   short Group, User, Year, Month, Day, Time;
   char Attributes[9];
   char Name[32];
   unsigned long FDSector;
   unsigned long Bytes;

   n = sscanf(line, " %hd.%hd %hd/%hd/%hd %hd %s %lx %ld %s",
      &Group, &User,
      &Year, &Month, &Day,
      &Time, Attributes, &FDSector,
      &Bytes, Name);
   if(n != 10){
      _errmsg(1, "Trouble finding file size.  Only %d fields parsed\n", n);
      return 0;
   }
   return Bytes;
}


AccumulateSize(Size)
{
   unsigned long Clusters, Sectors;
   register int i;

   ++FileCt;
   ByteCt += Size;

   for(i=0; i<PROPOSALS; ++i){
      /*At least one full cluster is allocated to the file.  */
      Sectors = (Size + Proposal[i].SectorSize − 1) /          /* ⌈Size/ SectSize⌉ */
         Proposal[i].SectorSize;
      Sectors++;                                                /* To a sector for the FD */
      Clusters = (Sectors + Proposal[i].ClusterSize − 1) /
         Proposal[i].ClusterSize;
      FDSpace[i] += Proposal[i].SectorSize;
```

17.12. PROGRAMS

```
            DataSpace[i] += ((Clusters * Proposal[i].ClusterSize - 1) *
                    Proposal[i].SectorSize);
    }
}


PrintResults()
{
    register int i;

    printf("\nThere are %u bytes of data or directory info on the disk.\n", ByteCt);
    printf("There are %u files and directories on the disk.\n\n", FileCt);

    printf("Sect Sect/ Data FD Overhead\n");
    printf("Size Clus Space Space percent\n");
    for(i=0; i<PROPOSALS; ++i){
        printf("%4d %4d %12.1fk %11.1fk %6.2f\n",
            Proposal[i].SectorSize,
            Proposal[i].ClusterSize,
            (double)DataSpace[i]/1024.0,
            (double)FDSpace[i]/1024.0,
            100.0 * ((double)(DataSpace[i] + FDSpace[i]) /
            (double)(DataSpace[0] + FDSpace[0])));
    }
}
```

17.12.3 Scavenge

This version of *scavenge* is a crude program. You may want to modify it to suit your needs. For instance, the SECT_SIZE constant might need a different value.

Scavenge works on ordinary files,[4] but only user 0 can use it on a raw device. Raw disks can only be read beyond sector zero by user 0.

```
/* scavenge */
#include <stdio.h>
#include <direct.h>
#include <modes.h>
#include <errno.h>
#include <ctype.h>

#define FALSE 0
```

---

[4] It's not clear that running *scavenge* against an ordinary file would serve any useful purpose.

```c
#define TRUE 1

#define REC_FILE "recover"
#define SECT_SIZE 256

main(argc, argv)
int argc;
char **argv;
{
    int diskpath;
    FILE *recover;
    char sector[SECT_SIZE];
    int This, c;

    /* Call for unbuffered I/O on standard input */
    stdin→_flag |= _UNBUF;

    /* Open the input file */
    if((diskpath = open(argv[1], S_IREAD)) == -1)
        exit(_errmsg(errno, "Error %d when opening %s\n",
            errno, argv[1]));

    /* Open the output file */ /*/
    if((recover = fopen(REC_FILE, "w")) == NULL)
        exit(_errmsg(errno, "Error %d opening %s\n",
            errno, REC_FILE));

    for(This = 0; GetSector(diskpath, This, sector); ++This){
        DisplaySector(This, sector);
        printf("\nKeep this? (yn) ");
        fflush(stdout);
        while((c = toupper(getchar())) != 'Y' && c != 'N');
        if(c == 'Y')
            if(fwrite(sector, SECT_SIZE, 1, recover) != 1)
                exit(_errmsg(errno, "Error %d writing %s\n",
                    errno, REC_FILE));
    }
    close(diskpath);
    fclose(recover);
    exit(0);
}
```

17.12. PROGRAMS

```
/* Get a specified sector from the input file */
GetSector(path, sect_number, sector)
int path;
int sect_number;
char *sector;
{
   if((lseek(path, sect_number * SECT_SIZE, 0)) == -1)
      if(errno == E_EOF)
         return FALSE;
      else
         exit(_errmsg(errno,
            "Error %d seeking to %d in source disk\n",
            errno, sect_number * SECT_SIZE));
   if(read(path, sector, SECT_SIZE) == -1)
      if(errno == E_EOF)
         return FALSE;
      else
         exit(_errmsg(errno,
            "Error %d in read of source disk\n",
            errno));
   return TRUE;
}


/*
   Display a sector in ascii and hexadecimal (like dump)
*/
DisplaySector(sect_number, sector)
int sect_number;
char *sector;
{
   int i;
   printf("\n Sector Number: %d\n", sect_number);
   for(i = 0; i < SECT_SIZE; i += 16){
      HexOut(sector + i);
      putchar('\t');
      CharOut(sector + i);
      putchar('\n');
   }
}
```

```
/*
    Print a 16-byte array of bytes in hexadecimal
*/
HexOut(s)
char *s;
{
    int i;
    for(i=0; i<16; i += 2)
        printf("%02x%02x ", s[i] & 0x0ff, s[i+1] & 0x0ff);
}


/*
    Print a 16-byte array of characters in ascii, displaying
    non-printable characters as dots.
*/
CharOut(s)
char *s;
{
    int i;
    for(i=0; i<16; ++i)
        if(isprint(s[i]))
            putchar(s[i]);
        else
            putchar('.');
}
```

17.12.4 ForceCopy

The following program skips bad sectors while copying a file.

```
/* ForceCopy */
#include <stdio.h>
#include <modes.h>
#include <direct.h>
#include <sgstat.h>
#include <errno.h>

#define TRUE        1
#define FALSE       0
#define RETRIES     4

typedef enum { Retry, Abort, OK, End} Codes;
```

17.12. PROGRAMS

```
/*
    Variables known throughout this file.
*/
static char *InFile = NULL, *OutFile = NULL;
static int InPath;
static int OutPath;
static int RetryCt=RETRIES;
static int Try=RETRIES;
static unsigned long Location=0;
static struct fildes InFDBuffer;           /*Shared by OpenFiles() and CleanUp() */
/*
    Declarations of functions
*/
void *malloc();
static Codes Read();
static Codes Write();
static Codes ForceRead();

main(argc, argv)
int argc;
char **argv;
{
    int SectorSize;
    unsigned char *buffer;
    int Length;

    /*
        Prepare
    */
    ParseArgs(argc, argv);
    OpenFiles();
    SectorSize = GetSectorSize(InPath);
    if((buffer = malloc(SectorSize)) == NULL)
        exit(_errmsg(errno, "cannot allocate %d bytes for sector buffer\n",
            SectorSize));

    /*
        Main loop
    */
    do{                                           /*Read/Write loop */
        do                               /*Repeat seek-read several times if required */
            Seek(InPath, Location);
        while(ForceRead(InPath, buffer, SectorSize, &Length) == Retry);
```

```
        if(Length > 0){                                            /* If not end of file */
            Location += Length;
            Write(OutPath, buffer, Length);
        }
    }while(Length > 0);
}


static ParseArgs(argc, argv)
int argc;
char **argv;
{
    register char *ptr;
    if(argc != 3){
        Usage();
        exit(0);
    }

    /*
        This version of ParseArgs is a bit heavy-weight
        for what's required here, but this makes it easy
        to add options later.
    */
    for(++argv ; *argv; ++argv){
        ptr = *argv;
        if(*ptr == '-')
            for(++ptr; *ptr; ++ptr)
                switch(*ptr){
                    case '?':
                    default:
                        Usage();
                        exit(0);
                }
        else if(InFile == NULL)                                    /* There's no - */
            InFile = ptr;
        else if(OutFile == NULL)
            OutFile = ptr;
        else
            exit(_errmsg(0, "Too many file names\n"));
    }
}
```

17.12. PROGRAMS

```
static OpenFiles()
{
    int InSize;

    /*
        Open the input file,
        Create the output file,
        and give it the input file's length.
        Don't clone grp.user or protection attributes yet;
        they might prevent this program from writing the file.
    */
    if((InPath = open(InFile, 1)) == -1)
        exit(_errmsg(errno, "error %d opening %s\n",
            errno, InFile));
    if(_gs_gfd(InPath, &InFDBuffer, 32) == -1)
        exit(_errmsg(errno, "error %d getting file descriptor of %s\n",
            errno, InFile));
    InSize = InFDBuffer.fd_fsize[3] + 256 
        (InFDBuffer.fd_fsize[2] + 256 
        (InFDBuffer.fd_fsize[1] + 256 * InFDBuffer.fd_fsize[0]));
    if((OutPath = creat(OutFile, S_IWRITE)) == -1)
        exit(_errmsg(errno, "error %d creating %s\n",
            errno, OutFile));
    if(_ss_size(OutPath, InSize) == -1)
        exit(_errmsg(errno, "error %d setting the size of %s\n",
            errno, OutFile));
}


static Seek(InPath, Location)
int InPath;
unsigned long Location;
{
    if(lseek(InPath, Location, 0) == -1)
        exit(_errmsg(errno, "Error %d seeking to %u in %s\n",
            errno, Location, InFile));
}


/*
    Read with some error recovery.
*/
static Codes ForceRead(InPath, buffer, SectorSize, Length)
int InPath, SectorSize, *Length;
```

```
unsigned char *buffer;
{
    switch(Read(InPath, buffer, SectorSize, Length)){
        case Retry:
            if(――Try <= 0){
                /* We cannot read this */
                AnnounceError(Location);
                PatchSector(buffer, SectorSize, Length);
                return OK;
            }else{                                                      /* try again */
                _ss_rest(InPath);
                return Retry;
            }
        case OK:
            Try = RetryCt;
            return OK;
        case End:
            CleanUp();
            exit(0);
        case Abort:
        default:
            _errmsg(errno, "Error %d on read\n", errno);
            CleanUp();
            exit(0);
    }
}


/*
    Read with error detection and analysis
*/
static Codes Read(InPath, buffer, SectorSize, Length)
int InPath;
char *buffer;
int SectorSize;
int *Length;
{
    *Length = read(InPath, buffer, SectorSize);
    if(*Length == ―1)
        switch(errno){
            case E_EOF:
                *Length = 0;
                return End;
                break;
```

17.12. PROGRAMS

```
            case E_SECT:
            case E_CRC:
            case E_READ:
            case E_NOTRDY:
            case E_SEEK:
                *Length = 0;
                return Retry;
                break;
            default:
                *Length = 0;
                return Abort;
        }
    else if(*Length == 0)
        return End;
    else
        return OK;
}



/*
    write() enhanced with error detection and
    quit in case of an error.
*/
static Codes Write(OutPath, buffer, SectorSize)
int OutPath;
char *buffer;
int SectorSize;
{
    if(write(OutPath, buffer, SectorSize) == -1)
        exit(_errmsg(errno, "Error %d writing %s\n", errno, OutFile));
    else
        return OK;
}




static AnnounceError(Location)
unsigned long Location;
{
    _errmsg(0, "Patching bad sector at %u in %s\n",
        Location, InFile);
}
```

```
/*
    Copy the last byte of the last sector successfully read throughout this buffer.
*/
PatchSector(buffer, SectorSize, Length)
register char *buffer;
register int SectorSize;
int *Length;
{
    register char c;
    register int i;

    c = buffer[SectorSize − 1];
    for(i = SectorSize; i > 0; −−i)
        *buffer++ = c;
    *Length = SectorSize;
}


/*
    Set the grp.user, last modified date, and protection
    attributes of the output file to the the same values as
    the input file.  Then close the files.
*/
static CleanUp()
{
    if(_ss_pfd(OutPath, &InFDBuffer) == −1)
        exit(_errmsg(errno, "error %d writing the fd of %s\n",
            errno, OutFile));
    if(_ss_attr(OutPath, InFDBuffer.fd_att) == −1)
        exit(_errmsg(errno, "error %d setting the permissions of %s\n",
            errno, OutFile));
    close(InPath);
    close(OutPath);
}


static GetSectorSize(InPath)
{
    struct sgbuf buffer;

    if(_gs_opt(InPath, &buffer) == −1)
        exit(_errmsg(errno, "Error %d in gs_opt for %s\n",
            errno, InFile));
    return buffer.sg_ssize;
}
```

17.12. PROGRAMS

```
static Usage()
{
    static char *Message[ ] = {
        "forcecopy",
        "usage: forcecopy [-?] <from_file> <to_file>",
        "\t-?\tdeliver this message",
        NULL
    };
    register char **ptr;

    for(ptr=Message; *ptr; ++ptr)
        fprintf(stderr, "%s\n", *ptr);
}
```

Chapter 18

Customizing OS-9

> *The ultimate descriptor in OS-9 is the init module. You can think of it as the OS-9 descriptor.*

18.1   The Init Module

The OS-9 coldstart code consults init. Fields in init tell the coldstart how much memory to allocate for internal tables. Initial values for the scheduler come from init. The name of the first program to run, an initial default directory, and the device it should use for the standard I/O paths are also in init.

Most of the fields in init provide ways to make small adjustments to OS-9. You can adjust it to fit the size of your system, and tune it a little by fiddling with init. The init module is not, however, limited to subtle adjustments. The module-name fields, M$SysGo and M$Extens, can change OS-9 in fundamental ways.

18.2   SysGo

The SysGo module is the best understood and most modified of these modules. It is the first non-system module to be executed, and it's responsible for maintaining the user interface. *SysGo* usually forks a shell to run the startup file. When startup is done, *SysGo* enters a loop in which it forks a shell, waits for it to terminate, then goes back and starts the shell again. This provides a safety net under the shell. If the shell terminates, *SysGo* will start a new shell immediately. This is not an excessive precaution. Users frequently terminate the shell accidentally. If a user hits the <eof> key by mistake while he's in the shell, the shell will clean up and exit.

The behavior of an OS-9 system can be changed drastically by replacing *SysGo* entirely, or altering *SysGo* so it starts some program other than the shell. Since the shell forms a user's view of OS-9, replacing it with some other program can make OS-9 seem entirely different. This is a useful option for people who run OS-9 for some specific task. *SysGo* can start that task when the system is coldstarted without messing with startup or the shell.

18.3 The Customization Modules

System state is a special, privileged state of both OS-9 and the processor processor. Some 68000 instructions can only be issued when the processor is in system (supervisor) state, and some OS-9 functions can only be used when OS-9 is in system state. The processor enters system state when it gets an exception (a hardware interrupt, a *trap* instruction or an execution exception such as a bus error or divide-by-zero). The exception transfers control to the OS-9 kernel and enters system state. System state remains in effect until the kernel returns control to a non-system process. The kernel and all the other components of the operating system are only executed in system state.

Any module can run in system state by requesting it in the module header's attribute byte. This is, however, insufficient for many purposes.

- A programmer may need a task accomplished early in the system-startup process.

- If the system code includes a SVC, it must not be removed from memory.

- Modules outside the operating system itself should not alter operating system structures.

The customization modules are system modules. They are called by the kernel as the last part of the coldstart process but before the first process is started, and can do anything the kernel can. Most things that a module might do before any programs are running aren't interesting. A customization module is mainly used to install new supervisor service requests (SVCs). The name of a customization module should be placed in the M$Extens field in the init module.

A customization module should execute the few statements necessary to issue a *F$SSvc* SVC, then exit. The bulk of the module should consist of new SVCs that you can use later. Supervisor services that are provided by the customization module have all the privileges of other SVCs.

Special SVCs installed by a customization module should avoid SVC numbers that OS-9 uses or is likely to use. At this time, the defined SVCs run up to 83, then skip to 128 for the I/O SVC's which end at 147. You could use any unused numbers for

18.3. THE CUSTOMIZATION MODULES

your new SVC's, but it would probably be a good idea to leave a wide margin after the nearest standard SVC. Starting at 200 might leave a safe margin.

OS-9 may require several levels of customization, so the coldstart code is able to run any number of customization modules. Provided that they don't clash in some way like redefining a SVC, there is no difficulty with this. The names of the customization modules can be concatenated in M$Extens with spaces or carriage returns between the module names, and a null to terminate the string. OS-9 calls the modules in the order they are named.

Chapter 19

Building a Device Descriptor

Device descriptors are OS-9's reference material for I/O devices. In this chapter we will talk about how they are constructed and what they do.

There is a device descriptor for every I/O device in an OS-9 system. As the name implies, each descriptor describes the attributes of a device. They each contain a description of the hardware for a device and other information specific to it. A new terminal port or graphics card will need a new device descriptor. Sometimes, just changing the type of terminal attached to a serial port requires some changes to the descriptor for that port.

Device descriptors contain all that OS-9 needs to know about a device. All device descriptors have some basic information in common: the address of the device, the interrupt vector it uses, the IRQ (interrupt) level and priority, which file manager to use with it, what device driver to use with it, which access modes are valid for the device, and what it is named. Also, there is always a place for a table, called the initialization table, which contains information that the file manager and device driver might find useful.

The contents of the initialization table vary from one kind of device to another. Devices that use the Random Block File manager (e.g., disk drives) have information like the device's stepping rate and the number of sectors per track. The initialization table for devices that use the Sequential Character File manager contains a list of editing characters, baud rate information, the number of lines on a page, and other similar information. A pipe device descriptor only has a device type (PIPE) and the default pipe buffer size in its initialization table.

19.1 How OS-9 Uses the Descriptor

When you first open a path to a device, OS-9 (the IOMan component) refers to the device descriptor. It has to start at the device descriptor because all it has is the name of the device you want to use. The descriptor gives IOMan the names of the file manager and device driver that it should use. If the device is uninitialized, IOMan attaches the device and calls the device driver's init routine with a pointer to the device descriptor.

For all *I$Open* system calls IOMan builds a path descriptor for the new path and copies much of the information contained in the device descriptor into the path descriptor. Then IOMan hands the request to the appropriate file manager with the address of the path descriptor.

A file manager has access to all the information in the path descriptor, but it ignores the device-specific path options. There is no rule governing what the file manager can use, but it generally avoids data that is specific to the I/O device, such as its port-address. The file manager uses the device driver named in the device descriptor to do physical-I/O operations. The driver reads values that might depend on the specific device from the device descriptor and the path descriptor. Some of the values device drivers read from the device descriptor are the device address, baud rate, stepping rate, and parity.

19.1.1 The /dd Device

Various utility programs work best if they know the name of the device that contains the various system directories; such as DEFS, SYS, SPOOL, and LIBS. Programs can run through a litany of common device names—/h0, /d0, /r0—but it is faster for the program and more predictable for the system administrator to always have a device named /dd. By convention, /dd is the default device, and programs will look there first for special directories.

The selection of a default device is confusing. System-related code (like *login*) usually selects the default device named in the init module. Other utility programs usually look for directories in the current directory and on /dd, then on various conventional disk device names; e.g., /h0, /d0, and /r0.

You can name any disk /dd even if it has another name. The /dd device descriptor is usually made by changing the device name from either h0 or d0 to dd. No other change is required. It is a fine idea to have /dd and another device descriptor for the same device both loaded and attached at the same time. IOMan will understand that the two descriptors refer to the same device and will treat them like one device.

19.2 Managing Device Descriptors

The device descriptors that come with your system should be adequate to describe your hardware. If the company that sold you the system is doing its job, you will find that your copy of OS-9 has more device descriptors than you need. You may also find a directory of alternate descriptors somewhere on your distribution disk.

OS-9 usually comes with device descriptors for all the hardware you might have. This probably includes surplus disk drive descriptors and terminal device descriptors. If your boot file contains descriptors for floppy drives /d0 through /d3 and you only have one disk drive, the space used for the /d1, /d2, and /d3 descriptors is wasted. You can remove unneeded descriptors by building a new bootstrap without them. If you save the modules on disk, you can load them if you ever need them.

Unless a device is hardly used at all, it is best to include its descriptor in the boot file. If you include a module in the boot file you can be certain that it will be packed into memory as efficiently as possible, and won't disappear if you unlink it by mistake. Also, the error messages you get when you try to use a device whose descriptor isn't in memory are sometimes hard to understand. I always seem to have trouble with missing descriptors when I am four or five hours overdue for bed. At times like that I only understand the simplest error messages. Sometimes I have gotten myself into a bit of a panic before I realized that the device descriptor was sitting safe on disk.

19.3 Making and Modifying Descriptors

It is sometimes a matter of judgment whether to generate a new device descriptor or use one that you already have. If you have a new serial card, disk controller, or whatever, you will definitely have to make a device descriptor for it. The device address isn't something you can change after a file has been opened. However, small changes to a device's configuration can be accomplished with little effort.

Information in the initialization table can be changed with the *I$SetStt* service request. The change isn't actually made to the device descriptor, just to the path descriptor's copy of the initialization table. If you aren't certain you want to make the change permanent, this is the way to do it.

If you choose to go the *I$SetStt* route you still have a few choices. You can do it all by yourself with a piece of code like:

```
        moveq   #0,D0           Standard input path number
        moveq   #SS_Opt,D1      Select the Read option getstat
        lea     OptBuff(A7),A0  Point at 32-byte buffer
        OS9     I$GetStt        Issue SVC
        bcs     IOError         If error; deal with it
```

```
***************
* Just by way of example let's turn on XOn/XOff
*
        move.b  #$11,PD_XON-PD_OPT(A0)  XOn
        move.b  #$13,PD_XOFF-PD_OPT(A0) XOff
        moveq   #SS_Opt,D1      SetStat
***************
* D0 and A0 are still set from the previous call
*
        OS9     I$SetStt        issue the SVC
        bcs     IOError
***************
* All set
```

If you mean to change the characteristics of a device in the middle of a program, a *I$SetStt* is surely the way to do it; but, since the change is only to the path descriptor, the change will go away when the path closes. Even this isn't as simple as it seems. The standard I/O paths are all "dups." The *I$Dup* call is used to give the same path several path numbers. All three standard I/O paths often use the same system path descriptor. Since standard I/O paths are inherited when a process is forked, the change made in this program is passed to the shell (or whatever program forked this one), and perhaps back through several generations. Clearly, path descriptors should be changed cautiously.

Still, the path will eventually be closed, and when that happens your change will go away. If that's fine with you and the device to change is an SCF device, there is an easy OS-9 command, *tmode,* which does just this kind of setstat for you. You can turn on XOn/XOff from the shell before starting a program and not have to worry about writing the setstat into it. I assume that you have used ***tmode*** by now; if you haven't, do it soon. There are some values that you can fool with without causing great trouble. Try turning echo off:

    $ tmode noecho

When you are convinced that its no fun typing without seeing the results turn echo back on:

    $ tmode echo

It's also useful to experiment with pause.

19.3.1 Xmode

If you want to make the change a little more permanent, you have to change the device descriptor. The ***xmode*** command makes changes to the initialization table in

19.3. MAKING AND MODIFYING DESCRIPTORS

the device descriptor instead of the copy in the path descriptor. Unlike *tmode*, it can be used to change the attributes of a device that isn't on one of the shell's standard paths, but like *tmode, xmode* only works with SCF devices. The syntax of *xmode* looks a lot like *tmode,* but they act on different control blocks. *Tmode* takes effect immediately but may not have a permanent effect. *Xmode* only takes effect when a new path to that device is opened, but the change continues in effect for every path opened to that device until OS-9 is rebooted or something else is done to alter the device descriptor.

If you don't have *xmode* you can still change device descriptors on the fly. *Debug* changes device descriptors as easily as it changes any other type of module (although it would be hard to change path descriptors with it). *Debug* can change anything about the descriptor, including the device address and the access mode—values that can't be altered by *xmode*.

19.3.2 Debug

You've got to keep your wits about you when you use *debug*. There is nothing to protect you from yourself. If you feel any doubt about it, plan out what you will do before you start. The following is a script for changing the device address for the device descriptor "/t2":

```
$ debug
dbg: l t2                            link to /t2
dbg: d1 .r7+30                       display the port address
00000030+r7 - 00FF 80A0 1B03 0323 0064 0068 0000 0000
dbg: c1 .r7+30                       change the port address
00000030+r7:00FF80A0 00FF80a4        to 00ff80a4
00000034+r7:1B030323 .               end of changes
dbg: q                               done with debugger
```

This is sufficient if you don't want to save the descriptor for another session. If you do want to save this modified version of /T2, you need to update its CRC bytes. *Debug* changed a byte in the module, and when it is next loaded OS-9 will reject it because the CRC will indicate that the module is flawed. The *fixmod* command will repair the CRC:

```
$ save t2 −f=new.t2
$ fixmod −u new.t2
```

One problem still remains. There are now two /T2 modules. One in the boot file, the other in the file new.t2. If we leave things just the way they are, there won't be any way to use the new /T2.

The version of /T2 in the boot can't be removed from memory by unlinking it. All modules in the boot are protected from that. It could be replaced by a module with a higher revision number, but the new version of /T2 we made has the same revision number.

There are two approaches we can take. If we really mean to change the address of /T2, the /T2 module in the boot file will have to be replaced. This can be done with *os9gen*.

The usual reason for changing the device address in a device descriptor is that there is a new port that needs a descriptor. In that case, what we really needed was a device descriptor with a new name as well as a new device address. *Debug* can be used to change the name as well as the address provided that the new name is no longer than the old one. The following *debug* statements could have been included at the end of the *debug* script for changing the address. They change the module name from T2 to T5:

```
$ debug
dbg: d1 .r7+[.r7+c]1                  display the module name
00000070+r7 - 7432 0000 005E 396C 4AFC 0001 0000 0078
dbg: c .r7+71                         change the module name
00000071+r7:32 35                     change 2 to 5
00000072+r7:00 .                      done with changes
```

If the module name needs lengthening, this trick won't work. In fact, this method is altogether too cumbersome for most purposes. The only time I use it is when I want to experiment with a modified device descriptor without making any permanent changes.

19.3.3 Module Permissions

If you have SSM, device descriptors are typically read-only. *Xmode, debug,* and every other tool that can modify modules in memory will fail with a bus error or some other error. The device descriptor must be made writable before it can be updated. This can be done with *fixmod* before the module is loaded, or when the module is created. Module permissions cannot be changed after the module is loaded.

19.3.4 Moded

Moded can modify all types of descriptor modules in disk files—system init modules as well as all types of device descriptors. It itemizes the fields in a module and lets you change them. It may even provide help with information about the meaning of each field. The advantages of *moded* are:

- It is easy to use.

- It provides a little protection against improper modification of a module.

- It can modify a module in a file that contains many modules; like a boot file.

Moded is not the perfect tool for module maintenance. It cannot change the length of a module name or modify a module in RAM. It is also unable to even limp through a module type that is not described in the moded.fields file. Since adding a new module type to moded.fields is a serious chore, *moded* is not a tool you'll want to use for a quick fix to a module type that isn't already defined.

Moded is a *great* way to modify things like the default process table size in the boot file version of init, or the stepping rate capability of a disk descriptor in the boot file. Before *moded* was available, *os9gen* was the recommended tool for such modifications. Now simple changes to modules in the boot file are easy to make.

19.4 Building a Descriptor From Scratch

The most powerful, and sometimes the easiest, way to create a device descriptor is with an editor and assembler. Choose the descriptor from the back of the *OS-9 Technical Manual* that is closest to what you need, type it in, making whatever changes are necessary to fit it to your needs, and assemble it. You can also find files in your SYSSRC directory that can make new descriptors with little or no typing. You can test the new descriptor by loading it into memory with the *load* command, and doing some I/O to it. If it doesn't perform as you hoped it would, use *unlink* to remove it from memory and try again. Don't build a new boot file including the new device descriptor until you are certain it is correct; it's much harder to build a new boot than it is to use *unlink* and *load* to replace a module that isn't part of the boot.

19.5 The Contents of a Device Descriptor

The values in the device descriptor are all important constants. They are covered in several other places in this book, but perhaps it would do no harm to run through them all together.

The device descriptor starts like any other module—with a module header. The only special part of the module header is the type/language field. The type is $F0, a type set aside for device descriptors. The language is $00, language unspecified.

Following the module header is the port address of the device. The port address is that memory address at which its I/O hardware can be reached. Since 68000-family processors use memory-mapped I/O, all devices have at least one reserved location in memory.

OS-9 can deal with I/O hardware that isn't interrupt-driven, but it works best when the devices use interrupts to indicate that they need service. The 68000-family of processor supports seven levels of interrupts, each of which might be caused by a list of devices. If there are several possible sources for an interrupt, OS-9 checks each possibility. More elaborate hardware can give the address of the routine that should handle each interrupt. Interrupts from those devices are called vectored interrupts.

The three fields after the port address have to do with interrupt service. The IRQ vector field tells OS-9 which interrupt vector to expect the device to use. Since the higher vectors are for vectored interrupts, this field also tells OS-9 whether the interrupt is vectored or not (although it really doesn't make any difference in the way the interrupt is handled). The interrupt level field tells the driver which hardware interrupt line the device will use. The driver uses this value to mask interrupts to the level of the device. The polling priority is used when several devices share an interrupt vector. Devices with lower priority numbers are placed before devices with higher priority numbers on the list of devices to check when an interrupt arrives.

Then comes the mode byte for this device. This byte can have any of the values used as file access modes:

read	$01
write	$02
execute	$04
public read	$08
public write	$10
public execute	$20
adjust size	$20
shareable	$40
directories	$80

These access mode bits are treated like the attributes of a disk file. When a process opens or creates a file on a device, the device's mode byte is checked to ensure that the device supports the access mode that the process requests.

The next field is the offset from the beginning of the module to the name of the file manager for this device (SCF, RBF, PipeMan, NFM, or whatever). Next is the offset from the start of the module to the name of the device driver for this device (sc68230, rbm20o, etc.).

The next field is the offset to a device-dependent value called the Device Configuration Offset. This could be any value that is convenient to store in a device descriptor. For instance, the device configuration field has been used to store offsets into I/O globals, the names of related modules and events, and device initialization commands.

After the eleven reserved bytes are two bytes that hold the length of the device's initialization table followed by the table. The first byte in every initialization table indicates the class of device the descriptor is for: SCF, RBF, Pipe, Net, or whatever.

19.5. THE CONTENTS OF A DEVICE DESCRIPTOR

19.5.1 SCF Initialization Table

The initialization table for SCF-type files contains all the bytes set by *tmode* and *xmode*.[1] Many of the fields reflect the kind of primitive teletypes in use when OS-9 was born. Today the idea of automatic translation to upper case seems silly, but in the seventies many people had to work with teletypes that only printed upper case and got confused if confronted with lower case letters.

- SCF can translate all lower-case letters to upper case.

- If the backspace character you choose erases the character it moves onto, PD_BSO can be set to zero. If you want SCF to erase the character with a non-destructive backspace, set PD_BSO to 1; SCF will echo backspace-space-backspace for input of backspace. Turning BSO off makes sense if you really do have a destructive backspace, or if you use a hard-copy terminal where printing a space over a character has no effect.

- If you have a hard-copy terminal, backspacing over a line to delete it is ineffective. For these terminals, set PD_DLO. SCF then "deletes" a line by moving to the next line. This might also be useful if you want to keep a record of deleted lines on your screen.

- Echo is a very useful thing to change. With echo on, SCF echoes every input character to the output device. With echo off, SCF echoes nothing. It is good to set echo off from inside programs (like text editors) that want to control what is displayed on the screen, and for slow terminals that can echo locally. Turning echo off cripples SCF's line editing ability, so leave it on by default unless there are strong advantages to having it off.

Many people recommend echoing locally when the computer is located on the other side of a packet-switched network such as Telenet. Echo time across such a network can be annoyingly long.

It is convenient not to echo input to simple prompts. For instance prompting

```
Enter y or n:
```

works rather well if you echo a bell character from your program for any character other than y or n. If you let SCF echo, you have to clear the display after each incorrect entry.

---

[1] One value in the initialization table can't be set by *tmode* or *xmode* (though it is accessible through *moded*), the offset to the "2nd device name string."

- If PD_ALF is non-zero, SCF's formatted output[2] follows each carriage return with a line feed character.

  You may want to set PD_ALF from your programs or in the device descriptor. A program may wish to have some of SCF's line editing power available, but still be able to use carriage return to return to the beginning of the current line.[3] PD_ALF tells the program whether the output device supports that operation (if PD_ALF is non-zero the device probably cannot do a carriage return without moving to the next line), and lets the program turn auto line feed off.

  Many terminals and printers can automatically do a carriage return/line feed when they receive a carriage return. If your output device has this option locked on, SCF lets you turn off automatic line feeds to prevent unintended double spacing.

- Printers, and even some CRT terminals, once needed padding to give them time after they received control characters that caused the print head to move. SCF supports padding after new lines. The value of PD_NUL is the number of bytes of nulls to send after a new line. Non-zero values for PD_NUL are rare with modern output devices.

- Three fields in the SCF device initialization table affect the way SCF pauses output. The idea is that humans seldom read as fast as SCF can display output, so SCF will pause. It will pause after displaying each page (with page length given in PD_PAG) and wait for any character of input before continuing if PD_PAU is non-zero. It will also pause any time it receives the character specified in PD_PSC.

  Page pause is also useful for sheet-fed printers.

- PD_BSP is the character SCF treats as backspace on input. For some terminals this is backspace, for others it is delete. Note that backspace input is separate from backspace output.

- Several other characters in the SCF initialization table are simply editing control characters. For each of these editing characters you may wish to turn the capability off (by zeroing the character), use the OS-9-standard character, or choose one that you like. The fields in this class are in table 19.1

---

[2]SCF uses formatted output for I$WriteLn and echoed characters.
[3]It would generally be better to use I$Write for the occasional output that should not be exposed to SCF line editing.

19.5. THE CONTENTS OF A DEVICE DESCRIPTOR

Table 19.1: SCF Edit Control Characters

Field	Meaning	Default
PD_BSP	Backspace	$08 control-H
PD_DEL	Delete line	$18 control-X
PD_EOR	End of record (line)	$0d carriage return
PD_EOF	End of file	$1b escape
PD_RPR	Reprint line	$04 control-D
PD_DUP	Duplicate last line	$01 control-A
PD_Tab	Tab	$09 control-I

- The PD_DUP field is an exceptionally useful editing character. Simply hitting the dup character at the beginning of a line of input will cause SCF to copy the last line of input into your input buffer and onto the screen. You can then edit that line.

  Dup shows very little intelligence and that turns out to be just the right thing. It keeps all input in the same buffer, terminated where the line ends. If you type

  $ copy –rx mycmds/beta/research_info /d0/foreddy/research_info
  $ dir –e

  The second command line has only wiped out the first seven characters of the long copy command. Typing

  $ copy –r

  followed by control-A will display the entire *copy* command on the command line ready for editing. You can then backspace to "research_info", type "research1.c   " over that, type control-A again to display the line to the end, and backspace to change the second file name.

  Line editing sounds confusing, but it isn't difficult when you actually use it. The SCF dup trick isn't as useful as real command line editing supported by the shell would be, but it works everywhere SCF's *I$ReadLn* is used and it is more useful than it looks.

- The keyboard interrupt character causes the device driver to send a SIGINT signal to the last process to read or write the device. If PD_INT is zero, there is no keyboard interrupt character.

- The keyboard abort character is also implemented by the driver. The driver should send a SIGQUIT when it sees this character in input.

Both keyboard interrupt and keyboard abort are sent by the driver's interrupt service routine. This means that the signals are sent when the character arrives at the device, not when it is read by the process.

- PD_BSE specifies the character that causes the output device to move a position to the left. This is useful for those terminals that want you to type the delete key to backspace, but expect to receive a backspace when they should move the cursor to the left.

- PD_OVF is usually set to the bell character. When a process uses *I$ReadLn* to get input, SCF rejects lines longer than the process requests. Each time the user presses a key that would make the line too long, SCF rejects the character and echoes the PD_OVF character.

- PD_PAR and PD_BAU set the parity and baud rate for the device. The codes are hardware independent. (See the *OS-9 Technical Manual* for the supported codes.) These values are the business of the device driver which goes to some trouble to let processes reset these hardware parameters with *I$SetStt SS_Opt*.

- The second device, PD_D2P, is the device used to echo input. Most terminal ports are set to echo to themselves. If you have a separate keyboard and a graphics display, the keyboard probably should echo to the display.

- The PD_XON and PD_XOFF fields control XOn/XOff processing by the driver. You can set them to unconventional values if your terminal has unusual requirements, or set them to zero if you don't want to use XOn/XOff.

  When my hardware and device driver support it, I prefer hardware flow-control to XOn/XOff.

- The PD_Tab and PD_Tabs fields combine to control SCF's tab processing. If PD_Tab is non-zero, it defines the tab character. When SCF encounters a tab character, it expands it to enough spaces to reach the next tab stop.

  The spacing of tab stops is controlled by PD_Tabs. Typical values would be 4 or 8.

19.5.2 RBF Initialization Table

The initialization area for an RBF device contains information about the type of disk drive attached to it:

19.5. THE CONTENTS OF A DEVICE DESCRIPTOR

- When multiple disk drives are attached to the disk controller, the drive number selects one of the disk drives. PD_DRV is a drive number used for communication between RBF and the driver. For non-SCSI disks, PD_DRV will usually be the same as the drive select number for the drive.[4] For SCSI drives, PD_DRV is just a number that must be unique for each drive and less than the maximum number of drives supported by the driver; PD_LUN and PD_CtrlrID select the drive.

- The stepping rate of the drive is entered as a code. Check the *OS-9 Technical Manual* for details.

- If bit 7 (the high-order bit) in PD_TYP is on, the field specifies hard-disk parameters, otherwise it specifies floppy parameters.

  Hard disks are comparatively simple. If bit 6 is on, the disk is removable. There are no other hard disk types. The driver freely caches sector zero if the disk is not removable. If it is removable, the driver can only cache sector zero if it finds a way to invalidate the cache whenever the disk changes.

  For floppy disks, the meaning of PD_TYP is either pre-version 2.4 of OS-9 or post version 2.4.

  For pre-2.4 descriptors the device type field contains two significant bits:

  bit zero Disk diameter

      1 the disk is eight inches

      0 the disk is five and a quarter or three and a half inches

  bit five Track-zero density

      1 non-standard disk format (double-density track 0)

      0 standard format

  In post-version 2.4 descriptors, PD_TYP for floppies contains more information:

  bits 1–3 Disk diameter

      0 It's a pre-2.4 descriptor

      1 eight-inch physical size

      2 five and a quarter-inch physical size

      3 three and a half-inch physical size

  bit five Track-zero density

---

[4]Whether PD_DRV identifies a physical drive is decided by the driver.

1 non-standard disk format (double-density track 0)
0 standard format

The definition of PD_TYP is upward and downward compatible. The extra information added at version 2.4 is invisible to pre-2.4 drivers and the bits that the definitions have in common are enough to give old drivers as much information about the disk as they used to get. Old drivers guessed the drive's rotational rate and data transfer rate based on the disk size. New drivers with old descriptors must still derive the rates based on the type information. New drivers with new descriptors look in PD_Rate for rotational and transfer rate and get the actual disk size from PD_TYP. The physical size of the disks is only used to let *format* give an accurate message about the physical size of the disk it is formatting.

- If the disk is a floppy, the media density field indicates the recording density:

  bit zero Bit density

  1 double density

  0 single density

  bit one Double track density. The default is single track density, 48 tracks per inch.

  1 double track density (96 tpi)

  bit two Quad (1.2M per floppy) track density. (192 tpi)

  1 quad density

  bit three Oct track density (384 tpi)

  1 oct density

- The number of cylinders is the number of tracks recorded on one side of a disk. This number is usually 35, 40, or 80. For hard disks the number is much larger. For autosize drives (see PD_Cntl), this field is ignored and is generally set to zero.

- The number of sides is one for single sided floppies and two for double sided floppies. Hard disks can have many sides. For autosize drives (see PD_Cntl), this field is ignored and is generally set to zero.

- Verification is usually used for floppy disks. If the disk controller or drive automatically verifies data it has written, verification need not be done, otherwise

19.5. THE CONTENTS OF A DEVICE DESCRIPTOR

it is strongly recommended. If you use good hardware you will seldom have data incorrectly written, but it is worth the check just to be sure. If the verify byte is zero, all writes are verified.

- The number of sectors per track affects how much can be written on a disk. Pushing the number of sectors per track higher than the standard requires excellent hardware, and may be unreliable. Find out what the hardware manufacturer recommends. For autosize drives (see PD_Cntl), this field is ignored and is generally set to zero.

- The number of sectors on track zero is special because, under the standard OS-9 floppy disk format, track zero is always written single density. By keeping the first track single density regardless of the density of the rest of the disk we make it easy for OS-9 to read enough of the disk to learn the characteristics of the rest of it. Since the density of track zero may be different from the rest of the tracks, the number of sectors on it may also differ. For autosize drives (see PD_Cntl), this field is ignored and is generally set to zero.

- The segment allocation size is part of another optimization trick. Most files start small and grow as more data is written to them. If the system is active with several processes writing to the disk, little pieces of files may get scattered around the disk. By making the segment allocation size greater than one, files can be made to start out with several sectors. Any unused clusters will be released when the file is closed. If most files are roughly some multiple of the segment allocation size, nice non-fragmented files are the result. Programs can request non-standard initial allocations when they open a file. The default is only important for programs that don't use this feature.

- Sector interleaving is a trick to improve performance. If sector two is written directly after sector one on the disk, there may be a serious performance penalty. After the computer reads the first sector in a file, there is usually a tiny pause before it requests the second sector. If the pause is longer than the amount of time it takes the disk to cross the boundary between the first and second sectors, the disk will have to spin all the way around before the second sector can be read. By putting some other sectors (say the eighth and fifteenth) between the first and second, we give the program time to process the first sector and ask for the second before the sector arrives under the disk's head, ready to be read. The interleave factor specifies how many sectors apart sequentially numbered sectors should be located.

- The Direct Memory Access (DMA) byte may be used to specify DMA[5] options. The use of PD_DMA is defined by the driver, and since DMA seldom has options, PD_DMA is usually ignored. This byte is not usually used to turn DMA on and off.

- Track base offset is the physical track number of the first accessible track on a disk.[6] Universal format uses a track offset of one to escape any special significance of track zero. A track offset of one will map logical track zero to physical track one. This wastes a track of disk space, but avoids constraints that the controller or driver might place on track zero.

- Sector base offset is the physical sector number of the first accessible sector. It can be used like the track base offset. Several common OS-9 disk formats (including the universal format) require a sector base offset of one. This offset is required by floppy disk controllers that only work well when sector numbers start at one. The original RBF physical disk format was designed for disk controllers that could start each track at sector zero. A sector offset of one will map the sector numbers from one of these IBM-style controllers into the zero-based array that RBF drivers assume.

- The default sector size is 256 bytes, but if the hardware and driver support it, other sector sizes can be specified in the PD_SSize field.

    The PD_SSize field specifies the *physical* sector size. This is the sector size that the driver expects to find on the disk. Drivers and hardware that support variable sector size always use a logical sector size equal to the physical sector size. Deblocking drivers only support 256-byte logical sectors, but they support different physical sector sizes by deblocking; e.g., 512-byte physical sectors are each divided into two 256-byte logical sectors. Less sophisticated drivers will just return an error when the physical sector size differs from 256 bytes.

    When variable sector size is supported by the driver and hardware, PD_SSize is used to set the physical sector size when the drive is formatted.

    When variable sector size is supported and PD_SSize is zero, the driver stores the actual sector size in that field.

---

[5] Devices that support DMA are able to access main memory. Entire blocks of data can be moved between a file and memory with no help from the processor. This feature is implemented by the hardware and the driver.

[6] Many device drivers for hard disks fail to support track base offset. These drivers simply ignore the value without comment. It is best to assume that your driver does not support a track base offset unless you *know* that it does.

19.5. THE CONTENTS OF A DEVICE DESCRIPTOR

The documentation for a driver should specify its degree of variable sector size support.

Zero is generally a good value for PD_SSize. Variable sector size drivers update the value to correspond to the disk, and non-variable sector size drivers ignore the field and use 256 bytes.

- The device control word is a multi-purpose field used to control the features of RBF and the drivers.

  bit 0 Format inhibit. This can be used to protect a disk from being accidentally reformatted. The idea is that you should normally use device descriptors that are format protected. If you want to format a disk you have to load a special device descriptor with formatting enabled. This extra step might prevent dreadful mistakes.

  bit 1 Multi-sector I/O is supported. If multi-sector I/O is supported, the PD_MaxCnt field should indicate the number of bytes the I/O hardware and driver can transfer per multi-sector operation.

  bit 2 is defined as Stable ID, but it is not implemented yet. It will probably mean that the sector zero information maintained by the device driver will be either invalid or correct. (If the sector-zero-read flag is true, the drive table information is correct and the sector zero buffer contains a true image of sector 0.) This requires the driver to be aware of disk changes.

  bit 3 The device size can be determined with SS_DSize, *format* will format the entire disk with one write track, and the disk geometry fields (sectors per track, cylinders per device, and so forth) for the device should be ignored.

  bit 4 The device can write a single track. Various disk-repair strategies only work for devices that let a program write tracks.

- An I/O error on a disk is not always repeatable. If you get an I/O error, trying the operation again might work. The Number of Tries field lets you override a driver's default number of tries. In particular it lets you insist on no retries.

- Many computers support a Small Computer System Interface (SCSI) bus. The devices on this bus are intelligent controllers and computers. A device descriptor can describe a device attached to a SCSI controller. The address of such a device contains two numbers in addition to the port address[7]:

---

[7]A computer can support many separate SCSI connections. The address of the SCSI interface identifies the bus.

- The SCSI ID of the controller on the bus. A SCSI bus can support up to eight devices (one of which is the computer), each identified by a SCSI ID number. The SCSI controller ID, PD_CtrlrID, is the SCSI ID of the SCSI controller for this device. This value is used by the device driver to address messages to the controller.
- The logical unit number of the device on the SCSI controller. A single SCSI controller might easily support two hard disks, a floppy disk, and a tape drive. These would be distinguished by their SCSI logical unit number.

- Some disk drives behave differently for the inner and outer tracks. If the controller needs to get involved, it will find values for the cylinder where it should begin reduced write current and the cylinder where it should begin write precompensation.

- Some hard disk drives leave their head resting on the surface of the disk when they stop. This will cause extra wear on the part of the disk where the head skids to a halt and takes off again. Important data can be protected by designating a region of the disk as the parking area. Some disk drives automatically move their heads into the parking area when they detect low power. The driver can protect drives that don't park their heads automatically by moving the heads to the cylinder specified in the PD_Park field. Disks can also be parked from outside the driver with the SS_SQD setstat.

- The total cylinders field reflects the number of physical cylinders on the device. If the disk is partitioned, the total number of cylinders will be the sum of the cylinders in all the partitions. On a partitioned drive, the number of cylinders in each partition is recorded in the PD_CYL field of the partition's descriptor.

  A disk with a track offset must have PD_TotCyls equal to the track offset plus PD_CYL.

- The LSN offset is also intended for use with partitioned drives. The LSN offset is added to the LSN by the driver before it uses the LSN for anything. The sector offset is a hardware-level constant; it is added to the sector number before the number is written to the controller hardware, but after range checks and so forth.

- SCSI driver options are passed to drivers for SCSI disks. The bits in the field are defined as follows:

  bit 0 ATN asserted (disconnect allowed)

19.5. THE CONTENTS OF A DEVICE DESCRIPTOR

bit 1 Device can operate as a target

bit 2 Synchronous data transfer is supported

bit 3 Parity on

- The PD_Rate field specifies the data rate and rotational speed of floppy disks. It defines data rates from 125k bits/sec to 5M bits/sec and rotational speeds from 300 RPM to 600 RPM. See the manual for details and check the disk drive's manual too before you assume that a particular bit rate corresponds to a rotation rate. Some drives change data rates by changing rotation rate, others don't.

- The PD_MaxCnt field is the maximum number of bytes that can be transferred in one multi-sector read or write. Note that this field specifies a number of *bytes* not sectors.

  RBF divides long multi-sector I/O requests into blocks of no more than PD_MaxCnt bytes.

19.5.3 RAM Disks

OS-9 uses a special RBF driver to manage RAM disks; it is an unusually simple driver. The device initialization entry causes the driver to allocate enough memory to contain a RAM image of an RBF disk, and the terminate entry frees the memory allocated by the initialization routine. The read and write entries simply treat the block of memory as an array of sector images.

Only two option fields in a RAM disk device descriptor are usually non-zero: the number of sectors per track, and the segment allocation size. The number of sectors per track controls the size of the RAM disk, and the segment allocation size primarily controls the minimum fragment size for files. The usual performance considerations are not as much a concern for RAM disks as for mechanical disks.

Since RAM disks use 256 byte sectors, the number of sectors per track is four times the RAM disk's capacity in kilobytes.

Single-user OS-9 systems can benefit from a collection of pre-configured RAM disk descriptors in the commands directory. I usually use a RAM disk with 1536 sectors per track and a segment allocation size of four sectors, but when I am doing exceptionally memory-hungry work I deiniz the RAM disk to free its 384k, and when I want to compile unusually large programs I sometimes *deiniz* the 384k RAM disk and load one with 2048 sectors (512k).

The port address of a RAM disk has two meanings. If the number is less than $400, it simply identifies the RAM disk. The memory for RAM disks with low port addresses is allocated with an *F$SRqMem* SVC when the disk is attached and freed when the device is detached.[8] These RAM disks could be called floating RAM disks because they may appear at a different location each time they are attached.

If the port address is greater than or equal to $400, the port address is the starting address of the RAM disk. This lets the RAM disk be locked into particular memory locations; e.g., non volatile RAM. Memory that will be used for a fixed RAM disk should not be available for general allocation. It can be left out of the memory table in the init module, or given a type and priority that prevents it from being allocated except by a special request.

---

[8]Yes, it is possible to have 1024 floating RAM disks at the same time. At least two or three RAM disks can be useful.

Chapter 20

File Managers

> *This chapter is an overview of file managers. Each of the main file managers is mentioned, and the role of a file manager in the OS-9 system is discussed.*

File managers are the level between the I/O manager and device drivers. Like device drivers, they hide some aspects of the I/O system from user programs. Some requests are passed on to device drivers with little intervention: Sequential Character File (SCF) *I$Write* requests would be an example. Other requests, such as the Delete request to the Random Block File (RBF) manager, are handled mainly in the file manager with only incidental requests going to the driver. The *I$Seek* request and some GetStat and PutStat calls don't go to the driver at all.

Much of SCF's function relates to editing. All special characters, like backspace and reprint-line, are handled here. SCF also handles contention between several processes wanting simultaneous access to a device.

RBF is the only part of OS-9 that knows anything about the structure of a disk. It handles directories, file descriptors, and the disk identification sector.

Pipeman does everything for pipes; the device driver for pipe files does exactly nothing. The device driver is necessary because IOMan wouldn't tolerate a path without one, but there isn't any actual device associated with a pipe. Pipes are manufactured entirely of mirrors.

Most devices can be fit into the SCF or RBF class. Devices in these classes can be added to an OS-9 system with little effort. At most, a device driver will need to be written, though usually a device descriptor will suffice.

A special file manager called NFM adds local area network support to OS-9. This permits several computers to be attached to each other. Resources like disk space and peripherals can be shared through the network. A single large-capacity disk can serve several computers, saving money on disks and making public files available to users of any computer on the network. Other high-priced peripherals like fast printers and graphics devices are easier to afford when they are shared by several computers on a network.

Networking involves more than a network file manager. Special processes need to run on each networked processor to do what a file manager can't. Still, the network looks just like any other device to a program. The network file manager is not a simple piece of code, but fitting it into OS-9's I/O structure was not a problem.

A file manager called SBF handles devices like tape drives. These devices don't support random access, so they can't properly be controlled by RBF. SCF isn't appropriate because tape drives handle data in blocks (very like disk sectors). Since streaming tape drives work best when they are fed a steady stream of data, the SBF file manager supports asynchronous I/O. It returns from a write before the data is actually written to the tape. If a program can assemble blocks of data fast enough, it can keep the file manager ahead of the tape drive. This will let the tape drive run without hesitations...a big advantage for streaming tape drives.

A few devices can benefit from an entirely new file manager. OS-9's architecture permits new file managers to be added without any disruption. Several ideas for alternative file managers come to mind.

20.1 Possibilities for New File Managers

An I/O processor file manager to replace SCF was once written for OS-9/6809. Many of the functions of a file manager can be pushed all the way down into a device if the device is intelligent enough. Intelligent controller boards that support terminals and printers have been made. The processor on the I/O board can handle line editing nicely without any help from the file manager. When this function can be placed in the device controller board and the file manager is stripped down to those functions that can't be moved to the controller, the I/O capabilities of the computer increase substantially. Each CPU cycle that can be made the responsibility of the I/O processor is another cycle available for user programs. Taking full advantage of an intelligent SCF device requires a special file manager with line-editing functions removed and possibly some additions to give the controller the information it needs.

RBF can benefit just as much from intelligent controllers as the SCF manager, perhaps more. Functions like file and directory handling—in fact, most of the functions of the RBF manager—could be moved to the controller. A dedicated processor could handle these operations more efficiently than the general purpose processor running the file manager. Even if the microprocessor on the controller is slower than the main

20.2. WRITING A FILE MANAGER

processor, unloading functions onto intelligent peripherals returns processor resources to other programs.

It is in the interest of the manufacturers of intelligent controller boards to write special file managers as well as device descriptors for their hardware. The special software makes their hardware look a lot better. Unfortunately, RBF is a good deal more complicated than it seems. The only straightforward way to move RBF's functions into an I/O board is to move RBF there.

A very intelligent terminal would do best with a file manager somewhere between SCF and the network file manager. You want to be able to send programs and non-display data to the terminal as well as normal terminal I/O. A good file manager would normally handle the terminal's special features for you. You could pretend it was a normal terminal. It would also give you a way to get at the terminal if you wanted to do something special to it.

OS-9 has local area networking, but it doesn't yet deal with dialup networks. It's an interesting question whether it will be better to extend the current software to handle phone lines or write a new file manager that supports such protocols as zmodem, and uucp.

There are dozens of other promising opportunities for file managers. A file manager for write-once-read-many-times (WORM) media would be fun to write, so would a file manager for Unix-format disks and a file manager for high-speed serial I/O.

20.2 Writing a File Manager

There is nothing inherently difficult about writing a file manager. The trickiest aspect of the job is that debug and srcdbg don't work for file managers. Three special debuggers can be used with file managers. The ROM debugger is part of an OS-9 Port-Pak. It is not nearly as powerful as debug, but it is barely enough.[1] The *Sysdbg* program is similar to *debug*, but it works with system modules. *Sysdbg* runs from inside OS-9. It can debug system code and it supports features like *debug*. Once a system is running well enough to load sysdbg and run it, *sysdbg* is much easier to use than the ROM debugger.

The best debugger for system state code is ***ROMBug***. It has all the features of *debug* and *sysdbg* but it uses polled I/O like the ROM debugger and I think it is the more reliable than *sysdbg*.

A file manager has thirteen entry vectors, each pointing to a routine that provides a specific service. All the entry vectors must be there, but the attached routines can be

---

[1] The ROM debugger can be invoked at system startup, when a processor trap takes place, or when the F$SysCall SVC is used. Access to the ROM debugger is controlled by hardware and software switches.

null procedures that only return with carry clear, or routines that set an error code and return with carry set.

If a new device driver will do what you want, don't write a file manager. A file manager is a much bigger project than a driver; look at the relative sizes of the file managers and drivers included with your system, or the examples later in this book. The device drivers in chapter 23 and appendix D are *real* device drivers written in assembly language. The file managers in chapter 21 and appendix C are simplified demonstrations mainly written in C, but they are still bulky programs.

A new file manager is about the most important addition that a user can make to OS-9. A new or modified file manager can add new functions to OS-9. A new file manager can be brought into use by adding a device descriptor that references it. Clearly this one of the directions in which OS-9 was meant to be expanded.

Chapter 21

A Simple File Manager

This chapter shows how to build a file manager by walking through a very simple file manager written in C.

The file manager in this chapter is the precursor to the much more complicated file manager in appendix C. This example is not useful in itself but it shows how a file manager can fit between IOMan and RBF device drivers.

The most difficult task for this file manager is interfacing to an RBF device driver. Device drivers are constructed with a particular file manager in mind, and fitting such a specific interface to a different file manager takes care. The trickiest aspects of this interface were the sector size (512 bytes instead of the OS-9 standard 256) and the driver's assumptions about the system sector.

The dummy file manager supports the open, close, and read entry points. All the other entries return a zero as if everything was fine. This is not a recommended practice, but it made the file manager easier to test.

21.1 Using the C Language

Until recently all file managers were written in assembly language, system-level code written in a high-level language is still unusual. The interface specification for a file manager assumes that the programmer has full control of the processor's registers, and that the programmer can insert values at particular spots in the module. It is difficult for a C program to get at the parameters passed in registers, particularly A6, where the system globals pointer is passed. The offset list at the module entry point is also challenging.

The complete list of problems with C for writing file managers is:

- C doesn't support access to registers, but the interface between IOMan and the file manager and the interface to existing device drivers is through parameters passed in registers.

- C doesn't support explicit constants in code. Furthermore, the C entry point is CStart. It definitely doesn't have a vector table at its entry point.

- C programs are slower and larger than equivalent assembly language programs.

- C programs tend to use static storage and initialized storage. Initialization is done by the fork SVC which will not be used for a file manager, and it is difficult to fit C static storage into a file manager's memory model.

A different CStart can deal with the parameter passing and vector table conventions. An assembly language interface routine can set up registers and call the device driver. The static storage problem could be addressed with some fancy linking, but I find it easier to simply avoid static storage. The only remaining problems are speed and size.

If the size of a C program is a problem, fall back to assembly language. A file manager written in C may be two to four times the size of an equivalent assembly language file manager, but that's still under 100K. Most systems can spare the memory. If you can't, use assembly language.

The slower speed of C programs is unlikely to be a problem for most file managers. The I/O rate is slow compared with the processor. Also, it is easier to make algorithm enhancements in C than in assembly language. Algorithm improvements can make performance improvements that bury the cost of high-level-language code.

21.2 A CStart for a File Manager

This version of cstart forms an interface between the kernel's interface to a file manager, and the C runtime environment. It uses entirely separate code for each interface to make debugging easier.

```
****************************
*
* cstart.a - C program startup routine for a file manager
*
           use      <oskdefs.d>
           opt      −l
00000001 Carry:     equ      %00000001 Carry bit
```

21.2. A CSTART FOR A FILE MANAGER

```
0000000d  Typ      equ    FlMgr
00000001  Edit     equ    1
00000400  Stk      equ    1024              a default stack size
00000101  Cerror   equ    257               arbitrary C error

          psect    cstart_a,(Typ<<8)!Objct,(ReEnt<<8)!1,Edit,Stk,_cstart

0000000d  cr       equ    $0d
00000020  space    equ    $20
0000002c  comma    equ    $2c
00000022  dquote   equ    $22
00000027  squote   equ    $27

*
* C Program entry point
*
* On entry we have:
*         a1       points to the path descriptor
*         a4       points to the current process descriptor
*         a5       points to the user's register stack
*         a6       points to the system global area
*
* To run a C program we must have:
*         a6       static storage base pointer
* The static storage is in the path descriptor
          _cstart:
0000 001a          dc.w   _Create-_cstart
0002 0032          dc.w   _Open-_cstart
0004 004a          dc.w   _MakDir-_cstart
0006 0062          dc.w   _ChgDir-_cstart
0008 007a          dc.w   _Delete-_cstart
000a 0092          dc.w   _Seek-_cstart
000c 00aa          dc.w   _Read-_cstart
000e 00c2          dc.w   _Write-_cstart
0010 00da          dc.w   _ReadLn-_cstart
0012 00f2          dc.w   _WriteLn-_cstart
0014 010a          dc.w   _GetStat-_cstart
0016 0122          dc.w   _SetStat-_cstart
0018 013a          dc.w   _Close-_cstart

          _Create
001a 48e7          movem.l a4/a6,-(sp)
001e 2009          move.l  a1,d0
0020 220d          move.l  a5,d1
0022=6100          bsr     Create            (pd, regs, ProcDesc, SysGlobs)
0026 4cdf          movem.l (sp)+,a4/a6
002a 4a40          tst.w   d0
```

```
           002c 6600         bne      _Error
           0030 4e75         rts
                _Open
           0032 48e7         movem.l  a4/a6,−(sp)
           0036 2009         move.l   a1,d0
           0038 220d         move.l   a5,d1
           003a=6100         bsr      Open         (pd, regs, ProcDesc, SysGlobs)
           003e 4cdf         movem.l  (sp)+,a4/a6
           0042 4a40         tst.w    d0
           0044 6600         bne      _Error
           0048 4e75         rts
                _MakDir
           004a 48e7         movem.l  a4/a6,−(sp)
           004e 2009         move.l   a1,d0
           0050 220d         move.l   a5,d1
           0052=6100         bsr      MakDir       (pd, regs, ProcDesc, SysGlobs)
           0056 4cdf         movem.l  (sp)+,a4/a6
           005a 4a40         tst.w    d0
           005c 6600         bne      _Error
           0060 4e75         rts
                _ChgDir
           0062 48e7         movem.l  a4/a6,−(sp)
           0066 2009         move.l   a1,d0
           0068 220d         move.l   a5,d1
           006a=6100         bsr      ChdDir       (pd, regs, ProcDesc, SysGlobs)
           006e 4cdf         movem.l  (sp)+,a4/a6
           0072 4a40         tst.w    d0
           0074 6600         bne      _Error
           0078 4e75         rts
                _Delete
           007a 48e7         movem.l  a4/a6,−(sp)
           007e 2009         move.l   a1,d0
           0080 220d         move.l   a5,d1
           0082=6100         bsr      Delete       (pd, regs, ProcDesc, SysGlobs)
           0086 4cdf         movem.l  (sp)+,a4/a6
           008a 4a40         tst.w    d0
           008c 6600         bne      _Error
           0090 4e75         rts
                _Seek
           0092 48e7         movem.l  a4/a6,−(sp)
           0096 2009         move.l   a1,d0
           0098 220d         move.l   a5,d1
           009a=6100         bsr      Seek         (pd, regs, ProcDesc, SysGlobs)
           009e 4cdf         movem.l  (sp)+,a4/a6
           00a2 4a40         tst.w    d0
           00a4 6600         bne      _Error
           00a8 4e75         rts
```

21.2. A CSTART FOR A FILE MANAGER

```
          _Read
00aa 48e7         movem.l  a4/a6,−(sp)
00ae 2009         move.l   a1,d0
00b0 220d         move.l   a5,d1
00b2=6100         bsr      Read         (pd, regs, ProcDesc, SysGlobs)
00b6 4cdf         movem.l  (sp)+,a4/a6
00ba 4a40         tst.w    d0
00bc 6600         bne      _Error
00c0 4e75         rts
          _Write
00c2 48e7         movem.l  a4/a6,−(sp)
00c6 2009         move.l   a1,d0
00c8 220d         move.l   a5,d1
00ca=6100         bsr      Write        (pd, regs, ProcDesc, SysGlobs)
00ce 4cdf         movem.l  (sp)+,a4/a6
00d2 4a40         tst.w    d0
00d4 6600         bne      _Error
00d8 4e75         rts
          _ReadLn
00da 48e7         movem.l  a4/a6,−(sp)
00de 2009         move.l   a1,d0
00e0 220d         move.l   a5,d1
00e2=6100         bsr      ReadLn       (pd, regs, ProcDesc, SysGlobs)
00e6 4cdf         movem.l  (sp)+,a4/a6
00ea 4a40         tst.w    d0
00ec 6600         bne      _Error
00f0 4e75         rts
          _WriteLn
00f2 48e7         movem.l  a4/a6,−(sp)
00f6 2009         move.l   a1,d0
00f8 220d         move.l   a5,d1
00fa=6100         bsr      WriteLn      (pd, regs, ProcDesc, SysGlobs)
00fe 4cdf         movem.l  (sp)+,a4/a6
0102 4a40         tst.w    d0
0104 6600         bne      _Error
0108 4e75         rts
          _GetStat
010a 48e7         movem.l  a4/a6,−(sp)
010e 2009         move.l   a1,d0
0110 220d         move.l   a5,d1
0112=6100         bsr      GetStat      (pd, regs, ProcDesc, SysGlobs)
0116 4cdf         movem.l  (sp)+,a4/a6
011a 4a40         tst.w    d0
011c 6600         bne      _Error
0120 4e75         rts
          _SetStat
0122 48e7         movem.l  a4/a6,−(sp)
```

```
0126 2009           move.l    a1,d0
0128 220d           move.l    a5,d1
012a=6100           bsr       SetStat       (pd, regs, ProcDesc, SysGlobs)
012e 4cdf           movem.l   (sp)+,a4/a6
0132 4a40           tst.w     d0
0134 6600           bne       _Error
0138 4e75           rts
       _Close
013a 48e7           movem.l   a4/a6,-(sp)
013e 2009           move.l    a1,d0
0140 220d           move.l    a5,d1
0142=6100           bsr       Close         (pd, regs, ProcDesc, SysGlobs)
0146 4cdf           movem.l   (sp)+,a4/a6
014a 4a40           tst.w     d0
014c 6600           bne       _Error
0150 4e75           rts
       _Error
0152 003c           ori       #Carry,ccr
0156 4e75           rts
```

The following routines are called from the C component of the file manager. They interface to the device driver and provide functions that are normally found in the C libraries. This file manager avoids the standard libraries to ensure that no static storage references sneak into the file manager code.

```
           * CallRead (ct, lsn, pd, DevStaticS, ProcD, regs, sysglobs)
           * puts
           *         ct in d0
           *         lsn in d2
           *         pd in a1
           *         DevStaticS in a2
           *         ProcD in a4
           *         regs in a5
           *         sysglobs in a6
           CallRead:
0158 48e7           movem.l   d2-d7/a0-a5,-(sp)
           * ct is already in d0
           * calculate the entry address in the device driver
015c 226f           move.l    13*4(sp),a1    pd to a1
0160=2069           move.l    PD_DEV(a1),a0  device table entry
0164=2068           move.l    V$DRIV(a0),a0  device driver address
0168=2428           move.l    M$Exec(a0),d2  device driver entry offset
016c=d0f0           add.w     D$READ(a0,d2),a0 Add read-ent offset to module base

0170 2401           move.l    d1,d2
0172 246f           move.l    14*4(sp),a2    DevStatic to a2
```

21.2. A CSTART FOR A FILE MANAGER

```
0176 286f              move.l   15*4(sp),a4     ProcD to a4
017a 2a6f              move.l   16*4(sp),a5     regs to a5
              * sysglobs is already in a6
017e=4e40              os9      F$SysDbg        look for errors

0182 4e90              jsr      (a0)
0184 6500              bcs      CallError
0188 6000              bra      CallOK


              * CallWrite (ct, lsn, pd, DevStaticS, ProcD, regs, sysglobs)
              * puts
              *        ct in d0
              *        lsn in d2
              *        pd in a1
              *        DevStaticS in a2
              *        ProcD in a4
              *        regs in a5
              *        sysglobs in a6
              CallWrite:
018c 4e75              rts


              * CallGetStat(code, pd, DevStaticS, pd, regs, sysglobs)
              * puts
              *        code in d0
              *        pd in a1
              *        DevStaticS in a2
              *        ProcD in a4
              *        regs in a5
              *        sysglobs in a6
              CallGetStat:
018e 4e75              rts


              * CallSetStat(code, pd, DevStaticS, pd, regs, sysglobs)
              * puts
              *        code in d0
              *        pd in a1
              *        DevStaticS in a2
              *        ProcD in a4
              *        regs in a5
              *        sysglobs in a6
              CallSetStat:
0190 4e75              rts

              CallOK
0192 4cdf              movem.l  (sp)+,d2–d7/a0–a5
0196 4280              clr.l    d0
```

```
                        CallError
0198 4e75               rts

019a 2001               move.l   d1,d0
019c 4cdf               movem.l  (sp)+,d2–d7/a0-a5
01a0 4e75               rts

                        _srqmem:
01a2 2f0a               move.l   a2,-(sp)
01a4=4e40               os9      F$SRqMem
01a8 6400               bcc      srqmemx1
01ac 70ff               moveq.l  #-1,d0
01ae 6000               bra      srqmemx
                        srqmemx1
01b2 200a               move.l   a2,d0
                        srqmemx
01b4 245f               move.l   (sp)+,a2
01b6 4e75               rts

        *
        * DoIOQ(process_id)
        *
        DoIOQ:
01b8=4e40               os9      F$IOQu
01bc 2001               move.l   d1,d0        return code
01be 4e75               rts

        *
        * DoSRtMem(ptr, size)
        *
        DoSRtMem:
01c0 2f0a               move.l   a2,-(sp)
01c2 2440               move.l   d0,a2
01c4 2001               move.l   d1,d0
01c6=4e40               os9      F$SRtMem
01ca 245f               move.l   (sp)+,a2
01cc 4e75               rts
000001ce                ends
```

The special CStart for file managers can be used for any file manager. There is no distinction between the different classes of file managers (RBF, SCF, etc.) or between one file manager and another within a class.

This version of CStart is much longer than it needs to be. It retains entirely separate code for each entry point. The refined CStart in appendix C acts like this

---

[†] *CStart*: see page 423

21.3 The Dummy File Manager

Most entries into a file manager are straightforward. IOMan finds the path descriptor for the call, assembles the parameters for the call, and *jsr*'s to the required entry in the file manager. In detail:

- IOMan finds the path descriptor for the given path number.

- It organizes contention for the path descriptor. If the path is already busy (consider duped paths), IOMan causes the current request to wait in the I/O Queue.

- It sets the PD_CPR and PD_LProc fields to the current user id.

- It calls the correct entry in the file manager.

- When the file manager returns, IOMan checks the I/O queue. If there are any processes waiting on the I/O queue, IOMan dequeues a process from the queue and signals it to wakeup.

This is IOMan's action for Delete, Seek, Read, Write, ReadLn, and WriteLn. IOMan takes a more active role in processing the other functions.

21.3.1 Preprocessor Includes and Defines

The file manager uses the OS-9 error codes from errno.h, and the process descriptor structure given in the procid.h include file.

```
/* A dummy file manager for an RBF-type file */
#include <errno.h>
#include <procid.h>
typedef char *POINTER;
#include "format.h"
#include "PathDesc.h"
#define SECTORSIZE 512
```

21.3.2 Open

Before calling the Open entry in the file manager, IOMan creates and initializes a path descriptor. In detail:

1. It finds a free path descriptor and a free path number for the process.

2. It sets the PD_COUNT and PD_CNT fields to 1.

3. It sets PD_MOD to the access mode passed with the *I$Open* SVC.

4. It initializes PD_USER to the current user.

5. If the device is non-sharable and already opened on some path, IOMan returns an error.

6. If the device is not initialized, IOMan attaches it.

7. It copies the options from the device descriptor into the path descriptor.

8. It sets PD_DEV to point to the device's device table entry.

9. IOMan maintains a linked list of open paths for each device. The linked list starts at V_Paths in device static storage and ends with a NULL. The links are through the PD_Paths field in the path descriptors.

The remainder of the path descriptor will be filled with zeroes.

The file manager may use the variables set by IOMan, but it should not change them.

A file manager that will use RBF device drivers must do some setup activity to keep the driver happy. This function duplicates PD_DEV into PD_DVT and sets PD_FD to 0 (there is no FD sector). It also sets PD_DTB to point to the correct drive table entry.

The function also sets some variables that will be used in the file manager. It allocates an I/O buffer and points PD_BUF at the buffer, sets PD_CP (current position) to 0, and indicates that there is no sector in the I/O buffer by claiming that sector -1 is buffered.

Since this file manager will read PC-DOS disks, it is constantly fighting the device driver's updates to the drive table. The device driver is normally responsible for the drive table. It maintains this table by copying a portion of sector 0 into the drive table every time it reads it. This works fine when the disk is in OS-9 format. A file manager that managed OS-9-format disks could read sector zero and trust the device driver to update the drive table. The first sector on a PC-DOS disk certainly does not contain

21.3. THE DUMMY FILE MANAGER

information in OS-9 system sector format. This file manager must read sector zero then shuffle data around to convert PC-DOS system information into a pseudo OS-9 system sector.

The open function should copy the file name into the path descriptor if file names have any meaning.

```
Open(pd, regs, procd, SysGlobs)
register PD_TYPE pd;
{
    register PD_OPTS OptionPtr;
    int RVal;


    /*
        Initialize the path descriptor.
    */
    if((pd→PD_BUF = (char *)_srqmem(SECTORSIZE)) == (char *)−1)
        return E_MEMFUL;

    OptionPtr = (PD_OPTS)(&pd→PD_OPT);
    OptionPtr→PD_DVT = (POINTER)pd→PD_DEV;
    OptionPtr→PD_FD = 0;

    pd→PD_DTB = (POINTER)&pd→PD_DEV→V_STAT→
            V_DRIVES[OptionPtr→PD_DRV];
    pd→PD_CP = 0;              /* current offset in file        */
    pd→PD_CSector = −1;        /* no sector in buffer           */

    if((RVal = ReadSector(pd, 0, pd→PD_BUF, regs, procd, SysGlobs)) == 0)
        InitFromBoot(pd, pd→PD_BUF);

    return RVal;
}
```

Properly, the open function should have called the open setstat in the device driver before returning.

21.3.3 Seek

IOMan takes no interest in *I$Seek*. It finds the path descriptor and passes the call to the file manager.

```
Seek(pd, regs, procd, SysGlobs)
register PD_TYPE pd;
register REGS regs;
{
    pd→PD_CP = regs→R_d1;
    return 0;
}
```

21.3.4 Read

This is another call that IOMan largely ignores. IOMan checks for possible security violations, finds the right path descriptor and calls the file manager. The file manager is responsible for deciding which sector(s) on the disk contains the data at the position specified in the path descriptor, reading the sector from the disk and copying the required data into the user's buffer.

File locking should be done in this function. This is also one of the places where cleverness about letting the device driver move data directly into the user's buffer would be hidden.

```
Read(pd, regs, procd, SysGlobs)
register PD_TYPE pd;
REGS regs;
{
    unsigned long length, i;
    register char *dest, *ptr;
    int ReturnVal=0;
    unsigned long Sector, offset;

    Sector = pd→PD_CP >>9;              /* divide current position by 512   */
    offset = pd→PD_CP & (SECTORSIZE −1);
    length = regs→R_d1;
    dest = regs→R_a0;

    while(length > 0){
        if(pd→PD_CSector != Sector)
            ReturnVal = ReadSector(pd, Sector, pd→PD_BUF,
                regs, procd, SysGlobs);
            if(Sector == 0 && ReturnVal == 0 )
                    InitFromBoot(pd, pd→PD_BUF);
            if(ReturnVal != 0)
                break;
        }else
```

21.3. THE DUMMY FILE MANAGER

```
            ReturnVal = 0;

    /*
            At least part of this sector should be copied to the caller's buffer. The "interesting"
            data starts at offset from the beginning of the sector and continues for length
            bytes, or to the end of the sector (whichever is least).
    */
            i = SECTORSIZE − offset;
            if(i>length)
                i = length;
            length −= i;

            pd→PD_CP += i;                      /* Update current position in pd         */

            /* Copy the data to the caller's buffer */
            for(ptr = pd→PD_BUF+offset;i>0; i−−) *dest++ = *ptr++;

            /* Now prepare to read the next sector */
            ++Sector;
            offset = 0;
        }
        return ReturnVal;
    }
```

21.3.5 Close

IOMan takes an interest in the *I$Close* SVC. Before it calls the file manager, IOMan decrements PD_COUNT. If the path isn't busy, IOMan calls the Close entry in the file manager. If the path has no remaining users, IOMan frees the path descriptor. If the device is now unused, IOMan detaches the device.

The file manager must free any memory it allocated at open if the path is unused (PD_COUNT of zero). IOMan is about to free the path descriptor and the file managers will never see it again.

If file management requires any action when a file is closed, such as flushing write buffers, this is the place to do it.

```
Close(pd, regs, procd, SysGlobs)
register PD_TYPE pd;
{
    if(pd→PD_CNT == 0)                   /* Is this path unused?           */
        if(pd→PD_BUF != 0){               /* Is there a buffer for this path?  */
            DoSRtMem(pd→PD_BUF, SECTORSIZE);          /*Free the buffer mem */
```

```
            pd→PD_BUF = 0;
      }
   return 0;
}
```

21.3.6 MakDir

IOMan does a great deal to help the file manager with the *I$MkDir* SVC. It creates and initializes a path descriptor as if this were an *I$Open* SVC. After calling the file manager's MakDir function, IOMan removes the path descriptor exactly as if it had returned from the file manager's Close function.

MakDir in IOMan is essentially a duplicate of Open processing up to the call to the file manager. After its call to the file manager's MakDir function, IOMan follows the same procedure it uses after calling the file manager's close function. The only difference is that MakDir knows the path descriptor doesn't have multiple users.

This file manager doesn't implement MakDir, but you can find an example in the PC-DOS file manager.

```
MakDir(pd, regs, procd, SysGlobs)
{
   return 0;
}
```

21.3.7 Create

From IOMan's point of view, the only difference between opening a path and creating a file is the entry in the file manager that it calls.

Inside the file manager the functions are usually similar. Often the create function is aliased to the open function. In any case, a file manager should perform the same path descriptor initialization as open.

```
Create(pd, regs, procd, SysGlobs)
{
   return 0;
}
```

21.3.8 ChdDir

The default directories are attributes of a process, not a path. As it does for MakDir, IOMan creates a temporary path for ChdDir.

21.3. THE DUMMY FILE MANAGER

IOMan will record the device that contains the default directory. The file manager must store enough information for it to find the directory on the device. It should store this information in the current process descriptor. The _dio area in the process descriptor may be used to store default directory information. This area holds information about both the default data directory and the default execution directory. The first 12 bytes are for the data directory, the next 12 for the execution directory.

IOMan puts a pointer to the device table entry for the directory in the first long word of each directory specification. The rest is for the file manager's use.

See the PC-DOS file manager for an example of ChdDir and the code in Open that respects the default directories.

```
ChdDir(pd, regs, procd, SysGlobs)
{
    return 0;
}
```

21.3.9 Delete

At the SVC level, file deletion operates on a file name, not a path descriptor. This function is another one that works almost like MakDir (which, in turn, is much like Open). It creates a temporary path descriptor for the call, calls the file manager with the temporary descriptor, then disposes of the descriptor.

In the file manager the Delete function should start by opening the file, or some very similar operation, and finish by closing the path.

See the PC-DOS example for a working Delete function.

```
Delete(pd, regs, procd, SysGlobs)
{
    return 0;
}
```

21.3.10 Write

IOMan only takes its minimum actions for writes. For a file manager, writing is like reading.

```
Write(pd, regs, procd, SysGlobs)
{
    return 0;
}
```

21.3.11 ReadLn and WriteLn

IOMan doesn't distinguish between read and readln or write and writeln. For the file manager as well, readln is very similar to read. One interesting option is to consider different line ending strategies. For instance, a line does not neccessarily end with a byte value. Lines could *start* with a count. ReadLn and WriteLn would be a clean interface to a message passing system.

```
ReadLn(pd, regs, procd, SysGlobs)
register REGS regs;
{
   return 0;
}


WriteLn(pd, regs, procd, SysGlobs)
{
   return 0;
}
```

21.3.12 GetStat and SetStat

IOMan handles some status functions: set and get options, and read device name. All setstat and getstat functions are passed to the file manager even when IOMan seems to have done what's required. This has proved to be a good policy. If you look at the SCF device driver you will see that IOMan passes set option setstats to the file manager who passes them on to the device driver. The device driver adjusts the hardware options to fit the path options.

```
GetStat(pd, regs, procd, SysGlobs)
{
   register STATICSTORETYPE DevStatic;

   DevStatic = pd→PD_DEV→V_STAT;

   /* Do things that don't require the device driver */
   /* ... and return ... or ... */
   /* Wait for the device to be idle */
   while(DevStatic→V_BUSY) DoIOQ(DevStatic→V_BUSY);
   DevStatic→V_BUSY = pd→PD_CPR;

   /* Call the device driver */
```

21.3. THE DUMMY FILE MANAGER

```
      DevStatic→V_BUSY = 0;            /* device not busy              */
      return 0;
}


SetStat(pd, regs, procd, SysGlobs)
{
   register STATICSTORETYPE DevStatic;

   DevStatic = pd→PD_DEV→V_STAT;

   /* Do things that don't require the device driver */
   /* ... and return ... or ... */
   /* Wait for the device to be idle */
   while(DevStatic→V_BUSY) DoIOQ(DevStatic→V_BUSY);
   DevStatic→V_BUSY = pd→PD_CPR;

   /* Call the device driver */

   DevStatic→V_BUSY = 0;               /* device not busy              */
   return 0;
}
```

21.3.13 Support Functions

This is the function that contains the high-level interface to the device driver.

```
ReadSector(pd, Sector, buffer, regs, procd, SysGlobs)
register PD_TYPE pd;
int Sector;
char *buffer;
{
   int ReturnVal;
   char *HoldBuffer;
   register STATICSTORETYPE DevStatic;

   DevStatic = pd→PD_DEV→V_STAT;

   /* Wait for the device to be idle */
   while(DevStatic→V_BUSY) DoIOQ(DevStatic→V_BUSY);
   DevStatic→V_BUSY = pd→PD_CPR;

   /* The supplied buffer might not be the one in the path descriptor */
```

```
    HoldBuffer = pd→PD_BUF;
    pd→PD_BUF = buffer;

    /* Call the device driver to read a sector */
    ReturnVal = CallRead(1,                    /* contig sectors          */
        Sector,                                /* sector number           */
        pd,
        DevStatic,                             /* device static storage   */
        procd,
        regs,
        SysGlobs);

    DevStatic→V_BUSY = 0;                      /* device not busy         */

    /* Deal with a strangeness of the driver */
    if(Sector == 0 && ReturnVal == E_BTYP)
        ReturnVal = 0;

    /* Update the Current Sector field in the path descriptor */
    if(ReturnVal == 0)
        pd→PD_CSector = Sector;
    else
        pd→PD_CSector = −1;
    return ReturnVal;
}
```

The following function is responsible for setting values in the drive table.

```
static InitDriveTable(pd, FATStart, FATCopies, DirSize, ClusterSize,
    FATSize, TrackSize, Sides, Size)
register PD_TYPE pd;
{
    register DriveTableType *DriveTable;

    DriveTable = (DriveTableType *)pd→PD_DTB;
    DriveTable→DD_TOT[0] = (Size >> 16) & 0x00ff;
    DriveTable→DD_TOT[1] = (Size >> 8) & 0x00ff;
    DriveTable→DD_TOT[2] = Size & 0x00ff;
    DriveTable→DD_TKS = DriveTable→DD_SPT[1] = TrackSize & 0x00ff;
    DriveTable→DD_SPT[0] = (TrackSize >> 8) & 0x00ff;
    DriveTable→DD_FMT =
        ((Sides == 2) ? 1 : 0) +               /* 1: double sided         */
        2 +                                    /* 2: always double density */
```

21.3. THE DUMMY FILE MANAGER

```
        ((Size > 720) ? 4 : 0);              /* 4: 80 track             */
    DriveTable→V_FATSz = FATSize;
    DriveTable→DD_DIR = FATStart + (FATSize * FATCopies);
    DriveTable→DD_FirstFAT = FATStart;
    DriveTable→DD_FATCnt = FATCopies;
    DriveTable→V_DirEntries = DirSize;
    DriveTable→DD_FATSIZ = FATSize;
    return;
}
```

The following function picks useful information out of the PC-DOS boot sector and converts it into values that OS-9 needs:

```
static InitFromBoot(pd, BootPtr)
PD_TYPE pd;
BootSectorType BootPtr;
{
    InitDriveTable(pd,
        2,                                   /* Start of FAT            */
        BootPtr→FATCopies,
        (BootPtr→RootDirSize[1] << 8) + BootPtr→RootDirSize[0],
        BootPtr→SectorsPerCluster,
        (BootPtr→SectorsPerFAT[1] << 8) + BootPtr→SectorsPerFAT[0],
        (BootPtr→SectorsPerTrack[1] << 8) + BootPtr→SectorsPerTrack[0],
        (BootPtr→Sides[1] << 8) + BootPtr→Sides[0],
        (BootPtr→TotSectors[1] << 8) + BootPtr→TotSectors[0]);
    return;
}
```

21.3.14 The Format.h Header File

```
#define BOOTSECTOR 0
#define FATSTART 1
#define FILERASED '\0xE5'
#define DEFAULT_DRIVES 2

    /* Attributes */
#define MS_READ_ONLY 0x1
#define MS_HIDDEN 0x2
#define MS_SYSTEM 0x4
#define MS_V_LABEL 0x8
#define MS_SUBDIR 0x10
```

```
#define MS_ARCHIVE 0x20

typedef unsigned char uchar;
typedef unsigned long ulong;

typedef struct {
   char Reserved1[3];               /*A branch instruction              */
   char SystemID[8];
   uchar SectorSize[2];             /*Bytes per sector                  */
   uchar SectorsPerCluster;
   uchar ReservedSectors[2];        /*Number of reserved sectors at start */
   uchar FATCopies;
   uchar RootDirSize[2];            /*Number of entries in root directory */
   uchar TotSectors[2];             /*Sectors on the disk               */
   uchar FormatID;                  /*F8..FF                            */
   uchar SectorsPerFAT[2];
   uchar SectorsPerTrack[2];
   uchar Sides[2];
   uchar S_ReservedSectors[2];      /*Special reserved sectors          */
} *BootSectorType;

typedef struct {
   char FileName[8];
   char FileExtension[3];
   uchar FileAttr;
   char Reserved[10];
   uchar Time[2];
   uchar Date[2];
   uchar StartCluster[2];
   uchar FileSize[4];
} *MSDirE;

/* File attributes */
#define VOL_LABEL 0x20
#define SUB_DIRECTORY 0x10
#define READ_ONLY 0x08
#define MODIFIED 0x04
#define HIDDEN 0x02
#define SYSTEM_FILE 0x01

typedef uchar SmallFAT_Entrys[3];
```

21.3. THE DUMMY FILE MANAGER

```c
typedef struct {
    long R_d0, R_d1, R_d2, R_d3, R_d4, R_d5, R_d6, R_d7;
    char *R_a0, *R_a1, *R_a2, *R_a3, *R_a4, *R_a5, *R_a6, *R_a7;
    uchar   R_ssr;              /* Status register – system part         */
    uchar   R_cc;               /* Status register – condition code part */
    short   *R_pc;              /* Program counter register              */
    short   R_fmt;              /* 68010 exception format and vector     */
} *REGS;

typedef struct {
    uchar     DD_TOT[3];        /* Total number of sectors on device     */
    uchar     DD_TKS;           /* Track size in sectors                 */
    ushort    DD_FATSIZ;        /* Number of bytes in FAT                */
    ushort    DD_SPC;           /* Number of sectors per cluster         */
    ushort    DD_DIR;           /* Address of root directory             */
                                /* The address is actually an lsn: 24 bits */
                                /* but since it is always around 16,     */
                                /* 16 bits more than suffice             */
    ushort    DD_OWN;           /* Owner ID (meaningless)                */
    ushort    DD_DSK;           /* Disk ID                               */
    ushort    DD_ATT;           /* Attributes, one extra byte to compensate for */
                                /* DD_DIR (which was short)              */
    uchar     DD_FMT;           /* Disk format; density/sides            */
    uchar     DD_SPT[2];        /* Sectors per track                     */
    uchar     DD_FATCnt;        /* Copies of FAT                         */
    uchar     DD_FirstFAT;      /* First FAT Sector                      */
    uchar     DD_Reserved;      /* Pad to an even boundary               */
    ushort    V_TRAK;           /* Current track                         */
    POINTER   V_FileHd;         /* Open file list for this drive         */
    ushort    V_DiskID;         /* Disk ID (duplicate of DD_DSK?)        */
    ushort    V_FATSz;          /* FAT size                              */
    ushort    V_FATSct;         /* Lowest FAT word to search             */
    ushort    V_FATB;           /* FAT busy flag                         */
    POINTER   V_ScZero;         /* Pointer to sector zero buffer         */
    uchar     V_ZeroRd;         /* Sector zero read flag                 */
    uchar     V_Init;           /* Drive initialized flag                */
    ushort    V_ResBit;         /* Reserved bitmap sector number (if any) */
    ulong     V_SoftEr;
    ulong     V_HardEr;
    ushort    V_DirEntries;
    ulong     V_Reserved[8];
} DriveTableType;
```

```
                /*I/O Device Static storage required by the kernel for all device types.    */
typedef struct {
    POINTER    V_PORT;              /*Device base port address                             */
    ushort     V_LPRC;              /*Last active process ID                               */
    ushort     V_BUSY;              /*Current process ID (0=idle)                          */
    ushort     V_WAKE;              /*Active process ID if driver must wakeup              */
    POINTER    V_Paths;             /*Linked list of open paths on device                  */
    ulong      V_Reserved[8];
                                    /*Static storage for RBF drivers                       */
    uchar      V_NDRV;              /*Number of drives                                     */
    uchar      V_DReserved[7];
    DriveTableType V_DRIVES[DEFAULT_DRIVES];        /* This may be the wrong
                                                       size but that's ok                  */
                                    /*Followed by device driver static storage             */
} *STATICSTORETYPE;
```

21.3.15 The Special PathDesc.h Header File

```
typedef struct PDTYPE {
    unsigned short   PD_PD;         /*Path number                                          */
    unsigned char    PD_MOD;        /*Mode (read/write/update)                             */
    unsigned char    PD_CNT;        /*Number of open images                                */
    struct DEVTAB    *PD_DEV;       /*Device table entry address                           */
    unsigned short   PD_CPR;        /*Current process id                                   */
    POINTER          PD_RGS;        /*Caller's register stack pointer                      */
    char             *PD_BUF;       /*Buffer address                                       */
    unsigned int     PD_USER;       /*User ID of path's creator                            */
    struct PDTYPE    *PD_Paths;     /*Linked list of open paths on device                  */
    unsigned short   PD_COUNT;      /*Actual number of open images                         */
    unsigned short   PD_LProc;      /*Last active process ID                               */
    short            PD_Reserved[6];
    /*
        File manager storage
    */
    unsigned char    PD_SMF;        /*State flags                                          */
    unsigned char    PD_Unused[3];
    unsigned long    PD_CSector;    /*Number of sector in the buffer                       */
    unsigned long    PD_CP;         /*Current logical byte position                        */
    unsigned long    PD_SIZ;        /*File size                                            */
    short            PD_Unused1[7]; /* To put PD_DTB in the right spot                     */
    POINTER          PD_DTB;        /*Drive table pointer                                  */
    /*
        The fields so far add up to 34 bytes of file manager storage.
```

21.3. THE DUMMY FILE MANAGER

```
        86 bytes are required to bring us up to the option area.
    */
    char          PD_Unused2[86];
    char          PD_OPT;              /* Dummy field to signify the beginning of
                                          the options section                    */

    /* additional fields go here */
} *PD_TYPE;

typedef struct {
    unsigned char   PD_DTP;           /* Device type                             */
    unsigned char   PD_DRV;           /* Drive number                            */
    unsigned char   PD_STP;           /* Step rate                               */
    unsigned char   PD_TYP;           /* Disk device type                        */
    unsigned char   PD_DNS;           /* Density capability                      */
    unsigned char   PD_reserved2;
    unsigned short  PD_CYL;           /* Number of cylinders                     */
    unsigned char   PD_SID;           /* Number of sides                         */
    unsigned char   PD_VFY;           /* 0=verify disk writes                    */
    unsigned short  PD_SCT;           /* Default sectors per track               */
    unsigned short  PD_TOS;           /* Default sectors per track (tr0, s0)     */
    unsigned short  PD_SAS;           /* Segment allocation size                 */
    unsigned char   PD_ILV;           /* Sector interleave offset                */
    unsigned char   PD_TFM;           /* DMA transfer mode                       */
    unsigned char   PD_TOffs;         /* Track base offset                       */
    unsigned char   PD_SOffs;         /* Sector base offset                      */
    unsigned short  PD_SSize;         /* Size of sector in bytes                 */
    unsigned short  PD_Cntl;          /* Control word                            */
    unsigned char   PD_Trys;          /* Number of tries (1=no error correction) */
    unsigned char   PD_LUN;           /* SCSI unit number of drive               */
    unsigned short  PD_WPC;           /* First cylinder using write precomp      */
    unsigned short  PD_RWC;           /* First cylinder using reduced write current */
    unsigned short  PD_Park;          /* Park cylinder for hard disks            */
    unsigned long   PD_LSNOffs;       /* Logical sector number offset for partition */
    unsigned short  PD_TotCyls;       /* Total number of cylinders on device     */
    unsigned char   PD_CtrlrID;       /* SCSI controller ID                      */
    unsigned char   PD_reserved3[14];
    unsigned char   PD_ATT;           /* File attributes                         */
    unsigned long   PD_FD;            /* File descriptor psn                     */
    unsigned long   PD_DFD;           /* Directory file descriptor psn           */
    unsigned long   PD_DCP;           /* Directory entry pointer                 */
    POINTER         PD_DVT;           /* Device table pointer (copy)             */
    unsigned char   PD_reserved4[26];
    char            PD_Name[32];      /* Filename                                */
} *PD_OPTS;
```

```
typedef struct DEVTAB {
    POINTER V_DRIV;
    STATICSTORETYPE V_STAT;
    POINTER V_DESC;
    POINTER V_FMGR;
    short V_USRS;
} *DEVTABTYPE;
```

Chapter 22

Adding a New Device Driver

> *In this chapter we discuss the reason for device drivers, then move on to reasons for creating new drivers. The actual business of writing a driver is left for chapters 23 and 24, and appendix D.*

Device drivers are operating system modules that deal with the actual hardware of an I/O device. Other parts of OS-9 deal with an idealized device. All SCF devices seem to perform the same operations in the same way from the point of view of every module except the device driver. The driver does whatever is necessary to make the real device look like the imaginary device that the rest of the OS-9 world sees.

This philosophy has some important implications. It gives OS-9 tremendous flexibility. Only one module has to be written to permit the system to use a new device. The only limit on the number of device drivers that OS-9 can support concurrently is the memory that they all take. Eventually, the drivers and their associated buffers and descriptors will use up more memory than you can tolerate; since drivers usually need only a little memory this is seldom an important limit.

There is a hidden cost for this flexibility. When you know the characteristics of the device you are working with there is a lot you can do to optimize your system. Isolating that knowledge in device drivers prevents the rest of the system from taking advantage of any special features a device might have.

On a system with memory-mapped video, positioning the cursor is a trivial operation. The screen is mapped into a block of memory; the cursor position is just an address. On a system with a terminal, positioning a cursor is a harder task. OS-9 doesn't concern itself with cursor positioning, not because it isn't important, but because a system general enough to work on systems with very "dumb" terminals would be wasteful on systems with memory-mapped video.

Cursor positioning[1] is an example of a device characteristic that OS-9 hasn't taken responsibility for, but there are other things like buffering and error handling that OS-9 hides in the device driver at some cost in speed and power. Terminal characteristics are left to programs and library routines.

The actual design of a device driver will be taken up in chapters 23 and 24, and appendix D. It isn't difficult, but must be done carefully. Sysdbg, ROMBug, and the ROM debugger work on system code, but many problems at the operating system level involve timing or unexpected dependencies. A defective driver for a serial port could easily only manifest its problem when it's running full tilt in a heavily loaded system. Any bugs you write into the driver tend to have hair and teeth!

22.1 Why Create New Drivers?

If you like to play with your operating system, device drivers are a good playground. The operating system is meant to be expanded by having drivers added to it, and there are many opportunities for expansion.

If this kind of thing excites you, study the drivers presented here, and customize your own. Two warnings:

- OS-9 is an evolving operating system. New features are the visible sign of evolution, but many changes only improve performance, fix bugs, or add support for new processors. Compatibility with old user-state code is almost an absolute rule at Microware. Compatibility with old system-state code is only an important goal.

  Microware considers device drivers part of the operating system. If they find compelling reasons to drop compatibility with their old drivers, they will.[2] However, Microware tries (maybe tries too hard) to remain compatible with old system code. OS-9's evolution is unlikely to break your drivers if you follow the design of Microware's drivers as closely as possible and stick carefully to documented interfaces.

- Make a special effort to keep the program interface of your driver compatible with Microware's distributed drivers. If you add enhancements that make you slightly incompatible, you may find that a program you buy relies on the feature you changed.

---

[1] The C termcap library supports almost any terminal with a termcap database and a set of C functions.
[2] I don't remember any OS-9/68000 changes that lost compatibility with well-behaved old drivers. The compat bytes in the init module support old behavior.

22.1. WHY CREATE NEW DRIVERS?

Device drivers are a particularly important part of a real-time control system. Not only do real-time systems sometimes have special devices to support, but device drivers are entered only a few cycles after an interrupt takes place. If you need to respond to an interrupt with some almost-instant action, the interrupt service routine of a device driver is the only place to do the processing. Normal processes are run and put to sleep at the whim of the dispatcher; interrupt service routines run as soon as the source of the interrupt is discovered.

If, for example, you are controlling an outgoing voltage based on an incoming voltage, the times required for A/D (Analog-to-Digital) and D/A (Digital-to-Analog conversion) may be almost more than you can afford. A device driver could be designed to drive both devices and perform some simple computations. It would pass information on to a normal program for low-priority processing, but would respond almost instantly to each interrupt.

If you create a new device driver with a new name, you must also build a device descriptor for it. No device can be used without a descriptor.

If you build or buy a new device driver, you may not want to install it in your boot file immediately. If you want to experiment first, or don't want to use space in the boot for a seldom-used device, device drivers can be loaded after the system is booted. Just make sure that both the device driver and the device descriptor stay linked as long as they are being used.

One good cause for inexplicable errors is that the driver has come unlinked and disappeared from memory. If this happens, unlink the descriptor and load and link both the descriptor and the driver again. Since modules in the bootstrap can't be dropped from memory no matter how many times they are unlinked, the problem doesn't show up with modules from OS9Boot. If you load parts of your I/O system after the system is booted, be careful.

Chapter 23

Sample SCF Device Driver

This chapter contains a complete device driver for the Motorola 68681 I/O device. It includes most of the common features of SCF device drivers.

The device driver in this chapter is Microware's standard 68681 device driver for OS-9/68000 version 2.1 updated to version 2.4 standards.[1] The version is important. Device drivers are parts of the operating system and the requirements they must meet change as OS-9 evolves. This driver is very likely to work with future versions of OS-9/68000, but it may require adjustments as OS-9 changes.

23.1 Module Header

A device driver should have a module type of Drivr and the ReEnt[2] and SupStat attributes.

The stack size in the psect directive should be zero. This doesn't mean that the device driver is expected to run with no stack. It will use the system stack for the calling process (except for the IRQ routine). Although the driver may have more than a kilobyte available on the stack, it shouldn't count on more than about 256 bytes of stack space. The driver gets the stack after the kernel, IOMan, and the file manager have each consumed what they need.

---

[1]This driver is copyright ©1984 by Microware Systems Corporation Reproduced Under License. This source code is the proprietary, confidential property of Microware Systems Corporation, and is provided to licensee solely for documentation and educational purposes. Reproduction, publication, or distribution in any form to any party other than the licensee is strictly prohibited.

[2]Reentrancy is not absolutely required for drivers, but it is strongly suggested. Since a non-reentrant driver will only accept one link, it can only be used for one device.

```
0000000e  Edition    equ    14                        current Edition number

00000e01  Typ_Lang   set    (Drivr<<8)+Objct
0000a000  Attr_Rev   set    ((ReEnt+SupStat)<<8)+0
                     psect  MzrMpsc,Typ_Lang,Attr_Rev,Edition,0,MpscEnt

                     use    defsfile
```

Defsfile includes oskdefs.d and systype.d. Some of the values in oskdefs.d and systype.d are also in sys.l, but the linker has limited expression-handling facilities (for instance it cannot shift or complement values), and some important values are not in sys.l.

```
00000e01  Typ_Lang   set    (Drivr<<8)+Objct
```

The linker only knows how to substitute values at given offsets. It can't do arbitrary arithmetic.

23.2 Definitions

A device driver is a cryptic piece of code at best. It helps if the driver explains and names the "magic" constants for the driver and its I/O device.

```
00000001  No_IRQ    set  1                     (non-zero enables IRQ code)
00000007  Signbit   set  7
00000050  InpSiz    set  80                    input buffer size
0000008c  OutSiz    set  140                   output buffer size
0000000a  MinBuff   equ  10                    send XON at MinBuff
00000046  MaxBuff   equ  InpSiz-MinBuff        send XOFF at MaxBuff
```

The read and write routines in an interrupt-driven device driver don't actually transfer data to or from the I/O hardware. In general, the IRQ routine manipulates the hardware and the read and write routines deal with I/O buffers. There is a grey area where buffer management involves interaction with the hardware.

The I/O buffers should be large enough to accommodate the next unit up from a character—generally, a line. If the output buffer is too small, processes will find themselves blocked while the driver's IRQ routine works. This affects performance, but it isn't catastrophic. If the input buffer is too small, unneccessary flow control may be used. In the worst case input can be lost. When the input buffer is nearly full the driver will transmit an XOff character to the sender (if the device descriptor shows XOff support). If there is no flow control, the IRQ routine will announce an error and start dropping input.

23.2. DEFINITIONS

A human at a keyboard is unlikely to overflow any buffer, but a 9600 baud modem or a terminal that can dump a buffer at 19.2 Kbaud will challenge a loaded system. If you expect 2K screen dumps or 256 byte xmodem buffers, make the input buffer slightly larger than the expected input block. This will let the IRQ routine run at full speed into the buffer, and let the program read an entire block without waiting.

```
00000004  ABbit     equ   4                bit #4 of port address tells the "side"
80000080  BrkTime   equ   $80000000+128    break sent for 500mSec.
00000080  RxDefault equ   RxRTS            RxRTS control enabled
00000010  TxDefault equ   TxCTS            TxCTS control enabled
```

The RxDefault and TxDefault values are used in the RTSmode and TXmode fields in device static storage.

All the device control registers are addressed relative to the device address that will be specified in the device descriptor. If the relative addresses of the I/O registers in the device were not fixed by the I/O device, it would be better to define all the addresses in the descriptor.

```
*******************
* Register offset definitions.
*

* these offsets are "side" offsets from "device side" address

00000000  MPSMode  equ   $00              68681 mode register
00000002  MPSBdSt  equ   $02              68681 baud rate/status register
00000004  MPSCntl  equ   $04              68681 control register
00000006  MPSData  equ   $06              68681 data register

* these offsets are "base" offsets from device "base" address

00000008  MPSAcr   equ   $08              68681 ACR register
0000000a  MPSImr   equ   $0a              68681 interrupt mask/status register
00000018  MPSVec   equ   $18              68681 interrupt vector register
0000001a  MPSOPCR  equ   $1a              68681 output port configuration reg.
0000001c  MPSOPSet equ   $1c              68681 output port SET register
0000001e  MPSOPClr equ   $1e              68681 output port CLEAR register
```

The following equates define the important values for each I/O register.

```
* MPSMode Register

00000080  RxRTS    equ   %10000000        MR1 - rx rts flow control enable
00000020  TxRTS    equ   %00100000        MR2 - tx rts flow control enable
```

```
00000010  TxCTS      equ    %00010000    MR2 - tx cts flow control enable
```

* MPSAcr Register

```
0000000f  DeltaMask  equ    %00001111    delta IPx change mask
00000070  CTMask     equ    %01110000    counter/timer source bits
00000080  Set2       equ    %10000000    select baud set #2
00000000  Set1       equ    %00000000    select baud set #1
00000080  ACRDeflt   equ    Set2         default acr mode (w/o timer values)
```

* MPSBdSt Register

```
00000002  TxE_Bit    equ    2            transmit RDY bit
00000000  RxA_Bit    equ    0            receive char avail bit
00000010  IPOverrun  equ    %00010000    input over-run status bit
00000070  InputErr   equ    $70          input error mask
```

* MPSCntl Register

```
00000001  RxEnabl    equ    $1           enable receiver
00000002  RxDisabl   equ    $2           disable receiver
00000004  TxEnabl    equ    $4           enable xmit
00000008  TxDisabl   equ    $8           disable xmit
00000020  RxReset    equ    $20          reset receiver
00000030  TxReset    equ    $30          reset transmitter
00000040  ErrorRst   equ    $40          error reset
00000050  BreakRst   equ    $50          break condition reset
00000060  StartBrk   equ    $60          start break
00000070  StopBrk    equ    $70          stop break
```

* MPSImr register

```
00000002  RxIRQEnA   equ    $2           enable channel A receiver interrupt
00000001  TxIRQEnA   equ    $1           enable channel A transmitter interrupt
00000020  RxIRQEnB   equ    $20          enable channel B receiver interrupt
00000010  TxIRQEnB   equ    $10          enable channel B transmitter interrupt
00000003  IRQP_BitA  equ    $03          xmit & rec channel A interrupt mask
00000030  IRQP_BitB  equ    $30          xmit & rec channel B interrupt mask
00000001  IRQ_RecA   equ    1            channel A rec bit no
00000005  IRQ_RecB   equ    5            channel B rec bit no
```

* MPSOPCR register

```
00000000  OPCRmode   equ    %00000000    default o/p port control register mode

00000001  OP0        equ    1<<0         OP0 set/reset pattern
00000002  OP1        equ    1<<1         OP1
```

23.3. STATIC STORAGE

```
00000004  OP2    equ    1<<2     OP2
00000008  OP3    equ    1<<3     OP3
00000010  OP4    equ    1<<4     OP4
00000020  OP5    equ    1<<5     OP5
00000040  OP6    equ    1<<6     OP6
00000080  OP7    equ    1<<7     OP7
```

23.3 Static Storage

A device driver can use storage from four pools.

- The system stack. There may not be room on the stack for substantial data structures, and data stored on the stack is effectively erased every time the driver returns to its caller. Stack storage is, however, convenient and efficient.

- Path descriptors can be used to store device driver variables, but it's not generally a good idea. Path descriptors are for the use of IOMan and the file manager. It is, however, reasonable to read the path descriptor as needed. The path descriptor provides static storage that lasts while the I/O path is open. If a path is duped, the duplicate paths share a path descriptor[3], but path descriptors generally correspond to a single path to a device. The device driver's storage in a path descriptor can be used to store values that should span calls to the driver.

- The device static storage is shared between IOMan, the file manager, and the device driver. It stores values that are specific to the device (as opposed to a path or the device driver). The device static storage area can be thought of as a writable extension to the device descriptor. It can be used to store values that don't apply to any particular path. The I/O buffers are good examples of data structures that are typically stored in the device static storage.

- The OEM global area is available to the entire operating system. It can be used to communicate between device drivers, or between drivers and other system modules such as the bootstrap, SysGo, the clock module, and custom SVCs. It should only be used as a last resort.

Many of the fields in static storage for this driver are for the I/O buffers. The other fields reflect the state of the device or are stored here because the device static storage is a good place to cache values.

---

[3]Duping is a common practice for standard I/O paths.

Table 23.1: SC68681 Device Static Storage

Fields	Application
InFill InEmpty InEnd OutFill OutEmpty OutEnd InCount OutCount InpBuf OutBuf	I/O buffer fields
BaseAddr IRQMask ChanelNo Otpt_On Otpt_Off Globl	Static fields: set at initialization time and kept here to avoid repeated recalculation
BaudRate Parity InHalt OutHalt RTSmode RTSstate TXmode SigPrc DCDPrc	Dynamic fields: describe the state of the device

```
**********
* Static storage offsets
*
                       vsect
00000000  InFill    ds.l  1        input buffer next-in pointer
00000004  InEmpty   ds.l  1        input buffer next-out pointer
00000008  InEnd     ds.l  1        end of input buffer
0000000c  OutFill   ds.l  1        output buffer next-in pointer
00000010  OutEmpty  ds.l  1        output buffer next-out pointer
00000014  OutEnd    ds.l  1        output buffer end of buffer pointer
00000018  BaseAddr  ds.l  1        base address of port

0000001c  InCount   ds.w  1        # of chars in input buffer
0000001e  OutCount  ds.w  1        # of chars in output buffer
00000020  IRQMask   ds.w  1        interrupt mask word
00000022  Globl     ds.w  1        offset to global masks
00000024  SigPrc    ds.w  3        signal on data ready process (pid, signal, path)
0000002a  DCDPrc    ds.w  3        signal for DCD transitions process (pid, signal, path)

00000030  ChanelNo  ds.b  1        channel number 0 = A  1 = B
00000031  BaudRate  ds.b  1        baud rate value
00000032  Parity    ds.b  1        current parity value
00000033  InHalt    ds.b  1        input halted flag (non-zero if XON has been Sent)
00000034  OutHalt   ds.b  1        output IRQ's disabled when non-Zero
00000035  Otpt_On   ds.b  1        value to enable acia output IRQs
00000036  Otpt_Off  ds.b  1        value to disable acia output IRQs
00000037  RTSmode   ds.b  1        RxRTS handshake mode
00000038  RTSstate  ds.b  1        RxRTS current state
00000039  TXmode    ds.b  1        Tx handshake mode
```

```
0000003a  InpBuf    ds.b    InpSiz      input buffer
0000008a  OutBuf    ds.b    OutSiz      output buffer
00000000           ends
```

* OutHalt bit numbers (causes of disabled output IRQ)

```
00000000  H_XOFF    equ     0           V_XOFF received; awaiting V_XON
00000001  H_Empty   equ     1           output buffer is empty
```

23.4 The Entry Vector Table

The device descriptor module only has one code entry point in its module header, but it contains seven separate routines. The single entry point is used for seven routines by using the module entry offset value to indicate a vector table. File managers (and IOMan) that use SCF device drivers know the structure of this vector table and will use it to reach each entry point.

```
0000 000e  MpscEnt  dc.w    Init
0002 0226           dc.w    Read
0004 02f2           dc.w    Write
0006 0346           dc.w    GetStat
0008 0380           dc.w    PutStat
000a 04d6           dc.w    Term
000c 0000           dc.w    0           Exception handler entry (0=none)
```

23.5 Init Routine

The device driver's init entry is not called by a file manager. It is called directly from IOMan. The init routine initializes the static data structures associated with a device and sets up the hardware for subsequent I/O.

Only the init and term entries are passed a pointer to the device descriptor. Although other entries can discover the address of the device descriptor with some effort, the init routine takes every value the driver will use from the device descriptor and saves it in the device static storage. This is particularly important for values that will be used in the IRQ handler component of the driver. The IRQ handler only has the address of the static storage; it does not see a path descriptor.[4]

---
[4]It would be difficult for the kernel to decide which path will get each character of input when the interrupt is being dispatched. Consider, the kernel doesn't even know which driver will catch the interrupt much less whether it is input, output, or error. It won't be able to assign a path until it is fairly into the driver.

```
* Initialize (Terminal) MPSC
*
* Passed:  (a1) = device descriptor address
*          (a2) = static storage address
*          (a4) = process descriptor ptr
*          (a6) = system global data ptr
*
* Returns: nothing
*
* Error Return: (cc) = carry set
*               d1.w = error code
*
* Destroys: (may destroy d0–d7, a0–a5)
*
```

Start by initializing the easy values in device static storage. Here the device is made idle with empty buffers. The code sets up data structures for the I/O buffers and calculates a value for IRQMask.

IRQMask is moved into the processor's SR register to mask interrupts when the driver must do an "atomic" operation.

```
               Init:
*                      Output IRQ's disabled; buffer empty
000e 157c              move.b  #(1<<H_Empty),OutHalt(a2)
0014 41ea              lea.l   InpBuf(a2),a0      init buffer pointers
0018 2548              move.l  a0,InFill(a2)
001c 2548              move.l  a0,InEmpty(a2)
0020 41e8              lea.l   InpSiz(a0),a0      figure size of buffer
0024 2548              move.l  a0,InEnd(a2)       mark end of input buffer
0028 41ea              lea.l   OutBuf(a2),a0      point to start of output buffer
002c 2548              move.l  a0,OutFill(a2)     init output buff pointers
0030 2548              move.l  a0,OutEmpty(a2)
0034 41e8              lea.l   OutSiz(a0),a0      figure size of out buffer
0038 2548              move.l  a0,OutEnd(a2)      mark end of output buffer
003c=1429              move.b  M$IRQLvl(a1),d2    get irq level
0040 e142              asl.w   #8,d2              shift into priority
0042=08c2              bset.l  #SupvrBit+8,d2     set system state bit
0046 3542              move.w  d2,IRQMask(a2)     save for future use
```

Now the driver reads the port address from the device static storage,[5] converts it to a base address, and saves it in device static storage. This device has two classes of registers. Some registers control the chip as a whole. These registers are addressed with offsets from the device's base address. The 68681 has two "sides" that can handle

---
[5]The port address is copied from the device descriptor into device static storage by IOMan.

23.5. INIT ROUTINE

separate streams of I/O. Each side has a separate set of registers which are addressed with offsets from V_PORT. The driver also calculates the channel number within the device. Bit 4 (ABit) in the port address specifies the channel. The channel is used to initialize the Otpt_On and Otpt_Off values. These are precalculated values that will be stored in device control registers to turn output on and off. Each channel has its own codes.

At the end of this block of code, the ChanelNo field is 0 (A) or 1 (B), the Otpt_On and Otpt_Off fields are set correctly for the channel, and BaseAddr is set to the the actual base address of the device (after the channel is masked out).

```
004a=266a            movea.l  V_PORT(a2),a3   I/O port address
004e 200b            move.l   a3,d0           save device absolute address
0050 422a            clr.b    ChanelNo(a2)    assume channel A
      * Set interrupt enable flags on channel A
0054 157c            move.b   #RxIRQEnA!TxIRQEnA,Otpt_On(a2)
005a 157c            move.b   #^TxIRQEnA,Otpt_Off(a2)  set xmit int disable flag
0060 0800            btst.l   #ABbit,d0       figure out which port 0 = A, 1 = B
0064 6712            beq.s    Init20
0066 157c            move.b   #1,ChanelNo(a2) set to B
      * Set interrupt enable flags for channel B
006c 157c            move.b   #RxIRQEnB!TxIRQEnB,Otpt_On(a2)
0072 157c            move.b   #^TxIRQEnB,Otpt_Off(a2)  set xmit int disable flag
0078 0200  Init20    andi.b   #$E1,d0         get base address of port
007c 2a40            movea.l  d0,a5           move to address register
007e 2540            move.l   d0,BaseAddr(a2) save base address
```

The 68681 supports two serial lines and can also serve as the system clock. Since the clock driver and two SCF devices share the same chip, they must communicate with one another. The problem is that device-control registers are often write-only. A read to the address does not return the value last written into the control register. Since the value written into a single control register effects the operation of the clock driver and the device driver, both drivers maintain a shadow copy of the register in OEM global storage.

A system might contain several 68681's. This is accommodated by keeping an array of shadow registers. Some space in the device static storage is saved by storing the offset of the shadow register from the system global storage instead of an absolute address for the shadow register. This code saves the offset value in the field named Globl.

```
0082=3029            move.w   M$DevCon(a1),d0  get offset of global masks
0086 6700            beq      BadMode10        ..return error if descriptor is not valid
008a 3031            move.w   (a1,d0.w),d0     get offset to global pair for this device
008e=d07c            add.w    #D_Start,d0      calc entry of the pair in OEM_Globals
```

```
0092 3540           move.w  d0,Globl(a2)    save it
```

Next, the driver registers the device in the system polling table. The base address of the device was left in register A5 earlier. This base address is used to get the device vector. If the device interrupt vector is uninitialized, the driver sets it to the value from the device descriptor. If the value is initialized, the driver checks it against the value in the descriptor and reports an error if they differ. It returns a bad mode error, but it really means that the device descriptor for this device, or for the other side of the chip is incorrect.

With the vector number in D0, the interrupt priority from the device descriptor in D1, the address of the IRQ service routine (included in the driver) in A0, the device static storage pointer in A2, and the port address of the device in A3, the driver issues the *F$IRQ* system call to register the interrupt service routine with the kernel.

The *F$IRQ* call must be done at the right time. It must be done before the driver does anything that might cause the device to generate an interrupt. Otherwise the device might assert an interrupt that the kernel will fail to dispatch. However, the device static storage must be initialized to a point where the interrupt service routine can run successfully before the service routine can be registered.

```
0096 102d           move.b  MPSVec(a5),d0           read current device vector
009a 0c00           cmpi.b  #$0f,d0                 is it uninitialized vector ?
009e 670c           beq.s   Init40                  ..yes; go write the register
00a0=1229           move.b  M$Vector(a1),d1         get descriptor's vector
00a4 b001           cmp.b   d1,d0                   is the descriptor in error ?
00a6 670c           beq.s   Init45                  ..no; continue
00a8 6000           bra     BadMode10               ..yes; return error for invalid descriptor

00ac=1029 Init40    move.b  M$Vector(a1),d0         get descriptor's vector
00b0 1b40           move.b  d0,MPSVec(a5)           setup IRQ vector in device
00b4=1229 Init45    move.b  M$Prior(a1),d1          get priority
00b8 41fa           lea.l   MPSCIRQ(pc),a0          address of interrupt service routine
00bc=4e40           os9     F$IRQ                   add to IRQ polling table
00c0 6556           bcs.s   InitExit                ..exit if error
```

Now that the device is registered with the kernel, the driver can start device configuration. The next block of code configures the device. It leaves the hardware initialized but disabled.

The sequence of operations is:

- Reset the chip.

- Set the baud rate from the value in the device descriptor.

23.5. INIT ROUTINE

- Set the parity, stop bits, and bits per byte from the device descriptor.

Since the device descriptor contains standard values for various baud rates and parity values, the device driver searches tables for the device parameters that correspond to the given characteristics. The baud rate and parity can be changed by setstat calls, so the code that actually determines and sets the configuration is encapsulated in separate routines.

```
00c2 157c              move.b   #RxDefault,RTSmode(a2) Set RxRTS h/w control
00c8 6704              beq.s    Init50         ..bra if no RTS to assert
00ca 50ea              st.b     RTSstate(a2)   signal RTS to be asserted
00ce 157c  Init50      move.b   #TxDefault,TXmode(a2) Set TxCTS h/w control
00d4 1b7c              move.b   #OPCRmode,MPSOPCR(a5) Set o/p port configuration
00da 613e              bsr.s    InitSP         first init the 68681
00dc=1029              move.b   PD_BAU−PD_OPT+M$DTyp(a1),d0 Get baud rate
00e0 615a              bsr.s    BaudCalc       set baud rate
00e2 6534              bcs.s    InitExit       ..exit if error
         * Get stop bits, bits per char and parity
00e4=1029              move.b   PD_PAR−PD_OPT+M$DTyp(a1),d0
00e8 6100              bsr      BitPar         set stop bits, parity, & bits per char
00ec 652a              bcs.s    InitExit       ..exit if error
```

At this point the device is configured but disabled. Enable the receiver. This involves an operation on the device control register and its shadow copy in the OEM global area. The transmitter will not be enabled until the write entry is called. At this point there is nothing in the output buffer. Operations on the control register and its shadow in the OEM globals should always be atomic. Serious (and mysterious) things can go wrong if several processes update the registers at roughly the same time. Updates to a register that are only one instruction long are inherently atomic. No update that involves both the control register and its shadow can be done in one instruction[6] so the chunk of code, a "critical section" protects itself by masking interrupts while it runs.

The instructions printed in capital letters are in the critical section.

```
00ee 40e7              move.w   sr,−(sp)       save irq status
00f0 46ea              move.w   IRQMask(a2),sr mask interrupts
00f4 177c              MOVE.B   #RxEnabl!TxEnabl,MPSCntl(a3) Enable xmit and rec.
00fa 162a              MOVE.B   Otpt_On(a2),d3 get enable flag
00fe 302a              MOVE.W   Globl(a2),d0   get offset to global
0102 8736              OR.B     d3,(a6,d0.w)   turn xmit and rec on
```

---

[6] A value could be moved from the shadow register into the control register, but that would be redundant. The shadow register is a copy of the control register.

† *Critical Section*: see page 186

```
0106 162a           MOVE.B  Otpt_Off(a2),d3  get disable mask
010a c736           AND.B   d3,(a6,d0.w)     turn xmit off
010e 1b76           MOVE.B  (a6,d0.w),MPSImr(a5) put into register
0114 46df           MOVE.W  (sp)+,sr
0116 7200           moveq.l #0,d1            no errors
0118 4e75  InitExit: rts
```

The subroutine that resets the 68681 device also contains a critical section. This routine does not affect the shadow register. It simply resets the chip in four different ways.

```
*********************
* InitSP: initialize receiver/transmitter to idle state
*
* Passed: (a3) = device port address
*
* Returns: nothing
*
011a 40e7  InitSP:  move.w  sr,-(sp)             save irq status
011c 46ea           move.w  IRQMask(a2),sr       mask irqs
0120 177c           MOVE.B  #RxReset,MPSCntl(a3) reset receiver
0126 177c           MOVE.B  #TxReset,MPSCntl(a3) reset xmit
012c 177c           MOVE.B  #ErrorRst,MPSCntl(a3) reset error status
0132 177c           MOVE.B  #BreakRst,MPSCntl(a3) reset channel break interrupt.
0138 46df           MOVE.W  (sp)+,sr             enable irqs
013a 4e75           rts
```

The BaudCalc subroutine is called from the init entry and the setstat entry. This code has three steps:

1. Use the baud rate table to find the 68681 code for the given baud rate.[7]

2. Store the code from the table into the MPSBdSt register. This is a one-instruction update. It doesn't need to have interrupts masked to be atomic. The table uses the code $ff to indicate that the device does not support the corresponding baud rate.

---

[7] OS-9/6809 kept device-dependent baud rate and protocol information in the device descriptor. The device driver could simply use the control bytes from the descriptor to initialize the device. This made the driver simpler, but it caused great difficulties for any software that needed to adjust the rate or protocol of a device. How was a terminal emulator program to know the code that would set each particular device to each baud rate? The current system forces the device driver to interpret a device-independent code into the appropriate action, but that is the proper job of a device driver. Now any piece of software can look at a path options section and determine the setup for that path.

23.5. INIT ROUTINE

3. Use the control register to signal the device to set the baud rate. The operation on the control register is atomic, but the entire sequence including changes to the shadow register is a critical section. This step is protected by masking interrupts.

The exact technique for baud rate adjustment is very hardware dependent. In this case the table contains codes that set one of two rates supported by the chip (baud-rate set 2). The operation on the status register instructs the device to use the baud rate in set two.

```
********************
* BaudCalc: initialize baud rate of device
*
* Passed: d0.b = OS-9 baud rate code
*          (a2) = static storage ptr
*          (a3) = device port address
*          (a6) = system global data ptr
*
* Returns: nothing
*
* Error Return: (cc) = carry set
*          d1.w = error code
*
013c 2f08  BaudCalc:  move.l   a0,-(sp)              save reg
013e 0240             andi.w   #$00ff,d0             mask out all except baud rate
0142 0c40             cmpi.w   #MaxBaud,d0           legal baud rate ?
0146 6c40             bge.s    BadMode               ..no; return error
0148 41fa             lea.l    BaudTable(pcr),a0     get table address
014c 1230             move.b   (a0,d0.w),d1          get baud rate value for chip
0150 0c01             cmpi.b   #$ff,d1               available baud rate ?
0154 6732             beq.s    BadMode               ..exit if unsupported rate
0156 1741             move.b   d1,MPSBdSt(a3)        set baud rate in device
015a 1540             move.b   d0,BaudRate(a2)       save current rate
015e 302a             move.w   Globl(a2),d0          get the global table entry ptr
0162 5240             addq.w   #1,d0                 acr image held in second byte
0164 40e7             move.w   sr,-(sp)              save irq masks (NOTE: carry is clear)
0166 46ea             move.w   IRQMask(a2),sr        mask interrupts
016a 1236             MOVE.B   (a6,d0.w),d1          get the current acr image (if any)
016e 0201             ANDI.B   #CTMask+DeltaMask,d1  keep the c/t, delta bits the same
0172 0001             ORI.B    #ACRDeflt,d1          add in default baud set
0176 1d81             MOVE.B   d1,(a6,d0.w)          update image
017a 206a             MOVE.L   BaseAddr(a2),a0       get device BASE address
017e 1141             MOVE.B   d1,MPSAcr(a0)         update the hardware
0182 46df             MOVE.W   (sp)+,sr              restore irqs
0184 205f             movea.l  (sp)+,a0              restore register
0186 4e75             rts                            return (carry clear)
```

CHAPTER 23. SAMPLE SCF DEVICE DRIVER

* here if illegal or unsupported baud-rate

```
0188 205f   BadMode   movea.l  (sp)+,a0            restore a0

018a=323c   BadMode10 move.w   #E$BMode,d1         get error code
018e=003c             ori.b    #Carry,ccr          set the carry
0192 4e75             rts                          return
```

The baud-rate code is in the range 0–15 with each number specifying a particular rate (see *The OS-9 Technical Manual*). This table gives the 68681 code for each of those rates.

* Baud rate table for Set 2 of MC68681:

```
            BaudTable
0194 ff               dc.b    $ff      0 – 50 baud unavailable
0195 00               dc.b    $00      1 – 75 baud
0196 11               dc.b    $11      2 – 110 baud
0197 22               dc.b    $22      3 – 134.5 baud
0198 33               dc.b    $33      4 – 150 baud
0199 44               dc.b    $44      5 – 300 baud
019a 55               dc.b    $55      6 – 600 baud
019b 66               dc.b    $66      7 – 1200 baud
019c aa               dc.b    $aa      8 – 1800 baud
019d 77               dc.b    $77      9 – 2000 baud
019e 88               dc.b    $88      A – 2400 baud
019f ff               dc.b    $ff      B – 3600 baud unavailable
01a0 99               dc.b    $99      C – 4800 baud
01a1 ff               dc.b    $ff      D – 7200 baud unavailable
01a2 bb               dc.b    $bb      E – 9600 baud
01a3 cc               dc.b    $cc      F – 19.2k baud

00000010    MaxBaud   equ     *−BaudTable
```

The following routine sets the number of bits per character, the number of stop bits and the parity mode. It is called from the Init entry and from the *SetOpt* setstat. This routine works like BaudCalc. The outline of its algorithm is:

- Isolate the parity code from D0.

- Find the parity in the parity table and retain the code for later use.

- Isolate the bits-per-character.

- Find the bits-per-character in the BC table (see page 302) and combine the code with the parity code. Retain the result for later use.

23.5. INIT ROUTINE

- Isolate the stop bit value.

- Find the stop bit code in the SB table (see page 302) and retain it for later use.

The parity and bit codes have been decoded with interrupts enabled. They must, however, be disabled before the device state is changed. This is not a one-instruction update. The sequence for the actual update is:

- Save the value of the status register.

- Mask interrupts.

- Update the device MPSMode register.

- Save the device state in device static storage.

- Restore the processor's status register (which restores the interrupt mask to its value before this routine masked interrupts).

```
******************************
* BitPar: set bits/character, # stop bits, parity mode
*
* Passed: d0.b = device configuration
*          bits 1,0: 0 = no parity
*                    1 = odd parity
*                    3 = even parity
*          bits 3,2: 0 = 8 bit data
*                    1 = 7 bit data
*                    2 = 6 bit data
*                    3 = 5 bit data
*          bits 5,4: 0 = 1 stop bit
*                    1 = 1.5 stop bits
*                    2 = 2 stop bits
*          (a2) = static storage pointer
*          (a3) = device port address
*
* Returns: nothing
*
* Error Return: (cc) = carry set
*          d1.w = error code
*
01a4 2f08  BitPar:   move.l   a0,-(sp)           save register
01a6 7400            moveq.l  #0,d2              sweep d2
01a8 0240            andi.w   #$00ff,d0          clear high end of word
01ac 3200            move.w   d0,d1              copy parity value
01ae 0241            andi.w   #3,d1              isolate parity code
01b2 41fa            lea.l    TabPar(pc),a0      point at parity mode table
```

```
01b6 1430              move.b   (a0,d1.w),d2        get parity code
01ba 6bcc              bmi.s    BadMode             ..exit if illegal value
01bc 3200              move.w   d0,d1               get data bit size
01be e449              lsr.w    #2,d1               make index value
01c0 0241              andi.w   #3,d1               make legal index
01c4 41fa              lea.l    TabBC(pc),a0        point at bits/char table
01c8 8430              or.b     (a0,d1.w),d2        add in bits/char
01cc 3200              move.w   d0,d1               get stop bit value
01ce e849              lsr.w    #4,d1               make index value
01d0 0241              andi.w   #3,d1               make legal index
01d4 41fa              lea.l    TabSB(pc),a0        point at stop bit table
01d8 1630              move.b   (a0,d1.w),d3        get stop bit value
01dc 6baa              bmi.s    BadMode             ..exit if illegal value
01de 40e7              move.w   sr,-(sp)            save irq masks (NOTE: carry is clear)
01e0 46ea              move.w   IRQMask(a2),sr      mask interrupts
01e4 177c              MOVE.B   #$10,MPSCntl(a3)    point to mode 1 register
01ea 842a              OR.B     RTSmode(a2),d2      add RxRTS h/w handshake mode
01ee 1742              MOVE.B   d2,MPSMode(a3)      set parity/bit per char/RxRTS control
01f2 862a              OR.B     TXmode(a2),d3       add Tx h/w handshake mode
01f6 1743              MOVE.B   d3,MPSMode(a3)      set no. of stop bits/Tx control
01fa 1540              MOVE.B   d0,Parity(a2)       save current mode
01fe 4a2a              TST.B    RTSstate(a2)        need to assert RTS ?
0202 6704              BEQ.S    BitPar20            ..no; bra on
0204 6100              BSR      EnabRTS             go assert RTS line manually
0208 46df BitPar20     MOVE.W   (sp)+,sr            restore irq masks
020a 205f              MOVEA.L  (sp)+,a0            restore a0
020c 4e75              rts                          return (carry clear)

          TabPar
020e 10                dc.b     $10                 no parity
020f 04                dc.b     $04                 odd parity
0210 ff                dc.b     $ff                 illegal value
0211 00                dc.b     $00                 even parity

          TabBC
0212 03                dc.b     $03                 8 bits per char
0213 02                dc.b     $02                 7 bits per char
0214 01                dc.b     $01                 6 bits per char
0215 00                dc.b     $00                 5 bits per char

          TabSB
0216 07                dc.b     $07                 1 stop bit
0217 07                dc.b     $07                 1.5 stop bits (for 5 bit data)
0218 0f                dc.b     $0F                 2 stop bits
0219 ff                dc.b     $ff                 illegal value
```

23.6 Read Routine

In this driver, the read routine does not actually touch the physical device. It is isolated from the device by the driver's interrupt routine. The interrupt routine places input characters on a queue. The read routine takes characters off the queue as required.

If the read routine were only responsible for reading, the code would be less than half its present size. It would follow this outline:

```
repeat
    mask interrupts
    if the queue is empty
        unmask interrupts
        sleep
        continue
until the queue is not empty
take a character off the queue
unmask interrupts
return the character
```

Flow control, XOn/XOff or hardware, is partly the responsiblility of the read routine. When the interrupt service routine notices that the queue is mostly full, it halts input by sending an XOff or dropping RTS and turning off input interrupts from the device. The interrupt service routine will set the InHalt flag to indicate that input is halted. When the queue is mostly empty and the driver is in InHalt state, the read routine will send an XOn, re-enable input interrupts, and turn off the InHalt flag.

When the read routine writes an XOn it does not go through the usual procedure. It checks the state of its output queue (that is, the output queue for the output part of the device). If the output queue is full, the read routine sets a flag that tells the output code to send an XOn. If the output queue is not full, the read routine enqueues an XOn on the output queue.[8]

The set-signal mechanism could put a driver in a position where it should give a character of input to two separate processes. It protects itself from this predicament with a policy. If there is a signal pending, the read routine declares the device "not ready" to any other readers. So, if any process tries to read from a *device* (not a path) with a set-signal pending, the driver returns an error to the reader.

The critical section right after Read_a spans the branch to Read00. If the queue is empty, the routine registers itself as an interested party before it unmasks interrupts. Then it sleeps until some input arives.

---

[8]There may be some possibility for trouble in the read routines technique of enqueuing an XOn directly on its output queue. What if the output for this device doesn't control its input?

If there is data in the queue the critical section was unneccessary. The routine re-enables interrupts and proceeds to take a character off the queue and adjust the counter and pointer. Although the dequeue involves several variables, the code that implements it is not a critical section. The variables it uses are either used only by this one section of code, or they are manipulated with one-instruction operations (the *sub.w* that is used to decrement InCount).

```
********************
* Read: Return one byte of input from the Mpsc
*
* Passed: (a1) = Path Descriptor
*         (a2) = Static Storage address
*         (a4) = current process descriptor
*         (a6) = system global ptr
*
* Returns: (d0.b) = input char
*
* Error Return: (cc) = carry set
*               d1.w = error code
*
* Destroys: a0
*
021a=356a Read00    MOVE.W  V_BUSY(a2),V_WAKE(a2) arrange wake up signal
0220 46df           MOVE.W  (sp)+,sr             restore IRQs
0222 6100           bsr     MpscSlep
0226 4a2a   Read    tst.b   InHalt(a2)           is input halted?
022a 6f48           ble.s   Read_a               branch if not
022c 0c6a           cmpi.w  #MinBuff,InCount(a2) buffer mostly emptied?
0232 6240           bhi.s   Read_a               ..no; continue
0234=122a           move.b  V_XON(a2),d1         get XOn char
0238=266a           movea.l V_PORT(a2),a3        get port address
023c 40e7           move.w  sr,-(sp)             save current IRQ status
023e 46ea           move.w  IRQMask(a2),sr       mask IRQs
0242 082b           BTST.B  #TxE_Bit,MPSBdSt(a3) transmit buffer empty?
0248 670a           BEQ.S   Read10               no, signal XON ready to send
024a 422a           CLR.B   InHalt(a2)           clean up XOFF flag
024e 1741           MOVE.B  d1,MPSData(a3)       transmit XON character
0252 601e           BRA.S   Read20               continue

0254=0001 Read10    ORI.B    #Sign,d1            set Sign bit
0258 1541           MOVE.B   d1,InHalt(a2)       flag input resume
025c 206a           MOVEA.L  BaseAddr(a2),a0     get port base address
0260 162a           MOVE.B   Otpt_On(a2),d3
0264 302a           MOVE.W   Globl(a2),d0        get offset to global
0268 8736           OR.B     d3,(a6,d0.w)        enable IRQs
026c 1176           MOVE.B   (a6,d0.w),MPSImr(a0) put into register
0272 46df  Read20   MOVE.W   (sp)+,sr            unmask IRQs
```

23.7. SLEEP

```
0274 4a6a  Read_a    tst.w    SigPrc(a2)           a process waiting for device?
0278 663c            bne.s    ErrNtRdy             ..yes; return dormant terminal error
027a 40e7            move.w   sr,-(sp)             save current IRQ status
027c 46ea            move.w   IRQMask(a2),sr       mask IRQs
0280 4a6a            TST.W    InCount(a2)          any data?
0284 6794            BEQ.S    Read00               branch if not
0286 46df            MOVE.W   (sp)+,sr             unmask IRQs
0288 206a            movea.l  InEmpty(a2),a0       point to next char
028c 1018            move.b   (a0)+,d0             get character
028e 536a            subq.w   #1,InCount(a2)       dec buffer size by one
0292 b1ea            cmpa.l   InEnd(a2),a0         at end of buffer?
0296 6504            blo.s    Read_b               branch if not
0298 41ea            lea.l    InpBuf(a2),a0        point to start of buffer
029c 2548  Read_b    move.l   a0,InEmpty(a2)       update buffer pointer
02a0=136a            move.b   V_ERR(a2),PD_ERR(a1) copy I/O status to PD
02a6 670c            beq.s    Read90               return if no error
02a8=422a            clr.b    V_ERR(a2)
02ac=323c            move.w   #E$Read,d1           signal read error
02b0=003c            ori.b    #Carry,ccr           return Carry set
02b4 4e75  Read90    rts

02b6=323c  ErrNtRdy  move.w   #E$NotRdy,d1
02ba=003c            ori.b    #Carry,ccr           return Carry set
02be 4e75            rts
```

23.7 Sleep

Sleep is called by the read and write entries. The routine sleeps until it issent a signal. When it receives a signal it classifies the signal. A wakeup signal means that input or output has arived and the sleep routine should return to whoever called it (their data is ready). The interrupt routine sent a wakeup signal (signal 1), but OS-9 does not treat the wakeup signal like other signals. It moves the process from the sleeping queue to the active queue without storing a value in the P$Signal field.

The sleep routine considers three cases:

1. It is a deadly signal (less than 32). In this case, the sleep routine pops its return address off the stack and returns to its caller's caller with an error. This would, for instance, skip it around the read routine and directly back to the file manager with a keyboard interrupt.

2. The process sleeping in the driver has died. In this case, it doesn't matter what the signal number is; the sleep routine returns as it does for a deadly signal.

3. It's not a deadly signal and the process has not expired. The sleep routine returns to its caller.

```
*********************
* MpscSlep: Sleep until interrupt occurs
*
* Passed: (a2) = driver global storage
*         (a4) = current process descriptor ptr
*         (a6) = system global data ptr
*
* Returns: nothing
*
* Error Return: (cc) = carry set
*               d1.w = error code (signal)
*
* Destroys: possibly PC
*
           MpscSlep
02c0 2f00           move.l   d0,-(sp)              save reg
02c2 7000           moveq.l  #0,d0                 sleep indefinitely
02c4=4e40           os9      F$Sleep               wait for interrupt
02c8=322c           move.w   P$Signal(a4),d1       signal present?
02cc 6706           beq.s    ACSL90                ..no; return
02ce=0c41           cmpi.w   #S$Deadly,d1          deadly signal?
 02d2 650c          blo.s    ACSLER                ..yes; return error
02d4=082c ACSL90    btst.b   #Condemn,P$State(a4)  has process died?
02da 6604           bne.s    ACSLER                ..yes; return error
02dc 201f           move.l   (sp)+,d0              restore register, clear carry
02de 4e75           rts

02e0 508f  ACSLER   addq.l   #8,sp                 exit to caller's caller
02e2=003c           ori.b    #Carry,ccr            return Carry set
02e6 4e75           rts
```

23.8 Write Routine

Like the read entry, the write entry relies on the interrupt service routine to do the low-level I/O. This write routine enqueues data on the write queue that feeds the interrupt routine. The basic outline of the write routine is:

```
repeat
    mask interrupts
    if the queue is full
        unmask interrupts
        sleep
```

23.8. WRITE ROUTINE

```
            continue
    until the queue is not full
    Put the output character on the queue
    if the device isn't active for output
        activate it
    unmask interrupts
    return
```

The full outline isn't much more complicated.

```
repeat
    mask interrupts
    if the queue is full
        unmask interrupts
        sleep
        continue
until the queue is not full
put the output character on the queue
clear the output buffer empty flag.
if the queue was empty and the device was not XOff'ed
    activate the device for output
unmask interrupts
return
```

Most of the write code is one big critical section. It doesn't strictly have to be all one critical section; for instance, the queue update could be separated from the interrupt enable code. In this case the cost of enabling interrupts, and then disabling them are not justified for the six instructions that enable output interrupts from the device.

The IMR device register may be shared with the clock and the instance of the driver handling the other side of the chip, so it is shadowed in OEM static memory and the shadow must be updated.

```
********************
* Write
* Output one character to Mpsc
*
* Passed: (a1) = Path Descriptor
*         (a2) = Static Storage address
*         (a4) = current process descriptor ptr
*         (a6) = system global data ptr
*         d0.b = char to write
```

```
*
* Returns: nothing
*
* Error Return: (cc) = carry set
*              d1.w = error code
*
02e8=356a Write00   MOVE.W  V_BUSY(a2),V_WAKE(a2) arrange wake up signal
02ee 46df           MOVE.W  (sp)+,sr              restore IRQs
02f0 61ce           bsr.s   MpscSlep              sleep a bit
02f2 40e7 Write     move.w  sr,-(sp)              save current IRQ status
02f4 46ea           move.w  IRQMask(a2),sr        mask IRQs
02f8 342a           MOVE.W  OutCount(a2),d2       get output buffer data count
02fc 0c42           CMPI.W  #OutSiz,d2            room for more data?
0300 64e6           BHS.S   Write00               ..no; wait for room
0302 526a           ADDQ.W  #1,OutCount(a2)       increment byte count
0306 206a           MOVEA.L OutFill(a2),a0        point to next char location
030a 10c0           MOVE.B  d0,(a0)+              store char and inc pointer
030c b1ea           CMPA.L  OutEnd(a2),a0         end of buffer?
0310 6504           BLO.S   Write10               branch if not
0312 41ea           LEA.L   OutBuf(a2),a0         point to start of buffer
0316 2548 Write10   MOVE.L  a0,OutFill(a2)        update buffer pointer
031a 08aa           BCLR.B  #H_Empty,OutHalt(a2)  clear output buffer empty flag
0320 671e           BEQ.S   Write80               ..if data was in buffer, no need to re-enable irqs
0322 082a           BTST.B  #H_XOFF,OutHalt(a2)   output currently halted ?
0328 6616           BNE.S   Write80               ..yes; don't enable irqs
032a 206a           MOVEA.L BaseAddr(a2),a0       get device address
032e 302a           MOVE.W  Globl(a2),d0          get offset to global
0332 162a           MOVE.B  Otpt_On(a2),d3        get enable flag
0336 8736           OR.B    d3,(a6,d0.w)          put into global register
033a 1176           MOVE.B  (a6,d0.w),MPSImr(a0)  put into register
0340 46df Write80   MOVE.W  (sp)+,sr              unmask IRQs
0342 7200           moveq.l #0,d1                 clear carry
0344 4e75           rts
```

23.9 GetStat Routine

In this driver, the getstat code is straightforward. It bounces along matching the option code against the option for blocks of code until it finds a match and executes a block, or gets to the end of the getstat code and returns an unknown SVC error code.

The most interesting entry in this device driver's getstat code is the getoptions block. Most of the work for getopts is done at a higher level—probably IOMan—but the driver is still called in this case. The driver synchronizes the path descriptor's option area with the device static storage. In particular, it updates the parity and format codes in the path descriptor.

23.9. GETSTAT ROUTINE

None of the getstat code is in a critical section. The only multi-instruction update is in getstat options. Critical sections are only needed when a block of code must not be disturbed by an interrupt handler, and the interrupt handler for this driver never updates the baud rate or port protocol values.

```
********************
* GetStat: get device status
*
* Passed:  (a1) = Path Descriptor
*          (a2) = Static Storage address
*          (a4) = process descriptor
*          (a5) = caller's register stack ptr
*          (a6) = system global data ptr
*          d0.w = status call function code
*
* Returns: varies with function code
*
* Error Return: (cc) = carry set
*               d1.w = error code
*
          GetStat

* return data available count
*
0346=0c40           cmpi.w  #SS_Ready,d0          ready status?
034a 6610           bne.s   GetSta10              ..no
034c=426d           clr.w   R$d1(a5)              sweep high word of register
0350=3b6a           move.w  InCount(a2),R$d1+2(a5) return input char count
0356 6700           beq     ErrNtRdy              ..no data; return not ready error
035a 4e75           rts                           (carry clear)


* return eof status
*
035c=0c40 GetSta10  cmpi.w  #SS_EOF,d0            end of file?
0360 671c           beq.s   GetSta99              ..yes; return (Carry clear)

* check for "get options"
*
0362=0c40           cmpi.w  #SS_Opt,d0            get options call ?
0366 660e           bne.s   Unknown               ..no; return error for unknown request

* update path descriptor for currently active baud, parity
*
0368=136a           move.b  BaudRate(a2),PD_BAU(a1) set currently active baud rate
036e=136a           move.b  Parity(a2),PD_PAR(a1)  set currently active comms mode
0374 4e75           rts                           (carry clear)
```

```
* return error for unknown service requests
*
0376=323c Unknown  move.w  #E$UnkSvc,d1   unknown service code
037a=003c          ori.b   #Carry,ccr     return Carry set
037e 4e75 GetSta99 rts
```

23.10 PutStat Routine

The driver includes most of the standard putstats arranged in the following order:

> SS_SSig
> SS_Relea
> SS_EnRTS
> SS_DsRTS
> SS_Opt
> SS_Open
> SS_Break

The order is important because the selection mechanism makes the earlier putstats slightly faster than those late in the list.

The device driver does not get called for every setstat code, but it may be called for things that don't interest it. For instance, an SCF device driver probably has no interest in path closings but it is called for each one. Many setstats are passed to the device driver as a hedge against unexpected developments in drivers. The appropriate response to an uninteresting setstat code is "unknown SVC."

```
********************
* PutStat: set device status
*
* Passed:  (a1) = Path Descriptor
*          (a2) = Static Storage address
*          (a4) = process descriptor
*          (a5) = caller's register stack ptr
*          (a6) = system global data ptr
*          d0.w = status call function code
*
* Returns: varies with function code
*
* Error Return: (cc) = carry set
*          d1.w = error code
*
          PutStat
```

23.10. PUTSTAT ROUTINE

The *SS_SSig* setstat code ensures that no path is already waiting for the device (see the read routine for another related test). If no other path has tied up the input for this device, the code checks for input waiting. If there is input waiting, the setstat sends a signal immediately.

The rest of this function enables input interrupts[9] and saves data that will be used by the interrupt handler when the time comes to actually *send* the signal.

For this function, one critical section covers three activities. The actions are:

- Send a signal and return if there is data ready.

- Save the process ID, signal code, and path number for the interrupt routine.

- Enable output interrupts (and reflect the device register in the shadow register).

To see the need for the part of the critical section that spans the check for input and the storage of data, consider the results of queuing some input between those points:

> The input queue is empty.
> A program requests a signal when data is ready.
> The call gets to the device driver which checks the input queue.
> Since the input queue is empty, the driver proceeds to register the signal.
> BUT, a character arrives before the driver gets to the movem.w instruction.
> The hardware interrupt from the 68681 is dispatched to the device driver's
>   interrupt routine.
> The interrupt routine checks for a pending signal and finds none.
> It just queues the input.
> The putstat code resumes execution and completes.

The driver is left with input in the queue and a signal that should be sent as soon as data appears in the input queue. If the program was waiting for that one character, it could now wait forever.

```
* signal process on data available
*
0380=0c40           cmpi.w   #SS_SSig,d0        signal process when ready?
0384 6648           bne.s    PutSta_A           ..no
0386 4a6a           tst.w    SigPrc(a2)         somebody already waiting?
038a 6600           bne      ErrNtRdy           ..yes; error
038e=3029           move.w   PD_CPR(a1),d0      get caller's process ID
0392=322d           move.w   R$d2+2(a5),d1      get signal code
0396 40e7           move.w   sr,-(sp)           save IRQ status
0398 46ea           move.w   IRQMask(a2),sr     disable IRQs
```

---

[9]Input and output interrupts are *both* enabled by storing Otpt_On into MPSImr.

```
039c 4a6a              TST.W    InCount(a2)         any Data available?
03a0 6626              BNE.S    PutSta10            yes, signal Data ready
03a2=3429              MOVE.W   PD_PD(a1),d2        get associated path #
03a6 48aa              MOVEM.W  d0-d2,SigPrc(a2)    save process id, signal, path #
03ac 206a              MOVEA.L  BaseAddr(a2),a0     point to base address
03b0 302a              MOVE.W   Globl(a2),d0        get offset to global
03b4 162a              MOVE.B   Otpt_On(a2),d3      get enable flag
03b8 8736              OR.B     d3,(a6,d0.w)        or into global register
03bc 1176              MOVE.B   (a6,d0.w),MPSImr(a0) put into register
03c2 46df              MOVE.W   (sp)+,sr            unmask IRQs
03c4 7200              moveq.l  #0,d1               clear carry
03c6 4e75              rts

03c8 46df  PutSta10    MOVE.W   (sp)+,sr            restore IRQ status
03ca 6000              bra      SendSig             send the signal
```

The release device function is a slightly tricky piece of coding. What it *does* is:

- If signal-on-data-ready is set for this path and this process, clear it by setting the process ID for the signal to zero.

- If there is a signal-on-DCD-loss set for this path and this process, clear it by setting the process ID for the signal to zero.

The program saves a half dozen statements by calling the check and clear code as a subroutine. It saves an extra *bsr.s* and a *rts* by dropping through the subroutine instead of calling it a second time.

```
* release all signal conditions
*
03ce=0c40 PutSta_A     cmpi.w   #SS_Relea,d0        release Device?
03d2 6622              bne.s    PutSta_B            bra if not
03d4=3029              move.w   PD_CPR(a1),d0       get process id
03d8=3429              move.w   PD_PD(a1),d2        get associated path #
03dc 47ea              lea.l    SigPrc(a2),a3       check SigPrc
03e0 6104              bsr.s    ClearSig
03e2 47ea              lea.l    DCDPrc(a2),a3       now check DCDPrc

03e6 b053  ClearSig    cmp.w    (a3),d0             is signal for this process ?
03e8 6608              bne.s    ClearSig20          ..no; exit
03ea b46b              cmp.w    4(a3),d2            does it concern this path ?
03ee 6602              bne.s    ClearSig20          ..no; exit
03f0 4253              clr.w    (a3)                clear down signal condition
03f2 7200  ClearSig20  moveq.l  #0,d1               flag no error
03f4 4e75              rts                          return
```

23.10. PUTSTAT ROUTINE

The 68681 can perform hardware flow control with its RTS line. A program can also manipulate the line with the following setstats. They involve straightforward manipulation of the hardware. A custom device driver often includes many setstats of this general type.[10]

```
* RTS control
*
0416=0c40 PutSta_D    cmpi.w   #SS_EnRTS,d0       enable RTS
041a 661a             bne.s    PutSta_E           branch if not.
041c 343c EnabRTS     move.w   #MPSOPSet,d2       get SET register offset
0420 50ea             st.b     RTSstate(a2)       flag RTS asserted
0424 122a EnabRTS10   move.b   ChanelNo(a2),d1    get channel number
0428 7000             moveq.l  #0,d0              sweep d0
042a 03c0             bset.l   d1,d0              select channel RTS o/p line
042c 206a             movea.l  BaseAddr(a2),a0    get device base address
0430 1180             move.b   d0,(a0,d2.w)       condition appropriate state on channel
0434 4e75             rts                         return (carry clear)

0436=0c40 PutSta_E    cmpi.w   #SS_DsRTS,d0       disable RTS
043a 660a             bne.s    PutSta_F           branch if not
043c 343c DisablRTS   move.w   #MPSOPClr,d2       get CLEAR register offset
0440 51ea             sf.b     RTSstate(a2)       flag RTS negated
0444 60de             bra.s    EnabRTS10          go negate the line
```

SS_Opt is new to device drivers. It has been handled by IOMan, which simply copied the path options from the supplied buffer into the path descriptor.

After IOMan copies the options and SCF does anything it likes, the setstat is passed to the device driver. The driver checks for changes to the hardware configuration values in the path options and makes any changes neccessary to bring the device into correspondence with the descriptor.

The function compares the baud rate and communication mode in the path descriptor with the values in device static storage. If neither has changed, the function returns without modifying the hardware setup. If either has changed, the function calls the same routines the Init entry used to set the device configuration.

This function has no critical section itself, but it calls InitSP, BaudCalc, and BitPar; all of which include critical sections when they write to the chip and update shadow registers.

---

[10] Setstat and getstat routines are the official place to put strange, device-dependent code. If a chip offers a special service, this is the place to put support for that function. If, on the other hand, the chip requires special support, that should be hidden in the init routine and elsewhere. A device should never require the use of a non-standard set/getstat.

* change path options
*
```
0446=0c40 PutSta_F    cmpi.w   #SS_Opt,d0                        set options call ?
044a 6634             bne.s    PutSta_G                          branch if not
```

* here to check whether baud/parity have changed

```
044c=1029 CheckMode   move.b   PD_BAU(a1),d0                     get baud rate current
0450 b02a             cmp.b    BaudRate(a2),d0                   has it changed ?
0454 660a             bne.s    ChngMode                          ..yes; attempt to re-configure
0456=1229             move.b   PD_PAR(a1),d1                     get port configuration
045a b22a             cmp.b    Parity(a2),d1                     has communication mode changed ?
045e 6760             beq.s    PutSta90                          ..no; exit (nothing to do)
0460=266a ChngMode    movea.l  V_PORT(a2),a3                     get device port address
0464 6100             bsr      InitSP                            disable rx/tx
0468 6100             bsr      BaudCalc                          attempt new baud rate
046c 6508             bcs.s    ChngExit                          ..exit if error
046e=1029             move.b   PD_PAR(a1),d0                     get parity, etc
0472 6100             bsr      BitPar                            attempt to change com. mode
0476 40e7 ChngExit    move.w   sr,-(sp)                          save ccr status
0478 177c             move.b   #RxEnabl!TxEnabl,MPSCntl(a3)      re-enable rx/tx
047e 4e77             rtr                                        restore ccr and return
```

When a new path is opened, the driver checks the path options against options in device static storage. Without this function and the previous function, the hardware options are only changed when the init entry is called (when the device is attached).

* new path open
*
```
0480=0c40 PutSta_G    cmpi.w   #SS_Open,d0                       new path opened ?
0484 67c6             beq.s    CheckMode                         ..yes; check for configuration changes
```

Serial chips usually have a command that sends the break value, but the command is not sufficient to send an actual break. A break signal has both a value and a duration (which should be longer than the time it takes to send a character). You can't just write a break (though a $00 at a low baud rate will usually do the trick). To make a break, the driver has to set the chip to send the break value, wait a while; then tell the chip to stop sending a break.

This driver supports a break in two ways. If timed sleeps are supported (i.e., there is a working system clock), the setstat starts sending a break, sleeps for a specified interval; then stops sending the break value. If timed sleeps are not supported, the setstat delays by busy waiting instead of sleeping.

* send BREAK out port

23.11. TERMINATE ROUTINE

```
*
 0486=0c40 PutSta_H   cmpi.w  #SS_Break,d0              send break ?
 048a 6600            bne     Unknown                   ..no; return error
 048e=266a            movea.l V_PORT(a2),a3             get device port address
 0492 177c            move.b  #StartBrk,MPSCntl(a3)     start the break
 0498 203c            move.l  #BrkTime,d0               get "break time"
 049e=4e40 Brk_Timed os9      F$Sleep                   delay while break being sent
 04a2 6506            bcs.s   Brk_manual                do manual timing if no clock
 04a4 4a80            tst.l   d0                        sleep the full time ?
 04a6 6710            beq.s   Brk_End                   ..yes; go stop the break
 04a8 60f4            bra.s   Brk_Timed                 ..else, wait for break-time to expire

 04aa 303c Brk_manual move.w  #5,d0                     outer counter
 04ae 72ff            moveq.l #-1,d1                    iniz inner counter
 04b0 51c9 Brk_a      dbra    d1,Brk_a
 04b4 51c8            dbra    d0,Brk_a
 04b8 177c Brk_End    move.b  #StopBrk,MPSCntl(a3)      stop the break
 04be 4e75            rts                               (carry clear)

 04c0 7200 PutSta90   moveq.l #0,d1                     clear Carry
 04c2 4e75            rts
```

23.11 Terminate Routine

When a device is detached, IOMan calls its terminate routine. This code is responsible for shutting the device down in good order. The procedure includes these steps:

1. Wait for the output queue to empty.

2. If the driver/device supports hardware flow contrl, turn off RTS.

3. Shut down the device. In particular, disable its interrupts.

4. Take the driver out of the polling table.

It's important to take the steps in that order. If, for instance, the terminate routine disabled interrupts before the output queue was empty, output would halt and the queue would never empty. Any data left in the output buffer would be lost.

```
*********************
* Term: Terminate Mpsc processing
*
* Passed: (a1) = device descriptor pointer
*         (a2) = static storage
*         (a4) = current process descriptor ptr
```

```
*              (a6) = system global data ptr
*
* Returns: none
*
* Error Return: (cc) = carry set
*              d1.w = error code

04c4=356a TRMN00   MOVE.W  V_BUSY(a2),V_WAKE(a2)  arrange wake up signal
04ca 46df          MOVE.W  (sp)+,sr               restore IRQs
04cc 487a          pea.l   Term(pc)               return to entry point if signals
04d0 6100          bsr     MpscSlep               wait for interrupt
04d4 588f          addq.l  #4,sp                  toss return address if no signals
04d6=302c Term     move.w  P$ID(a4),d0
04da=3540          move.w  d0,V_BUSY(a2)
04de=3540          move.w  d0,V_LPRC(a2)
04e2 40e7          move.w  sr,-(sp)               save current IRQ status
04e4 46ea          move.w  IRQMask(a2),sr         mask IRQs
04e8 4a6a          TST.W   OutCount(a2)           any data?
04ec 66d6          BNE.S   TRMN00                 sleep if there is
04ee 4a2a          TST.B   RTSstate(a2)           RTS asserted ?
04f2 6704          BEQ.S   Term20                 ..no; no need to negate
04f4 6100          BSR     DisablRTS              go negate RTS line
04f8 206a Term20   MOVEA.L BaseAddr(a2),a0        get port base address

04fc 122a          MOVE.B  Otpt_On(a2),d1         get enable bits
0500 4601          NOT.B   d1                     complement it
0502 302a          MOVE.W  Globl(a2),d0           get offset to global
0506 670a          BEQ.S   Term40                 ..if zero; never got iniz'd
0508 c336          AND.B   d1,(a6,d0.w)           disable interrupts
050c 1176          MOVE.B  (a6,d0.w),MPSImr(a0)   move to register
0512 46df Term40   MOVE.W  (sp)+,sr               restore IRQ masks
0514=1029          move.b  M$Vector(a1),d0        get vector #
0518 91c8          suba.l  a0,a0
051a=4e40          os9     F$IRQ                  remove acia from polling tbl
051e 4e75          rts
```

23.12 Interrupt Handler

The interrupt handler has two primary tasks. It must determine whether an interrupt could have come from its device, and move data between the input/output queues and the device when the device originates an interrupt.

If several devices share an interrupt vector, the kernel will call each driver's interrupt handler until a driver finds that his device has asserted an interrupt. When a driver accepts the interrupt, the kernel assumes that the driver will deal with the interrupt.

23.12. INTERRUPT HANDLER

The interrupt handler is entered with its interrupt masked. This means that the entire interrupt handler is one big critical section. The driver should keep its interrupt handler code as fast as possible to prevent lost interrupts. If the interrupt handler must be long, consider ending the critical section early by enabling the device's interrupt.

First the interrupt handler classifies the interrupt. Is it from "my" device? Is it input or output for channel A or B?

```
********************
* MPSCIRQ: Process interrupt (input or output) from Mpsc
*
* Passed: (a2) = Static Storage addr
*         (a3) = port address ptr
*         (a6) = system global data ptr
*
* Returns: (cc) = carry set if false interrupt, else clear
*
* Destroys: May only destroy D0, D1, A0, A2, A3 and A6. Any
*           other registers used MUST be preserved.
*

* Exit here if no interrupts

0520=003c MPSIRQEx ori.b   #Carry,ccr         return with carry set
0524 4e75          rts

0526 206a MPSCIRQ  movea.l BaseAddr(a2),a0    point to base of port
052a 1228          move.b  MPSImr(a0),d1      get IRQ status register
052e 302a          move.w  Globl(a2),d0       get offset to global
0532 c236          and.b   (a6,d0.w),d1       mask out disabled interrupts
0536 200b          move.l  a3,d0              get port address
0538 0800          btst.l  #ABbit,d0          is this channel B?
053c 670e          beq.s   MIRQ.a             if channel A, branch

* Note! Check for receive interrupt first.
*
053e 0201          andi.b  #IRQP_BitB,d1      mask off all except B interrupts
0542 67dc          beq.s   MPSIRQEx           if no interrupts, branch
0544 0801          btst.l  #IRQ_RecB,d1       is this an rec interrupt?
0548 6736          beq.s   OutIRQ             if not, branch
054a 600c          bra.s   MPSIRQ.c           branch if rec irq

054c 0201 MIRQ.a   andi.b  #IRQP_BitA,d1      mask off all except A interrupts
0550 67ce          beq.s   MPSIRQEx           if no interrupts, branch.
0552 0801          btst.l  #IRQ_RecA,d1       is this a recv interrutpt?
0556 6728          beq.s   OutIRQ             if not, branch
```

For both input and output interrupts, the interrupt handler will attempt to send XOn or XOff values that are pending. These values are saved as pending output if the output buffer is full. The objective is to write them as soon as possible, so the interrupt handler looks for an opportunity to write the pending character. It doesn't write the character by enqueuing it; this routine writes the control character directly into the output register.

```
0558 122a  MPSIRQ.c move.b  InHalt(a2),d1          XOn or XOff waiting to be sent?
055c 6a00           bpl     InIRQ                  handle input IRQ if not
0560 082b           btst.b  #TxE_Bit,MPSBdSt(a3)   transmit buffer empty?
0566 6700           beq     InIRQ                  handle input IRQ if not
056a 0881           bclr.l  #Signbit,d1            clear Sign bit
056e 1741           move.b  d1,MPSData(a3)         send character
0572=102a           move.b  V_XON(a2),d0           get XOn value
0576 b101           eor.b   d0,d1                  get Zero if XOn
0578 1541           move.b  d1,InHalt(a2)          mark it sent
057c 6000           bra     InIRQ                  handle input IRQ
```

InHalt can be in one of three states:

- If the sign bit (high-order bit) is set, the remainder of the byte holds an XOn or XOff. This character is pending.

- If the sign bit is off but the byte is not zero, input has been halted by an XOff.

- If the byte is zero, the device is not halted and there is no XOff pending.

The following code is entered if the entry code of the interrupt handler determines that this is an output interrupt. First the routine handles any pending XOn/XOff characters. Since the driver knows that it just got an output interrupt, it does not need to check to know that the output buffer is empty. It simply writes the pending character and returns to the kernel just as if it had taken a character out of the output queue.

```
*********************
* OutIRQ: Mpsc output interrupt service
*
* Passed:  (a0) = device base address
*          (a2) = static storage address
*          (a3) = device port address
*          (a6) = system global data ptr
*          d1.b = device status register contents
*
```

23.12. INTERRUPT HANDLER

```
0580 102a  OutIRQ   move.b  InHalt(a2),d0         send XOn or XOff?
0584 6a1a           bpl.s   OutI_a                branch if not
0586 0880           bclr.l  #Signbit,d0           clear Sign bit
058a 1740           move.b  d0,MPSData(a3)        send character
058e=122a           move.b  V_XON(a2),d1          get XOn value
0592 b300           eor.b   d1,d0                 get Zero if XOn
0594 1540           move.b  d0,InHalt(a2)         mark it sent
0598 4a2a           tst.b   OutHalt(a2)           is output halted?
059c 6640           bne.s   OutIRQ3               branch if so
059e 4e75           rts
```

The simplified overview of the output interrupt handler is:

- If there is any data in the output queue, the handler dequeues one byte and writes it to the output device.

- If there is no data in the output queue, the handler turns off output interrupts.

The actual code is only slightly more complicated than the simplified version. If output is suspended, it must have been suspended after the last character was written (at most one character can be written after output is suspended). The interrupt routine responds to the suspended output flag by disabling output interrupts, even if there is still data in the output queue.

When the output queue is almost full, the write routine will sleep when it attempts to enqueue more data. The interrupt handler must detect that a process is sleeping in write and signal him that there is now room to continue.

The writer could be wakened whenever the queue has any space at all, but the driver lets the queue empty substantially before releasing the writer. This prevents a busy writer from sleeping on every character written. Since a write that includes a sleep and a signal is slower than a write that simply enqueues a byte, the lag in the queue improves efficiency.

If there is no data in the queue awaiting output, the code shuts down output interrupts from the device and sets a flag that indicates that output is halted because of an empty buffer (the other reason for halted output is an XOff from the other end).

```
05a0 082a  OutI_a   btst.b   #H_XOFF,OutHalt(a2)   is output suspension requested ?
05a6 6636           bne.s    OutIRQ3               ..yes; go disable interrupts
05a8 322a           move.w   OutCount(a2),d1       any Data in buffer?
05ac 672a           beq.s    OutIRQ2               branch if not
05ae 5341           subq.w   #1,d1                 taking one char
05b0 2f09           move.l   a1,-(sp)              save a1
05b2 226a           movea.l  OutEmpty(a2),a1       get pointer to next char
05b6 1759           move.b   (a1)+,MPSData(a3)     put Data in acia
```

```
05ba b3ea              cmpa.l   OutEnd(a2),a1       end of buffer?
05be 6504              blo.s    OutI_1              branch if not
05c0 43ea              lea.l    OutBuf(a2),a1       point to start
05c4 2549   OutI_1     move.l   a1,OutEmpty(a2)     update pointer
05c8 225f              movea.l  (sp)+,a1
05ca 3541              move.w   d1,OutCount(a2)     update char count
05ce 0c41              cmpi.w   #MinBuff,d1         ready for more data?
05d2 622c              bhi.s    Wake90              exit if not
05d4 4a41              tst.w    d1                  output buffer empty?
05d6 6618              bne.s    WakeUp              just wake up if not
05d8 08ea   OutIRQ2    bset.b   #H_Empty,OutHalt(a2) flag halted; buffer empty

05de 302a   OutIRQ3    move.w   Globl(a2),d0        get offset to global
05e2 122a              move.b   Otpt_Off(a2),d1     get disable mask
05e6 c336              and.b    d1,(a6,d0.w)        disable interrupts in global register
05ea 1176              move.b   (a6,d0.w),MPSImr(a0) write to register

05f0=302a   WakeUp     move.w   V_WAKE(a2),d0       owner waiting?
05f4 670a              beq.s    Wake90              ..no; return
05f6=426a              clr.w    V_WAKE(a2)
05fa=7200              moveq.l  #S$Wake,d1          wake up signal

05fc=4e40   SendSig    os9      F$Send              wake up process

0600 7200   Wake90     moveq.l  #0,d1               clear carry
0602 4e75              rts
```

The simplified action of the input interrupt handler is:

Fetch a byte from the 68681's input register.
Enqueue the character in the input queue.
If there is a process waiting for input, wake it.

Three features are added to this simplified outline. The input character is checked against a set of special characters: quit, pause, XOff, etc., a signal on data ready request is accommodated, and there is a special case to deal with a full input queue.

The input byte is checked against special values stored in the device static storage. These values are copies of codes from the path descriptor which the file manager copies into the static storage every time it calls the driver. This sounds inefficient, but the interrupt handler does not get access to a path descriptor (it would be difficult to determine which path descriptor to use for a given character of input). If it matches any of these characters, the handler branches off to special code for that control character.

The code for a null control character is $00. The input routine must pass null characters through without treating them as the first null control character. Several

23.12. INTERRUPT HANDLER

drivers have failed because they were careless about null values in input. Since terminals don't ordinarily send nulls, the drivers would cause mysterious problems when XModem or some other binary-transfer program was running.

If the input queue is almost full, the interrupt routine will notice the condition and set an XOff-pending in InHalt. If the queue is actually full, the routine will declare an error. (See the second half of InIRQ1.)

```
********************
* InIRQ: Mpsc input interrupt service
*
* Passed:  (a0) = device base address
*          (a2) = static storage address
*          (a3) = device port address
*          (a6) = system global data ptr
*

* Notice the Absence of Error Checking Here

0604 122b  InIRQ     move.b  MPSBdSt(a3),d1       get error status
0608 0201            andi.b  #InputErr,d1         any errors?
060c 670a            beq.s   InIRQ.a              branch if not
060e=832a            or.b    d1,V_ERR(a2)         update cumulative errors
0612 177c            move.b  #ErrorRst,MPSCntl(a3) reset special error condition
0618 102b  InIRQ.a   move.b  MPSData(a3),d0       read input char
061c 6728            beq.s   InIRQ1               ..NULL, impossible ctl chr
061e=b02a            cmp.b   V_INTR(a2),d0        keyboard Interrupt?
0622 6700            beq     InAbort              ..Yes
0626=b02a            cmp.b   V_QUIT(a2),d0        keyboard Quit?
062a 6700            beq     InQuit               ..Yes
062e=b02a            cmp.b   V_PCHR(a2),d0        keyboard Pause?
0632 6700            beq     InPause              ..Yes
0636=b02a            cmp.b   V_XON(a2),d0         XOn continue?
063a 6700            beq     InXON                ..Yes
063e=b02a            cmp.b   V_XOFF(a2),d0        XOff Immediate Pause request?
0642 6700            beq     InXOFF               ..Yes

0646 2f09  InIRQ1    move.l  a1,-(sp)             save a1
0648 226a            movea.l InFill(a2),a1        point to current char
064c 12c0            move.b  d0,(a1)+             put Data in buffer
064e 526a            addq.w  #1,InCount(a2)       count character
0652 0c6a            cmpi.w  #InpSiz,InCount(a2)  buffer full?
0658 6310            bls.s   InIRQ10              branch if not
065a 536a            subq.w  #1,InCount(a2)       uncount character
065e=002a            ori.b   #IPOverrun,V_ERR(a2) simulate ip over-run error
0664 225f            move.l  (sp)+,a1             restore a1
0666 6000            bra     WakeUp               exit
066a b3ea  InIRQ10   cmp.l   InEnd(a2),a1         end of buffer?
```

```
066e 6504              blo.s    InIRQ30             branch if not
0670 43ea              lea.l    InpBuf(a2),a1       point to start of buffer
0674 2549 InIRQ30      move.l   a1,InFill(a2)       update next in pointer
0678 225f              move.l   (sp)+,a1            restore a1
```

If any process requested a signal on data ready, send that signal. This is done *before* the queue is checked for impending overflow. Since a send signal on data ready can only be set when the queue is empty and it will be turned off after it is sent, the branch to send the signal (and not check for queue overflow) will only be taken when there is exactly one character in the queue.

```
067a 302a              move.w   SigPrc(a2),d0       any process to notify?
067e 670c              beq.s    InIRQ4              ..no
0680 322a              move.w   SigPrc+2(a2),d1     get signal code
0684 426a              clr.w    SigPrc(a2)          disable signal sending
0688 6000              bra      SendSig             signal waiting process & return
```

If the input queue is almost full, arrange to have an XOff sent—unless one has already been sent. The procedure is:

> If the input queue is almost full
>> Get the XOff character from static storage.
>>> If XOff has not been sent already
>>>> Clear the sign bit in the static storage XOff value.
>>>> Store XOff with the sign bit set in InHalt.
>>>> Enable output interrupts (so the XOff can be written).

```
068c=102a InIRQ4       move.b   V_XOFF(a2),d0       get XOff char
0690 6730              beq.s    InIRQ9              branch if not enabled
0692 0c6a              cmpi.w   #MaxBuff,InCount(a2) is buffer almost full?
0698 6528              blo.s    InIRQ9              bra if not
069a 122a              move.b   InHalt(a2),d1       have we sent XOFF?
069e 6622              bne.s    InIRQ9              yes then don't send it again
06a0 0880              bclr.l   #Signbit,d0         insure Sign clear
06a4=1540              move.b   d0,V_XOFF(a2)
06a8=0000              ori.b    #Sign,d0            set Sign bit
06ac 1540              move.b   d0,InHalt(a2)       flag input halt
06b0 302a              move.w   Globl(a2),d0        get offset to global
06b4 122a              move.b   Otpt_On(a2),d1      get enable flag
06b8 8336              or.b     d1,(a6,d0.w)        write into global register
06bc 1176              move.b   (a6,d0.w),MPSImr(a0) write to device register
```

23.12. INTERRUPT HANDLER

If more input is waiting in the 68681, handle it immediately. This is more efficient than returning to the kernel and getting another input interrupt.

```
06c2 082b   InIRQ9   btst.b    #RxA_Bit,MPSBdSt(a3)  any more input available?
06c8 6700            beq       WakeUp                exit if not
06cc 6000            bra       InIRQ                 go get it if so
```

Each input control character branches into one of the blocks below. They take the appropriate action, then branch back into the main input handler where they are treated like any other input. XOn and XOff are an exception to this rule, *XOn and XOff are not queued as ordinary input.*

XOn and XOff are flow-control characters. They refer specifically to a single serial port. The pause character is an OS-9 protocol character. It refers to the associated output device. The output device may not be the output part of a serial connection. The V_DEV2 field in the static storage (and the corresponding field in the device descriptor) are used to indicate the output device that corresponds to an input device. This will usually be the output side of the same device, but not always.

```
********************
* Control character routines
*
* Passed: (a0) = device base address
*         (a2) = static storage ptr
*         (a3) = device port address
*         (a6) = system global data ptr
*         d0.b = received input character
*

06d0=4aaa   InPause   tst.l     V_DEV2(a2)       any echo device?
06d4 6700             beq       InIRQ1           buffer char and exit if not
06d8 2f09             move.l    a1,-(sp)         save it
06da=226a             movea.l   V_DEV2(a2),a1    get echo device static ptr
06de=1340             move.b    d0,V_PAUS(a1)    request pause
06e2 225f             move.l    (sp)+,a1         restore it
06e4 6000             bra       InIRQ1           buffer char and exit

06e8=7200   InAbort   moveq.l   #S$Intrpt,d1     keyboard INTERRUPT signal
06ea 6002             bra.s     InQuit10

06ec=7200   InQuit    moveq.l   #S$Abort,d1      abort signal

06ee 1f00   InQuit10  move.b    d0,-(sp)         save input char
06f0=302a             move.w    V_LPRC(a2),d0    last process ID
06f4 6708             beq.s     InQuit90         ..none; exit
06f6=426a             clr.w     V_WAKE(a2)
06fa=4e40             os9       F$Send           send signal to last user
```

06fe 101f	InQuit90	move.b	(sp)+,d0	restore input char
0700 6000		bra	InIRQ1	buffer char, exit
0704 08aa	InXON	bclr.b	#H_XOFF,OutHalt(a2)	enable output
070a 4a2a		tst.b	OutHalt(a2)	still halted (buffer empty)?
070e 663a		bne.s	InXExit	exit if so
0710 302a		move.w	Globl(a2),d0	get offset to global
0714 122a		move.b	Otpt_On(a2),d1	get enable flag
0718 8336		or.b	d1,(a6,d0.w)	write into global register
071c 1176		move.b	(a6,d0.w),MPSImr(a0)	write into register
0722 082b		btst.b	#TxE_Bit,MPSBdSt(a3)	output buffer empty?
0728 6720		beq.s	InXExit	exit if not
072a 6000		bra	OutIRQ	start output if so
072e 08ea	InXOFF	bset.b	#H_XOFF,OutHalt(a2)	flag output restricted
0734 206a		movea.l	BaseAddr(a2),a0	
0738 302a		move.w	Globl(a2),d0	get offset to global
073c 122a		move.b	Otpt_Off(a2),d1	get transmit disable flag
0740 c336		and.b	d1,(a6,d0.w)	write into global register
0744 1176		move.b	(a6,d0.w),MPSImr(a0)	write to device register
074a 7200	InXExit	moveq.l	#0,d1	clear carry
074c 4e75		rts		
0000074e		ends		

This driver is a full-featured SCF driver. It is a typical driver for an ordinary serial port. A much simpler driver can be constructed by leaving out the interrupt handling and queuing capability and simply polling for input and output. This driver would waste system resources, but it is a fast way to get a device driver written. This is a good way to write an experimental driver, but it should not be used in a real driver unless the I/O device does not generate interrupts, or the device reponds to all requests in no more than about a tenth of a millisecond.

Much complexity might be added to a driver. First, the driver reflects the complexity of the underlying hardware. If the I/O device were more intelligent and the driver chose to take advantage of it, the driver would be likely to grow quite elaborate. The getstat and putstat routines are especially likely to grow. They are the areas where special tricks are normally inserted.

Sometimes device drivers include chunks of logic that would ordinarily go in a program. This is done when response time requirements don't permit control to travel out to a higher level in the system, then back. The driver in this chapter, and every other SCF driver, includes code for flow control on an associated device: a good example of code that has been placed in a driver for efficiency.

Chapter 24

An RBF Device Driver

This chapter presents a complete RBF device driver written almost entirely in C.

By far the most difficult part of writing the driver in this chapter was understanding the controller and disk drive well enough to write code to control them.

Although this driver is a good starting point for other drivers, it is not a generic driver. I chose simple hardware and made simplifying assumptions whenever they didn't hide important aspects of driver construction. Still, more than half of the driver is specific to the GMX Micro-20 SCSI board, the Western Digital WD33C93A SCSI controller chip, and the Quantum Prodrive 105S hard disk drive. This is an example, not a general-purpose SCSI driver.

I try to avoid explanations of my hardware, but a driver is so hardware-specific that some of the code looks magical or senseless without some understanding of the underlying hardware.

24.1 Hardware Overview

The GMX Micro-20 uses a MC68020 processor, but since the bulk of the driver is written in C, the driver is mostly independent of the processor. I know of one processor-dependency: the code that sets the disk's sector size uses an I/O buffer with odd alignment. This causes the code (in the Exec() function) that copies data between the SCSI board and memory to use the 68020's ability to handle unaligned data.

The GMX SCSI interface board is memory mapped to a block of 32 bytes (see table 24.1.)

The SCSI controller cannot DMA directly into the Micro-20's memory, but it has DMA access to 128 kilobytes of RAM on the SCSI board. The driver could use

Table 24.1: SCSI Board Memory Map

Offset	Mode	Size	Description
0	Read	byte	WD33C93A Auxiliary Status Register
0	Write	byte	WD33C93A Address Register
1	Read/Write	byte	WD33C93A Internal Registers
2	Read	byte	Board Status Register
2	Write	byte	Board Control Register
8	Read/Write	word/long	Data buffer
12	Write	word	Data buffer address

The remainder of the 32-byte block is reserved

Two bits in the board control register are useful: the high-order bit enables interrupts from the SCSI board, and bit six asserts the SCSI bus reset line and resets the WD33C93A.

The high-order bit in the board status register is set if the WD33C93A interrupt output is asserted.

WD33C93A programmed I/O, but performance would suffer. The higher performance option is to use DMA between the WD33C93A and the SCSI board's memory and use the processor to copy data between main memory and the SCSI board.

Both DMA and access by the CPU depend on the address selected by the *Data buffer address*. This register in the SCSI board's memory map controls the starting address for DMA or CPU access. Reads or writes by the WD33C93A or by the driver will start at the address placed in the data buffer address register and hit successive addresses on subsequent accesses. For instance, setting the data buffer address to 20 and reading a word from the data buffer four times:

for(i=0;i<4;++i)
 *ptr++ = Board_Data_Buffer;

will get data from the board's memory in the address range from 20 to 27.

The WD33C93A's internal registers are described in figure 24.1. There are several classes of register:

- The first two registers don't have register numbers. They have private memory mapped addresses. All the other registers share a single memory mapped address. They are accessed by writing a register number into the register select register, then reading or writing the address allocated to the selectable registers.

  The selected register auto-increments. If a program writes 3 to the register select register, then reads a byte from the "Internal registers" address four times, the program will receive the values of registers 3, 4, 5, and 6.

24.1. HARDWARE OVERVIEW

- Registers three through fourteen are dual-use registers. When the WD33C93A is given a *translate address* command, the registers use their main descriptions. The alternate descriptions are used for *Select and transfer* commands.

- Register 0 can also used by select and transfer, but it is only required for SCSI command blocks that are not known to the WD33C93A.

This driver uses *select and transfer* for all SCSI commands. This is a powerful simplifying rule. In particular, it avoids a problem with register selection: there is no way for the interrupt service routine to save and restore the number of the WD33C93A's selected register. If the interrupt service routine needs to use any WD33C93A register other than auxiliary status, it may disrupt the interrupted code. Even if the interrupt service routine only reads whatever register has been selected by the body of the driver, the auto-increment will change the selected register and the interrupted code's next access to a selectable register will get the register after the last register accessed by the interrupt service routine (due to auto-increment) unless the register select register is written before accessing another register.

The only general solutions to this problem are: don't write the register select register from the interrupt service routine, or mask interrupts to the level of the device over every interval from register select through the last access depending on that selection.

The simplest type of select and transfer runs with no intervention from the interrupt service routine; since this driver uses only simple select and transfer, the interrupt service routine's only access to the WD33C93A is a read of the auxiliary status register. This is safe.

24.1.1 The Quantum Disk Drive

The hardware details of the Quantum Prodrive 105S used to test this driver had little impact on the driver (which speaks well for the drive). The mode-sense/mode-select code that the driver uses to set the sector size threads its way through vendor-specific pages of information, but I think this driver's mode select and mode set code is fairly generic.

The driver contains at least one assumption that is true for most embedded-SCSI devices, but not a SCSI rule. The driver silently uses a constant zero as the logical unit number of the target device. To make this driver handle devices with a logical unit number other than zero, the pd_lun field from device options would have to be stored in the CDB for each SCSI command.

Figure 24.1: WD33C93A Device Registers

Mode	Description	Other Description	Register Number
R	Auxiliary status		
W	Register select		
R/W	Own ID	CDB size	0
R/W	Control register		1
R/W	Timeout period		2
R/W	Total sectors	CDB 1st byte	3
R/W	Total heads	CDB 2nd byte	4
R/W	Total cylinders (msb)	CDB 3rd byte	5
R/W	Total cylinders (lsb)	CDB 4th byte	6
R/W	Logical address (msb)	CDB 5th byte	7
R/W	Logical address (byte 2)	CDB 6th byte	8
R/W	Logical address (byte 3)	CDB 7th byte	9
R/W	Logical address (lsb)	CDB 8th byte	10
R/W	Sector number	CDB 9th byte	11
R/W	Head number	CDB 10th byte	12
R/W	Cylinder number (msb)	CDB 11th byte	13
R/W	Cylinder number (lsb)	CDB 12th byte	14
R/W	Target LUN		15
R/W	Command phase		16
R/W	Synchronous transfer		17
R/W	Transfer count (msb)		18
R/W	Transfer count (byte 2)		19
R/W	Transfer count (lsb)		20
R/W	Destination ID		21
R/W	Source ID		22
R	SCSI Status		23
R/W	Command		24
R/W	Data register		25
R	Auxiliary status		31

24.2 The Driver's Main Entries

24.2.1 Init

The driver's init routine has three tasks:

- IOMan initializes device static storage to 0, then sets V_Port. The driver's init routine should initialize any other fields in the driver's part of device static storage that should not have an initial value of 0.

- If the hardware for the device will trigger an interrupt, init() should install an interrupt service routine.

- Initialize the *controller* hardware.

The init routine is not responsible for drive initialization; its hardware duties are limited to controller initialization.

The SCSI controller may be shared by drivers for RBF and SBF file managers.[1] The kernel does not protect against interactions among drivers for different file managers, so the drivers are left responsible for device locking. The init routine creates an event that will be used to lock the controller. The ClaimController() and ReleaseController() functions use the event as a semaphore to get exclusive use of the SCSI controller (provided that other drivers use the same protocol.)

The device locking provided by RBF will prevent multiple processes from entering this driver concurrently, but SCSI is not an exclusively RBF bus. An SBF driver for this controller could be called by SBF to read a tape while this driver is active on behalf of RBF. If both drivers collided at the controller, the result would not be pretty. The solution is to implement contention for the controller in all drivers that will use the controller. So long as there are only RBF drivers, the contention code will never block.

```
#include <rbf.h>
#include <errno.h>
#include "drvr.h"
#include "lowlevel.h"

int IRQRtn();
void InitStatics();
```

---

[1] Microware only supplies SCSI drivers for RBF and SBF. That is not a limitation of SCSI. Microware, or someone else, might write additional drivers to add SCSI support for SCF, networking, and other things.

```
Init(dd, DevStatics, SysGlobs)
mod_dev *dd;                    /*device descriptor */
MyStatics DevStatics;
{
    register struct rbf_opt *Options;
    Board port;
    int Error;

    InitStatics(DevStatics);                                              /* pg. 331 */
    Options = (struct rbf_opt *)&(dd→_mdtype);
    port = (Board)DevStatics→v_sysio.v_port;

    if((Error = SetIRQ(dd→_mvector, dd→_mpriority,                        /* pg. 382 */
            IRQRtn, DevStatics, port)) != 0)
        return Error;
    if((DevStatics→EvID = MakeEvent((ulong)port, &Error)) == -1){         /* pg. 357 */
        DevStatics→EvID = 0;
        return Error;
    }
    ClaimController(DevStatics→EvID);                                      /* pg. 386 */

    if(QueryWDOwn(SysGlobs) == 0){/*Has the chip been initialized? */     /* pg. 379 */
        Error = Init33C93A(port, (Options→pd_scsiopt & SCSI_PARITY) != 0); /* pg. 331 */
        SetWDOwn((port→BD_STATUS & 0x07) |                                 /* pg. 380 */
            WD_OWNID_EAF | WD_OWNID_FS2, SysGlobs);
    }
    ReleaseController(DevStatics→EvID); /*Don't want the I/O board after all */ /* pg. 386 */
    return Error;
}
```

The driver will use the v_ndrv field to range-check the drive number whenever the driver is about to write a drive table entry. This is now a redundant check because RBF validates the drive number (using the value the driver stores in v_ndrv) before it sets the drive table pointer, pd_dtb. Before version 2.4 of OS-9, the drive number was only validated by the driver.

The dd_tot field in each drive table entry will contain the number of sectors on that drive. RBF will use this field to check for sector numbers that are beyond the end of the drive. The init routine initializes these field to the largest possible number to ensure that the entire drive is reachable even before the driver reads sector zero and puts actual data into the drive table entry.

24.2. THE DRIVER'S MAIN ENTRIES

```
void InitStatics(DevStatics)
register MyStatics DevStatics;
{
    register int i;

    DevStatics→v_ndrv = RBF_MAXDRIVES;

    for(i = 0 ; i < RBF_MAXDRIVES; ++i){
        DevStatics→drv[i].v_0.dd_tot[0] = 0x0ff;
        DevStatics→drv[i].v_0.dd_tot[1] = 0x0ff;
        DevStatics→drv[i].v_0.dd_tot[2] = 0x0ff;
    }
}


Init33C93A(port, ParityP)
register Board port;
boolean ParityP;
{
    uchar OwnVal;

    (void)GET_SCSI_STATUS(port);        /* Touch the SCSI status register */   /* pg. 386 */
    /*
        Store the right value in the 33C93A OwnID register This includes the SCSI ID
        for this board and a bit to tell the 33C93A to turn on its advanced features.
    */
    OwnVal =(port→BD_STATUS & 0x07) | WD_OWNID_EAF | WD_OWNID_FS2;
    SET_OWNID(port, OwnVal);                                                    /* pg. 386 */
    /* Now reset the chip. */
    if(Do_WD_Reset(port) != 1)                                                  /* pg. 363 */
        return E_NOTRDY;                                        /* Couldn't reset */
    SET_SYNCTRANS(port, WD_STR_INIT_VALUE);                                     /* pg. 386 */
    Set_Control(port, (uchar)(ParityP ?                                         /* pg. 363 */
        (WD_CTL_DMWD | WD_CTL_EDI | WD_CTL_HSP) :
        (WD_CTL_DMWD | WD_CTL_EDI)));
    return 0;
}
```

24.2.2 Term

The driver terminate routine releases resources claimed by the driver. In this case it:

- removes the driver's interrupt service routine from the polling list,

- frees any sector-zero buffers that have been allocated,
- and deletes the event that was created by init().

The terminate routine is called when the device is detached and after a call to init() fails. Init() and term() must interact such that init() always leaves the device and device static storage in a state that term() can handle smoothly.

```
#include <module.h>
#include <rbf.h>
#include "drvr.h"

Term(dd, DevStatics)
register mod_dev *dd;                              /* device descriptor */
register MyStatics DevStatics;
{
    register Rbfdrive DTableE;
    register int i;

    /* Take this controller out of the IRQ list */
    if(DevStatics→EvID != 0)
        ClaimController(DevStatics→EvID);                      /* pg. 386 */
    SetIRQ(dd→_mvector, 0, (void *)0, DevStatics, (Board)0);   /* pg. 382 */

    /* Free any memory attached to pointers in static storage */
    for(i=0; i < RBF_MAXDRIVES; ++i){
        DTableE= &(DevStatics→drv[i]);
        if(DTableE→v_sczero != (Sector0)0)                     /* Free sector 0 buffer */
            DoSRtMem(DTableE→v_sczero, DTableE→v_dtext);       /* pg. 378 */
    }
    if(DevStatics→EvID != 0){
        ReleaseController(DevStatics→EvID);                    /* pg. 386 */
        /* Delete the event */
        DeleteEvent((ulong)DevStatics→v_sysio.v_port, DevStatics→EvID);  /* pg. 358 */
    }
    return 0;
}
```

24.2.3 Read

The driver's read routine is comparatively complicated. It manages the hardware to read sectors from the disk and handles the special case processing required for sector zero.

24.2. THE DRIVER'S MAIN ENTRIES

Every read, write, getstat, or putstat entry to the driver will call Cond_InitDrive() to ensure that the drive accessed by this operation has been initialized and to validate some drive parameters. If the drive has not be initialized, Cond_InitDrive() will prepare it for I/O.

The RBF logical sector number presented to ReadDisk() must be mapped to a disk logical sector number. Addoffsets() adds pd_lsnoffs and the number of sectors corresponding to any track offset value to lsn.

The actual value of the LSN is important for disk access, but the lsn passed by the file manager corresponds to the file structure on the disk. Consequently, if the lsn number passed to ReadDisk() is 0, even if addoffsets() reveals that the actual sector number is in the thousands, ReadDisk() should give the read special treatment. The special treatment is covered in section 24.3.1. The effect here is to read the first sector.

If the read was not for sector 0, or it was for more than one sector, ReadDisk() continues to prepare for I/O.

- It checks the range of sector numbers covered by the read and returns an error if the sectors extend past the end of the disk. This check is usually redundant two ways. The disk will return an error for access that are out of range, and RBF checks disk addresses against dd_tot. The only time the driver is the sole protection against out-of-bounds disk access is for raw access to a partitioned disk before sector zero has been read.

- It activates the hardware to read the sectors.

- It attempts to recover from errors.

```
#include <rbf.h>
#include <machine/reg.h>
#include <path.h>
#include <errno.h>
#include "drvr.h"

int BoundsCheck();

ReadDisk(ct, lsn, pathd, DevStatics, SysGlobs)
int ct;
ulong lsn;
Pathdesc pathd;
register MyStatics DevStatics;
void * SysGlobs;
{
    register uchar *Buffer;
```

```
    register struct rbf_opt *Options;
    register Rbfdrive DTableE;
    register ulong StartAddr = lsn;
    int Error, retries;

    if(ct == 0)                                    /* If read is for no sectors, do no work */
        return 0;

    /* Make some useful pointers */
    Buffer = pathd→path.pd_buf;
    Options = (struct rbf_opt *)&(pathd→path.fm_opt);
    DTableE = pathd→path.fm_pvt.rbf.pd_dtb;

    if((Error = Cond_InitDrive(DevStatics, Options, DTableE, SysGlobs)) != 0)    /* pg. 348 */
        return Error;

    /* Make a "real" lsn by adding lsnoffset and trackoffset */
    StartAddr = addoffsets(lsn, Options→pd_lsnoffs,                              /* pg. 358 */
        (Options→pd_cntl & CNTL_AUTOSIZE) != 0,
        Options→pd_toffs, Options→pd_t0s,
        Options→pd_sct, Options→pd_sid);

    /*
        If the caller thought he was asking for sector 0 do special sector 0 things.
    */

    if(lsn == 0)
        if((Error = ReadSector0(StartAddr, DevStatics,                           /* pg. 346 */
                Buffer DTableE, Options)) == 0){
            ++StartAddr;
            ++lsn;
            ct--;
            Buffer += Options→pd_ssize;
        }else
            return Error;

    if(ct == 0)                                    /* Nothing left to read */
        return 0;

    if((Error = BoundsCheck(lsn, ct, DTableE→v_0.dd_tot[2] +                     /* pg. 359 */
            256 * (DTableE→v_0.dd_tot[1] +
            256 * DTableE→v_0.dd_tot[0]),
            DevStatics→v_Bytes > Options→pd_maxcnt)) != 0)
        return Error;
```

24.2. THE DRIVER'S MAIN ENTRIES

```
        for(retries = RETRY_MAX; retries > 0; --retries){
            Error = BaseRead(ct, StartAddr, Buffer, Options,           /* pg. 336 */
                DevStatics);
            switch(Error){
                case E_DIDC:
                    /* disk ID change (perhaps reset)          */
                    /* Re-init drive and try again.            */
                    (void)InitDrive(                                    /* pg. 349 */
                        (Board)DevStatics->v_sysio.v_port,
                        (Options->pd_cntl & CNTL_NOFMT) != 0,
                        (Options->pd_scsiopt & SCSI_PARITY) != 0,
                        &(Options->pd_ssize),
                        Options->pd_ctrlrid,
                        DevStatics,
                        (void **)&(DTableE->v_sczero),
                        &(DTableE->v_init),
                        &(DTableE->v_dtext),
                        SysGlobs);
                    break;
                case E_HARDWARE:
                    ClaimController(DevStatics->EvID);                  /* pg. 386 */
                    Error = Init33C93A((Board)DevStatics->v_sysio.v_port, /* pg. 331 */
                        (Options->pd_scsiopt & SCSI_PARITY) != 0);
                    ReleaseController(DevStatics->EvID);                /* pg. 386 */
                    if(Error == 0)
                        break;
                    else
                        return Error;
                default:
                    return Error;
            }
        }

    return Error;
}
```

BaseRead() is called by ReadDisk() and ReadSector0(). It sets some values in device static storage and calls Exec(), a routine that places a SCSI command on the SCSI bus.

This driver uses 6-byte SCSI read commands. This only supports reads of up to 256 sectors.[2] Since I chose to use 64 kilobytes of the SCSI board's memory for DMA,

---

[2] 6-byte SCSI commands specify the number of sectors to be tranferred with a one-byte field.

256 sectors will fill the memory even with 256-byte sectors. A more general driver would probably use the 10-byte extended read command with its 2-byte sector count. This choice is tied to the value of the PD_MaxCnt field in the path descriptor's options section. PD_MaxCnt protects the driver from over-large multi-sector I/O requests. My choice of the short read command block forces PD_MaxCnt to 65535 unless some other choice forces it lower.

```
BaseRead(ct, StartAddr, Buffer, Options, DevStatics)
int ct;
ulong StartAddr;
register uchar *Buffer;
register struct rbf_opt *Options;
register MyStatics DevStatics;
{
    int Error;

    DevStatics→v_Sectors = ct;
    DevStatics→v_Bytes = ct * Options→pd_ssize;

    SETUP_CMD(DevStatics→V_CDB, SCSI_READOP, StartAddr, ct);     /* pg. 385 */
    ClaimController(DevStatics→EvID);

    Error = Exec(READ_CMD_LEN, WD_DPD_In,                         /* pg. 360 */
            (ulong *)Buffer, Options→pd_ctrlrid,
            DevStatics);
    ReleaseController(DevStatics→EvID);                           /* pg. 386 */
    return Error;
}
```

24.2.4 Write

WritDisk() is very similar to ReadDisk.

WritDisk() only permits sector zero to be written if the disk is not format protected, and when sector zero is written WritDisk() notes that the copy of sector zero cached in v_sczero is out-of-date. This will cause a subsequent read of sector zero to update the sector zero buffer and reset drive parameters if the new values in sector zero indicate that the drive should be reconfigured.[3]

---
[3]Changes to sector zero will not cause hard disks to need reconfiguration, but sector-zero parameters may call for floppy disk drives to change density, or switch in or out of double stepping mode.

24.2. THE DRIVER'S MAIN ENTRIES

```
#include <rbf.h>
#include <machine/reg.h>
#include <path.h>
#include <errno.h>
#include "drvr.h"

int BoundsCheck();

WritDisk(ct, lsn, pathd, DevStatics, SysGlobs)
int ct;
ulong lsn;
Pathdesc pathd;
register MyStatics DevStatics;
void *SysGlobs;
{
    register uchar *Buffer;
    register struct rbf_opt *Options;
    register Rbfdrive DTableE;
    register ulong StartAddr = lsn;
    int Error, Retries;

    if(ct == 0)                              /* If write is for no sectors, do no work */
        return 0;

    /* Make some useful pointers */
    Buffer = pathd→path.pd_buf;
    Options = (struct rbf_opt *)&(pathd→path.fm_opt);
    DTableE = pathd→path.fm_pvt.rbf.pd_dtb;

    if((Error = Cond_InitDrive(DevStatics, Options, DTableE, SysGlobs)) != 0)   /* pg. 348 */
        return Error;

    if(lsn == 0)
        if((Options→pd_cntl & CNTL_NOFMT) != 0)
            /* Can't write sector zero if format is inhibited */
            return E_FORMAT;
        else
            DTableE→v_zerord = FALSE;

    /* Make a "real" lsn by adding lsnoffset and trackoffset */
    StartAddr = addoffsets(lsn, Options→pd_lsnoffs,        /* pg. 358 */
        (Options→pd_cntl & CNTL_AUTOSIZE) != 0,
        Options→pd_toffs, Options→pd_t0s,
        Options→pd_sct, Options→pd_sid);
```

```
    if((Error = BoundsCheck(lsn, ct, DTableE→v_0.dd_tot[2] +           /* pg. 359 */
            256 * (DTableE→v_0.dd_tot[1] +
            256 * DTableE→v_0.dd_tot[0]),
            DevStatics→v_Bytes > Options→pd_maxcnt)) != 0)
        return Error;

    for(Retries = RETRY_MAX; Retries > 0; --Retries){
        Error = BasicWrite(ct, StartAddr, Buffer, Options,             /* pg. 339 */
            DevStatics);
        switch(Error){
            case E_DIDC:
                /* disk ID change (perhaps reset)                 */
                /* Re-init drive and try again.                   */
                (void)InitDrive(                                       /* pg. 349 */
                    (Board)DevStatics→v_sysio.v_port,
                    (Options→pd_cntl & CNTL_NOFMT) != 0,
                    (Options→pd_scsiopt & SCSI_PARITY) != 0,
                    &(Options→pd_ssize),
                    Options→pd_ctrlrid,
                    DevStatics,
                    (void **)&(DTableE→v_sczero),
                    &(DTableE→v_init),
                    &(DTableE→v_dtext),
                    SysGlobs);
                break;
            case E_HARDWARE:
                ClaimController(DevStatics→EvID);                      /* pg. 386 */
                Error = Init33C93A((Board)DevStatics→v_sysio.v_port,   /* pg. 331 */
                    (Options→pd_scsiopt & SCSI_PARITY) != 0);
                ReleaseController(DevStatics→EvID);                    /* pg. 386 */
                if(Error == 0)
                    break;
                else
                    return Error;
            default:
                return Error;
        }
    }

    return Error;
}
```

24.2. THE DRIVER'S MAIN ENTRIES

```
BasicWrite(ct, StartAddr, Buffer, Options, DevStatics)
int ct;
ulong StartAddr;
uchar *Buffer;
register struct rbf_opt *Options;
register MyStatics DevStatics;
{
    int Error;

    DevStatics→v_Sectors = ct;
    DevStatics→v_Bytes = ct * Options→pd_ssize;

    SETUP_CMD(DevStatics→V_CDB, SCSI_WRITEOP, StartAddr, ct);      /* pg. 385 */

    ClaimController(DevStatics→EvID);                               /* pg. 386 */

    if((Error = Exec(WRITE_CMD_LEN, WD_DPD_Out,                    /* pg. 360 */
            (ulong *)Buffer, Options→pd_ctrlrid,
            DevStatics)) == 0)
        if(Options→pd_vfy == 0){                  /* verification requested */
            SETUP_CMD_10(DevStatics→V_CDB, SCSI_VERIFY,            /* pg. 386 */
                0, StartAddr, ct);
            DevStatics→v_Bytes = 0;
            Error = Exec(VERIFY_CMD_LEN, WD_DPD_In, (void *)0,     /* pg. 360 */
                Options→pd_ctrlrid, DevStatics);
        }
    ReleaseController(DevStatics→EvID);                             /* pg. 386 */
    return Error;
}
```

24.2.5 GetStat and PutStat

This driver understands three getstat requests:

1. a request to return the number of sectors on the disk,

2. a request to set or validate the pd_ssize field in the path descriptor

3. and a "direct command" getstat.

The direct command getstat (and setstat) permit user code to issue SCSI commands. It is intended for debugging and configuration commands, but it supports all SCSI operations. The *Quantumcache* program in section 24.11 illustrates correct usage of the direct command interface.

The VarSect function is implemented here as a simple call to the device initialization function. This works because every device initialization checks (and if necessary sets) the pd_ssize field. The varsect getstat is used during the path initialization phase by the file manager to determine the drive's sector size. It is called before the path has an I/O buffer attached. The driver should discover the drive's sector size without using any path descriptor fields other than the drive table pointer.

```
#include <rbf.h>
#include <machine/reg.h>
#include <path.h>
#include <errno.h>
#include <sg_codes.h>
#include "drvr.h"

GetStat(Code, pathd, DevStatics, procd, regs, SysGlobs)
int Code;
Pathdesc pathd;
register MyStatics DevStatics;
void *procd;
REGISTERS *regs;
void *SysGlobs;
{
    register struct rbf_opt *Options;
    register Rbfdrive DTableE;
    int Error;

    Options = (struct rbf_opt *)&(pathd→path.fm_opt);
    DTableE = pathd→path.fm_pvt.rbf.pd_dtb;
    switch(Code){
       case SS_DCmd:
          if((Error = Cond_InitDrive(DevStatics,            /* pg. 348 */
               Options, DTableE, SysGlobs)) != 0)
             return Error;
          return direct_command(regs, procd, Options);     /* pg. 371 */
       case SS_DSize:
          if((Error = Cond_InitDrive(DevStatics,            /* pg. 348 */
               Options, DTableE, SysGlobs)) != 0)
             return Error;
          return DSize(DevStatics, Options, regs);          /* pg. 343 */
```

24.2. THE DRIVER'S MAIN ENTRIES

```
        case SS_VarSect:
            return Cond_InitDrive(DevStatics, Options,        /* pg. 348 */
                DTableE, SysGlobs);
        default:
            return E_UNKSVC;
    }
}
```

24.2.6 PutStat

This driver understands three putstat requests: direct command, reset, and write track. The reset setstat converts to the SCSI rezero command. The write track setstat starts a disk format operation.

The format putstat insures that the device is not format protected before it does anything. Since a single format command formats the entire device, a write track for the first accessible track issues a SCSI format command. All other write tracks succeed without doing anything.

In case the path descriptor specifies that the disk's sector size should be changed, the write track putstat calls a function that changes the device's sector size.

Write track also clears both the v_zerord and v_init fields. This will cause any subsequent I/O call to start this drive from scratch.

```
PutStat(Code, pathd, DevStatics, procd, regs, SysGlobs)
int Code;
Pathdesc pathd;
register MyStatics DevStatics;
void *procd;
REGISTERS *regs;
void *SysGlobs;
{
    register struct rbf_opt *Options;
    register Rbfdrive DTableE;
    int Error;
    int retryct;

    Options = (struct rbf_opt *)&(pathd→path.fm_opt);
    DTableE = pathd→path.fm_pvt.rbf.pd_dtb;
```

```
switch(Code){
    case SS_DCmd:
        if((Error = Cond_InitDrive(DevStatics,                    /* pg. 348 */
                Options, DTableE, SysGlobs)) != 0)
            return Error;
        return direct_command(regs, procd, Options);
    case SS_Reset:
        if((Error = Cond_InitDrive(DevStatics,                    /* pg. 348 */
                Options, DTableE, SysGlobs)) != 0)
            return Error;
        for(retryct = 2; retryct != 0; retryct--){
            SETUP_CMD(DevStatics→V_CDB, SCSI_REZERO_UNIT, 0,0);   /* pg. 385 */
            DevStatics→v_Bytes = 0;
            ClaimController(DevStatics→EvID);                     /* pg. 386 */
            Error = Exec(REZERO_CMD_LEN, 0, (void *)0,            /* pg. 360 */
                Options→pd_ctrlrid, DevStatics);
            ReleaseController(DevStatics→EvID);                   /* pg. 386 */
            if(Error == 0)
                return 0;
            if(Error == E_DIDC)
                InitDrive((Board)DevStatics→v_sysio.v_port,       /* pg. 349 */
                    (Options→pd_cntl & CNTL_NOFMT) != 0,
                    (Options→pd_scsiopt & SCSI_PARITY) != 0,
                    &(Options→pd_ssize),
                    Options→pd_ctrlrid,
                    DevStatics,
                    (void **)&(DTableE→v_sczero),
                    &(DTableE→v_init),
                    &(DTableE→v_dtext),
                    SysGlobs);
        }
        return Error;
    case SS_WTrk:
        if((Options→pd_cntl & CNTL_NOFMT) != 0)
            return E_FORMAT;
        if((regs→d[2] != (unsigned int)Options→pd_toffs) ||
                (((regs→d[3] >> 8) & 0x0ff) != 0))
            /* Ignore write tracks for non-cyl 0 -head 0 */
            return 0;
        if((Error = InitDrive((Board)DevStatics→v_sysio.v_port,   /* pg. 349 */
                (Options→pd_cntl & CNTL_NOFMT) != 0,
                (Options→pd_scsiopt & SCSI_PARITY) != 0,
                &(Options→pd_ssize),
                Options→pd_ctrlrid,
```

24.2. THE DRIVER'S MAIN ENTRIES

```
                    DevStatics,
                    (void **)&(DTableE→v_sczero),
                    &(DTableE→v_init),
                    &(DTableE→v_dtext),
                    SysGlobs)) != 0)
                return Error;
            DTableE→v_zerord = FALSE;
            DTableE→v_init = FALSE;
            if((Error = SetSectorSize(DevStatics,                    /* pg. 353 */
                    (int)Options→pd_ctrlrid,
                    (int)Options→pd_ssize)) != 0)
                return Error;
            DevStatics→V_CDB[0] = SCSI_FORMAT_UNIT;
            DevStatics→V_CDB[1] = 0;
            DevStatics→V_CDB[2] = 0;
            DevStatics→V_CDB[3] = 0;
            DevStatics→V_CDB[4] = regs→d[4];
            DevStatics→V_CDB[5] = 0;
            ClaimController(DevStatics→EvID);                        /* pg. 386 */
            Error = Exec(FORMAT_CMD_LEN, 0, (void *)0,               /* pg. 360 */
                    Options→pd_ctrlrid, DevStatics);
            ReleaseController(DevStatics→EvID);                      /* pg. 386 */
            return Error;
        default:
            return E_UNKSVC;
    }
}


DSize(DevStatics, Options, regs)
register MyStatics DevStatics;
register struct rbf_opt *Options;
REGISTERS *regs;
{
    ulong Sectors;
    ushort SectSize=0;
    int Errno;

    if((Errno = GetCapacity(DevStatics→EvID,                         /* pg. 351 */
            (Options→pd_cntl & CNTL_NOFMT) != 0,
            &SectSize, &Sectors, Options→pd_ctrlrid,
            DevStatics)) != 0)
        return Errno;
    regs→d[2] = Sectors;
```

            return 0;
}

24.2.7 IRQ Service

This driver uses the WD33C93A's select and transfer operation with no disconnect allowed. This causes the chip to run the entire SCSI protocol without assistance. The WD33C93A does not raise an interrupt until the SCSI command has completed or has terminated due to an error. In either case all the interrupt service routine can do is start the waiting process. The less sophisticated WD33C93A commands raise interrupts as each SCSI phase completes. The interrupt service routine for these commands must actually operate the I/O hardware.

This interrupt service routine simply checks that this driver is waiting for an interrupt (by comparing v_wake to zero), and checks the SCSI board's interrupt bit to see if the interrupt actually came from this hardware. If the interrupt is indeed the responsibility of this driver, the interrupt service routine sends a wakeup signal to the process that is waiting in Exec().

```
#include <rbf.h>
#include "drvr.h"

C_IRQRtn(DevStatics, port)
register MyStatics DevStatics;
Board port;
{
    register ushort process;

    if((process = DevStatics→v_sysio.v_wake) == 0)
        return −1;                  /*Not our interrupt */
    if(port→BD_STATUS > 0)
        return −1;                  /*Not our interrupt */

    /*It is our interrupt */
    port→BD_CONTROL = 0;                    /*Disable interrupts from the board */
    DevStatics→v_sysio.v_wake = 0;          /*We are responsible for waking this process */
    AWake(process);                         /* pg. 381 */
     return 0;
}
```

24.3 Drive Management

24.3.1 Read Sector 0

This routine is called whenever the file manager wants to read sector 0. The outline of ReadSector0() is:

1. If sector zero has already been read (and is therefore cached in the sector zero buffer), don't read the disk. Copy the cached sector zero into the caller's buffer and return. RBF checks for disk changes by reading sector zero frequently. The driver can improve performance noticeably by satisfing these reads from the sector zero cache. However, if the disk is removeable, the driver must take care not to cripple RBF's disk change detection mechanism.

   - Executing every sector zero read is the simple approach; it works and is often sufficient. It is slow.

   - If the drive can raise an interrupt when its door is opened, the driver can use a sector zero cache and interrupt service routine for the "door opened" interrupt can invalidate the sector zero cache; that is about as efficient as sector zero management can be made with a removeable disk.

   - The driver can choose a reasonable time-out for the sector zero cache. The driver's designer should add head unload time, drive spin-up time, drive spin-down time, and some estimate of the minumum time required to yank the disk out of the drive and slap another in. The cache timeout interval should be somewhat less than the calculated minimum disk change time. The driver can use an alarm or a time stamp on the cache to invalidate the cache every time the disk has gone unused long enough to change disks.

     If the driver uses a cache timestamp
         In the code for every disk access:
             Reset the cache timeout stamp to now + interval
         In ReadSector0()
             If sector zero is not cached yet or
                 cache timeout < current time
                     Refresh the sector zero cache from disk
             Return sector zero from the cache
     If the driver uses a timeout alarm
         In the code for every disk access:
             Cancel any alarm
             Set an inteval alarm for one timeout interval
         In the alarm service routine:
             Clear the sector-zero-cached flag

> In ReadSector0()
> If sector zero is not cached yet
> Refresh the sector zero cache from disk
> Return sector zero from the cache

2. Read sector zero into the caller's buffer.

3. If the disk is a fixed hard disk, Copy the sector 0 from the caller's buffer into v_sczero in the drive table entry, and set v_zerord in the drive table entry to TRUE.

4. Copy the first 21 bytes of the caller's buffer into the beginning of the drive table entry. (This configures the drive table entry for the disk.) RBF refers to the drive table entry for disk configuration information.

5. Validate the disk format. At this point we could check the newly-set fields in the drive table entry against information in the device descriptor for compatibility with the controller and drive. For instance, if the drive were a floppy drive and could not handle double-sided disks, ReadSector0() should return an error whenever it reads a sector zero that shows a double sided disk.

    SCSI hard disk drives can handle all ordinary configuration details without help from the driver, so this driver can ignore all physical configuration parameters in sector zero. Even non-SCSI hard disks can ignore many configuration parameters.

    This driver only checks the number of sectors on the disk as stated in sector zero. If the number of sectors indicated in sector zero, plus the actual sector number of sector zero is greater than the number of sectors on the disk, the disk structure is broken.

```
#include <rbf.h>
#include <machine/reg.h>
#include <path.h>
#include "drvr.h"

ReadSector0(Block, DevStatics,
        Buffer, DTableE, Options)
ulong Block;
register MyStatics DevStatics;
uchar *Buffer;
register Rbfdrive DTableE;
register struct rbf_opt *Options;
```

24.3. DRIVE MANAGEMENT

```
{
    register ulong *lptr, *lptr2, *limit;
    ulong Sectors;
    int Error = 0;

    if(DTableE→v_zerord != FALSE){                          /* sector 0 already read */
        /* Just copy data out of sector 0 buffer */
        lptr = (ulong *)Buffer;
        (uchar *)limit = (uchar *)lptr + Options→pd_ssize;
        lptr2 = (ulong *)DTableE→v_sczero;

        while(lptr != limit)
            *lptr++ = *lptr2++;
        return 0;
    }
    if((Error = BaseRead(1, Block, Buffer, Options, DevStatics)) == 0){   /* pg. 336 */
        if(((Options→pd_typ & TYP_HARD) != 0) &&
            ((Options→pd_typ & TYP_HREMOV) == 0)){
            DTableE→v_zerord = TRUE;
            lptr = (ulong *)Buffer;
            (uchar *)limit = (uchar *)lptr + Options→pd_ssize;
            lptr2 = (ulong *)DTableE→v_sczero;
            while(lptr != limit)
                *lptr2++ = *lptr++;
        }
        /*
            Initialize the drive table from the buffer
        */
        MoveData(DTableE, Buffer, 21);                      /* pg. 379 */
        /*
            Validate the disk format and make certain it is compatible
            with this hardware.
        */
        if((Error = GetCapacity(DevStatics→EvID, TRUE,      /* pg. 351 */
                &(Options→pd_ssize),
                &Sectors, Options→pd_ctrlrid,
                DevStatics)) != 0)
            return Error;

        return BoundsCheck(Block, DTableE→v_0.dd_tot[2] +   /* pg. 359 */
                256 * (DTableE→v_0.dd_tot[1] +
                256 * DTableE→v_0.dd_tot[0]), Sectors,
                FALSE);
    } else
```

return Error;
}

24.3.2 Initialize a Drive

Cond_InitDrive() is called frequently. The function always checks the values of pd_drv,[4] pd_lun, and pd_ctrlrid and returns an error if any of the values are out-of-range.

If the drive has not yet been initialized (v_init is false), Cond_InitDrive() calls InitDrive() to initialize the drive hardware and data structures.

if pd_ssize is zero, it is set to the sector size indicated by the disk.

```
#include <types.h>
#include <rbf.h>
#include <errno.h>
#include "drvr.h"
#include "lowlevel.h"
#define NOTRDY_TO           10              /* Not ready timeout value */

void ResetQ();

Cond_InitDrive(DevStatics, Options, DTableE, SysGlobs)
register MyStatics DevStatics;
register struct rbf_opt *Options;
register Rbfdrive DTableE;
void *SysGlobs;
{
   if((Options→pd_drv >= DevStatics→v_ndrv) ||
        (Options→pd_lun > MAXLUN) ||
        (Options→pd_ctrlrid > MAXSCSI))
      return E_UNIT;                        /* bad unit number */

   if(DTableE→v_init == FALSE)
      return InitDrive((Board)DevStatics→v_sysio.v_port,        /* pg. 349 */
         (Options→pd_cntl & CNTL_NOFMT) != 0,
         (Options→pd_scsiopt & SCSI_PARITY) != 0,
         &(Options→pd_ssize),
         Options→pd_ctrlrid,
         DevStatics,
         (void **)&(DTableE→v_sczero),
```

---

[4]Pd_ndrv is a counter, and pd_drv is an index. Pd_drv must be in the range 0 to pd_ndrv −1.

24.3. DRIVE MANAGEMENT

```
                &(DTableE→v_init),
                &(DTableE→v_dtext),
                SysGlobs);
   if(Options→pd_ssize == 0)
      Options→pd_ssize = DTableE→v_dtext;
   return 0;
}
```

InitDrive()'s outline is:

1. If the I/O board detected a SCSI reset, reinitialize the WD33C93A.

2. Start the drive and wait for it to become ready.

3. Get the sector size on the drive. If it is the same as the value in pd_ssize, do nothing. If the value in pd_ssize is zero, copy the actual sector size in pd_ssize. if the value in pd_ssize is non-zero and different from the actual sector size of the disk, complain unless the disk is format enabled.

Our assumption is that the caller is preparing to format the disk with a new sector size if he calls the driver with a format-enabled path and an "incorrect" sector size, so we change the sector size to match the path descriptor's suggestion.

```
/*
   The init() function initialized the 33C93A and the entire drive table. This
   function initializes a specific drive attached to the 33C93A and some data
   structures associated with that specific drive.
*/

InitDrive(port, NoFmt, Parity, SectSize, ctrlrid,
        DevStatics, DTv_sczero, DTv_init, DTv_ext, SysGlobs)
Board port;
boolean NoFmt, Parity;
register ushort *SectSize;
uchar ctrlrid;
register MyStatics DevStatics;
register void **DTv_sczero;
uchar *DTv_init;
unsigned int *DTv_ext;
void *SysGlobs;
{
   int Errno;
   ulong Sectors;
   int Retries;
```

```
        for(Retries = RETRY_MAX; Retries >= 0; --Retries){
            ResetQ(port, Parity, DevStatics→EvID);                          /* pg. 351 */

            if((Errno = Make_UnitReady(DevStatics→EvID, ctrlrid,            /* pg. 351 */
                DevStatics)) == 0)
                Errno = GetCapacity(DevStatics→EvID, NoFmt,                 /* pg. 351 */
                    SectSize, &Sectors, ctrlrid, DevStatics);
            switch(Errno){
                case E_DIDC:
                    continue;
                case E_HARDWARE:
                    ClaimController(DevStatics→EvID);                       /* pg. 386 */
                    BdReset(port, SysGlobs);                                /* pg. 364 */
                    Errno = Init33C93A(port, Parity);                       /* pg. 331 */
                    ReleaseController(DevStatics→EvID);                     /* pg. 386 */
                    if(Errno != 0)
                        return Errno;
                    continue;
                case 0:
                    break;
                default:
                    return Errno;
            }
            break;
        }
        /* Allocate the sector zero buffer                      */
        if(*DTv_sczero == (void *)0){
            if((*DTv_sczero = (void *)_srqmem(*SectSize)) == (void *)-1){   /* pg. 378 */
                *DTv_sczero = (void *)0;
                return E_NORAM;
            }
            *DTv_ext = *SectSize;
        }
        *DTv_init = TRUE;
        return 0;
    }




/*
    Has a SCSI reset happened? If it has, reset the 33C93A.
*/
```

24.3. DRIVE MANAGEMENT

```
void ResetQ(port, Parity, Event)
register Board port;
boolean Parity;
ulong Event;
{
    ClaimController(Event);                                     /* pg. 386 */
    if(port→BD_STATUS < 0){                    /*An unexplained interrupt */
        if((GET_SCSI_STATUS(port) & 0xf0) == 0)
            Init33C93A(port, Parity);                           /* pg. 331 */
    }
    ReleaseController(Event);                                   /* pg. 386 */
}




Make_UnitReady(Event, SCSI_ID, DevStatics)
ulong Event;
uchar SCSI_ID;
register MyStatics DevStatics;
{
    ushort TimeCtr;
    int Errno;

    SETUP_CMD(DevStatics→V_CDB, SCSI_TEST_UNIT_READY, 0, 0);   /* pg. 385 */
    TimeCtr = NOTRDY_TO;
    do{
        DevStatics→v_Bytes = 0;
        ClaimController(Event);                                 /* pg. 386 */
        Errno = Exec(READY_CMD_LEN, WD_DPD_In, (void *)0,       /* pg. 360 */
            SCSI_ID, DevStatics);
        ReleaseController(Event);                               /* pg. 386 */
    }while((Errno != 0) && (TimeCtr-- != 0));
    return Errno;
}




GetCapacity(Event, NoFmt, SectSize, Sectors, ctrlrid, DevStatics)
register ulong Event;
boolean NoFmt;
register ushort *SectSize;
ulong *Sectors;
uchar ctrlrid;
register MyStatics DevStatics;
```

```
{
    struct {
        ulong Size;
        ulong SSize;
    } RCData;
    int Errno;

    SETUP_CMD_10(DevStatics→V_CDB, SCSI_READ_CAPACITY, 0, 0, 0);   /* pg. 386 */
    DevStatics→v_Bytes = sizeof(RCData);
    ClaimController(Event);                                         /* pg. 386 */
    Errno = Exec(READCAP_CMD_LEN, WD_DPD_In, (ulong *)&RCData,     /* pg. 360 */
        ctrlrid, DevStatics);
    ReleaseController(Event);                                       /* pg. 386 */
    if(Errno != 0)
        return Errno;
    *Sectors = RCData.Size;

    if(*SectSize == 0)
        *SectSize = RCData.SSize;
    else if(NoFmt){                                                 /* Format protected */
        if(*SectSize != RCData.SSize)                               /* Mismatch */
            return E_SECTSIZE;
    } else                                                          /* Format enabled */
        if(*SectSize != RCData.SSize)                               /* Mismatch */
            /* Change the sector size */
            return SetSectorSize(DevStatics, ctrlrid, *SectSize);   /* pg. 353 */

    return 0;
}
```

24.3.3 Set Sector Size

The sector size of a SCSI disk is altered with the MODE_SELECT SCSI command. The following functions attempt to change the logical block size and physical block size. If the drive will not permit changes to the physical block size, only the logical block size is changed.

The Quantum drive I used to test this driver only supports a 512-byte physical sector size, so the part of this code that changes the physical sector size has not been tested.

```
#include <rbf.h>
#include <machine/reg.h>
```

24.3. DRIVE MANAGEMENT

```
#include <path.h>
#include "drvr.h"

typedef struct {
    uchar length;
    uchar type;
    unsigned wp                     :1;
    unsigned res1                   :7;              /*reserved */
    uchar block_desc_length;
    /*Block descriptor */
    uchar density_code;
    unsigned blocks                 :24;
    uchar res2;
    unsigned block_length           :24;             /*logical block length */
} block_desc_type;


typedef struct {
    block_desc_type hdr;
    unsigned parameter_savable      :1;
    unsigned reserved               :1;
    unsigned page_code              :6;
    uchar page_length;
    ushort tracks_per_zone,
           alternate_sectors_per_zone,
           alternate_tracks_per_zone,
           alternate_tracks_per_vol,
           sectors_per_track,
           bytes_per_sector,                         /*Physical block length */
           interleave,
           track_skew,
           cylinder_skew;
    unsigned dt_ssec                :1,              /*Drive type bits */
             dt_hsec                :1,
             dt_rmb                 :1,
             dt_surf                :1,
             dt_ins                 :1,
                                    :27;
} page3_type;


SetSectorSize(DevStatics, SCSI_ID, sector_size)
register MyStatics DevStatics;
uchar SCSI_ID;
ushort sector_size;
```

```
{
    int error;
    union {
        page3_type page3;
        block_desc_type block_desc;
    } status_info;
    int set_length;

    if((error = GetChangeable((void *)&status_info, sizeof(status_info),     /* pg. 355 */
            DevStatics, SCSI_ID)) != 0)
        return error;

    if(status_info.page3.bytes_per_sector != 0){
        if((error = GetMode((void *)&status_info, sizeof(status_info),       /* pg. 355 */
                DevStatics, SCSI_ID)) != 0)
            return error;
        status_info.page3.bytes_per_sector = sector_size;
        status_info.page3.sectors_per_track = 0;                              /*drive will set */
        status_info.page3.parameter_savable = 0;
        status_info.page3.reserved = 0;
        set_length = sizeof (page3_type);
    } else
        set_length = sizeof (block_desc_type);

    init_blk_header(&status_info.block_desc, sector_size);                    /* pg. 354 */
    return mode_set((void *)&status_info, set_length, DevStatics, SCSI_ID);   /* pg. 356 */
}


init_blk_header(status_info, blk_size)
block_desc_type *status_info;
int blk_size;
{
    status_info→length = 0;
    status_info→type = 0;
    status_info→wp = 0;
    status_info→res1 = 0;
    status_info→block_desc_length = 8;
    status_info→density_code = 0;
    status_info→blocks = 0;
    status_info→res2 = 0;
    status_info→block_length = blk_size;
}
```

24.3. DRIVE MANAGEMENT

```
GetChangeable(data, datasize, DevStatics, SCSI_ID)
void *data;
int datasize;
register MyStatics DevStatics;
int SCSI_ID;
{
    register struct {
        uchar cmd;
        unsigned lun             :3,
                 res1            :5,
                 pcf             :2,
                 code            :6;
        uchar res2;
        uchar allocation_length;
        unsigned res3            :6,
                 flag            :1,
                 link            :1;
    } *CDB = DevStatics→V_CDB;

    CDB→cmd = SCSI_MODE_SENSE;
    CDB→flag = CDB→link = CDB→lun = CDB→res1 = CDB→res2 = CDB→res3 = 0;
    CDB→pcf = 1;                    /* this is the magic number for return changeable */
    CDB→code = 3;                   /* Page 3 is format parameters */
    CDB→allocation_length = 36;
    DevStatics→v_Bytes = datasize;
    return Exec(sizeof(*CDB), WD_DPD_In, (ulong *)data,      /* pg. 360 */
        (uchar)SCSI_ID, DevStatics);
}


GetMode(data, datasize, DevStatics, SCSI_ID)
void *data;
register MyStatics DevStatics;
int SCSI_ID;
{
    register struct {
        uchar cmd;
        unsigned lun             :3,
                 res1            :5,
                 pcf             :2,
                 code            :6;
        uchar res2;
        uchar allocation_length;
        unsigned res3            :6,
```

```
                flag                    :1,
                link                    :1;
    } *CDB = DevStatics→V_CDB;
    CDB→cmd = SCSI_MODE_SENSE;
    CDB→flag = CDB→link = CDB→lun = CDB→res1 = CDB→res2 = CDB→res3 = 0;
    CDB→pcf = 0;               /*this is the magic number for return current values */
    CDB→code = 3;                           /*Page 3 is format parameters */
    CDB→allocation_length = 36;
    DevStatics→v_Bytes = datasize;
    return Exec(sizeof(*CDB), WD_DPD_In, (ulong *)data, (uchar)SCSI_ID,   /* pg. 360 */
        DevStatics);
}




mode_set(data, set_length, DevStatics, SCSI_ID)
void *data;
int set_length;
register MyStatics DevStatics;
int SCSI_ID;
{
    register struct {
        uchar cmd;
        unsigned lun                    :3,
                 pf                     :1,
                 res1                   :3,
                 smp                    :1;
        ushort res2;
        uchar param_length;
        unsigned res3                   :6,
                 flag                   :1,
                 link                   :1;
    } *CDB = DevStatics→V_CDB;
    CDB→cmd = SCSI_MODE_SELECT;
    CDB→smp = 1;
    CDB→link = CDB→lun = CDB→res1 = CDB→res2 = CDB→res3 = 0;
    CDB→pf = 0;
    CDB→param_length = set_length;
    DevStatics→v_Bytes = set_length;
    return Exec(sizeof(*CDB), WD_DPD_Out, (ulong *)data, (uchar)SCSI_ID,   /* pg. 360 */
        DevStatics);
}
```

24.4 Miscellaneous

```
#include <rbf.h>
#include <errno.h>
#include "drvr.h"

/*
    Return an event ID number for the event corresponding to this port/SCSI_ID.
    The event will be made if it does not exist. return -1 if there is an error.
    Use Microware naming conventions for port event:
    <c><portaddress>
    This event claims the entire controller, so the SCSI ID suffix is not required.
    Convention is <c> = 'i' for interrupt service events. This is a non interrupt
    service mutex event for locking the controller, so we invent the convention that
    <c> = 'c' for controller locking.
*/

MakeEvent(port, Errno)
register ulong port;
int *Errno;
{
    char EvName[10];
    ulong EventID;

    MakeEvName(EvName, port);                                  /* pg. 357 */

    if((EventID = _Ev_link(EvName)) == -1)                     /* pg. 380 */
        return(_Ev_Creat(EvName, Errno));                      /* pg. 380 */
    else
        return EventID;
}




MakeEvName(EvName, port)
char *EvName;
ulong port;
{
    register int i;
    extern int HexTbl();

    EvName[0] = 'c';
    EvName[9] = '\0';
```

```
    for(i=8; i != 0; i--){
        EvName[i] = ((uchar *)HexTbl)[port & 0x0f];          /* pg. 380 */
        port >>= 4;
    }
}


DeleteEvent(port, EvID)
ulong port;
ulong EvID;
{
    char EvName[10];

    MakeEvName(EvName, port);                                /* pg. 357 */
    _Ev_Unlink(EvID);                                        /* pg. 381 */
    _Ev_Del(EvName);                                         /* pg. 381 */
}
```

For non-partitioned hard disks, offsets will generally be zero. If the disk is partitioned, it will either use an LSN offset or a track base offset. The two are not strictly mutually exclusive, but in practice a device descriptor will use one or the other. Track offset is not useful for autosize devices (which will probably claim to have zero sectors per track). Although an LSN offset will always do the expected thing, it does not automatically place partitions on track boundaries, and formatting considerations favor partitions on track boundaries.

Floppy disks need to consider sector offset. It can be added to lsnoffset.[5]

```
addoffsets(Sector, lsnoffset, AutoSize, TrackOffset, T0Sects, SectPerTrack,
    Sides)
ulong Sector;
unsigned int lsnoffset;
boolean AutoSize;
uchar TrackOffset;
ushort T0Sects;
ushort SectPerTrack;
uchar Sides;
```

---

[5]It is not important for SCSI disks, but for non-SCSI disks the sector offset should be added *after* the track is calculated. The sector offset applies *per track*. A 16 sector per track disk with a sector offset of 1 has sectors labeled from 1 to 16. A 16 sector per track disk with a sector offset of 0 has sectors labeled from 0 to 15. The driver should calculate the track and sector without considering the sector offset (though it may consider LSN offset and track base offset), then add the sector offset to the resulting sector number.

24.5. SCSI MANAGEMENT

```
{
   Sector += lsnoffset;
    if(!AutoSize && (TrackOffset != 0)){
       Sector += T0Sects;                          /*Sectors on track 0 side 0 */
       Sector += (SectPerTrack * (Sides − 1));     /*Rest of sectors on track 0 */
       Sector += (TrackOffset − 1) * Sides * SectPerTrack;
    }
    return Sector;
}


int BoundsCheck(lsn, ct, high, OverMaxCt)
ulong lsn;
int ct, high;
boolean OverMaxCt;
{
   if(OverMaxCt)
      /*Not what E_PARAM is meant for, but there's no better error */
      return E_PARAM;
   if(ct + lsn > high)
      return E_SECT;
   return 0;
}
```

24.5 SCSI Management

The Exec() function is responsible for the operation of the SCSI I/O board. Its outline is:

1. If the I/O direction is out, copy any output data to the I/O board.

2. Load the SCSI command, the transfer count (number of bytes to read or write), and target into the WD33C93A.

3. Reset the board's DMA address so reads or writes will take place at the right location in the board's address space.

4. Set v_wake equal to v_busy (so the interrupt service routine will know what process to awaken).

5. Enable interrupts from the I/O board.

6. Start a select and transfer operation.

7. Sleep until the interrupt service routine sends a wakeup signal.

8. Check for errors, and handle any that are detected.

9. If the command is an input command, copy data from the I/O board into a buffer that was passed to Exec().

```
#include <rbf.h>
#include "drvr.h"
#include "lowlevel.h"

Exec(Len, Direction, Buffer, SCSI_ID, DevStatics)
int Len;
uchar Direction;
ulong *Buffer;
uchar SCSI_ID;
register MyStatics DevStatics;
{
    register Board port;
    register int i;
    int Errno;

    port = (Board)DevStatics→v_sysio.v_port;

    /* First move any data to the I/O board that will be written */

    if((DevStatics→v_Bytes > 0) && (Direction == WD_DPD_Out)){
        port→BD_Address = BD_PUBLIC_BUF;
        if((((ulong)Buffer & 0x02) == 0) &&              /* addr is multiple of 4 */
            ((DevStatics→v_Bytes & 0x03) == 0)){         /* So is length */
            register ulong *lptr, *limit;
            lptr = (ulong *)Buffer;
            (uchar *)limit = (uchar *)lptr + DevStatics→v_Bytes;
            while(lptr != limit)
                port→Databuffer.L_DataBuf = *lptr++;
        } else {                                          /* Multiple of two */
            register ushort *sptr, *limit;
            sptr = (ushort *)Buffer;
            (uchar *)limit = (uchar *)sptr + DevStatics→v_Bytes;
            while(sptr != limit)
                port→Databuffer.W_DataBuf = *sptr++;
        }
    }
```

24.5. SCSI MANAGEMENT

```
/*
    Then do the I/O operation with retries if required.
*/
while(TRUE){
    port→WD_SELECT = WD_CDB1;
    for(i = 0 ; i <Len ; ++i)
        port→WD_WRITE_REG = DevStatics→V_CDB[i];
    /*Fill the rest of the CDB registers */
    Errno = 0;
    for(;i<10;++i)
        port→WD_WRITE_REG = Errno;

    Set_XFrCt(port, DevStatics→v_Bytes);                    /* pg. 364 */

    SET_TARGET(port, SCSI_ID | Direction);                  /* pg. 386 */

    while(TRUE){
        port→BD_Address = BD_PUBLIC_BUF;
        DevStatics→v_sysio.v_wake = DevStatics→v_sysio.v_busy;
        BD_EnableInt(port);                                 /* pg. 386 */
        SET_CMD(port, SCSI_X_SAT); /*Select and transfer */ /* pg. 386 */
        do{
            dosleep(0);                                     /* pg. 381 */
        }while(DevStatics→v_sysio.v_wake != 0);

        if((Errno = GET_SCSI_STATUS(port)) != WD_SAT_OK)    /* pg. 386 */
            if((Errno = SAT_Error(Errno, port,              /* pg. 365 */
                    DevStatics)) == 0)
                /*SAT_Error() wants a retry */
                continue;
            else
                return Errno;
        else
            break;
    }
    Errno = GET_SCSI_TARGETSTAT(port);                      /* pg. 386 */
    if(Errno == 0)
        break;                              /*Break out of while(TRUE) loop */
    else {
        if((Errno & 0x02) != 0)
            if((Errno = DeviceCheck(DevStatics, SCSI_ID)) != 0)  /* pg. 367 */
                return Errno;
        if((Errno & 0xC0) != 0){                /*Busy or reservation conflict */
            dosleep(0x8000007f);   /*wait about .5 seconds */    /* pg. 381 */
```

```
                    continue;                              /*and retry */
                }
            }
        }

        /*Copy any data that was read */

        if((DevStatics→v_Bytes > 0) && (Direction == WD_DPD_In)){
            /*Move data from board */
            port→BD_Address = BD_PUBLIC_BUF;
            if((((ulong)Buffer & 0x02) == 0) &&             /*Addr is multiple of 4 */
               ((DevStatics→v_Bytes & 0x03) == 0)){         /*So is length */
                register ulong *lptr, *limit;
                lptr = (ulong *)Buffer;
                (uchar *)limit = (uchar *)lptr + DevStatics→v_Bytes;
                while(lptr != limit)
                    *lptr++ = port→Databuffer.L_DataBuf;
            } else {                                        /*Multiple of two */
                register ushort *sptr, *limit;
                sptr = (ushort *)Buffer;
                (uchar *)limit = (uchar *)sptr + DevStatics→v_Bytes;
                while(sptr != limit)
                    *sptr++ = port→Databuffer.W_DataBuf;
            }
        }
        return 0;
    }
```

The following functions operate on SCSI board's I/O registers.

```
#include <rbf.h>
#include <machine/reg.h>
#include <path.h>
#include "drvr.h"
#include <errno.h>

#define RESET_LOOPS        256*10           /* 10 seconds */
#define RESET_DELAY        0x80000001       /* 1/256 second */

void LL_Put(port, value, reg)
register Board port;
uchar value;
uchar reg;
```

24.5. SCSI MANAGEMENT

```
{
   port→WD_SELECT = reg;                              /*Select register */
   @ nop
   port→WD_WRITE_REG = value;
}



LL_Get(port, reg)
register Board port;
uchar reg;
{
   port→WD_SELECT = reg;
   @ nop
   return (port→WD_READ_REG);
}
```

/*
   The value returned from a successful Do_WD_Reset should
   be 0x00000001 "The device has successfully completed a
   reset command..." A value of −1 signifies that it timed out.
*/
```
Do_WD_Reset(port)
register Board port;
{
   int ctr;
   LL_Put(port, WD_RESET, WD_CMDREG);/*Start a 33C93A reset */        /* pg. 362 */

   for(ctr= 0; ctr < RESET_LOOPS; ++ctr)
      if((port→BD_STATUS & 0x80) != 0)
         /*Reset is done */
         return(LL_Get(port, WD_SCSI_STAT)); /*Touch SCSI status */    /* pg. 363 */
      else
         dosleep(RESET_DELAY);                                         /* pg. 381 */
   return −1;
}


void Set_Control(port, value)
register Board port;
uchar value;
```

```
{
    LL_Put(port, value, WD_CONTROL);              /* pg. 362 */
    /* Register auto-increments */
    port→WD_WRITE_REG = WD_TIMEOUT;
}


void Set_XFrCt(port, value)
register Board port;
ulong value;
{
    port→WD_SELECT = WD_XFRCT1;
    port→WD_WRITE_REG = ((value >> 16) & 0x0ff);
    port→WD_WRITE_REG = ((value >> 8) & 0x0ff);
    @ nop
    port→WD_WRITE_REG = value & 0x0ff;
}


int Get_XFrCt(port)
register Board port;
{
    register int accum;
    port→WD_SELECT = WD_XFRCT1;
    accum = port→WD_READ_REG;
    accum <<= 8;
    accum += port→WD_READ_REG;
    accum <<= 8;
    accum += port→WD_READ_REG;
    return accum;
}


/* reset the controller and the SCSI bus */

BdReset(port, SysGlobs)
Board port;
void *SysGlobs;
{
    register uchar zero=0;

    port→BD_CONTROL = BD_RESET;
    dosleep(0x80000000 | 5);        /* Wait about .02 seconds */       /* pg. 381 */
    port→BD_CONTROL = zero;                  /* Stop resetting. Leave interrupts disabled */
```

24.5. SCSI MANAGEMENT

}

24.5.1 Error Handling

The usual reaction of this driver to any detected error is:

1. Try the operation again.

2. Reinitialize the drive and try again.

3. Reinitialize the WD33C93A and try again.

4. Do a SCSI bus reset, reinitialize the WD33C93A, reinitialize the drive and try again.[6]

5. If none of those tricks work, return an error to the caller.

The error-handling functions, SAT_Error() and DeviceCheck(), attempt to identify errors that can be ignored, unit attention errors (that can often be resolved by reinitializing the drive), and not ready errors that should cause the driver to wait a while and try again. Beyond that, the functions convert error codes from the WD33C93A and the SCSI device into OS-9 error codes.

```
#include <rbf.h>
#include <errno.h>
#include "drvr.h"
#include "lowlevel.h"
/*
    A SCSI protocol error caused a command failure.  The error
    code is in Errno.
*/

SAT_Error(Errno, port, DevStatics)
int Errno;
Board port;
register MyStatics DevStatics;
{
    int Count;

    switch(Errno & 0x0f0){
```

---

[6]A SCSI bus reset is a serious thing. All devices on the bus will need reinitialization, and any other initiators on the bus will have to handle unexpected resets. If there are multiple initiators, it might be better to return an error and get human help instead of resetting the bus.

```
        case 0x040:                    /*Status group 4 */
        /*
            The command terminated prematurely due to an error or other unexpected
            condition. Now we try to find a way to restart the command.
        */
        switch(Errno & 0x0f){
            case 0: /*Invalid command */
                break;
            case 1: /*Unexpected disconnect by the target */
                break;
            case 2: /*A timeout during (re)select */
                return E_NOTRDY;

            case 3: /*Parity error */
                break;
            case 4: /*Parity error with ATN asserted */
                break;
            case 5: /*Sector number off disk */
                break;
            case 6: /*WD33C93A in non-advanced mode */
                break;
            case 7: /*Incorrect status byte was received */
                break;
            /*
                The following cases are all in a family with values depending
                on which phase got the error.
            */
            /* An unexpected information phase was requested. */
            case 8: /*Data out phase] */
                break;
            case 9: /*[Data in phase ] */
                break;
            case 10: /*[Command phase] */
                break;
            case 11: /*[Status phase] */
                /*
                    Reselect and transfer
                    Resume after the data phase has been completed.
                */
                SET_CMDPHASE(port, (uchar)0x046);              /* pg. 386 */
                Count = Get_XFrCt(port);                        /* pg. 364 */
                /*Calculate amount left */
                DevStatics→v_Bytes − = Count;
                Set_XFrCt(port, (ulong)0);                      /* pg. 364 */
```

24.5. SCSI MANAGEMENT

```
                    return 0;                    /*Zero means try to continue */
                case 12: /*[Unspecified info out phase] */
                    break;
                case 13: /*[Unspecified info in phase] */
                    break;
                case 14: /*[Message out phase] */
                    break;
                case 15: /*[Message in phase] */
                    break;
                default:
                    break;
            }
        case 0x020: /*Status group 2 */
            break;
        default:
            break;
    }
    /*
        There's no way to deal with this error so return this useless
        error code
    */
    return E_HARDWARE;
}


/*
    A device error caused a SCSI command failure.
*/
DeviceCheck(DevStatics, SCSI_ID)
register MyStatics DevStatics;
uchar SCSI_ID;
{
    struct {
        unsigned validity:1,
            Class :3,
                :4,
            Segment_Num:8,
            FileMark:1,
            EOM :1,
            ILI :1,
                :1,
            Sense_Key:4;
        uchar InfoByte[4];
        uchar AdditionalLength;
        uchar Reserved[4];
```

```
        uchar ErrorCode;
        uchar Reserved2;
        uchar FRUCode;
        unsigned FPV :1,
            CD :1,
                :2,
            BPV :1,
            BitPtr :3;
        uchar FieldPtr[2];
} Req_Sense_Return;

if(DevStatics→V_CDB[0] == SCSI_REQUEST_SENSE)
    /*Don't recurse */
    return E_HARDWARE;

SETUP_CMD(DevStatics→V_CDB, SCSI_REQUEST_SENSE, 0, 18);       /* pg. 385 */
DevStatics→v_Bytes = sizeof(Req_Sense_Return);

if(Exec(SENSE_CMD_LEN, WD_DPD_In,                              /* pg. 360 */
        (ulong *)&Req_Sense_Return, SCSI_ID, DevStatics) != 0)
    return E_HARDWARE;

switch(Req_Sense_Return.Sense_Key){
    case 0:
        return 0;
    case 1: /*Recovered error */
        return 0; /*Happy */
    case 2: /*Not ready */
        switch(Req_Sense_Return.ErrorCode){
            case 4: /*not ready */
                return E_NOTRDY;
            case 0x44: /*Internal controller error */
                return E_HARDWARE;
            default: /*Mystery: return real data */
                return ((Req_Sense_Return.Sense_Key <<8) |
                    Req_Sense_Return.ErrorCode);
        }
    case 3: /*Medium error */
        switch(Req_Sense_Return.ErrorCode){
            case 0x10: /*ID CRC or ECC error */
            case 0x12: /*No address mark in ID field */
            case 0x13: /*No address mark in data field */
            case 0x14: /*No record found */
```

24.5. SCSI MANAGEMENT

```
            case 0x15:  /*Seek error */
                return E_SEEK;
            case 0x11:  /*Uncorrectable data error */
                return E_READ;
            case 0x19:  /*Defect list error */
            case 0x1c:  /*Primary defect list missing */
                return E_READ;
            case 0x31:  /*Medium format corrupted */
                return E_BTYP;
            case 0x32:  /*No defect spare available */
                return E_FULL;
            default:  /*Mystery: return real data */
                return ((Req_Sense_Return.Sense_Key <<8) |
                    Req_Sense_Return.ErrorCode);
        }
    case 4:  /*Hardware error */
        switch(Req_Sense_Return.ErrorCode){
            case 1:  /*No index from drive */
                return E_NOTRDY; /*Say not ready */
            case 2:  /*No seek complete */
            case 0x10:  /*ID CRC or ECC error */
            case 0x15:  /*Seek error */
                return E_SEEK;
            case 3:  /*Write fault received from drive */
                return E_WRITE;
            case 8:  /*LUN communication failure */
            case 9:  /*Track following error */
            case 0x40:  /*RAM failure */
            case 0x41:  /*Data path diagnostic failure */
            case 0x42:  /*Power-on diagnostic failure */
            case 0x44:  /*Internal controller error */
            case 0x47:  /*SCSI interface parity error */
                return E_HARDWARE;
            default:  /*Mystery: return real data */
                return ((Req_Sense_Return.Sense_Key <<8) |
                    Req_Sense_Return.ErrorCode);
        }
    case 5:  /*Illegal request */
        switch(Req_Sense_Return.ErrorCode){
            case 0x20:  /*Invalid command code */
            case 0x22:  /*Illegal function for drive type */
                return E_BTYP;
            case 0x21:  /*Illegal logical block address */
                return E_SECT;
```

```
                    case 0x24: /*Illegal field in CDB */
                    case 0x26: /*Invalid field in param list */
                        return E_PARAM;
                    case 0x25: /*Invalid LUN */
                        return E_UNIT;
                    default: /*Mystery: return real data */
                        return ((Req_Sense_Return.Sense_Key <<8) |
                            Req_Sense_Return.ErrorCode);
                }
            case 6: /*Unit attention */
                return E_DIDC; /*Always treat as disk ID change */
            case 11: /*Aborted command */
                switch(Req_Sense_Return.ErrorCode){
                    case 0x43: /*Message reject error */
                    case 0x45: /*Select/reselect failed */
                    case 0x48: /*Initiator detected error */
                    case 0x49: /*Inappropriate/illegal message */
                        return E_DEVBSY;
                    default: /*Mystery: return real data */
                        return ((Req_Sense_Return.Sense_Key <<8) |
                            Req_Sense_Return.ErrorCode);
                }
            case 13: /*Volume overflow */
                return E_FULL;
            case 14: /*Data miscompare */
                return E_WRITE;
            default:
                return ((Req_Sense_Return.Sense_Key <<8) |
                    Req_Sense_Return.ErrorCode);
        }
}
```

24.6 Direct Command Interface

This function implements the SCSI direct command setstat and getstat functions. The function checks its parameters extensively. This is required because IOMan cannot validate parameters for new getstat and setstat functions. Direct_command() validates parameters as follows:

- Can the caller read the data pointed to by A0?

24.6. DIRECT COMMAND INTERFACE

- Are the file manager code, device code, and command sync code specified in the direct command block correct?

- Is the caller in group 0?

- Are all the other pointer parameters valid?

```
#include <rbf.h>
#include <machine/reg.h>
#include <path.h>
#include <procid.h>
#include <errno.h>
#include <modes.h>
#include "drvr.h"
#include "dcmd.h"

#define SENSE_LEN            6


direct_command(regs, procd, Options, DevStatics, DTableE)
REGISTERS *regs;
procid *procd;
struct rbf_opt *Options;
MyStatics DevStatics;
Rbfdrive DTableE;
{
    register Dcmd dcmd;                    /*direct command structure */
    register Cmdblk cmd;
    int i;
    int Errno;
    uchar *ptr;

    dcmd = regs→a[0];
    /* Is dcmd a valid pointer?  */
    if(_chkMem(sizeof(struct d_cmd), S_IREAD, dcmd, procd))        /* pg. 382 */
        return E_PERMIT;
    cmd = (Cmdblk)dcmd→dcmdblk;
    /*
        Preliminary checks.
    */
    if((dcmd→manager != Options→pd_dtp) ||
        (dcmd→device != SCSIdevice) ||
        (dcmd→dcmdsync != DCMDSYNC))
        return E_PARAM;
```

```
/*
    The constants seem correct.  Now make certain that the caller
    is in the super group.
*/
if(procd→_group != 0)
    return E_PERMIT;
/*
    Now check the other pointers.
*/
if(_chkMem(sizeof(struct cmdblk), S_IREAD | S_IWRITE, cmd, procd))    /* pg. 382 */
    return E_PERMIT;
if(_chkMem(cmd→_cb_cmdlen, S_IREAD | S_IWRITE,                        /* pg. 382 */
        cmd→_cb_cmdptr, procd))
    return E_PERMIT;
if(cmd→_cb_datlen)                                  /* Will data be transferred? */
    if(_chkMem(cmd→_cb_datlen, S_IREAD | S_IWRITE,                    /* pg. 382 */
        cmd→_cb_datptr, procd))
        return E_PERMIT;
if(cmd→_cb_errlen)                                  /* Is there an error block? */
    if(_chkMem(cmd→_cb_errlen, S_IWRITE, cmd→_cb_errptr, procd))      /* pg. 382 */
        return E_PERMIT;
/* More parameter checking        */
if((cmd→_cb_cmdlen != 6) && (cmd→_cb_cmdlen != 10))
    return E_PARAM;
if((cmd→_cb_xfer != INPUT) && (cmd→_cb_xfer != OUTPUT))
    return E_PARAM;
/*
    Fill in values to be returned in the cmd block
*/
cmd→_cb_pd_lun = Options→pd_lun;
cmd→_cb_scsi_id = Options→pd_ctrlrid;
for(i=0, ptr=cmd→_cb_cmdptr;i<cmd→_cb_cmdlen;++i)
    DevStatics→V_CDB[i] = (*ptr)++;
DevStatics→V_CDB[1] = Options→pd_lun << 5;
DevStatics→v_Bytes = cmd→_cb_datlen;
Errno = Exec(cmd→_cb_cmdlen, (cmd→_cb_xfer == INPUT) ?                /* pg. 360 */
        WD_DPD_In : WD_DPD_Out,
        cmd→_cb_datptr,
        Options→pd_ctrlrid,
        DevStatics);
if((Errno != 0) && (cmd→_cb_errlen != 0)){
    SETUP_CMD(DevStatics→V_CDB, SCSI_REQUEST_SENSE,                   /* pg. 385 */
        0, cmd→_cb_errlen);
    DevStatics→v_Bytes = cmd→_cb_errlen;
```

24.7. ASSEMBLY LANGUAGE GLUE

```
        Exec(SENSE_LEN, WD_DPD_In, cmd→_cb_errptr,              /* pg. 360 */
             Options→pd_ctrlrid, DevStatics);
    }
    return Errno;
}
```

24.7 Assembly Language Glue

This assembly language is the "glue" that lets a C program fit into the interfaces designed for an assembly language driver. It replaces cstart and any functions that might possibly use static storage.

C-language system code can use the static storage class, but I think it is a dangerous practice. The C compiler makes no guarantees about how it will arrange static variables. It happens to leave the variables in device static storage in the order they are declared, but it may not always do that. I prefer to avoid static variables and pass device static storage around as a pointer to a structure (which C will not reorder). I make certain that no static data crept into the driver by inspecting the output of *rdump* for each .r file in the driver and each library function the driver invokes.

Device drivers written in C tend to use too much stack space. This causes nasty and sometimes non-obvious system crashes, so I allocate a large stack just for this drive. Since only one process at a time can use a device static storage for an RBF driver,[7] I leave space for the stack in device static storage. Each call to the driver moves to the driver's stack on entry and moves back to its original stack when it leaves the driver.

```
            ******************************
            *
            * cstart.a - C program startup routine for a device driver
            *
00000001    Edit        equ     1

                        use     <oskdefs.d>
                        opt     -l
00000001    Carry:      equ     %00000001       Carry bit

0000000e    Typ         equ     Drivr
00001000    Stk         equ     4096            Memory size
00000101    Cerror      equ     257             arbitrary C error
```

---

[7]RBF locks device static storage before every call to the driver, but SCF leaves device static storage unlocked for getstat calls to the driver. Although the outline of this RBF driver is generally usable for SCF drivers, the getstat entry for an SCF driver should either use the stack passed to it, or allocate a special getstat stack on entry and free it before returning to SCFMan.

```
                              psect    drmain_a,(Typ<<8)!Objct,((ReEnt+SupStat)<<8)!1,Edit,0,_Entry

c0dee0e0   Sflag        equ      $C0DEE0E0


           * NEWSTACK clobbers d1 and a3
           NEWSTACK macro
           *
           * Move the stack
                        move.l   a2,a3
                        add.l    #Stk-1,a2       Get the address of the end of the stack.
                        move.l   sp,-(a2)        Put old stack address on the new stack
                        move.l   a2,sp           The actual stack switch
                        move.l   a3,a2
                        endm

           OLDSTACK macro
                        move.l   (sp)+,sp old sp
                        endm

00000000                align
           *
           * C Program entry point
           *
           * On entry we have:
           * a2 points to the device static storage
           * a6 points to the system global area
           *
           _Entry:
0000 000e               dc.w     _InitDisk
0002 003a               dc.w     _ReadDisk
0004 0066               dc.w     _WritDisk
0006 0098               dc.w     _GetStat
0008 00c4               dc.w     _PutStat
000a 00f2               dc.w     _Term
000c 0000               dc.w     0

           *
           * On entry we have:
           * a1 points to the device descriptor
           * a2 points to the device static storage
           * a6 points to the system global area
           *
           _InitDisk
                        NEWSTACK
           *
```

24.7. ASSEMBLY LANGUAGE GLUE

```
001c 48e7           movem.l  a4/a6,-(sp)
0020 2009           move.l   a1,d0
0022 220a           move.l   a2,d1
0024 2f0e           move.l   a6,-(sp)
0026=6100           bsr      Init        (dd, statics, sysglobs)      /* pg. 330 */
002a 588f           addq.l   #4,sp                throw away arg space
002c 4cdf           movem.l  (sp)+,a4/a6
0030 3200           move.w   d0,d1
                    *
                    * restore the old stack
                            OLDSTACK
0034 6600           bne      _Error
0038 4e75           rts

                    *
                    * On entry we have:
                    *
                    * (d0.l) number of contiguous sectors to read
                    * (d2.l) logical sector number
                    * (a1) path descriptor
                    * (a2) static storage
                    * (a4) process descriptor
                    * (a5) caller's registers
                    * (a6) system globals
                    *
                    _ReadDisk
                            NEWSTACK
                    *
0048 48e7           movem.l  a4/a6,-(sp)
004c 2202           move.l   d2,d1
004e 48e7           movem.l  a1/a2/a6,-(sp)     prepare parameters

0052=6100           bsr      ReadDisk    (ct, lsn, pathd, statics, sysglobs)  /* pg. 333 */
0056 4fef           lea.l    (3*4)(sp),sp       throw away arg space
005a 4cdf           movem.l  (sp)+,a4/a6
005e 3200           move.w   d0,d1
                    *
                    * restore the old stack
                    *
                            OLDSTACK
0062 662e           bne.s    _Error
0064 4e75           rts
                    *
                    * On entry we have:
                    *
                    * (d0.l) number of contiguous sectors to write
                    * (d2.l) logical sector number
```

```
         * (a1) path descriptor
         * (a2) static storage
         * (a4) process descriptor
         * (a5) caller's registers
         * (a6) system globals
         *
         _WritDisk
                   NEWSTACK
         *
0074 48e7          movem.l  a4/a6,-(sp)
0078 2202          move.l   d2,d1
007a 48e7          movem.l  a1/a2/a6,-(sp)

007e=6100          bsr      WritDisk     (ct, lsn, pathd, statics, sysglobs)   /* pg. 337 */
0082 4fef          lea.l    12(sp),sp    throw away arg space
0086 4cdf          movem.l  (sp)+,a4/a6
008a 3200          move.w   d0,d1
         *
         * restore the old stack
         *
                   OLDSTACK
008e 6602          bne.s    _Error
0090 4e75          rts



0092 003c _Error   ori      #Carry,ccr
0096 4e75          rts


         *
         * On entry we have:
         *
         * (d0.w) Code
         * (a1) path descriptor
         * (a2) static storage
         * (a4) process descriptor
         * (a5) caller's registers
         * (a6) system globals
         *
         _GetStat
                   NEWSTACK
         *
00a6 48e7          movem.l  a4/a6,-(sp)
00aa 2209          move.l   a1,d1
00ac 48e7          movem.l  a2/a4/a5/a6,-(sp)

00b0=6100          bsr      GetStat      (code, pathd, statics, procd, regs, sglobs)/* pg. 340 */
```

24.7. ASSEMBLY LANGUAGE GLUE

```
00b4 4fef           lea.l    16(sp),sp           throw away arg space
00b8 4cdf           movem.l  (sp)+,a4/a6
00bc 3200           move.w   d0,d1
                    *
                    * restore the old stack
                    *
                             OLDSTACK
00c0 66d0           bne.s    _Error
00c2 4e75           rts


                    *
                    * On entry we have:
                    *
                    * (d0.w) Code
                    * (a1) path descriptor
                    * (a2) static storage
                    * (a4) process descriptor
                    * (a5) caller's registers
                    * (a6) system globals
                    *
                    _PutStat
                             NEWSTACK
                    *
00d2 48e7           movem.l  a4/a6,-(sp)
00d6 2209           move.l   a1,d1
00d8 48e7           movem.l  a2/a4/a5/a6,-(sp)

00dc=6100           bsr      PutStat             (code, pathd, statics, procd, regs, sglobs)/* pg. 341 */
00e0 4fef           lea.l    16(sp),sp           throw away arg space
00e4 4cdf           movem.l  (sp)+,a4/a6
00e8 3200           move.w   d0,d1
                    *
                    * restore the old stack
                    *
                             OLDSTACK
00ec 6600           bne      _Error
00f0 4e75           rts


                    *
                    * On entry we have:
                    *
                    * (a1) device descriptor
                    * (a2) static storage
                    * (a6) system globals
                    *
                    _Term
                             NEWSTACK
```

```
                *
0100 48e7       movem.l  a4/a6,-(sp)
0104 2009       move.l   a1,d0
0106 220a       move.l   a2,d1

0108=6100       bsr      Term          (dd, statics, sysglobs)      /* pg. 332 */
010c 4cdf       movem.l  (sp)+,a4/a6
0110 3200       move.w   d0,d1
                *
                * restore the old stack
                *
                OLDSTACK
0114 6600       bne      _Error
0118 4e75       rts
```

Most of the following functions are the glue that interfaces the driver to various system calls. The exceptions are SetWDOwn and QueryWDOwn. Those functions read and write a value in the I/O globals area of system globals. GMX defined the WDOwn field and uses it to indicate whether the WD33C93A is initialized. This driver maintains the field to help it interact with GMX drivers.

The HexTable data declaration is defined here because C doesn't offer any obvious way to allocate a constant in the program area without using static initialized data. HexTable is referenced as a function pointer in section 24.4.

```
            _srqmem:
011a 2f0a       move.l   a2,-(sp)
011c=4e40       os9      F$SRqMem
0120 6404       bcc.b    srqmemx1
0122 70ff       moveq.l  #-1,d0
0124 6002       bra.b    srqmemx
            srqmemx1
0126 200a       move.l   a2,d0
            srqmemx
0128 245f       move.l   (sp)+,a2
012a 4e75       rts

                *
                *       DoSRtMem(ptr, size)
                *
            DoSRtMem:
012c 2f0a       move.l   a2,-(sp)
012e 2440       move.l   d0,a2
0130 2001       move.l   d1,d0
0132=4e40       os9      F$SRtMem
0136 6404       bcc.b    DoSrtMx
```

24.7. ASSEMBLY LANGUAGE GLUE

```
0138=4e40            os9    F$SysDbg
         DoSrtMx
013c 245f            move.l (sp)+,a2
013e 4e75            rts
```

The SysDebug function is not called by this driver... any more. While the driver was under development it was liberally sprinkled with calls to SysDebug. They generally looked like:

if(something_unexpected_happened)
   SysDebug(ID_Number, More_information)

These *assertions* would drop me into ROMbug each time my code detected a likely bug or unexpected event. The assertions were a substantial part of the code. Ordinarily, I would have left the assertions in the code with conditional compilation deactivating the calls to SysDebug. I took them out because they made the driver too long and confusing.

Calls to SysDebug are only useful if a system debugger (ROMbug or sysdbg) is active. Without a system state debugger, a call to SysDebug will panic (usually reboot) the system. (And don't count on ROMbug unless your startup terminal is logged on as user 0.0.)

```
         SysDebug:
0140=4e40            os9    F$SysDbg
0144 4e75            rts

         * MoveDate(dest, src, length)
         MoveData:
0146 48e7            movem.l d2/a0/a2,-(sp)
014a 2440            move.l  d0,a2              destination
014c 2041            move.l  d1,a0              source
014e 242f            move.l  4*4(sp),d2         length
0152 7200            moveq.l #0,d1              sweep for error code
0154=4e40            os9     F$Move
0158 2001            move.l  d1,d0              move error code to d0
015a 4cdf            movem.l (sp)+,d2/a0/a2
015e 4e75            rts

         * QueryWDOwn(SysGlobs) returns uchar D_SCOwn
         QueryWDOwn:
0160 2f0e            move.l  a6,-(a7)           being very careful
0162 2c40            move.l  d0,a6
0164 7000            moveq.l #0,d0
0166=102e            move.b  D_SCOwn(a6),d0
```

```
016a 2c5f            move.l   (a7)+,a6
016c 4e75            rts

            * SetWDOwn(new, SysGlobs) returns new
            SetWDOwn:
016e 2f0e            move.l   a6,-(a7)           being very careful
0170 2c41            move.l   d1,a6
0172=1d40            move.b   d0,D_SCOwn(a6)
0176 2c5f            move.l   (a7)+,a6
0178 4e75            rts


017a 3031  HexTbl:   dc.b     '0','1','2','3','4','5','6','7','8','9','A','B','C','D','E','F'

            *
            * _Ev_link(name) returns an event ID number or -1
            *
018a 48e7  _Ev_link:  movem.l  d1/a0,-(sp)
018e 2040            move.l   d0,a0
0190=323c            move.w   #Ev$Link,d1
0194=4e40            os9      F$Event
0198 6402            bcc.b    evlinkX
019a 70ff            moveq.l  #-1,d0              Error return
019c 4cdf  evlinkX   movem.l  (sp)+,d1/a0
01a0 4e75            rts


            *
            * _Ev_creat(name, *Errno) returns an event ID number or -1
            *
01a2 48e7  _Ev_Creat: movem.l  d1-d3/a0/a1,-(sp)
01a6 2040            move.l   d0,a0               Event name
01a8 2241            move.l   d1,a1               Error number pointer
01aa 7000            moveq.l  #0,d0               Initial event variable value (semaphore open)
01ac=323c            move.w   #Ev$Creat,d1
01b0 7401            moveq.l  #1,d2               Autoinc for wait
01b2 76ff            moveq.l  #-1,d3              Autoinc for signal
01b4=4e40            os9      F$Event
01b8 640a            bcc.b    evcreatX
01ba 70ff            moveq.l  #-1,d0              Error return
01bc 32bc            move.w   #0,(a1)             sweep high-order word of Errno
01c0 3341            move.w   d1,2(a1)            place error code
01c4 4cdf  evcreatX  movem.l  (sp)+,d1-d3/a0/a1
01c8 4e75            rts


            *
            * _Ev_Unlink(EvID)
            *
```

24.7. ASSEMBLY LANGUAGE GLUE

```
01ca 2f01   _Ev_Unlink: move.l  d1,-(sp)
01cc=323c               move.w  #Ev$UnLnk,d1
01d0=4e40               os9     F$Event
            * ignore errors
01d4 221f               move.l  (sp)+,d1
01d6 4e75               rts


            *
            * _Ev_Del(Name)
            *
01d8 48e7   _Ev_Del:    movem.l d1/a0,-(sp)
01dc 2040               move.l  d0,a0
01de=323c               move.w  #Ev$Delet,d1
01e2=4e40               os9     F$Event
01e6 4cdf               movem.l (sp)+,d1/a0     ignore errors
01ea 4e75               rts


            *
            * _Ev_Wait(EvID)
            *
01ec 48e7   _Ev_Wait:   movem.l d1-d3,-(sp)
01f0=323c               move.w  #Ev$Wait,d1
01f4 7400               moveq.l #0,d2
01f6 7600               moveq.l #0,d3
01f8=4e40               os9     F$Event
01fc 4cdf               movem.l (sp)+,d1-d3
0200 4e75               rts
            *
            * _Ev_Signal(EvID)
            *
0202 2f01   _Ev_Signal: move.l  d1,-(sp)
0204=323c               move.w  #Ev$Signl,d1
0208=4e40               os9     F$Event
020c 221f               move.l  (sp)+,d1
020e 4e75               rts


            dosleep:
0210=4e40               os9     F$Sleep
0214 6402               bcc.b   dosleepX
0216 70ff               moveq.l #-1,d0          only one error's possible: NoClk
0218 4e75   dosleepX    rts


            *
            * Awake(process)
            *
021a 2f01   AWake:      move.l  d1,-(sp)
```

```
021c=323c              move.w   #S$Wake,d1
0220=4e40              os9      F$Send
0224 221f              move.l   (sp)+,d1
0226 4e75              rts


             * SetIRQ(vector, priority, IRQRtn, DevStatics, port)
0228 48e7 SetIRQ:      movem.l  a0/a2/a3,−(sp)
022c 206f              move.l   (4*4)(sp),a0    IRQ service routine pointer
0230 246f              move.l   (4*5)(sp),a2    Device static storage
0234 266f              move.l   (4*6)(sp),a3    Port address
0238=4e40              os9      F$IRQ
023c 6508              bcs.b    SetIRQE
023e 7000              moveq.l  #0,d0           Signal no error
0240 4cdf SetIRQX      movem.l  (sp)+,a0/a2/a3
0244 4e75              rts

0246 7000 SetIRQE      moveq.l  #0,d0           sweep d0
0248 3001              move.w   d1,d0           Put error where it's expected
024a 60f4              bra.b    SetIRQX


             *
             * IRQRtn
             * Called by the kernel
             * a2 points to static storage
             * a3 is the port address
             * a6 points to system globals
             *
             * d2-d7/a4-a5/a7 must be preserved
024c 200a IRQRtn:      move.l   a2,d0           Dev statics
024e 220b              move.l   a3,d1           port address
             * skip sysglobs.  The C routine doesn't use them.
0250=6100              bsr      C_IRQRtn
0254 4a40              tst.w    d0              Is d0 0? (and clear carry)
0256 6704              beq.b    IRQX
0258 003c              ori.b    #Carry,ccr
025c 4e75 IRQX         rts


             *
             * _chkMem(size, permissions, ptr, proc_desc)
             *
             _chkMem:
025e 48e7              movem.l  a2/a4,−(sp)
0262 246f              move.l   3*4(sp),a2      ptr
0266 286f              move.l   4*4(sp),a4      proc_desc
             * d0 and d1 are already loaded
026a=4e40              os9      F$ChkMem
```

24.8. HEADER FILES 383

```
026e 6508            bcs.b    ChkMemEr
0270 7000            moveq    #0,d0           return 0 if OK
        ChkMemX
0272 4cdf            movem.l  (sp)+,a2/a4
0276 4e75            rts
        ChkMemEr
0278 3001            move.w   d1,d0           return the error code from ChkMem
027a 48c0            ext.l    d0
027c 60f4            bra.b    ChkMemX
0000027e             ends
```

24.8 Header Files

24.8.1 drvr.h

```
#define RBF_MAXDRIVES    3
#define MAXLUN           0        /* Only handle one logical unit per controller */
#define MAXSCSI          7        /* Support all SCSI ids                        */
#define RETRY_MAX        2        /* Number of retries on I/O errors             */
#ifndef TRUE
#define TRUE             1
#define FALSE            0
#endif

typedef unsigned char uchar;
typedef unsigned long ulong;
typedef char boolean;

typedef struct mstatics {
    sysioStatic v_sysio;                     /* kernel static storage  */
    uchar v_ndrv;                            /* number of drives       */
    uchar v_dumm1[7];                        /* reserved               */
    struct rbfdrive drv[RBF_MAXDRIVE];       /* drive table            */
    /*
        Driver static storage
    */
    uchar V_CDB[10];                         /* CDB (SCSI Command block ) */
    ulong v_Sectors;
    ulong v_Bytes;
    ulong EvID;
} *MyStatics;
```

```
/*
    GMX SCSI I/O Board constants
*/

typedef struct GMXBd {
    uchar chip1, chip2;
    char chip3;
    uchar reserved[4];
    union {
        ushort W_DataBuf;
        ulong L_DataBuf;
    } Databuffer;
    ushort BD_Address;
} *Board;
#define WD_SELECT           chip1
#define WD_AUX              chip1
#define WD_READ_REG         chip2
#define WD_WRITE_REG        chip2


#define BD_STATUS           chip3
#define BD_CONTROL          chip3

#define BD_PUBLIC_BUF       0x08000
#define BD_ENABLE_INT       0x080
#define BD_RESET            0x040
/*
    WD 33C93A constants
*/

#define WD_OWNID_FS2        0          /* Clock divider for 8-- 10 mhz clock      */
#define WD_TIMEOUT          32         /* Timeout value for chip                  */
#define WD_OWNID_EAF        0x08       /* Enable advanced features                */
#define WD_STR_INIT_VALUE   0x020      /* No sync transfers,
                                          but use shortest transfer period       */
#define WD_CTL_DMWD         0x040      /* DMA will use a WD bus                   */
#define WD_CTL_EDI          0x08       /* Generate endiing disconnect interrupt   */
#define WD_CTL_HSP          0x01       /* Hold on parity error                    */
#define WD_SAT_OK           0x16       /* SAT command completed successfully      */

#define WD_OWNID            0          /* Owner ID and general initialization register */
#define WD_CONTROL          1
#define WD_TOTSECTS         3
#define WD_CDB1             3
```

24.8. HEADER FILES

```
#define WD_TARGET_STAT   15
#define WD_TARGET_LUN    15
#define WD_CMD_PHASE     16
#define WD_SYNCTRANS     17      /*Synchronous transfer register           */
#define WD_XFRCT1        18
#define WD_DESTID        21      /*Destination ID register                 */
#define WD_SCSI_STAT     23      /*SCSI status register                    */
#define WD_CMDREG        24      /*33C93A commands go here                 */

/*33C93A Commands*/
#define WD_RESET         0x0
#define SCSI_X_SAT       9       /*33C93A Select and transfer              */

#define WD_DPD_In        0x040   /*Data phase direction                    */
#define WD_DPD_Out       0x00    /* The other data phase direction         */

/*
   SCSI Commands
 */
#define SCSI_TEST_UNIT_READY 0
#define SCSI_REZERO_UNIT     1
#define SCSI_REQUEST_SENSE   3
#define SCSI_FORMAT_UNIT     4
#define SCSI_READOP          8
#define SCSI_WRITEOP         10
#define SCSI_TARGET_STAT     15
#define SCSI_MODE_SELECT     21
#define SCSI_MODE_SENSE      26
#define SCSI_START_UNIT      27
#define SCSI_READ_CAPACITY   37
#define SCSI_VERIFY          47

#define SENSE_CMD_LEN    6
#define READ_CMD_LEN     6
#define REZERO_CMD_LEN   6
#define FORMAT_CMD_LEN   6
#define WRITE_CMD_LEN    6
#define READY_CMD_LEN    6
#define VERIFY_CMD_LEN   10
#define READCAP_CMD_LEN  10


#define SETUP_CMD(CDB,op,lsn,len) CDB[0] = op, CDB[1] = (lsn >> 16),\
                                  CDB[2] = (lsn >> 8), CDB[3] = lsn,\
```

```
                              CDB[4] = len, CDB[5] = 0

#define SETUP_CMD_10(CDB,op,b2,lsn,len)  CDB[0] = op, CDB[1] = b2,\
                              CDB[2] = (lsn >> 24),\
                              CDB[3] = (lsn >> 16),\
                              CDB[4] = (lsn >> 8),\
                              CDB[5] = lsn, CDB[6] = 0,\
                              CDB[6] = (len >> 8), CDB[8] = len,\
                              CDB[9] = 0
#define ClaimController(EvID)    _Ev_Wait(EvID)              /* pg. 381 */
#define ReleaseController(EvID)  _Ev_Signal(EvID)            /* pg. 381 */

/*
    Function declarations
*/
LL_Get();
Do_WD_Reset();
void LL_Put();
void Set_XFrCt();
int Get_XFrCt();
void Set_Control();
```

24.8.2 lowlevel.h

```
#define GET_SCSI_STATUS(port)      LL_Get(port, WD_SCSI_STAT)        /* pg. 363 */
#define GET_SCSI_TARGETSTAT(port)  LL_Get(port, SCSI_TARGET_STAT)    /* pg. 363 */
#define SET_OWNID(port,value)      LL_Put(port, value, WD_OWNID)     /* pg. 362 */
#define SET_SYNCTRANS(port,val)    LL_Put(port, val, WD_SYNCTRANS)   /* pg. 362 */
#define SET_TARGET(port,value)     LL_Put(port, value, WD_DESTID)    /* pg. 362 */
#define SET_CMD(port,value)        LL_Put(port, value, WD_CMDREG)    /* pg. 362 */
#define SET_CMDPHASE(port,value)   LL_Put(port, value, WD_CMD_PHASE) /* pg. 362 */
#define BD_EnableInt(port)         port->BD_CONTROL = BD_ENABLE_INT
```

24.8.3 dcmd.h

```
/*
    This is the structure that is passed to the getstat and putstat
    routines.
*/
typedef struct d_cmd {
    int dcmdsync,              /* sink code—must be DCMDSYNC           */
        manager,               /* file manager code, pd_dtype from _gs_opts() */
```

24.8. HEADER FILES

```
        device;                    /* device type code                  */
    void *dcmdblk;                 /* device driver specific command    */
} *Dcmd;
```

/*
    General definitions
*/

```
#define DCMDSYNC 0xCA7CA11         /* this code validates the command block  */
```

/* device type codes:
    These are specific to the devices. The drivers can use this
    field to validate that the call that arrived is for the device
    that they control.
*/
```
#define SCSIdevice 0x5C51          /* SCSI bus device                   */
```

/*
    definitions for SCSI direct command structure.
*/

/*
    scsi command block definitions.
    this block is the SCSI command specification block used to
    communicate between the calling program and the driver.
*/
```
typedef struct cmdblk {
    uchar *_cb_cmdptr;             /* pointer to the scsi command       */
    void  *_cb_datptr;             /* pointer to the data area          */
    void  *_cb_errptr;             /* pointer to the error data area    */
    ulong _cb_cmdlen;              /* length of the command block       */
    ulong _cb_datlen;              /* expected data length              */
    ulong _cb_errlen;              /* expected error length             */
    ulong _cb_scsi_id;             /* the target id (filled in by driver) */
    uchar _cb_pd_lun;              /* the target lun ( also filled in by driver ) */
    uchar _cb_xfer;                /* data input/output flag            */
#define INPUT          0
#define OUTPUT         1
} *Cmdblk;
```

24.9 Makefile

```
CSRC    =   Errors.c Init.c InitDrive.c term.c\
            exec.c irq.c misc.c read.c read0.c\
            scsi.c setmode.c static. write.c direct.c
ASRC    =   drmain.a

GLUE    =   drmain.r

FILES   =   Errors.r Init.r term.r\
            InitDrive.r exec.r irq.r misc.r\
            read.r read0.r setmode.r stat.r direct.r write.r scsi.r

CFLAGS  =   −qs −k2wcw −O=2
RFLAGS  =   −q
LFLAGS  =   −g
SLIB    =   /h0/lib/sys.l
MLIB    =   /h0/lib/math.l


tstdrvr:    $(FILES) $(GLUE)
            l68 $(LFLAGS) $(GLUE) $(FILES) −l=$(SLIB) −l=$(MLIB)\
                −o=tstdrvr −msw >−map.tst
            patchmod tstdrvr 4096

Errors.r:   Errors.c

Init.r :    Init.c

term.r :    term.c

InitDrive.r: InitDrive.c

exec.r:     exec.c

irq.r:      irq.c

misc.r:     misc.c

read.r:     read.c

read0.r:    read0.c

setmode.r:  setmode.c
```

```
stat.r:      stat.c

direct.r:    direct.c

write.r:     write.c

scsi.r:      scsi.c
```

If the driver is not made by the super user, the super user must run a script to "claim" the driver module:

```
chown −o=0.0 /h0/cmds/peter/tstdrvr
fixmod −uo=0.0 /h0/cmds/peter/tstdrvr
attr /h0/cmds/peter/tstdrvr −prpwperwe
```

24.10 Patchmod

The driver module must request enough static storage for the device static storage plus enough stack space. Since C doesn't know that there is any static storage, the amount of device static storage must be set by hand. The actual device static storage structure is fairly small—around 300 bytes, but the makefile requests four kilobytes of device static storage to leave plenty of space for the driver's stack. The value passed to *Patchmod* by the makefile must be the same as the *Stk* equate in drmain.a.

Patchmod is a simple program that updates the memory requirement field in a file containing a module.

```
#include <stdio.h>
#include <module.h>
#include <errno.h>

main(argc, argv)
int argc;
char **argv;
{
   int size;
   char *Name;
   int pathnum;
```

```
    if(argc != 3){
       Usage();
       exit(1);
    }
    if(strcmp(argv[1], "-?") == 0){
       Usage();
       exit(0);
    }
    Name = argv[1];
    if((pathnum = open(Name, 7)) == -1)
       exit(_errmsg(errno, "Cannot open %s\n", Name));

    if((size = atoi(argv[2])) == 0){
       Usage();
       exit(1);
    }
    lseek(pathnum, 0x38, 0);                        /* Seek to memory-amount location */
    if(write(pathnum, &size, sizeof(size)) == -1)
       exit(_errmsg(errno, "Cannot update memory amount in %s\n", Name));
    close(pathnum);
    exit(0);
}


Usage()
{
    printf("Patchmod <file> <mem>\n");
    printf("\tUpdate the memory requirement of <file> to <mem>\n");
}
```

24.11 QuantumCache

Microware uses a version of the following program to demonstrate the SCSI direct command interface. The official version operates on CDC Wren disk drives. This version is slightly modified to work with Quantum Prodrive disk drives.

```
/*
    Quantumcache—enable the cache on Quantum prodrive
*/

/* Copyright 1990 by Microware Systems Corporation
   Reproduced Under License.
```

24.11. QUANTUMCACHE

This source code is the proprietary confidential property of Microware Systems Corporation, and is provided to licensee solely for documentation and educational purposes. Reproduction, publication, or distribution in any form to any party other than the licensee is strictly prohibited.
*/

/*
This utility, besides being useful in manipulating the cache on Quantum drives, provides an example of the direct command feature of the Microware drivers.
  Edition History:

Ed	Date	Reason	Who
1	90/04/09	Created (for Wren)	Rwb
2	90/06/01	Modified to allow it to work with Swift 126	Rwb
		—OS–9/68K V2.4 released—	
3	91/12/28	Converted from Wren to Quantum	pcd

*/
@_sysedit: equ 3

```
#include <stdio.h>
#include <sgstat.h>
#include <sg_codes.h>
#include <modes.h>
#include <errno.h>
typedef unsigned char uchar;
typedef unsigned long ulong;
#include "../dcmd.h"

#define TRUE            1
#define FALSE           0
#define CACHEON         TRUE
#define CACHEOFF        !CACHEON

#define NOCACHEPAGE     FALSE
#define SHOWCACHEPAGE   TRUE
#define CDB_STD         6
#define SC_INQUIRY      0x12
#define SC_MODESENSE    0x1a
#define SC_MODESELECT   0x15

static char devs[14][16];              /* device names from command line      */
```

```c
static char *nulstr = "";                   /* a nice way to print nothing at all    */
static char *equstr = "===================================";
static *cpagestr = "====== Cache page information =====";

static struct d_cmd dcd;                    /* direct command structure              */
static struct cmdblk cmd;                   /* command block for the driver          */
static struct sgbuf opt;                    /* place for the options info from drive */

static union scsipkt {
    struct std_str {
        uchar sp_opcode;                    /* the opcode                            */
        unsigned sp_lun : 3;                /* logical unit (filled in by driver)    */
        unsigned sp_lbamsbs : 5;            /* the block address (msbs)              */
        char sp_lba[2];                     /* (the rest of) the block address       */
        char sp_blkcnt;                     /* the block count                       */
        uchar sp_options;                   /* command options                       */
    } std;
    struct ext_str {
        uchar sp_opcode;                    /* the opcode                            */
        unsigned sp_lun : 3;                /* logical unit (filled in by driver)    */
        unsigned sp_zero : 5;               /* zero                                  */
        ulong sp_lba;                       /* logical block address                 */
        uchar sp_zero2;                     /* zero                                  */
        uchar sp_count[2];                  /* transfer count                        */
        uchar sp_options;                   /* command options                       */
    } ext;
} spkt;                                     /* This structure is the SCSI command block */

/*
    This is the structure that defines request sense information from the Quantum
    drives.
*/
static union errdetails {
    struct rbferr {
        unsigned ed_valid : 1,              /* error is valid                        */
            ed_class : 3,                   /* error class = 7                       */
            ed_zero : 4;                    /* always 0                              */
        uchar ed_seg;                       /* segment number always 0               */
        unsigned ed_filemrk : 1,            /* filemark                              */
            ed_eom : 1,                     /* end of medium                         */
            ed_ili : 1,                     /* incorrect length indicator            */
            ed_zero2 : 1,                   /* always zero                           */
            ed_main : 4;                    /* main sense key                        */
        uchar ed_info[4],                   /* info byte [lba]                       */
```

24.11. QUANTUMCACHE

```c
            ed_senslen;                 /* additional sense info length    */
        ulong ed_zero3;                 /* always zero                     */
        uchar ed_code,                  /* error code                      */
            ed_zero4,                   /* always 0                        */
            ed_fru;                     /* fru code                        */
        unsigned ed_fpv : 1,            /* field pointer valid             */
            ed_cd : 1,                  /* command/data bit                */
            ed_zero5 : 2,               /* always zero                     */
            ed_bpv : 1,                 /* block pointer valid             */
            ed_bitptr : 3;              /* bit pointer                     */
        uchar ed_fptr[2];               /* field pointer                   */
    } rerr;
    struct sbferr {
        unsigned ed_valid : 1,          /* error is valid                  */
            ed_class : 3,               /* error class = 7                 */
            ed_zero : 4;                /* always 0                        */
        uchar ed_seg;                   /* segment number always 0         */
        unsigned ed_filemrk : 1,        /* filemark                        */
            ed_eom : 1,                 /* end of medium                   */
            ed_ili : 1,                 /* incorrect length indicator      */
            ed_zero2 : 1,               /* always zero                     */
            ed_main : 4;                /* main sense key                  */
        uchar ed_info[4];               /* info byte [lba]                 */
        uchar ed_senslen;               /* additional sense info length    */
        uchar ed_cpsrc;                 /* COPY source sense data ptr      */
        uchar ed_cpdest;                /* COPY destination sense data ptr */
        uchar ed_zero3[2];              /* always zero                     */
        uchar ed_recov[2];              /* # recoverable errors            */
        uchar ed_cptstat;               /* COPY target status              */
        uchar ed_cptsens[8];            /* COPY target sense data (0-7)    */
    } serr;
} edat;


/*
    inquiry data structure
*/
struct inquirdat {
    uchar iq_type;                      /* device type                     */
    unsigned iq_rmb : 1,                /* always 0                        */
        iq_typqual : 7,                 /* device type qualifier           */
        iq_iso : 2,                     /* ISO version                     */
        iq_ecma : 4,                    /* ECMA version                    */
        iq_ansi : 2,                    /* ANSI version                    */
```

```
        iq_zero : 4,                    /* always 0                         */
        iq_datfmt : 4;                  /* response data format             */
    char iq_addlen,                     /* additional length                */
        iq_quantres1,                   /* Quantum uniq = 0                 */
        iq_quantres2[2],                /* Quantum reserved = 0             */
        iq_vendid[8],                   /* vendor id QUANTUM                */
        iq_prodid[16],                  /* product id                       */
        iq_revlev[4];                   /* revision level                   */
} idat;


/* definitions used to access parameters in mode sense */
#define PCF_CURRENT         0x00    /* current paramters                    */
#define PCF_CHANGE          0x01    /* changeable drive parameters          */
#define PCF_DEFAULT         0x02    /* default drive parameters             */

/*
    mode sense data structure (basic, must add pages to be complete )
*/
typedef struct modesen_str {
    /* parameter list header */
    uchar msn_datlen;                   /* length of sense info             */
    uchar msn_medtype;                  /* medium type                      */
    unsigned msn_wp : 1;                /* write protect 1=WP ON            */
    unsigned msn_res1 : 7;              /* unused                           */
    uchar msn_bdlen;                    /* block descriptor length          */
    /* block descriptor */
    uchar msn_denscode;                 /* density code                     */
    uchar msn_numblks[3];               /* number of blocks                 */
    uchar msn_res2;                     /* reserved                         */
    uchar msn_blklen[3];                /* block length                     */
} modesense;



static struct page37 {
    modesense mds;
    /* page 37—The Quantum vender-specific cache information */
#define PAGE_37             0x37
    uchar msn_p37code,                  /* page code                        */
        msn_p37plen;                    /* page length (0x0e)               */
    unsigned msn_p37res:2,              /* reserved bits                    */
        msn_p37psm:1,                   /* preserve synchronous mode        */
        msn_p37ssm:1,                   /* send synchronous message         */
        msn_p37wie:1,                   /* write index enable               */
```

24.11. QUANTUMCACHE

```
        msn_p37po:1,           /* prefetch only             */
        msn_p37pe:1,           /* prefetch enable           */
        msn_p37ce:1;           /* cache enable              */
    uchar msn_p37ncache,       /* number of cache segments  */
        msn_p37mnpf,           /* minimum pre-fetch         */
        msn_p37mxpf,           /* max pre-fetch             */
        msn_p37resvb[10]       /* 10 reserved bytes         */
} cpag;

static char *devtypes[ ] = {
    "Direct Access (disk drive)",
    "Sequential Access (mag tape)",
    "Printer",
    "Processor",
    "Write once, Read Multiple (WORM)",
    "CD-ROM",
    "Scanner",
    "optical Memory Device (some optical disks)",
    "Changer Device (jukeboxes)",
    "Communications Device"
};


static char *ansiver[ ] = {
    "Not compliant to ANSI standards.",
    "ANSI X3.131-1986 (SCSI 1)",
    "ANSI X3.131 X3T9.2/86-109 (SCSI 2 working draft)"
};


static char *helpline[ ] = {
"Syntax: .../quantumcache {<opts>} <device> {<opts>>
        "Function: view/enable/disable cache on Quantum Prodrive drives.\n",
        " no options specified will print current cache condition\n",
        "Options:\n",
        " -e enable cache\n",
        " -d disable cache\n",
        " -v printout information from inquiry command\n",
        "\n"
    };

/*
    printuse — print argument list
*/
```

```c
printuse( outfilepath )
FILE *outfilepath;
{
    register int i;

    for( i = 0; i < sizeof(helpline)/sizeof(helpline[0]); i++ )
        fprintf(outfilepath, helpline[i]);
}


/*
    setcmdblk—set parameters in the command block
*/
void setcmdblk( datptr, datsize, scsize , direction )
char *datptr;                       /* buffer for I/O                      */
ulong datsize;                      /* number of bytes to transfer         */
int scsize;                         /* SCSI command block size             */
int direction;                      /* either INPUT or OUTPUT              */
{
    /*set up the direct command structure */
    dcd.manager = opt.sg_class;     /* device manager                      */
    dcd.dcmdsync = DCMDSYNC;        /* set sync to validate the call       */
    dcd.device = SCSIdevice;        /* this is indeed a SCSI specific op   */
    dcd.dcmdblk = &cmd;             /* pointer to command block            */

    /*and now the SCSI driver required block */
    cmd._cb_cmdptr = &spkt;         /* pointer to the command              */
    cmd._cb_datptr = datptr;        /* place for the data                  */
    cmd._cb_cmdlen = CDB_STD;       /* 6 byte command block                */
    cmd._cb_datlen = datsize;       /* the number of data bytes to xfer    */
    cmd._cb_xfer = direction;       /* read data flag                      */
    cmd._cb_errptr = &edat;         /* pointer to the error block          */
    cmd._cb_errlen = sizeof edat;   /* and the size reserved for it        */
}


/*
    execute—prepare the command block for the driver and do the status call.
*/
int execute( pn, command, lbam, lba0, lba1, size )
    int pn;                         /* path number                         */
    uchar command;                  /* scsi command to perform             */
    uchar lbam;                     /* logical unit                        */
    uchar lba0;
```

24.11. QUANTUMCACHE

```
    uchar lba1;
    int size;                              /* number of bytes to transer              */
    {
        spkt.std.sp_opcode = command;
        spkt.std.sp_lbamsbs = lbam;
        spkt.std.sp_lba[0] = lba0;
        spkt.std.sp_lba[1] = lba1;
        spkt.std.sp_blkcnt = size;

        if( cmd._cb_xfer == INPUT )
            return _gs_dcmd( pn, &dcd);
        else
            return _ss_dcmd( pn, &dcd);
    }


    /*
        identify—prepare an inquiry command and send it.
    */
    identify( pn )
    int pn;                                /* path number                             */
    {
        /*set up the command block for the driver */
        setcmdblk( &idat, sizeof idat, CDB_STD, INPUT );

        /*now set up the SCSI command packet for inquiry command */
        return execute( pn, SC_INQUIRY, 0, 0, 0, sizeof idat );
    }


    /*
        getcachepage—read the cache page from the device
    */
    getcachepage( pn )
    int pn;                                /* path number                             */
    {
        /*set up the command block for the driver */
        setcmdblk( &cpag, sizeof cpag, CDB_STD, INPUT );

        /*now set up the SCSI command packet for inquiry command */
        return execute( pn, SC_MODESENSE, 0, (PCF_CURRENT << 5) | (PAGE_37),
            0, sizeof cpag );
    }
```

```
/*
    setcache—enable/disable the cache for the device.
*/
int setcache(pn, condition)
int pn;                                 /* path number to the device            */
int condition;
{
    cpag.mds.msn_datlen = 0;            /* This field is reserved for modeset   */
    cpag.msn_p37code = PAGE_37;         /* insure that ps not set               */

    /*set the cache enable bit in the page information */
    if(condition){
        cpag.msn_p37ce = condition;     /* Set cache enable                     */
        cpag.msn_p37pe = condition;
        cpag.msn_p37mnpf = 0;           /* Minimum prefetch                     */
        cpag.msn_p37mxpf = 16;          /* Maximum prefetch                     */
        cpag.msn_p37ncache = 8;         /* Number of cache entries              */
    } else
        cpag.msn_p37ce = condition;     /* Set cache enable                     */


    /*set up the command block for the driver */
    setcmdblk( &cpag, sizeof cpag, CDB_STD, OUTPUT );

    /*now set up the SCSI command packet for inquiry command */
    return execute( pn, SC_MODESELECT, 0, 0, 0, sizeof cpag );
}


/*
    fieldcopy—copy requested number of characters and null terminate dest.
*/
void fieldcopy( dest, src, size )
register char *dest,*src;
register int size;
{
    while( --size >= 0 )
        *dest++ = *src++;

    *dest++ = 0;
}


/*
```

24.11. QUANTUMCACHE

```
        prdevbits—print device information bits, only applies to SCSI 2 devices.
*/
prdevbits()
{
    register int shifter;

    shifter = (uchar)idat.iq_quantres2[1];     /* the info byte                      */

    puts(" Device Capabilities");
    shifter >>= 4;
    if( shifter & 1 )
        puts("Synchronous operation supported.");
    shifter >>= 1;

    switch( shifter & 0x3 ) {
        case 0:
            puts("8 bit wide transfers");
            break;
        case 1:
            puts("16 bit wide transfers");
            break;
        case 2:
            puts("32 bit wide transfers");
            break;
    }
}


/*
    This is a subroutine that will print out the inquiry information.
*/
show_inq( devname, cpflag )
char *devname;
int cpflag;                                    /* cache page flag, if FALSE, don't print   */
{
    char devstr[64];


    printf("========= Device %s =============\n",devname);

    if( idat.iq_ansi > 2 )
        printf(" Responds with illegal Ansi compliance code.\n");
    else
        printf("Compliance: %s\n",ansiver[idat.iq_ansi]);
```

```
    switch ( idat.iq_datfmt ) {
        case 0:                          /* SCSI I                          */
        case 1:                          /* sccs definition                 */
            if( idat.iq_type > 9 )
                printf("Device type is UNDEFINED!\n");
            else
                printf("Device Type: %s\n", devtypes[idat.iq_type]);
            break;

        case 2:                          /* SCSI II                         */
            if( idat.iq_typqual > 9 )
                printf("Device type is UNDEFINED!\n");
            else
                printf("Device Type: %s\n", devtypes[idat.iq_typqual]);
            break;

        default:
            printf("Format of remaining data does not comply with any standard\n");
            break;
    }

    /*device function bits  */
    if(idat.iq_datfmt == 2)
        prdevbits();                     /* only works on SCSI II devices    */

    /*  inquiry vender specific fields (pre SCSI II)
        but are defined for SCSI II as the same.
     */
    if(idat.iq_datfmt < 2) {
        printf(" ISO: %x ECMA: %x\n", idat.iq_iso, idat.iq_ecma);
        printf(" Media is %s.\n",idat.iq_rmb ? "removable" : "fixed");
        fieldcopy( devstr, &idat.iq_vendid[0], 8 );
        printf(" Vendor: %s\n", devstr );
        fieldcopy( devstr, &idat.iq_prodid[0], 16 );
        printf(" Product: %s\n", devstr );
        fieldcopy( devstr, &idat.iq_revlev[0], 4 );
        printf(" Revision: %s\n", devstr );
    }

    if( cpflag ) {                       /* only if it is a valid page       */
        puts( cpagestr );
        printf("Page code: 0x%x page length: 0x%x\n",
        cpag.msn_p37code & 0x3f,cpag.msn_p37plen);
```

24.11. QUANTUMCACHE

```
            printf(" Cache is %s\n", cpag.msn_p37ce ? "ENABLED" : "Disabled");
            printf("Number of cache segments: 0x%x\n",cpag.msn_p37ncache );
            printf("Maximum Pre-fetch: 0x%x\n",cpag.msn_p37mxpf );
            printf("Minimum Pre-fetch: 0x%x\n",cpag.msn_p37mnpf );
            printf("Write index: %s\n",cpag.msn_p37wie == 0 ? "DISABLED" : "ENABLED");
            printf("Prefetch only: %s\n",cpag.msn_p37po == 0? "DISABLED" : "ENABLED");
            printf("Prefetch: %s\n",cpag.msn_p37pe == 0? "DISABLED" : "ENABLED");
        }
        puts(equstr);
}


/*
    show_sense — print results of a request sense if valid
*/
show_sense()
{
    int mainstat,errorcode;
    uchar *infop;
    int i;

    if( edat.rerr.ed_valid != 0 ) {
        fputs(equstr,stderr);
        fprintf(stderr,"\n Sense Results\n");

        switch( opt.sg_class ) {
            case DT_RBF:
                mainstat = edat.rerr.ed_main;
                errorcode = edat.rerr.ed_code;
                infop = &edat.rerr.ed_info[0];
                break;
            case DT_SBF:
                mainstat = edat.serr.ed_main;
                errorcode = 0;
                infop = &edat.serr.ed_info[0];
                break;
            default:
                fprintf(stderr,"Unknown device type\n");
                break;
        }
        fprintf(stderr," This is an %s Device\n",
                (opt.sg_class == DT_RBF) ? "RBF":"SBF");;

        fprintf(stderr," Main Status: 0x%x\n",mainstat);
```

```
            fprintf(stderr," Error Code: 0x%x\n",errorcode);
            fprintf(stderr," Info bytes (in HEX): ");
            for( i = 0; i < 4; i++ )
                fprintf(stderr," %x",*infop++);
            fprintf(stderr,"\n");
            fputs(equstr,stderr);
            fprintf(stderr,"\n");
        } else
            fprintf(stderr,"Error did not produce a valid sense result.\n");
}


/*
    Mainline
*/
main(argc,argv)
int argc;
char *argv[];
{
    register char *p;
    int pn,error;                       /* path number and error                       */
    int nooptions = TRUE;               /* no options requested (by default)           */
    int disable = FALSE,enable = FALSE; /* condition to set the cache                  */
    int index = 0;                      /* start at 0 always                           */
    int verbose = FALSE;                /* don't print inquiry data                    */
    int nodevnames = TRUE;              /* no devices defined until user does it       */
    int errvalue;                       /* temporary holder on error occurences        */
    char i;
    char devname[24];                   /* hope they don't have huge device names      */

    if( argc < 2 ) {
        printuse(stderr);
        fprintf(stderr,"Must provide at least one device name.\n");
        exit(0);
    }

    argv++;
    while (--argc > 0) {
        if (*(p = *argv++) == '-') {
            p++;
            while (i = *p++) {
                switch (i | 0x60) {
                    /*disable cache request */
                    case 'd':
```

24.11. QUANTUMCACHE

```
                    nooptions = FALSE;
                    disable = TRUE;
                    break;

                /*enable cache request */
                case 'e':
                    nooptions = FALSE;
                    enable = TRUE;
                    break;

                /*verbose mode—print cache and inquire info */
                case 'v':
                    verbose = TRUE;
                    break;

                /*get useage */
                case ('?' | 0x60):
                    printuse(stdout);
                    exit(0);
                    break;

                /*just fishing? */
                default:
                    printuse(stderr);
                    _errmsg(errno," unknown option %c\n\n", i);
                    exit(0);
                    break;
            } /*end switch */
        } /*end while chars left */
    } else {
        /*must be a device name */
        if( index > 13 ) {
            printuse(stderr);
            fprintf(stderr, "Too many devices!\n");
            exit(0);
        }
        if( *p == '/' ) {
            strcpy( &devs[index++][0], p ); /*copy string for use */
            nodevnames = FALSE;
        } else {
            printuse(stderr);
            printf(" Illegal argument: \"%s\"\n",p);
            exit(0);
        }
```

```
        } /*end if */
    } /*end while args */

    /*insure no conflict in arguments */
    if( (enable == disable) && !(nooptions) ) {
        printuse(stderr);
        fprintf(stderr, "Conflicting options: -d -e\n");
        exit(0);
    }

    /*insure at least one device specified */
    if( nodevnames ) {
        printuse(stderr);
        fprintf(stderr,"Must provide at least one device name.\n");
        exit(0);
    }

    index = 0;
    while( *(p = &devs[index][0]) != 0 ) {

        /*get a path to the device ( need to open @ form of device ) */
        strcpy( devname, p );
        strcat( devname, "@" );
        if( (pn = open(devname, S_IREAD)) < 0 )
            _exit(_errmsg(errno,"Could not open \"%s\"\n",p));

        do {
            /*read in the options for this device */
            if( (error = _gs_opt(pn, &opt)) < 0 ) {
                _errmsg(errno,"Error occured durring read options.\n");
                break;
            }

            /*now try the identify command */
            if( (error = identify( pn )) ) {
                _errmsg(errno,"Error occured durring Identify command.\n");
                break;
            }

            /*if this is a Quantum drive, try to enable the cache */
            if( !(strncmp( "QUANTUM", &idat.iq_vendid[0], 3 )) ) {
                /*if it is a Quantum disk, we can at least try. */
                if( (error = getcachepage(pn)) ) {
                    _errmsg(errno,"Error attempting to read the cache page.\n");
```

24.11. QUANTUMCACHE

```
                    break;
                }

                if( nooptions ) {
                    /* if not verbose, then print the current condition */
                    if( !verbose )
                        fprintf( stdout, "%s: Cache %s\n", p,
                                    cpag.msn_p37ce ? "ENABLED" : "Disabled");
                } else {
                    /* wants to enable or disable the cache */
                    if( enable )
                        error = setcache(pn, CACHEON );
                    else
                        error = setcache( pn, CACHEOFF );

                    if( error ) {
                        _errmsg(errno,"Error durring cache %s on %s.\n",
                                    enable ? "enable" : "disable", p);
                        break;
                    }
                }

                /* if requested, print the inquiry info and cache pages */
                if( verbose )
                    show_inq(p, SHOWCACHEPAGE);         /* print out the information */

            } else {
                show_inq(p, NOCACHEPAGE);
                fprintf( stderr, "%s is not a Quantum drive!\n",p);
            }

        } while(0);
        close(pn);                              /* close path for this pass        */
        index++;                                /* next device                     */
    }
    errvalue = errno;
    if( error )
        show_sense();
    exit(errvalue);

}
```

```
/*
    This is slated to become part of the standard library, but it hasn't happened yet.
*/
#asm
**  _gs_dcmd()
**  _ss_dcmd()
**
**  'C' bindings for direct command to a device.
**
*
* Function:  _gs_dcmd — get information from a device via direct command
*            _ss_dcmd — send information to a device via direct command
*
* Syntax: int _gs_dcmd( pn, cmd )
* int pn;                           /* path number to the device as returned by open() */
* void *cmd;                        /* the direct command to be performed              */
*
* int _ss_dcmd( pn, cmd )
* int pn;                           /* path number to the device as returned by open() */
* void *cmd;                        /* the direct command to be performed              */
*
* Returns:  0 if all went well
*          -1 on error, errno set to error number from driver
*
* Description:
* This is a mechanism where by a direct command can be issued to
* a device. The type of device of course determines the requirements of the
* command being sent. Refer to the documentation concerning the driver
* for the device to be communicated with.
*
* Caveats:
* Garbage in.... Garbage (possibly crash) out
*

_ss_dcmd:
    link a5,#0
    move.l a0,-(sp)
    move.l d1,a0 the command pointer
    move.l #SS_DCmd,d1 direct command code
    os9 I$SetStt
    bcs.s _gs_dcmderr
    clr.l d0 return all ok
    bra.s _gs_dcmdex
```

24.11. QUANTUMCACHE

```
_gs_dcmd:
    link a5,#0
    move.l a0,-(sp)
    move.l d1,a0 the command pointer
    move.l #SS_DCmd,d1 direct command code
    os9 I$GetStt
    bcs.s _gs_dcmderr
    clr.l d0 return all ok
    bra.s _gs_dcmdex

* common code for both calls
_gs_dcmderr
    move.l #-1,d0 set error flag for return
    move.l d1,errno(a6) set errno to value from driver
_gs_dcmdex
    move.l (sp)+,a0
    unlk a5
    rts

#endasm
```

Chapter 25

The Philosophy of OS-9

Small and *flexible* are OS-9's primary design goals. For many operating systems small and flexible work against each other, but since OS-9 interprets flexible as configurable, small and flexible fit together very well.

The most important parts of the OS-9 kernel consist of "glue" expressed as hooks and interfaces. The only I/O services in the OS-9 kernel are those services that must be in the kernel to insure that I/O systems can be installed and removed without interfering with one another. The collection of file managers from Microware, the file managers in this book, and the several commercially available file managers demonstrate that OS-9 accommodates a wide range of file managers smoothly. It does this precisely because there is very little code in the kernel that has anything to do with I/O.

Memory protection and cache control were added to the OS-9 kernel with only minor changes—calls to the MMU and cache control SVCs were added where appropriate—which were not dependent on the cache and MMU hardware. This update to the OS-9 kernel is a good example of the OS-9 design philosophy. The kernel remains small because the kernel has almost no cache or MMU control code, and flexible because the kernel will support a wide variety of configurations with hardware-specific SysCache and SSM modules.

The main avenue for user expansion of the OS-9 system is the I/O subsystem, but some services are not appropriate for the I/O subsystem. Occasionally the kernel is expanded to accommodate these services, but unless the service will be needed by a large part of the OS-9 community, special needs are met with system calls installed in a P2 module. This is a powerful tool. If a community needs a new kernel service, they can add it without changing OS-9; the kernel does not become bigger or slower. Those who don't need the new service are completely unaffected by it.

It is not an OS-9 rule that flexible must always be interpreted as configurable. The way the kernel handles various CPU and FPU chips is a case in point. One kernel will run any 68000-family CPU combined with no FPU, a 68881, or a 68882. The kernel includes code that recognizes the type of CPU and FPU and adjusts to the environment. This feature used several hundred bytes of code in the kernel, but the space cost of supporting all known 68xxx hardware in the kernel was seen as a good trade for the simplicity and slight speed advantage this approach had over building interfaces to CPU and FPU handler modules.

25.1 Weaknesses

Worst-Case Interrupt Latency   Probably because of OS-9's imperative to be as configurable as possible, it defines almost no restrictions on interrupt service routines. Although Microware suggests vigorously that interrupt service routines should be short and simple, almost any behavior is permitted: an interrupt service routine can allocate and free memory; there are rumors that you can even fork a new process.

The result of this lack of regulation is that the kernel can be interrupted by an ISR that can execute an arbitrary set of SVCs. This requires a reentrant kernel (code and data), and since kernel data structures cannot practically be locked against interrupt code[1] the kernel is forced to mask interrupts for some operations on kernel data structures.

The maximum amount of time during which all interrupts can be masked in the kernel is too high. It can probably be reduced as the kernel is further tuned and improved, but it will be difficult to make worst case interrupt latency as good as it would have been if interrupt service routines were restricted to a small set of SVCs.[2]

File System Interface   The kernel is quite unrestrictive about file managers and device drivers, but the utilities and drivers that support Microware file managers are tightly bound to those file managers. Consider the ugly hoops PCFM traverses to fit the expectations of RBF utilities and device drivers. It would be nice if the standard file manager interfaces went further than a set of system calls. An abstract file structure would let a single *dir* utility work with every file manager without alteration

---

[1]Locks that shut out code in an interrupt service routine would require the ISR code to wait. If is possible to make that work at all, the complexity it would cause would be frightening, to say **nothing** of what it would do to the execution time of the ISR.

[2]When interrupt latency is a serious concern, the worst case latency can be greatly decreased by avoiding operations that allocate or free memory: calls to the memory allocator, signals that queue, event creation or deletion, and I/O device attach and detach. These operations should be performed before and after real time activities.

25.2 Strengths

Passing over OS-9's practical strengths and moving directly to the philosophical advantages; the small and configurable philosophy works. It has done well at protecting the OS-9 kernel from ill-considered feature additions.[3] Features can be, and almost always are, added *outside* the OS-9 kernel. The kernel on my Micro-20 is 27562 bytes long. The OS-9 configuration for a minimal embedded system would use perhaps another kilobyte of miscellaneous modules and around 8 kilobytes of data. This has only grown by around 8 kilobytes since OS-9 came to the 68000.

25.3 Application of this Philosophy to User Code

The tools that the kernel uses to build interfaces are available to the other system components. They are, consequently, available to all programs. These facilities (e.g., subroutine modules, data modules, and trap handlers) support OS-9 configurable applications just as they support a configurable operating system.

Small applications that are tightly bound to particular hardware and have have no possibility for other configuration changes, should probably be written as monolithic programs. Programs that are divided into several modules bear a tiny performance penalty. Large, complicated, or volatile programs should be divided into modules. Programs that are carefully divided into modules are much easier to update than monolithic programs. OS-9 forms an excellent practical example of this strategy.

Composite/Structured Design by Glenford J. Myers is a rather old book, but it includes good guidelines for partitioning a program into modules. (Though the book doesn't actually mention modules.)

Trap handlers are an especially convenient tool for partitioning programs. The difference in cost between calling a function and calling a trap handler (see page 143) is large when the functions are trivial, but invisible for a typical C function.

---

[3] Although it is hard to justify the Julian and Gregorian date-handling code in the OS-9 kernel.

Appendix A

Recent History

This appendix reviews the highlights of the past five years of OS-9 evolution.

A.1 Version 1.2

OS-9 version 1.2 was released in mid-1985. The kernel featured new system calls for events. RBF and IOMan relaxed the rules for file names to permit letters, numbers, period, underscore, and dollar-sign. The only remaining restriction was that file names must contain at least one letter or number somewhere. Pipeman was extended to support named pipes.

IOMan was merged with the kernel.

The format-inhibit attribute was added to disk device descriptors; so was a sector size field.

SCF added a bunch of modem-control setstats.

F$STrap let user programs catch bus errors and address exceptions.

The kernel now tries to expand system tables when they overflow. This lets the system administrator configure the system for a reasonable maximum number of processes and devices without experiencing odd program failures whenever the estimated table sizes are too small.

A.2 Version 2.0

OS-9 version 2.0 was released in late 1986. The big excitement was support for the 68020/68881. The 020 support included the obvious handling for different exception stack formats, also emulation for the *move ccr,ea* instruction, and adjustments of alignments in system data structures to improve performance with the 68020.

System state processes first appeared in version 2.0.

Before version 2.0, signal broadcast reached all processes with no consideration for their group.user. The broadcast facility was also unprotected: any process could broadcast signals. Version 2.0 restricted processes to broadcasting to all processes with their group.user.

Sysdbg appeared, and kernel support for *debug* improved.

Security was tightened. In particular, module access permissions are now checked.

The memory allocator was improved. It now merges adjacent blocks in the process memory list. Overflowing the list is much less likely.

Interrupt service routines are expected to save and restore some registers. This gives a big performance improvement. OS-9 was saving and restoring everything even though the typical interrupt service routine only used about three registers.

RBF supports multi-sector I/O and I/O direct from the device to the user's buffer.

The FD segment list of deleted files is not zeroed. This makes an *undelete* utility possible.

A.3 Version 2.1

OS-9 version 2.1 was released in mid-1987. It featured the *F$SigMask* and *F$CCtl* system calls.

These were significant new system calls. *F$SigMask* was an indication that the 2.1 kernel supported signal queuing and masking.

F$CCtl resulted from a major restructuring of the kernel. Cache control operations for the 68020 had been inserted in the kernel. This strategy was inadequate. With *F$CCtl*, the kernel can keep all its cache-control code in a separate module. OEMs can now configure OS-9 to take advantage of their external cache without major kernel surgery.

When version 2.1 was released, MMUs for 68020 boards were not common, but version 2.1 included support for an SSM module[1] that would add memory protection for processes.

F$SetSvc now allows a static data area to be associated with each system call. Combined with the startup code's new ability to allocate storage for each P2 module

---

[1] When version 2.1 was released Microware only supported an SSM module for the 68851 MMU coprocessor.

and leave the storage allocated after the P2 module returns, version 2.1 gives P2 system calls a way to allocate private static storage.

The "ghost" module attribute was added.

On the 68020, OS-9 uses VBR to locate its system globals and interrupt vectors.

A.4 Version 2.2

OS-9 version 2.2 was released in early 1988 as a maintenance release. All the new stuff since 1.2 was cleaned up in the light of experience. For instance, pipes behave like SCF and RBF when they receive signals. Pipes used to abort when they received a signal. It's also possible to:

    $ dir –e /pipe

I$GetStt SS_Opt now calls the driver. This lets the driver keep track of the path options section more easily.

Timed sleeps are handled by the system process instead of the clock tick IRQ routine, and timed sleep handling is more efficient.

The system ticking variables have been lengthened from 8 bits to 16 bits. This lets the tick rate go above 256 ticks per second.

(The C compiler was greatly enhanced, but that's a different story.)

A.5 Version 2.3

OS-9 version 2.3 was released in mid-1989. It featured *F$Alarm*, colored memory, and an extensively revised *F$CCtl*.

The first two features are discussed at length elsewhere in this book. The *F$CCtl* SVC let the kernel move cache control into a P2 module that could contain an *F$CCtl* to control any combination of on-chip and off-chip cache.

F$Trans was also added to OS-9. It translates between local addresses and external bus addresses. This is important when an off-board DMA device must reference on-board RAM.

F$Panic was implemented to let a P2 module attempt to recover from conditions that the kernel cannot handle.

The "Universal Disk Format" is first explained in the version 2.3 Release Notes. It is a disk format that should work with any known or likely disk controller:

Table A.1: Processor Support

Version	Processor
2.0	68020
2.2	68030
	68882
2.4	CPU32 family
2.4.2	68040

Device Descriptor Option	Value
PD_TotCyls	80
PD_CYL	79
PD_SCT	16
PD_DNS	MFM and 96 tpi
PD_SOffs	1
PD_TOffs	1

The most remarkable feature of the universal disk format is that it avoids track zero completely. This makes the various behavior of controllers on track zero a non-issue.

A.6 Version 2.4

OS-9 version 2.4 is almost exactly CD-RTOS version 1.1. It was released in late 1990.

Version 2.4 features support for the 683xx chips.

RBF added variable sector size support and caching of disk sectors.

Boot files larger than 64k and non-contiguous boot files are now supported by *os9gen* and the boot code.

The kernel's understanding of cache memory is further enhanced.

Incremental releases start here. Microware decided to release software without waiting for grand checkpoints. Too much good stuff (like 68040 support) was being held up by the extreme effort involved in a full OS-9 release.

The first incremental release was version 2.4.2 (early 1991). It introduced initial, and quite tentative, support for the 68040.

Support for the 68040 is improved in version 2.4.3, released in mid-1991. The 68040 runs much faster with copy-back caching turned on. (Though it only works for user code.)

Appendix B

Technical Appendix

> *This appendix contains a number of bits of information that did not deserve a chapter of their own or fit into another chapter.*

B.1 The Arithmetic of XOR

The effect of an XOR operation on two words is to leave on (i.e., with the bit set to one) only those bits which are on in only one of the two words. For example, if the binary numbers $A =$ %0101011001101010 and $B =$ %0101010110101010 were XOR'ed together, the result would be %0000001111000000. Working from the most significant (rightmost) bit to the least significant bit:

The first six bits in A and B are identical, %010101 in both,
    so the result is 0 for each bit: %000000.
The seventh bit in A is 1 and the seventh bit in B is 0.
    Since one of them is 1, the result is 1.
The eighth bit in A is 0 and the eighth bit in B is 1.
    Since one of them is 1, the result is 1.
The ninth bit in A is 0 and the ninth bit in B is 1.
    Since one of them is 1, the result is 1.
The tenth bit in A is 1 and the tenth bit in B is 0.
    Since one of them is 1, the result is 1.
The last six bits in A and B are identical, %101010 in both,
    so the result is 0 for each bit: %000000.

The one's complement operation reverses the state of each bit in a number. Each 1 becomes a 0, and each 0 becomes a 1. If a number is XOR'ed with its one's complement, the result is all 1's:

A	=	%11001101 10101100
Ones complement of A	=	%00110010 01010011
A XOR Complement of A	=	%11111111 11111111

B.2 Bootlist

Os9gen is usually used with a bootlist file:

$ os9gen –z=bootlist.h0 /h0

The bootlist file contains the list of files that *os9gen* should include in the boot file it makes. It is possible, but less common, to type the list of files into *os9gen*'s standard input, or to redirect its standard input from a bootlist file.

It usually takes a few tries before the bootlist is right, so it is best to make boot files on a floppy or extra hard disk until you have tested it and know that the system will boot correctly with the new boot file. If you replace your working boot file with a broken file, you will have to reconstruct your world rather painfully.

I have two bootlist files that differ mainly in the device they use for initial data and execution directories.

Both of the bootlists shown in figure B.1 are quite fully configured (though I leave the RAM disk descriptor out of the boot file so I can conveniently load a RAM disk of the right size when I need it.) The list labeled bootlist.d0 includes an experimental P2 module and its stb module, and bootlist.h0 includes a descriptor for the default device.

The main difference is that the init module for bootlist.d0 keeps all activity on the /d0.

The boot file described by bootlist.d0 (without the test P2 module) is the bootfile I use on my emergency disk. This is the disk I use to rescue my system when I cannot boot from my hard disk (probably because I broke some important file on /h0). The emergency disk contains everything I need to rescue my system: a boot file that only relies on the one floppy drive, a CMDS directory with enough files in it to get the system going, and a SYS directory with a useful set of files. If the disk has enough space, it is good to add a BOOTOBJS directory with the raw materials to build a new master boot file. Figure B.3 contains a list of the structure of my emergency disk. The .login file and startup file on the emergency disk are as simple as possible. The emergency disk should boot as quickly as possible... furthermore, there are better ways to use disk space than storing fortunes or other login fluff.

The following is a useful .login suitable for the emergency disk:

B.2. BOOTLIST

Figure B.1: Two Bootlists

Comment	Bootlist.d0	Bootlist.h0
	Kernel	Kernel
	../peter/os9p2	
	../peter/stb/os9p2.stb	
	Init.d0.020	Init.h0.020
	syscache020	syscache020
	m20clk	m20clk
Sequential Block File Manager	Scf	Scf
SCF Drivers and Descriptors		
Serial Driver	sc68681	sc68681
Serial Descriptors	Term	Term
	t1	t1
	t2	t2
	t3	t3
Parallel Driver	sc68230	sc68230
Parallel Descriptor	P	P
Null Driver	Null	Null
Null Descriptor	Nil	Nil
Pipe File Manager	Pipeman	Pipeman
Pipe Descriptor	Pipe	Pipe
Random Block File Manager	Rbf	Rbf
RBF Drivers and Descriptors		
Floppy Disk Driver	rb1772	rb1772
SCSI Disk Driver	rbm20vsl	rbm20vsl
Floppy Disk Descriptors	D0	D0
SCSI Disk Descriptor	h0_vs_4	h0_vs_4
Default Device Descriptor		dd_h0_vs_4
RAM Disk Driver	ram	ram
SBF file manager	sbf	sbf
SBF device driver	sbm20	sbm20
SBF device descriptor	mt0.teac	mt0.teac
Initial System Process	Sysgo	Sysgo

Figure B.2: Two Init Modules

Description	Init.d0.020	Init.h0.020
reserved	0	0
number of irq polling entries	64	64
device table size	64	64
initial process table size	64	64
initial path table size	64	64
startup parameter string		
first executable module	Sysgo	Sysgo
default directory name	/D0	/H0
console terminal name	/Term	/Term
customization module list	OS9P2 SYSCACHE	OS9P2 SYSCACHE
clock module name	M20CLK	M20CLK
ticks per time slice	2	2
reserved	$0000	$0000
site code	0	0
installation name	GMX Micro-20	GMX Micro-20
cpu type	68020	68020
operating system level	$01020401	$01020401
os-9 revision name	OS-9/68K V2.4	OS-9/68K V2.4
initial system priority	128	128
minimum priority	0	0
maximum age	0	0
module directory size (unused)	$00000080	$00000080
initial event table size	0	0
compatability flag #1	$08	$08
compatibility flag #2	$8b	$8b
irq stack size (longwords)	1024	1024
coldstart "chd" retry count	0	0

B.2. BOOTLIST

Figure B.3: Directory of an Emergency Disk

```
             Directory of /D0 01:02:13
     .login     CMDS       OS9Boot    SYS        startup
             Directory of CMDS 01:02:16
     attr      break      cio        copy       date
     dd_d0     dd_h0      del        devs       dir
     dump      emacs      fixmod     format     frestore
     link      list       load       login      makdir
     math881   mdir       moded      mt0        os9gen
     pd        r0         save       sectsize   setime
     shell     tape       tmode      tsmon      unlink
     utils
             Directory of SYS 01:02:36
     errmsg    moded.fields   motd    password   termcap
     termset
```

```
setenv TERM ansi
setenv _sh 0
setenv PROMPT "@$"
setenv PATH /h0/cmds
setenv TZ EST
-e
```

and the minimal startup that I use for my floppy boot disk:

```
-np
-nt
load utils
link shell cio                          ;* make shell and cio stay in memory
setime -s                               ;* read clock & start "ticks"
iniz d0 h0
```

Appendix C

Building a File Manager

Chapter 21 discussed a simple RBF-type file manager. This appendix contains the successor to that file manager. This file manager falls somewhere between a simple example and a serious tool. It illustrates many of the tricks needed to write a real file manager. Regrettably, it also fusses extensively with the PC-DOS disk format.

This file manager[1] reads and writes PC-DOS disks. It even makes them look enough like OS-9 disks that many system utilities work on them. It is definitely *not* a production-quality file manager.

- This program has been tested in ordinary use on several PC-DOS formats with a GMX Micro-20. It may have difficulties with some PC-DOS formats. It will certainly fail with device drivers that have difficulties with 512-byte sectors. The GMX driver simply ignores the sector length. This works unless verify-after-write is requested. Drivers that respect the sector-size field in the device descriptor should work better than drivers that ignore it, but such drivers are uncommon.

- There is no obvious way to detect a new disk in the drive. This file manager doesn't worry about it. Be very cautious if you change disks.

- The file manager creates virtual OS-9 file descriptors, but the simulation is not good enough. Some utilities (e.g., *pd*, *dcheck*, and *deldir*) don't work.

To delete a directory on an PC-DOS-format disk, follow these steps:

---

[1] This source code is the proprietary confidential property of Microware Systems Corporation, and is provided to licensee solely for documentation and educational purposes. Reproduction, publication, or distribution in any form to any party other than the licensee is strictly prohibited.

- Empty the directory.
- Use the *attr -nd* command from the parent directory to remove the directory attribute.
- Delete the file.

- There is no locking of records or files.

- The file manager seems to handle large numbers of active files, but this is difficult to test.

- There are many ways the I/O performance could be improved.

You do, however, have the source. If you need an additional feature, add it!

Perhaps I have given in slightly to the "It was hard to write. It should be hard to read." policy. Another theory is that this appendix was already long with few comments. In either case, you will probably want to refer to chapter 21 for additional comments.

C.1 Interface to the C File Manager

The OS-9 kernel was written in assembly language, and its interfaces are defined in assembly-language terms. This file manager was written in C with consideration for the limits imposed by the assembly language environment. You won't find any static storage declared in this file. You definitely won't find any initialized statics.

I avoided the standard C libraries because I didn't want to risk a static variable slipping in from the library (errno was a particular problem). Some functions that would normally be library functions are in the fmmain.a file; others are in utils.c; some are even coded in line.

A file manager gets a stack whenever it is called, but it doesn't get stack-size information. Stack-size checking would pose a nasty set of problems, so I didn't do it. Note that the makefile specifies no stack checking.

C.1.1 fmmain.a

Fmmain is the equivalent of cstart. It is the entry point for the file manager. All interfaces that are defined in assembly language are made through the fmmain file.

If you look carefully you will find that this fmmain is a considerably compressed version of the code in chapter 21.

[†] *fmmain*: see page 260

C.1. INTERFACE TO THE C FILE MANAGER

```
                   ****************************
                   *
                   * cstart.a - C program startup routine for a file manager
                   *
                          use      <oskdefs.d>
                          opt      -l
00000001  Carry:          equ      %00000001       Carry bit

0000000d  Typ             equ      FlMgr
00000001  Edit            equ      1
00000400  Stk             equ      1024            a default stack size
00000101  Cerror          equ      257             arbitrary C error

                          psect    cstart_a,(Typ<<8)!Objct,(ReEnt<<8)!1,Edit,Stk,_cstart

                   *
                   * C Program entry point
                   *
                   * On entry we have:
                   *        a1 points to the path descriptor
                   *        a4 points to the current process descriptor
                   *        a5 points to the user's register stack
                   *        a6 points to the system global area
                   *
          _cstart:
0000 001a         dc.w     _Create-_cstart
0002 0020         dc.w     _Open-_cstart
0004 0026         dc.w     _MakDir-_cstart
0006 002c         dc.w     _ChgDir-_cstart
0008 0032         dc.w     _Delete-_cstart
000a 0038         dc.w     _Seek-_cstart
000c 003e         dc.w     _Read-_cstart
000e 0044         dc.w     _Write-_cstart
0010 005c         dc.w     _ReadLn-_cstart
0012 0062         dc.w     _WriteLn-_cstart
0014 0068         dc.w     _GetStat-_cstart
0016 006e         dc.w     _SetStat-_cstart
0018 0074         dc.w     _Close-_cstart

          _Create
001a=41fa         lea.l    Create(pc),a0    on page 449
001e 6028         bra.s    fmCommon

          _Open
0020=41fa         lea.l    Open(pc),a0      on page 444
0024 6022         bra.s    fmCommon
```

```
              _MakDir
0026=41fa              lea.l      MakDir(pc),a0      on page 450
002a 601c              bra.s      fmCommon

              _ChgDir
002c=41fa              lea.l      ChgDir(pc),a0      on page 455
0030 6016              bra.s      fmCommon

              _Delete
0032=41fa              lea.l      Delete(pc),a0      on page 454
0036 6010              bra.s      fmCommon

              _Seek
0038=41fa              lea.l      Seek(pc),a0        on page 455
003c 600a              bra.s      fmCommon

              _Read
003e=41fa              lea.l      Read(pc),a0        on page 434
0042 6004              bra.s      fmCommon

              _Write
0044=41fa              lea.l      Write(pc),a0       on page 438
      *                bra.s      fmCommon           a trivial branch

              fmCommon
0048 48e7              movem.l    a4/a6,-(sp)
004c 2009              move.l     a1,d0
004e 220d              move.l     a5,d1
0050 4e90              jsr        (a0)               (pd, regs, ProcDesc, SysGlobs)
0052 4cdf              movem.l    (sp)+,a4/a6
0056 4a40              tst.w      d0
0058 6620              bne.s      _Error
005a 4e75              rts

              _ReadLn
005c=41fa              lea.l      ReadLn(pc),a0      on page 436
0060 60e6              bra.s      fmCommon

              _WriteLn
0062=41fa              lea.l      WriteLn(pc),a0     on page 441
0066 60e0              bra.s      fmCommon

              _GetStat
0068=41fa              lea.l      GetStat(pc),a0     on page 456
006c 60da              bra.s      fmCommon
```

C.1. INTERFACE TO THE C FILE MANAGER

```
                _SetStat
006e=41fa       lea.l       SetStat(pc),a0    on page 457
0072 60d4       bra.s       fmCommon

                _Close
0074=41fa       lea.l       Close(pc),a0      on page 453
0078 60ce       bra.s       fmCommon

                _Error
007a 3200       move.w      d0,d1
007c 003c       ori         #Carry,ccr
0080 4e75       rts

        *       CallRead (ct, lsn, pd, DevStaticS, ProcD, regs, sysglobs)
        * Sets up to call read in the device driver. Puts:
        *           ct in d0
        *           lsn in d2

        *           pd in a1
        *           DevStaticS in a2
        *           ProcD in a4
        *           regs in a5
        *           sysglobs in a6
        CallRead:
0082 48e7       movem.l     d2-d7/a0-a5,-(sp)
        * ct is already in d0
        * calculate the entry address in the device driver
0086 226f       move.l      13*4(sp),a1       pd to a1
008a=2069       move.l      PD_DEV(a1),a0     device table entry
008e=2068       move.l      V$DRIV(a0),a0     device driver address
0092=2428       move.l      M$Exec(a0),d2     device driver entry offset
0096=d0f0       add.w       D$READ(a0,d2),a0  Add read-entry offset to module base
009a 2401       move.l      d1,d2
009c 246f       move.l      14*4(sp),a2       DevStatic to a2
00a0 286f       move.l      15*4(sp),a4       ProcD to a4
00a4 2a6f       move.l      16*4(sp),a5       regs to a5
        * sysglobs is already in a6

00a8 4e90       jsr         (a0)
00aa 6534       bcs.s       CallError
00ac 602a       bra.s       CallOK

        * CallWrite (ct, lsn, pd, DevStaticS, ProcD, regs, sysglobs)
        * Sets up to call the write entry in the device driver. Puts:
        *           ct in d0
```

```
                   *        lsn in d2
                   *        pd in a1
                   *        DevStaticS in a2
                   *        ProcD in a4
                   *        regs in a5
                   *        sysglobs in a6
                CallWrite:
00ae 48e7                   movem.l  d2-d7/a0-a5,-(sp)
                * ct is already in d0
00b2 226f                   move.l   13*4(sp),a1       pd to a1
                * calculate the entry address in the device driver
00b6=2069                   move.l   PD_DEV(a1),a0     device table entry
00ba=2068                   move.l   V$DRIV(a0),a0     device driver address
00be=2428                   move.l   M$Exec(a0),d2     device driver entry offset
00c2=d0f0                   add.w    D$WRIT(a0,d2),a0  add read-entry offset to module base

00c6 2401                   move.l   d1,d2             lsn to d2
00c8 246f                   move.l   14*4(sp),a2       DevStatic to a2
00cc 286f                   move.l   15*4(sp),a4       ProcD to a4
00d0 2a6f                   move.l   16*4(sp),a5       regs to a5
                * sysglobs is already in a6
00d4 4e90                   jsr      (a0)
00d6 6508                   bcs.s    CallError
                   *        bra.s    CallOK

                CallOK
00d8 4cdf                   movem.l  (sp)+,d2-d7/a0-a5
00dc 4280                   clr.l    d0
00de 4e75                   rts

                CallError
00e0 2001                   move.l   d1,d0
00e2 4cdf                   movem.l  (sp)+,d2-d7/a0-a5
00e6 4e75                   rts

                * CallGetStat(code, pd, DevStaticS, procd, regs, sysglobs)
                * Sets up to call the getstat entry in the device driver. Puts:
                   *        code in d0
                   *        pd in a1
                   *        DevStaticS in a2
                   *        ProcD in a4
                   *        regs in a5
                   *        sysglobs in a6
                CallGetStat:
00e8 48e7                   movem.l  d2-d7/a0-a5,-(sp)
                * code is already in d0
00ec 2241                   move.l   d1,a1             pd to a1
```

C.1. INTERFACE TO THE C FILE MANAGER

```
              * calculate the entry address in the device driver
00ee=2069       move.l    PD_DEV(a1),a0   device table entry
00f2=2068       move.l    V$DRIV(a0),a0   device driver address
00f6=2428       move.l    M$Exec(a0),d2   device driver entry offset
00fa=d0f0       add.w     D$GSTA(a0,d2),a0 add read-entry offset to module base

00fe 246f       move.l    13*4(sp),a2     DevStatic to a2
0102 286f       move.l    14*4(sp),a4     ProcD to a4
0106 2a6f       move.l    15*4(sp),a5     regs to a5
              * sysglobs is already in a6
010a 4e90       jsr       (a0)
010c 65d2       bcs.s     CallError
010e 60c8       bra.s     CallOK

              * CallSetStat(code, pd, DevStaticS, procd, regs, sysglobs)
              * Sets up to call the putstat entry in the device driver.  Puts:
              *         code in d0
              *         pd in a1
              *         DevStaticS in a2
              *         ProcD in a4
              *         regs in a5
              *         sysglobs in a6
              CallSetStat:
0110 48e7       movem.l   d2-d7/a0-a5,-(sp)
              * code is already in d0
0114 2241       move.l    d1,a1           pd to a1
              * calculate the entry address in the device driver
0116=2069       move.l    PD_DEV(a1),a0   device table entry
011a=2068       move.l    V$DRIV(a0),a0   device driver address
011e=2428       move.l    M$Exec(a0),d2   device driver entry offset
0122=d0f0       add.w     D$PSTA(a0,d2),a0 add read-entry offset to module base
0126 246f       move.l    13*4(sp),a2     DevStatic to a2
012a 286f       move.l    14*4(sp),a4     ProcD to a4
012e 2a6f       move.l    15*4(sp),a5     regs to a5
              * sysglobs is already in a6
0132 4e90       jsr       (a0)
0134 65aa       bcs.s     CallError
0136 60a0       bra.s     CallOK


              _srqmem:
0138 2f0a       move.l    a2,-(sp)
013a=4e40       os9       F$SRqMem
013e 6404       bcc.b     srqmemx1
0140 70ff       moveq.l   #-1,d0
0142 6002       bra.b     srqmemx
```

```
                srqmemx1
0144 200a               move.l   a2,d0
                srqmemx
0146 245f               move.l   (sp)+,a2
0148 4e75               rts


           *
           *            DoIOQ(processid)
           *
                DoIOQ:
014a=4e40               os9      F$IOQu
014e 2001               move.l   d1,d0           return code
0150 4e75               rts


           *
           *            DoSRtMem(ptr, size)
           *
                DoSRtMem:
0152 2f0a               move.l   a2,-(sp)
0154 2440               move.l   d0,a2
0156 2001               move.l   d1,d0
0158=4e40               os9      F$SRtMem
015c 6404               bcc.b    DoSrtMx
015e=4e40               os9      F$SysDbg
                DoSrtMx
0162 245f               move.l   (sp)+,a2
0164 4e75               rts


                SysDebug:
0166=4e40               os9      F$SysDbg
016a 4e75               rts


                GetUser:
016c 2f02               move.l   d2,-(sp)
016e=4e40               os9      F$ID
0172 241f               move.l   (sp)+,d2
0174 2001               move.l   d1,d0
0176 4e75               rts


                GetDate:
0178 48e7               movem.l  d0-d2/a0,-(sp)
017c 7000               moveq    #0,d0           Gregorian
017e=4e40               os9      F$Time
0182 2057               move.l   (sp),a0         get the pointer from d0
0184 2401               move.l   d1,d2
0186 4242               clr.w    d2
0188 4842               swap     d2
```

C.1. INTERFACE TO THE C FILE MANAGER

```
018a 84fc          divu.w    #100,d2
018e 4842          swap      d2              put the remainder in the low-ord word
0190 10c2          move.b    d2,(a0)+        save YY
0192 e159          rol.w     #8,d1           Move MM into position
0194 10c1          move.b    d1,(a0)+        save MM
0196 e159          rol.w     #8,d1           Move DD into position
0198 10c1          move.b    d1,(a0)+        save DD
019a e198          rol.l     #8,d0
019c e198          rol.l     #8,d0           Move HH into position
019e 10c0          move.b    d0,(a0)+        save HH
01a0 e198          rol.l     #8,d0           Move MM into position
01a2 1080          move.b    d0,(a0)         save MM
01a4 4cdf          movem.l   (sp)+,d0-d2/a0
01a8 4e75          rts

                 * MoveData(dest, src, length)
                 MoveData:
01aa 48e7          movem.l   d2/a0/a2,−(sp)
01ae 2440          move.l    d0,a2           destination
01b0 2041          move.l    d1,a0           source
01b2 242f          move.l    4*4(sp),d2      length
01b6 7200          moveq.l   #0,d1           sweep for error code
01b8=4e40          os9       F$Move
01bc 2001          move.l    d1,d0           move error code to d0
01be 4cdf          movem.l   (sp)+,d2/a0/a2
01c2 4e75          rts
000001c4           ends
```

C.1.2 Makefile

```
# Make file to produce an PC-Dos disk file manager
LIB = /dd/lib/sys.l
DEBUG = −g
CFLAGS = $(DEBUG) −qjsk0 −t=/r0 −w=.
RFILES = fmmain.r msfm.r msopen.r ReadSector.r drivetable.r MakDir.r\
    Read.r ReadLn.r Close.r FATSupport.r Create.r Delete.r\
    dir.r utils.r TransDir.r GetFD.r Write.r WriteLn.r WriteSector.r

all: pcfm msD0

pcfm: $(RFILES)
    l68 $(DEBUG) −l=/dd/lib/clibn.l −l=$(LIB) −l=/dd/lib/math.l −o=pcfm\
    $(RFILES)

fmmain.r: fmmain.a
```

```
    r68 fmmain.a −o=fmmain.r

msD0: DevDesc.r
    l68 DevDesc.r −l=/dd/lib/sys.l −o=msD0

msfm.r: msfm.c format.h PathDesc.h
    cc −r $(CFLAGS) msfm.c

msopen.r: msopen.c format.h PathDesc.h
    cc −r $(CFLAGS) msopen.c

DevDesc.r: DevDesc.a
    r68 DevDesc.a −o=DevDesc.r

ReadSector.r: ReadSector.c format.h PathDesc.h
    cc −r $(CFLAGS) ReadSector.c

drivetable.r: drivetable.c format.h PathDesc.h
    cc −r $(CFLAGS) drivetable.c

Read.r: Read.c format.h PathDesc.h
    cc −r $(CFLAGS) Read.c

ReadLn.r: ReadLn.c format.h PathDesc.h
    cc −r $(CFLAGS) ReadLn.c

Close.r: Close.c format.h PathDesc.h
    cc −r $(CFLAGS) Close.c

FATSupport.r: FATSupport.c format.h PathDesc.h
    cc −r $(CFLAGS) FATSupport.c

dir.r: dir.c format.h PathDesc.h
    cc −r $(CFLAGS) dir.c

utils.r: utils.c
    cc −r $(CFLAGS) utils.c

TransDir.r: TransDir.c
    cc −r $(CFLAGS) TransDir.c

GetFD.r: GetFD.c format.h PathDesc.h
    cc −r $(CFLAGS) GetFD.c
```

C.2. MAIN ENTRY POINTS 433

SysUtils.r: SysUtils.a
   r68 SysUtils.a −o=SysUtils.r

Create.r: Create.c format.h PathDesc.h
   cc −r $(CFLAGS) Create.c

WriteSector.r: WriteSector.c format.h PathDesc.h
   cc −r $(CFLAGS) WriteSector.c

Write.r: Write.c format.h PathDesc.h
   cc −r $(CFLAGS) Write.c

WriteLn.r: WriteLn.c format.h PathDesc.h
   cc −r $(CFLAGS) WriteLn.c

Delete.r: Delete.c format.h PathDesc.h
   cc −r $(CFLAGS) Delete.c

MakDir.r: MakDir.c format.h PathDesc.h
   cc −r $(CFLAGS) MakDir.c

C.2 Main Entry Points

Each file manager function has a corresponding C function. These functions are for the most part generic, and should work with small changes for any RBF-style file system.

C.2.1 Read.c

There is an extensive *if* statement near the end of the Read() function. The *if* statement deals with an odd feature of the PC-DOS root directory. Unlike all other PC-DOS directories, the root directory doesn't have . and .. entries. OS-9 doesn't like that at all, so the Read() and Readln() functions insert . and .. entries at the beginning of the root directory.

```
#include <errno.h>
#include <procid.h>
#include <modes.h>
typedef char *POINTER;
```

[†] *read*: see page 270

```
#include "format.h"
#include "PathDesc.h"

Read(pd, regs, procd, SysGlobs)
register PD_TYPE pd;
REGS regs;
{
    ushort PartialLength;
    register ushort Sector, offset;
    register long length;
    char *dest;
    int ReturnVal=0;

    if((pd→PD_Accs & S_IREAD) == 0)
        return(E_BMODE);

    length = regs→R_d1;
    dest = regs→R_a0;

    if((length + pd→PD_CP) >= pd→PD_SIZ)
        if(pd→PD_CP >= pd→PD_SIZ)
            return E_EOF;
        else
            length = regs→R_d1 = (pd→PD_SIZ − pd→PD_CP);

    offset = OffsetInSector(pd);                                    /* pg. 435 */

    while(length > 0){
        /* Now prepare to read a sector */
        if((Sector = CheckSector(pd)) >= (T_FAT_BADTRACK)){          /* pg. 486 */
            ReturnVal = Errno(Sector);                               /* pg. 481 */
            break;
        }
        if((ReturnVal = ReadSector(pd, Sector, pd→PD_BUF,            /* pg. 469 */
            regs, procd, SysGlobs)) != 0)
            break;

        /*
            At least part of this sector should be copied to the caller's buffer. The
            "interesting" data starts at offset from the beginning of the sector and
            continues for length bytes, or to the end of the sector (whichever is
            least).
        */
        PartialLength = SECTORSIZE − offset;
```

C.2. MAIN ENTRY POINTS 435

```
            if(PartialLength > length)
                PartialLength = length;
            length -= PartialLength;


            /* Copy the data to the caller's buffer.                    */
            if((pd→PD_SMF & PD_DIR_MODE) &&
                    !(pd→PD_SMF & PD_RAWMODE) &&
                    (pd→PD_CP < (2 * sizeof(MSDirEntry))) &&
                    (Sector == MS_SECTOR(pd→PD_DTB→DD_DIR)))
                pd→PD_CP = FakeRootDir(pd→PD_CP,                        /* pg. 479 */
                    &PartialLength, &dest);

            pd→PD_CP += PartialLength; /* Update current position in pd */
            MoveData(dest, pd→PD_BUF+offset, PartialLength);
            dest += PartialLength;
            offset = 0;
        }
        return ReturnVal;
}


OffsetInSector(pd)
register PD_TYPE pd;
{
    if((pd→PD_SMF & PD_DIR_MODE) &&
            !(pd→PD_SMF & PD_RAWMODE) &&
            (pd→PD_SMF & PD_RDIR_MODE))
        if(pd→PD_CP <= (2 * sizeof(MSDirEntry)))
            return(pd→PD_CP & 31); /* note that sizeof msdirentry = 32 */
        else
            return((pd→PD_CP-(2*sizeof(MSDirEntry))) & (SECTORSIZE - 1));

    return (pd→PD_CP & (SECTORSIZE −1));
}
```

C.2.2 ReadLn.c

The ReadLn() function resembles the Read() function. It must, however, transfer bytes one at a time while looking for the end-of-line character.

ReadLn(), like Read(), generates fake entries for the root directory.

[†] *readln*: see page 274

```
#include <errno.h>
#include <procid.h>
#include <modes.h>
typedef char *POINTER;
#include "format.h"
#include "PathDesc.h"

ReadLn(pd, regs, procd, SysGlobs)
register PD_TYPE pd;
REGS regs;
{
   unsigned long length;
   ushort i, j;
   register unsigned long Sector, offset;
   char *dest, *ptr;
   int ReturnVal=0;
   int eol;

   if((pd→PD_Accs & S_IREAD) == 0)
      return(E_BMODE);

   length = regs→R_d1;
   dest = regs→R_a0;
   regs→R_d1 = 0;

   if((length + pd→PD_CP) >= pd→PD_SIZ)
      if(pd→PD_CP >= pd→PD_SIZ)
         return E_EOF;
      else
         length = (pd→PD_SIZ − pd→PD_CP);

   offset = OffsetInSector(pd);                              /* pg. 435 */

   eol = FALSE;
   while((length > 0) && !eol){
      /* Now prepare to read a sector */
      if((Sector = CheckSector(pd)) >= T_FAT_BADTRACK){      /* pg. 486 */
         ReturnVal = Errno(Sector);                          /* pg. 481 */
         break;
      }
      if((ReturnVal = ReadSector(pd, Sector, pd→PD_BUF,      /* pg. 469 */
            regs, procd, SysGlobs)) != 0)
         break;
```

C.2. MAIN ENTRY POINTS

```
    /*
        At least part of this sector should be copied to the caller's buffer. The
        "interesting" data starts at offset from the beginning of the sector and
        continues for length bytes, or to the end of the sector (whichever is
        least).
    */
    i = SECTORSIZE − offset;
    if(i>length)
        i = length;

    /*
        Copy the data to the caller's buffer
    */
    if((pd→PD_SMF & PD_DIR_MODE) &&
        !(pd→PD_SMF & PD_RAWMODE) &&
        (pd→PD_CP < (2 * sizeof(MSDirEntry))) &&
        (Sector == pd→PD_DTB→DD_DIR))
        pd→PD_CP = FakeRootDir(pd→PD_CP, &i, &dest);        /* pg. 479 */

    for(ptr = pd→PD_BUF+offset, j=0 ; j<i ; ++j)
        if(*ptr != pd→PD_NewLine)
            *dest++ = *ptr++;
        else{
            *dest++ = '\n';
            eol = TRUE;
            ++j;
            break;
        }
    length −= j;
    pd→PD_CP += j;          /* Update current position in pd */
    regs→R_d1 += j;         /* Update the amount read */
    offset = 0;
    }
    return ReturnVal;
}
```

C.2.3 Write.c

Ordinary data is written without excitement. Directory entries require special processing. PC-DOS hides what amounts to a file descriptor in each directory entry. The file manager must not allow OS-9 utilities (e.g., *rename*) to obliviously write directory

---

† *write*: see page 273

entries. They could easily destroy file descriptor information. Write() and WriteLn() note directory writes and use a special function that protects and reconstitutes PC-DOS file information.

```
#include <errno.h>
#include <procid.h>
#include <modes.h>
typedef char *POINTER;
#include "format.h"
#include "PathDesc.h"

Write(pd, regs, procd, SysGlobs)
register PD_TYPE pd;
REGS regs;
{
    register long length;
    register ushort PartialLength, offset;
    register ulong Sector;
    register char *from;
    int ReturnVal=0;

    if((pd→PD_Accs & S_IWRITE) == 0)
        return E_BMODE;

    length = regs→R_d1;
    from = regs→R_a0;


    if(pd→PD_CP + length > pd→PD_SIZ)
        SetFileSize(pd, pd→PD_CP + length);                         /* pg. 439 */

    if((Sector = WritePrepare(pd,1)) >= T_FAT_BADTRACK)             /* pg. 440 */
        return(E_FULL));

    offset = OffsetInSector(pd);                                    /* pg. 435 */

    while(length > 0){
        /*
            At least part of this sector should be updated. The "interesting" data
            starts at offset from the beginning of the sector and continues for length
            bytes, or to the end of the sector (whichever is least).
        */
        PartialLength = SECTORSIZE − offset;
        if(PartialLength > length)
```

C.2. MAIN ENTRY POINTS

```
                    PartialLength = length;
                length -= PartialLength;
                /*
                    Adjust the file length if necessary
                */
                if((Sector = WritePrepare(pd, PartialLength))    /* pg. 440 */
                        >= T_FAT_BADTRACK)
                    return(E_FULL);

                /*
                    Copy the data from the caller's buffer
                */
                RawReadSector(pd, Sector, pd→PD_BUF,             /* pg. 469 */
                    regs, procd, SysGlobs);
                pd→PD_CP += PartialLength;    /* Update current position in pd */
                if(pd→PD_SMF & PD_DIR_MODE) {
                    if(WriteIntoDir(offset, PartialLength,       /* pg. 479 */
                            pd→PD_BUF+offset, from) != 0)
                        return -1;           /* ad hoc error msg */
                } else{
                    MoveData(pd→PD_BUF+offset, from, PartialLength);
                    from += PartialLength;
                }

                if((ReturnVal = WriteSector(pd, Sector, pd→PD_BUF,  /* pg. 471 */
                        regs, procd, SysGlobs)) != 0)
                    break;
                offset = 0;
            }
            if(ReturnVal == 0)
                if(pd→PD_CP > pd→PD_SIZ)
                    return SetFileSize(pd, pd→PD_CP);            /* pg. 439 */
            return ReturnVal;
        }


SetFileSize(pd, length)
register PD_TYPE pd;
register ulong length;
{
    register int RVal;

    if((RVal = FATSetFileLength(pd, length)) == 0)               /* pg. 484 */
        DirSetFileLength(pd, length);                            /* pg. 465 */
```

```
      return RVal;
}


WritePrepare(pd, length)
register PD_TYPE pd;
register ushort length;
{
   register ulong Sector;
   register ulong n;

   if(pd→PD_SMF & PD_DIR_MODE)
      return W_PrepareDir(pd, length);                          /* pg. 440 */
   else{
      n = SectorInFile(pd→PD_CP, pd→PD_SMF);                    /* pg. 486 */
      if((Sector = SectorOnDisk(pd, n)) >= (T_FAT_BADTRACK))    /* pg. 486 */
         if(Errno(Sector) == E_EOF)                             /* pg. 481 */
            if(FATSetFileLength(pd, pd→PD_SIZ) != 0)            /* pg. 484 */
               return T_FAT_LASTSECTOR;
            else
               Sector = SectorOnDisk(pd, n);                    /* pg. 486 */
      if(pd→PD_CP > pd→PD_SIZ)
         DirSetFileLength(pd, pd→PD_CP);                        /* pg. 465 */
      return(Sector);
   }
}


W_PrepareDir(pd, length)
register PD_TYPE pd;
register ushort length;
{
   register ulong Sector;
   register ulong n;

   n = SectorInFile(pd→PD_CP, pd→PD_SMF);                       /* pg. 486 */
   if((Sector = SectorOnDisk(pd, n)) >= (T_FAT_BADTRACK))       /* pg. 486 */
      if(Errno(Sector) == E_EOF)                                /* pg. 481 */
         if(FATSetFileLength(pd, pd→PD_CP+length) != 0)         /* pg. 484 */
            return T_FAT_LASTSECTOR;
         else
            Sector = SectorOnDisk(pd, n);                       /* pg. 486 */
   return(Sector);
}
```

C.2. MAIN ENTRY POINTS

C.2.4 WriteLn.c

WriteLn() operates under the foolish assumption that nobody will use I$WritLn to update a directory entry. It doesn't check for directory-write mode.

```
#include <errno.h>
#include <procid.h>
#include <modes.h>
typedef char *POINTER;
#include "format.h"
#include "PathDesc.h"

WriteLn(pd, regs, procd, SysGlobs)
register PD_TYPE pd;
REGS regs;
{
    unsigned long length, i, j;
    unsigned long Sector;
    unsigned short offset;
    char *from, *ptr;
    int ReturnVal=0;
    int eol;

    if((pd→PD_Accs & S_IWRITE) == 0)
        return E_BMODE;

    length = regs→R_d1;
    from = regs→R_a0;
    regs→R_d1 = 0;


    if(pd→PD_CP + length > pd→PD_SIZ)
        SetFileSize(pd, pd→PD_CP + length);                   /* pg. 439 */

    if((Sector = WritePrepare(pd, 1)) >= T_FAT_BADTRACK)      /* pg. 440 */
        return(E_FULL));
    offset = OffsetInSector(pd);                              /* pg. 435 */

    eol = FALSE;
    while((length > 0) && !eol){
```

---

† *write*: see page 274

```
    /*
        At least part of this sector should be updated from the caller's buffer.
        The "interesting" data starts at offset from the beginning of the sector
        and continues for length bytes, or to the end of the sector (whichever
        is least).
    */
    i = SECTORSIZE - offset;
    if(i>length)
        i = length;

    if((Sector = WritePrepare(pd, i)) >= T_FAT_BADTRACK)        /* pg. 440 */
        return(E_FULL);
    RawReadSector(pd, Sector, pd→PD_BUF, regs, procd,           /* pg. 469 */
            SysGlobs);
    /*
        Copy the data from the caller's buffer
    */

    for(ptr = pd→PD_BUF+offset, j=0 ; j<i ; ++j)
        if(*from != pd→PD_NewLine)
            *ptr++ = *from++;
        else{
            *ptr++ = '\n';
            eol = TRUE;
            ++j;
            break;
        }
    length -= j;
    pd→PD_CP += j;          /* Update current position in pd */
    regs→R_d1 += j;         /* Update the amount written */
    if((ReturnVal = WriteSector(pd, Sector, pd→PD_BUF,          /* pg. 471 */
            regs, procd, SysGlobs)) != 0)
        break;

    offset = 0;
    }
    if(ReturnVal == 0)
        if(pd→PD_CP > pd→PD_SIZ)
            return SetFileSize(pd, pd→PD_CP);                   /* pg. 439 */

    return ReturnVal;
}
```

C.2.5 MsOpen.c

The MsOpen.c file contains the open() function and a number of closely-related service functions. The Open() function serves the *I$Open* SVC. The FindFile() function is used by Open(), and all the functions that initialize a path descriptor (e.g., Create(), Delete(), and Makdir()).

FindFile initializes a path descriptor as far as it can without binding it to a file. When preliminary initialization is finished, FindFile() parses the file name and locates it on the disk. It finishes by checking for protection violations and setting the file's access mode.

The outline of FindFile() is:

>   if file-name-independent path initialization succeeds
>   write the FAT cached in device static storage
>   if Reset the drive table entry is successful
>   if Reload of the FAT is successful
>   if the file name is valid
>   find it on the disk
>   if the file is found
>   if the caller has access rights
>   set the file access mode
>   return success

When this function is called by Create() or MakDir()—functions that need not find the file they are trying to open—it returns a path descriptor that is initialized as far as putting the parsed file name into the path descriptor, and an error code describing its failure mode. When it is called by Open(), it returns a fully initialized path descriptor.

The name-parsing rules used by ParseName() are more rigid than are necessary. PC-DOS does not restrict file names to alphanumeric characters.

```
#include <errno.h>
#include <procid.h>
#include <modes.h>
typedef char *POINTER;
#include "format.h"
#include "PathDesc.h"

#define OS9_WRITE 0x02
#define OS9_DIR 0x080
```

---

† *open*: see page 268

```
char *CopyToken();
char *CopyFName();
char *GetName();

Open(pd, regs, procd, SysGlobs)
register PD_TYPE pd;
register REGS regs;
{
   register int RVal;

   if(pd→PD_CNT > 1) return 0;                          /* The path's already open.  */

   if((RVal = FindFile(pd, regs, procd, SysGlobs)) != 0)   /* pg. 444 */
      Close(pd, regs, procd, SysGlobs);                    /* pg. 453 */
   return RVal;
}


FindFile(pd, regs, procd, SysG)
register PD_TYPE pd;
register REGS regs;
{
   register int RVal;

   if((RVal = InitPD(pd)) == 0){                        /* pg. 444 */
      FlushDevice(pd, procd, SysG);                     /* pg. 489 */
      if((RVal = ReadSector(pd, 0,                      /* pg. 469 */
            pd→PD_BUF, regs, procd, SysG)) == 0)
         if((RVal = ReadFAT(pd, regs, procd, SysG)) == 0)   /* pg. 487 */
            if((RVal = ParseName(pd, regs, procd, SysG)) == 0)   /* pg. 445 */
               if((RVal = CheckSecurity(pd, (uchar)regs→R_d0))   /* pg. 446 */
                     ==0)
                  pd→PD_Accs = regs→R_d0;
   }
   return RVal;
}

/*
   Initialize the path descriptor.
*/
InitPD(pd)
register PD_TYPE pd;
{
   if((pd→PD_BUF =                                      /* pg. 429 */
```

C.2. MAIN ENTRY POINTS   445

```
              (char *)_srqmem(SECTORSIZE)) == (char *)-1)
        return E_MEMFUL;
    if((pd→PD_FDBUF =                                              /* pg. 429 */
              (MSDirE)_srqmem(SECTORSIZE)) == (MSDirE)-1)
        return E_MEMFUL;

    pd→PD_DVT = (POINTER)pd→PD_DEV;
    pd→PD_SMF = 0;
    pd→PD_DTB = &(pd→PD_DEV→V_STAT→V_DRIVES[pd→PD_DRV]);
    pd→PD_CP = 0;                                    /* current offset in file */
    pd→PD_Accs = S_IREAD | S_IFDIR;

    return 0;
}
```

```
/*
   Get the file name from *R_a0, Ensure that it is in the msdos name.ext
   form and put the resulting name/extension into PD_Name.
*/

ParseName(pd, regs, procd, SysGlobs)
register PD_TYPE pd;
REGS regs;
{
    register char *Name;
    register char *NextName;
    int RVal;
    boolean InTree;
    char Delim;

    NextName = regs→R_a0;
    if((Delim = *NextName) == PATHDELIM)
        ++NextName;

    InTree = FALSE;
    RVal = 0;

    do {
        Name = NextName;
        if((NextName = GetName(pd, Name, &RVal)) == NULL)          /* pg. 447 */
            return RVal;

        if(!InTree){
```

```
            InTree = TRUE;
            SetRootDir(pd, procd, Delim);                           /* pg. 462 */
            if((RVal = CheckAccess(pd, regs→R_d0)) != 0)            /* pg. 446 */
                break;
            if(Delim == PATHDELIM)
                continue;
        }

        if((RVal = DirLookup(pd, regs, procd, SysGlobs)) == 0){     /* pg. 459 */
            if((RVal = CheckAccess(pd, regs→R_d0)) == 0)            /* pg. 446 */
                continue;
        } else if(RVal == E_EOF)
            RVal = E_PNNF;

        return RVal;
    } while(*NextName > ' ');


    regs→R_a0 = NextName;
    return 0;
}


CheckAccess(pd, AccessMode)
register PD_TYPE pd;
ulong AccessMode;
{
    /* If rawmode, only give superuser write access */
    /* Everyone gets read access through the end of the root directory */
    if((pd→PD_SMF & PD_RAWMODE) && (AccessMode & OS9_WRITE)){
        if(GetUser() == 0)                                          /* pg. 430 */
            return 0;
        else
            return E_FNA;
    }
    return 0;
}


CheckSecurity(pd, mode)
register PD_TYPE pd;
register uchar mode;
{
    register uchar x;
```

C.2. MAIN ENTRY POINTS

```
        if(!(pd→PD_SMF & PD_RAWMODE) &&
            ((pd→PD_SMF & PD_DIR_MODE) || (mode & S_IFDIR)) &&
            !((pd→PD_SMF & PD_DIR_MODE) && (mode & S_IFDIR)))
          return E_FNA;
        x = pd→PD_ATT & (S_IFDIR | S_IWRITE | S_IREAD);
        if((x | mode) != x)    /*no public/private distinction */
          return E_FNA;
        return 0;
}


static char *GetName(pd, Name, RVal)
register PD_TYPE pd;
register char *Name;
int *RVal;
{
        *pd→PD_Name = '\0';   /*Initialize */

        Name = CopyFName(pd→PD_Name, Name);                         /* pg. 448 */
        if(islegal(*Name)){ /*Names more than 8 characters long are bad */   /* pg. 467 */
          *RVal = E_BPNAM;
          return(NULL);
        }

        if(strcmp(pd→PD_Name, "..") == 0)
          return Name;   /*Stop after . . */

        if(*Name == '.'){   /*Non-null extension */
          Name = CopyToken(pd→PD_Name, Name, 4);                    /* pg. 448 */
          if(islegal(*Name)){  /*extensions are limited to 3 characters */  /* pg. 467 */
            *RVal = E_BPNAM;
            return(NULL);
          }
        }

        switch(*Name){
          case ENTIRE_DELIM:
            pd→PD_SMF |= PD_RAWMODE;
            /*Fall through intentionally */
          case PATHDELIM:
            ++Name;
            break;
          default:
```

```
            break;
    }

    return Name;
}


char *CopyToken(to, from, length)
register char *to, *from;
register int length;
{
    while(*to) ++to; /*skip to 0 */

    if(*from == '.'){
        *to++ = *from++;
        length--;
    }

    for(; length > 0; length--)
        if(islegal(*from))                                      /* pg. 467 */
            *to++ = toupper(*from++);                           /* pg. 467 */
        else
            *to++ = '\0';

    *to = '\0';
    return from;
}


char *CopyFName(to, from)
register char *to, *from;
{
    register int length=8;

    if(*from == PATHDELIM)
        ++from;
    if(*from == '.'){                                           /* One dot          */
        *to++ = *from++;
        length--;
        if(*from == '.'){                                       /* Two dots         */
            *to++ = *from++;
            length--;
            if(*from == '.'){                                   /* More dots        */
                *to = '\0';
```

C.2. MAIN ENTRY POINTS 449

```
                return (from − 1);
            }
        }
        *to = '\0';
    }

    return CopyToken(to, from, length);                              /* pg. 448 */
}
```

C.2.6 Create.c

```
#include <errno.h>
#include <procid.h>
#include <modes.h>

typedef char *POINTER;

#include "format.h"
#include "PathDesc.h"

Create(pd, regs, procd, SysGlobs)
register PD_TYPE pd;
register REGS regs;
{
    register int RVal;

    switch(RVal = FindFile(pd, regs, procd, SysGlobs)){             /* pg. 444 */
        case E_PNNF:   /*A new file. We can create it */
            /*Build a directory entry. */
            if(regs→R_d1 & S_IFDIR)    /*a directory */
                pd→PD_SMF |= PD_DIR_MODE;
            RVal = MakDirEntry(pd, regs, procd, SysGlobs);          /* pg. 463 */
            break;
        case 0:    /*An old file that we can access.  */
            /*Empty it and return as if we just opened */
            RVal = SetFileSize(pd, 0);                              /* pg. 439 */
            break;
        default:    /*Probably not accessible. Return the error code */
            break;
    }
    if(Rval){
```

---

† *create*: see page 272

```
            CLEANFD(pd);                           /* Don't update the fd for this file. */
            Close(pd, regs, procd, SysGlobs);                              /* pg. 453 */
            return RVal;
        }
    }
```

C.2.7 MakDir.c

PC-DOS directories are allocated a sector at a time. They don't have a specified length, so the directory sectors must be initialized with null directory entries when they are allocated.

```
#include <errno.h>
#include <procid.h>
#include <modes.h>
typedef char *POINTER;
#include "format.h"
#include "PathDesc.h"

#define INIT_DIR_SIZE(pd) ((pd)→PD_SAS*2*(pd)→PD_DTB→DD_SPC)

MakDir(pd, regs, procd, SysGlobs)
register PD_TYPE pd;
register REGS regs;
{
    int RVal;
    register ushort i;
    register uchar *ptr;
    REGISTERS RegsCopy;
    MSDirEntry DirEntry;

    /* Create the file in directory mode.                              */

    RegsCopy = *regs;
    RegsCopy.R_d1 |= S_IFDIR;         /*Make this create into directory mode */
    RegsCopy.R_d0 |= S_IWRITE;

    if((RVal = Create(pd, &RegsCopy, procd, SysGlobs)) != 0)           /* pg. 449 */
        return RVal;
    regs→R_a0 = RegsCopy.R_a0;
```

---

†*makdir*: see page 272

C.2. MAIN ENTRY POINTS 451

```
    if(FATSetFileLength(pd,                                    /* pg. 484 */
        (ulong)(INIT_DIR_SIZE(pd)*SECTORSIZE)) >= FAT_BADTRACK)
       RVal = E_FULL;    /*media full */
    else
       RVal = 0;

    /* Set up a directory entry for .                          */

    if(RVal == 0){
       MakDotDir(&DirEntry, pd);                               /* pg. 452 */
       RVal = MakDirBlanks(&DirEntry, 1, pd,                   /* pg. 451 */
           &RegsCopy, procd, SysGlobs);
    }

    /* Patch the . entry into a . . entry.                     */

    if(RVal == 0){
       DirEntry.FileName[1] = '.';
       change_sex_2ia(DirEntry.StartCluster, pd→PD_Parent);    /* pg. 468 */
       RVal = MakDirBlanks(&DirEntry, 1, pd,                   /* pg. 451 */
           &RegsCopy, procd, SysGlobs);
    }

    /* Fill the rest of the directory with empty entries.      */

    if(RVal == 0){
       for(ptr=(uchar*)&DirEntry, i=sizeof(DirEntry); i>0; i——)
          *ptr++ = '\0';

       RVal = MakDirBlanks(&DirEntry,                          /* pg. 451 */
           (int)(INIT_DIR_SIZE(pd)*(SECTORSIZE/sizeof(DirEntry))—2),
           pd, &RegsCopy, procd, SysGlobs);

       DirSetFileLength(pd, 0L);    /*Directories show zero length */   /* pg. 465 */
    }

    Close(pd, regs, procd, SysGlobs);                          /* pg. 453 */
    return RVal;
}


MakDirBlanks(DirEntry, n, pd, regs, procd, SysGlobs)
register MSDirE DirEntry;
register int n;
```

```
    register PD_TYPE pd;
    register REGS regs;
{
    int RVal;
    register uchar *ptr;
    register short i;

    regs→R_a0 = (char *)DirEntry;
    regs→R_d1 = sizeof(*DirEntry);


    for(RVal = 0; n > 0; n−−)
        if((RVal = Write(pd, regs, procd, SysGlobs)) != 0)              /* pg. 438 */
            break;
    return RVal;
}


MakDotDir(DirEntry, pd)
register MSDirE DirEntry;
register PD_TYPE pd;
{
    register uchar *ptr;
    register short i;

    for(ptr = (uchar *)DirEntry, i = sizeof(*DirEntry); i > 0; i−−)
        *ptr++ = '\0';
    DirEntry→FileName[0] = '.';

    for(i=1;i<8; ++i)
        DirEntry→FileName[i] = ' ';
    for(i=0;i<3; ++i)
        DirEntry→FileExtension[i] = ' ';

    DirEntry→FileAttr = MS_SUBDIR;
    change_sex_2ia(DirEntry→StartCluster,pd→PD_FCluster);               /* pg. 468 */
}
```

C.2.8 Close.c

The Close() function has two roles:

---

†*close*: see page 271

C.2. MAIN ENTRY POINTS

- It writes dirty cached data to the disk—the file descriptor image and the FAT.

- It frees the memory InitPD() allocated for the path.

```
typedef unsigned short ushort;
typedef char *POINTER;

#include "format.h"
#include "PathDesc.h"

Close(pd, regs, procd, SysGlobs)
register PD_TYPE pd;
REGS regs;
{
    register DriveTableType *DriveTable;

    DriveTable = pd→PD_DTB;

    if(pd→PD_SMF & PD_DIRTYFD)
        UpdateFD(pd, regs, procd, SysGlobs);                    /* pg. 464 */

    if(DriveTable→V_FATDirty)
        WriteFAT(pd, regs, procd, SysGlobs);                    /* pg. 488 */

    if(pd→PD_CNT == 0){     /* Is anyone still using this path? */
        if(pd→PD_BUF != 0)  /* Is there a buffer for this path? */
            DoSRtMem(pd→PD_BUF, SECTORSIZE);    /* Free it */   /* pg. 430 */
        pd→PD_BUF = NULL;

        if(pd→PD_FDBUF != 0)   /* Is there an FD buffer for this path? */
            DoSRtMem(pd→PD_FDBUF, SECTORSIZE);                  /* pg. 430 */
        pd→PD_FDBUF = NULL;
        FreeFAT(DriveTable);                                    /* pg. 489 */
    }

    return 0;
}
```

C.2.9 Delete.c

---

†*delete*: see page 273

Delete opens the file to ensure that it exists, the caller has write access to it, and so forth. The open also saves the location of the directory entry in the path descriptor. The actual deletion is done by the Close() function. Delete() primes the path descriptor by giving the file a zero length, freeing FAT entries as required, and changing the file name to ERASED in the path descriptor.

```
typedef unsigned short ushort;
typedef void *POINTER;
#include "format.h"
#include "PathDesc.h"

Delete(pd, regs, procd, SysGlobs)
register PD_TYPE pd;
REGS regs;
{
    int RVal;

    /*
        It would be consistent with OS-9 policy to refuse to delete a directory file.
    */
    /* Open the file for read */
    if((RVal = Open(pd, regs, procd, SysGlobs)) != 0)          /* pg. 444 */
        return RVal;

    /* Shorten the file to zero */
    FATSetFileLength(pd, 0L);    /* Free the entire file */     /* pg. 484 */

    /*
        Write a $E5 into the first byte of the file name in the directory. This
        signifies that the file has been erased.
    */
    *(pd→PD_Name) = FILERASED;
    DIRTYFD(pd);
    Close(pd, regs, procd, SysGlobs);                           /* pg. 453 */
    return 0;
}
```

C.2.10   Msfm.c

Most of the functions in this file are "easy." Seek() is certainly the simplest function this file manager implements. It is supposed to update the current position in the file.

[†] *seek*: see page 269

C.2. MAIN ENTRY POINTS

It does that—in one statement—and returns.

The ChgDir() function finds the requested directory and saves information in the process descriptor. FindFile() can use the the data saved by ChgDir() to find the default directories on the disk. IOMan has already taken care of saving the default *device*.

```
#include <errno.h>
#include <procid.h>
#include <modes.h>
#include <sg_codes.h>
#include <direct.h>

typedef char *POINTER;

#include "format.h"
#include "PathDesc.h"


ChgDir(pd, regs, procd, SysGlobs)
 register PD_TYPE pd;
procid *procd;
REGS regs;
{
    int RVal;
    register DefaultDescriptor *dptr;

    regs→R_d0 |= S_IFDIR;                           /* Call for directory mode */
    if((RVal = Open(pd, regs, procd, SysGlobs)) != 0)   /* pg. 444 */
        return RVal;

    dptr = (DefaultDescriptor *)procd→_dio;
    if(regs→R_d0 & S_IEXEC)
        ++dptr;

    dptr→DirCluster = pd→PD_FCluster;

    Close(pd, regs, procd, SysGlobs);               /* pg. 453 */
    return 0;
}


Seek(pd, regs, procd, SysGlobs)
register PD_TYPE pd;
register REGS regs;
```

```
{
    pd→PD_CP = regs→R_d1;
    return 0;
}



GetStat(pd, regs, procd, SysGlobs)
register PD_TYPE pd;
register REGS regs;
{
    short limit;
    int RVal;

    switch((ushort)regs→R_d1){
        case SS_Size:
            regs→R_d2 = pd→PD_SIZ;
            break;
        case SS_Pos:
            regs→R_d2 = pd→PD_CP;
            break;
        case SS_EOF:
            if(pd→PD_CP >= pd→PD_SIZ)
                return E_EOF;
            else
                regs→R_d1 = 0;
            break;
        case SS_FDInf:
            if((RVal = GetFD(pd, regs, procd, SysGlobs, regs→R_d3)) != 0)      /* pg. 475 */
                return RVal;
            /*Drop through */
        case SS_FD:
            limit = regs→R_d2;
            if(limit > 256)
                return E_UNKSVC;
            MoveData(regs→R_a0, &(pd→PD_FD), limit);                            /* pg. 431 */
            break;
        case SS_Opt:
            break;
        case SS_DevNm:
            break;
        default:
            return DriverGetStat(pd, regs, procd, SysGlobs);                    /* pg. 458 */
    }
}
```

C.2. MAIN ENTRY POINTS

```
      return 0;
}


SetStat(pd, regs, procd, SysGlobs)
register PD_TYPE pd;
register REGS regs;
register procid *procd;
{
   int RVal;
   REGISTERS CopyRegs;

   switch((ushort)regs→R_d1){
      case SS_Size:
         return SetFileSize(pd, regs→R_d2);                        /* pg. 439 */
      case SS_FD:    /* Write FD sector */
         return WriteFD(pd, regs→R_a0, procd→_user);               /* pg. 457 */
      case SS_Attr:  /* Set the file attributes */
         DirSetFileAttr(pd, regs→R_d2);                            /* pg. 466 */
         break;
      case SS_Opt:   /* This is ioman's business */
         break;
      case SS_Reset:
      case SS_WTrk:  /* Not supported here. Pass it
                       to the device driver */
      default:
         return DriverSetStat(pd, regs, procd, SysGlobs);          /* pg. 458 */
   }
   return 0;
}


static WriteFD(pd, fd, User)
register PD_TYPE pd;
register struct fildes *fd;
short User;
{
   if(pd→PD_Accs & S_IWRITE){
      DirSetFileDate(pd, fd→fd_date);                              /* pg. 465 */
      DirSetCrDate(pd, fd→fd_dcr);                                 /* pg. 465 */
      if(User == 0)
         DirSetFileOwner(pd, *(ushort *)(fd→fd_own));              /* pg. 465 */
      return 0;
   }else
```

```
        return E_BMODE;
}


DriverSetStat(pd, regs, procd, SysGlobs)
register PD_TYPE pd;
register REGS regs;
register procid *procd;
{
   int RVal;
   register STATICSTORETYPE DevStatic;

   DevStatic = pd→PD_DEV→V_STAT;

   /* Wait for the device to be idle */
     while(DevStatic→V_BUSY) DoIOQ(DevStatic→V_BUSY);         /* pg. 430 */
   DevStatic→V_BUSY = pd→PD_CPR;

   RVal = CallSetStat(regs→R_d1, pd, pd→PD_DEV→V_STAT,        /* pg. 429 */
        procd, regs, SysGlobs);

   DevStatic→V_BUSY = 0;    /*device not busy */

   return RVal;
}


DriverGetStat(pd, regs, procd, SysGlobs)
register PD_TYPE pd;
register REGS regs;
{
   int RVal;
   register STATICSTORETYPE DevStatic;

   DevStatic = pd→PD_DEV→V_STAT;

   /* Wait for the device to be idle */
   while(DevStatic→V_BUSY) DoIOQ(DevStatic→V_BUSY);
   DevStatic→V_BUSY = pd→PD_CPR;

   RVal = CallGetStat(regs→R_d1, pd, pd→PD_DEV→V_STAT,        /* pg. 428 */
        procd, regs, SysGlobs);

   DevStatic→V_BUSY = 0;    /*device not busy */
```

```
        return RVal;
}
```

C.3 Service Functions

The service functions are called by the main functions. The functions in this group are distinguished by the separate files into which they are grouped. Some service functions share a file with one of the file manager's main entry points. The functions in this section are shared by several of the main functions.

C.3.1 Dir

The functions in the file, dir.c, manipulate directory files. There are functions here that search a directory for a given file name or an empty entry. Other functions update the virtual file descriptor in the path descriptor and update the directory entry on disk.

A large part of the action of FindFile is encapsulated in DirEntryFound(). This function applies information from (and about) a directory entry to the path descriptor.

MakDirEntry() handles most of the work for Create().

```
#include <errno.h>
#include <procid.h>
#include <modes.h>
#include <direct.h>
typedef char *POINTER;
#include "format.h"
#include "PathDesc.h"

void SetRootDir();


#define HUGE 0xFFFFFFFF; /*BIG number ... unsigned */

DirLookup(pd, regs, procd, SysGlobs)
register PD_TYPE pd;
{
    struct dirent DirEntry;
    register int RVal;
```

---

†*makdirentry*: see page 463

```
    if(pd→PD_SMF & PD_RAWMODE){
        pd→PD_SIZ = HUGE;
        return(0);
    }

    pd→PD_Parent = pd→PD_FCluster;

    /*
        A special case: If the current directory is the root directory, the parent
        is also the root directory even though no parent is given in the directory
        structure.
    */
    if(pd→PD_SMF & PD_RDIR_MODE)
        if((NameMatch(".", pd→PD_Name) == 0) ||                /* pg. 460 */
            (NameMatch("..", pd→PD_Name) == 0)){
            SetRootDir(pd, procd, PATHDELIM);                   /* pg. 462 */
            pd→PD_CP = 0;
            return 0;
        }

        while(ReadEntry(&DirEntry, pd, procd, SysGlobs) == 0)   /* pg. 463 */
            if(NameMatch(DirEntry.dir_name, pd→PD_Name) == 0){  /* pg. 460 */
                if((RVal = GetFD(pd, regs, procd,               /* pg. 475 */
                    SysGlobs, DirEntry.dir_addr)) != 0)
                    return RVal;
                return DirEntryFound(pd, &DirEntry, procd);     /* pg. 461 */
            } else if(DirEntry.dir_addr == 0)  /*no further entries */
                break;

        return E_PNNF;
    }

NameMatch(Name1, Name2)
register char *Name1, *Name2;
{
    /*empty name: match empty or erased */
    if((*Name2 == '\0') || (*Name2 == '\345'))
        if((*Name1 == '\0') || (*Name1 == '\345'))
            return 0;    /*a match */
        else
            return 1;    /*no match */

    return (ncstrcmp(Name1, Name2));
}
```

C.3. SERVICE FUNCTIONS

```
DirEntryFound(pd, DirEntry, procd)
register PD_TYPE pd;
register struct dirent *DirEntry;
{
   pd→PD_FDSector = pd→PD_CSector;
   pd→PD_DCP = pd→PD_CP − sizeof(MSDirEntry);
   pd→PD_FDOffset = FDOFFSET(DirEntry→dir_addr);
   pd→PD_ATT = pd→PD_FD.vfd_att;
   pd→PD_FCluster = array_to_int(pd→PD_FD.vfd_cluster,2);
   pd→PD_SIZ = array_to_int(pd→PD_FD.vfd_fsize, 4);
   pd→PD_CP = 0;
   if(pd→PD_ATT & S_IFDIR){    /*a directory */
      pd→PD_SMF |= PD_DIR_MODE;
      if(pd→PD_FCluster == 0)
         SetRootDir(pd, procd, PATHDELIM);            /* pg. 462 */
      else{
         pd→PD_SMF &= ~PD_RDIR_MODE;
         pd→PD_SIZ = HUGE;
      }
   } else
      pd→PD_SMF &= ~(PD_DIR_MODE | PD_RDIR_MODE);
   return 0;
}


AdjustAttributes(msAttr)
register uchar msAttr;
{
   register int attr;

   attr = 0x03f;    /* %00111111 RWErwe */
   if(msAttr & 0x01)    /*read only */
      attr &= 0x2d;
   if(msAttr & 0x010)    /*directory file */
      attr |= 0x80;
   return attr;
}


ReAdjustAttributes(osAttr)
register uchar osAttr;
{
```

```
    register uchar attr;

    attr = 0;
    if(!(osAttr & 0x12))    /*read only */
        attr |= 0x01;
    if(osAttr & 0x80)    /*directory */
        attr |= 0x010;
    return attr;
}


/*
    Set up for reading the "root directory." If the path name begins with
    a slash, the root directory is the disk's root directory. If the path name
    does not begin with a slash, the root directory is a current directory.
*/
void SetRootDir(pd, procd, Delim)
register PD_TYPE pd;
procid *procd;
char Delim;
{
    pd→PD_SIZ = HUGE;
    if(Delim == PATHDELIM)
        pd→PD_SMF |= (PD_RDIR_MODE | PD_DIR_MODE);    /*root Dir*/
    else {
        register DefaultDescriptor *dptr;

        dptr = (DefaultDescriptor *)procd→_dio;
        if(pd→PD_Accs & S_IEXEC)
            ++dptr;
        if(dptr→DirCluster == 0)    /*Root Directory */
            pd→PD_SMF |= (PD_RDIR_MODE | PD_DIR_MODE);
        else {
            pd→PD_FCluster = dptr→DirCluster;
            pd→PD_SMF |= PD_DIR_MODE;
        }
    }
    if(pd→PD_SMF & PD_RDIR_MODE)
        pd→PD_FCluster = 0;    /*Root directory */

    pd→PD_ATT = AdjustAttributes(MS_SUBDIR);    /*Directory */        /* pg. 461 */
    return;
}
```

C.3. SERVICE FUNCTIONS

```
ReadEntry(Entry, pd, procd, SysGlobs)
PD_TYPE pd;
char *Entry;
{
    REGISTERS regs;

    regs.R_d1 = sizeof(MSDirEntry);
    regs.R_a0 = Entry;

    return Read(pd, &regs, procd, SysGlobs);                    /* pg. 434 */
}



FindEmpty(pd, regs, procd, SysGlobs)
register PD_TYPE pd;
{
    struct dirent DirEntry;

    pd→PD_CP = 0;
    pd→PD_SIZ = HUGE;     /* This must be a directory */
    pd→PD_SMF |= PD_DIR_MODE;

    while(ReadEntry(&DirEntry, pd, procd, SysGlobs) == 0)       /* pg. 463 */
        if(NameMatch(DirEntry.dir_name, "") == 0)               /* pg. 460 */
            return 0;
    return E_PNNF;
}



MakDirEntry(pd, regs, procd, SysGlobs)
PD_TYPE pd;
REGS regs;
procid *procd;
{
    int RVal;
    char Date[5];
    MSDirEntry DirEntry;
    short Offset;

    /*get an empty directory entry */
    if((RVal = FindEmpty(pd, regs, procd, SysGlobs)) != 0){     /* pg. 463 */
        /*did not find an empty spot */
        /*try extending the directory file */
```

```
        SYSDEBUG(5, pd);
        return RVal;
    }
    DirSetFileLength(pd, 0);                                        /* pg. 465 */
    DirSetFileOwner(pd, 0);                                         /* pg. 465 */
    DirSetFileLink(pd, 1);                                          /* pg. 465 */
    DirSetFileAttr(pd, (ushort)regs→R_d1);                          /* pg. 466 */
    GetDate(Date);
    DirSetFileDate(pd, Date);                                       /* pg. 465 */
    DirSetCrDate(pd, Date);                                         /* pg. 465 */
    DirSetFCluster(pd, FAT_LASTSECTOR);                             /* pg. 465 */
    UpdateDirEntFromPD(&DirEntry, pd);                              /* pg. 477 */
    Offset = ((pd→PD_SMF & PD_RDIR_MODE) ?
        (pd→PD_CP / sizeof(DirEntry) - 3):
        (pd→PD_CP / sizeof(DirEntry) - 1)) &
        ((SECTORSIZE / sizeof(DirEntry)) - 1);
    if((RVal = WriteDirEntry(&DirEntry, pd→PD_CSector, Offset,      /* pg. 466 */
            pd, regs, procd, SysGlobs)) != 0)
        return RVal;
    /* Set up the path descriptor for the new file */
    pd→PD_SMF = pd→PD_CP = pd→PD_SIZ = 0;
    pd→PD_FCluster = FAT_LASTSECTOR;
    pd→PD_FDOffset = Offset;
    pd→PD_FDSector = pd→PD_CSector;
    pd→PD_Accs = regs→R_d0;
    return 0;
}


UpdateFD(pd, regs, procd, SysGlobs)
register PD_TYPE pd;
{
    char Date[5];
    MSDirEntry DirEntry;

#ifdef ALWAYS_STAMP
    GetDate(Date);
    DirSetFileDate(pd, Date);                                       /* pg. 465 */
#endif ALWAYS_STAMP
    UpdateDirEntFromPD(&DirEntry, pd);                              /* pg. 477 */
    CLEANFD(pd);

    return (WriteDirEntry(&DirEntry, pd→PD_FDSector,                /* pg. 466 */
        pd→PD_FDOffset, pd, regs, procd, SysGlobs));
```

C.3. SERVICE FUNCTIONS

```
}


DirSetFileOwner(pd, owner)
register PD_TYPE pd;
register int owner;
{
    int_to_array(pd→PD_FD.vfd_own, owner, 2);
}


DirSetFileLink(pd, link)
register PD_TYPE pd;
register int link;
{
    pd→PD_FD.vfd_link = link;
}


DirSetFileDate(pd, Date)
register PD_TYPE pd;
register char Date[5];
{
    _strass(pd→PD_FD.vfd_date, Date, 5);
}


DirSetCrDate(pd, Date)
register PD_TYPE pd;
register char Date[5];
{
    _strass(pd→PD_FD.vfd_dcr, Date, 3);
}


DirSetFCluster(pd, Cluster)
register PD_TYPE pd;
register ushort Cluster;
{
    int_to_array(pd→PD_FD.vfd_cluster, Cluster, 2);
}


DirSetFileLength(pd, length)
```

register PD_TYPE pd;
register long length;
{
    int_to_array(pd→PD_FD.vfd_fsize, length, 4);
    pd→PD_SIZ = length;
    DIRTYFD(pd);
}

DirSetFileAttr(pd, Attr)
register PD_TYPE pd;
register short Attr;
{
    pd→PD_FD.vfd_att = Attr;
    pd→PD_ATT = Attr;
    DIRTYFD(pd);
}

WriteDirEntry(DirEntry, Sector, Offset, pd, regs, procd, SysGlobs)
register MSDirE DirEntry;
long Sector;
register short Offset;
register PD_TYPE pd;
{
    register MSDirE DirPtr;
    int RVal;

    if(Sector < 5) SYSDEBUG(2, Sector);

    /* This sector may be in the buffer — translated */
    /* Get it again */
    if((RVal = RawReadSector(pd, Sector, pd→PD_BUF,   /* pg. 469 */
        regs, procd, SysGlobs)) != 0){
      SYSDEBUG(Sector, pd); /* bad trouble */
      return(RVal);
    }

    DirPtr = ((MSDirE)pd→PD_BUF) + Offset;
    *DirPtr = *DirEntry;

C.3. SERVICE FUNCTIONS

```
        if((RVal = RawWriteSector(pd, Sector, pd→PD_BUF,         /* pg. 471 */
                regs, procd, SysGlobs)) != 0){
            SYSDEBUG(Sector, pd);   /*bad trouble */
            return RVal;
        }
        return 0;
}
```

C.3.2   Utils

```
strncmp(s1, s2, n)
register char *s1, *s2;
register int n;
{
    for(; n> 0; n−−)
        if(*s1++ != *s2++)
            return (*(s1−1) − *(s2−1));
    return 0;
}


ncstrcmp(s1, s2) /* Case independent comparison */
register char *s1, *s2;
{
    while(*s2)
        if(toupper(*s1++) != toupper(*s2++))               /* pg. 467 */
            return(*(s1−1) − *(s2−1));
    return(*s1);
}


toupper(c)
register char c;
{
    c &= 0x7F;
    return (((c >='a') && (c <= 'z')) ? (c & 0x005f) : c);
}


islegal(c)
{
    return (((c >= 'a') && (c <= 'z')) ||
        ((c >= 'A') && (c <= 'Z')) ||
```

```
        ((c >= '0') && (c <= '9')) ||
        (c == '_') || (c == '-') || (c == '$'));
}


u_bound_div(a,b)    /* Upper bound of quotient. */
register unsigned long a;
register int b;
{
    return ((a+b-1)/b);
}


array_to_int(a,l)   /* Convert an array of bytes to an int */
register unsigned char *a;
register unsigned short l;
{
    register int acc;

    for(acc=0;l>0;--l)
        acc = (acc << 8) + *a++;
    return acc;
}




int_to_array(a,i,len)
register unsigned char *a;          /* The array. May not be aligned */
unsigned int i;                     /* The integer. Aligned */
register int len;
{
    register unsigned char *ptr;

    ptr = (unsigned char *)&i;
    len = sizeof(int) - len;
    for(;len<sizeof(int);++len)
        *a++ = ptr[len];
}


change_sex_2ia(a,b)                 /* change byte order and convert short to array of bytes */
register unsigned char *a;
int b;
{
    a[0]= (unsigned char)b;
```

C.3. SERVICE FUNCTIONS

```
    a[1]= (unsigned char)(b >> 8);
}
```

C.3.3 ReadSector

This file contains the low-level interface to the device driver's read-sector entry. ReadSector contains part of the code that makes PC-DOS directories look like OS-9 directories. Note that RawReadSector() is careful to mark sectors that haven't been through the PC-DOS to OS-9 mapping not-good. This prevents raw PC-DOS directories from being cached and used as if they had been mapped.

The loop that calls DoIOQ() before the read is important. This is where paths queue up for access to a device.

```
#include <errno.h>
#include <procid.h>
typedef char *POINTER;
#include "format.h"
#include "PathDesc.h"

RawReadSector(pd, Sector, buffer, regs, procd, SysGlobs)
register PD_TYPE pd;
ulong Sector;
char *buffer;
{
    uchar HoldSMF;
    int RVal;

    HoldSMF = pd→PD_SMF;
    pd→PD_SMF = PD_RAWMODE;
    RVal= ReadSector(pd, Sector, buffer, regs, procd, SysGlobs);      /* pg. 469 */
    pd→PD_SMF = HoldSMF & ~PD_GOODBUF;
    return RVal;
}


ReadSector(pd, Sector, buffer, regs, procd, SysGlobs)
register PD_TYPE pd;
register ulong Sector;
register char *buffer;
REGS regs;
{
    int ReturnVal;
```

```
    char *HoldBuffer;
    register STATICSTORETYPE DevStatic;

    if((Sector == pd→PD_CSector) && (pd→PD_SMF & PD_GOODBUF))
        return 0;

    DevStatic = pd→PD_DEV→V_STAT;

    /* Wait for the device to be idle */
    while(DevStatic→V_BUSY) DoIOQ(DevStatic→V_BUSY);            /* pg. 430 */
    DevStatic→V_BUSY = pd→PD_CPR;

    /* The supplied buffer might not be the one in the path descriptor */
    HoldBuffer = pd→PD_BUF;
    pd→PD_BUF = buffer;

    /* Call the device driver to read a sector */
    ReturnVal = CallRead(1,   /* contig sectors */                /* pg. 427 */
        Sector,    /* sector number */
        pd,
        DevStatic,    /* device static storage */
        procd,
        regs,
        SysGlobs);

    DevStatic→V_BUSY = 0;   /* device not busy */

    pd→PD_BUF = HoldBuffer;

    /* Deal with a strangeness of the driver */
    if((Sector == 0) && (ReturnVal == E_BTYP))
        ReturnVal = 0;

    if((Sector == 0) && (ReturnVal == 0 ))
        InitFromBoot(pd, pd→PD_BUF, regs, procd, SysGlobs);       /* pg. 474 */

    /* Update the Current Sector field in the path descriptor */
    if(ReturnVal == 0){
        pd→PD_CSector = Sector;
        pd→PD_SMF |= PD_GOODBUF;
        if((pd→PD_SMF & PD_DIR_MODE) &&
            !(pd→PD_SMF & PD_RAWMODE))
            SectorMs2os9(pd, buffer);                              /* pg. 476 */
    }else
```

C.3. SERVICE FUNCTIONS

```
      pd→PD_SMF &= ~PD_GOODBUF;
   return ReturnVal;
}
```

C.3.4 WriteSector

WriteSector() implements the low-level interface to the device driver's write-sector entry.

The RawwriteSector() function pretends that some writes might pass through a OS-9 to PC-DOS mapping. It doesn't. Data must be mapped before it is passed to WriteSector().[2]

```
#include <errno.h>
#include <procid.h>
typedef char *POINTER;
#include "format.h"
#include "PathDesc.h"

RawWriteSector(pd, Sector, buffer, regs, procd, SysGlobs)
register PD_TYPE pd;
ulong Sector;
char *buffer;
{
   uchar HoldSMF;
   int RVal;

   HoldSMF = pd→PD_SMF;
   pd→PD_SMF = PD_RAWMODE;
   RVal= WriteSector(pd, Sector, buffer, regs, procd, SysGlobs);      /* pg. 471 */
   pd→PD_SMF = HoldSMF;
   return RVal;
}


WriteSector(pd, Sector, buffer, regs, procd, SysGlobs)
register PD_TYPE pd;
register int Sector;
register char *buffer;
{
   int ReturnVal;
   char *HoldBuffer;
```

---

[2]The Write() function does mapping as required.

```
    register STATICSTORETYPE DevStatic;

    DevStatic = pd→PD_DEV→V_STAT;
#ifndef WRITEBOOT
    if(Sector == 0)    /* we shouldn't be doing this */
        return 99;
#endif

    /* Wait for the device to be idle */
    while(DevStatic→V_BUSY) DoIOQ(DevStatic→V_BUSY);           /* pg. 430 */
    DevStatic→V_BUSY = pd→PD_CPR;

    /* The supplied buffer might not be the one in the path descriptor */
    HoldBuffer = pd→PD_BUF;
    pd→PD_BUF = buffer;

    /* Call the device driver to write a sector */
    ReturnVal = CallWrite(1       /* contig sectors */,        /* pg. 428 */
        Sector             /* sector number */,
        pd,
        DevStatic,         /* device static storage */
        procd,
        regs,
        SysGlobs);

    DevStatic→V_BUSY = 0;    /* device not busy */

    pd→PD_BUF = HoldBuffer;

    /* Update the Current Sector field in the path descriptor */
    if(ReturnVal == 0)
        pd→PD_CSector = Sector;
    return ReturnVal;
}
```

C.4 Artifacts of PC-DOS

A file manager contains knowledge about the file system it implements. The functions in this section do most of the PC-DOS-specific operations. This is not the place to learn about PC-DOS. I recommend the Norton book *Programmer's Guide to the IBM PC*. I used it to write this driver.

C.4. ARTIFACTS OF PC-DOS

One adjustment from the PC-DOS file structure is repeated often. The Intel 80x8x line of processors uses a different byte ordering from the Motorola 680xx line. These functions convert integers between formats.

C.4.1 Drivetable.c

The device driver updates the drive table whenever the driver is asked to read sector zero. It updates the drive table by copying the beginning of sector zero into the table. Since the beginning of the PC-DOS boot sector is nothing like an OS-9 disk ID sector, the file manager has to rework what the driver did.

This file contains functions that inspect the PC-DOS boot sector and the beginning of the FAT, and generate a drive table entry from that information.

```
#include <errno.h>
#include <procid.h>
typedef char *POINTER;
#include "format.h"
#include "PathDesc.h"

    static InitDriveTable(pd, FATStart, FATCopies, DirSize, ClusterSize,
FATSize, TrackSize, Sides, Size)
    register PD_TYPE pd;
{
    register DriveTableType *DriveTable;

    DriveTable = (DriveTableType *)pd→PD_DTB;
    int_to_array(DriveTable→DD_TOT, Size, 3);
    DriveTable→DD_TKS = TrackSize & 0x00ff;
    int_to_array(DriveTable→DD_SPT, TrackSize, 2);
    pd→PD_TOS = TrackSize;              /* Sectors-in-track-0 is the same as Tracksize */
    DriveTable→DD_FMT =
        ((Sides == 2) ? 1 : 0) +        /* 1: double sided               */
        2 +                             /* 2: always double density      */
        ((Size > 720) ? 4 : 0);         /* 4: 80 track                   */
    DriveTable→V_FATSz = FATSize;
    DriveTable→DD_DIR = FATStart + (FATSize * FATCopies);
    DriveTable→DD_FirstFAT = FATStart;
    DriveTable→DD_FATCnt = FATCopies;
    DriveTable→V_DirEntries = DirSize;
    DriveTable→DD_FATSIZ = FATSize;
    DriveTable→DD_SPC = ClusterSize;
    /*
```

The first sector of data is after the boot (1 sector), the FAT, and the directory.
*/
   DriveTable→V_DataStart = (FATSize * FATCopies) + (DirSize/16) − 2;
}

InitFromBoot(pd, BootPtr, regs, procd, SysGlobs)
PD_TYPE pd;
BootSectorType BootPtr;
{
   char *ptr;
   uchar id;
   int RVal;

   /* Make the drive table look sane. */
   InitDriveTable(pd, 2, 2, 64, 1, 1, 8, 1, 320);   /* pg. 473 */
   if((ptr = (char *)_srqmem(SECTORSIZE)) == (char *)−1){   /* pg. 429 */
      SysDebug(E_MEMFUL, pd);
      id = 0x0FD;   /*desperate attempt */
   } else {
      if((RVal = RawReadSector(pd, 1, ptr,   /* pg. 469 */
            regs, procd, SysGlobs)) != 0){
         SysDebug(RVal, pd);   /*nothing's supposed to go wrong here */
         id = 0x0FD;   /*Another deperate attempt */
      } else
         id = *ptr;
      DoSRtMem(ptr, SECTORSIZE);   /* pg. 430 */
   }

   switch(id){
      case 0xff: /*double sided 8 sector */
         InitDriveTable(pd, 2, 2, 112, 2, 1, 8, 2, 640);   /* pg. 473 */
         break;
      case 0xfe: /*single sided 8 sector */
         InitDriveTable(pd, 2, 2, 64, 1, 1, 8, 1, 320);   /* pg. 473 */
         break;
      default:
         InitDriveTable(pd,   /* pg. 473 */
            2, /*Start of FAT */
            BootPtr→FATCopies,
            (BootPtr→RootDirSize[1] << 8) + BootPtr→RootDirSize[0],
            BootPtr→SectorsPerCluster,
            (BootPtr→SectorsPerFAT[1] << 8) + BootPtr→SectorsPerFAT[0],

C.4. ARTIFACTS OF PC-DOS

```
            (BootPtr→SectorsPerTrack[1] << 8) + BootPtr→SectorsPerTrack[0],
            (BootPtr→Sides[1] << 8) + BootPtr→Sides[0],
            (BootPtr→TotSectors[1] << 8) + BootPtr→TotSectors[0]);
         break;
   }
}
```

C.4.2 GetFD.c

PC-DOS doesn't use file descriptors as such, but OS-9 insists on them. This file manager creates a virtual file descriptor whenever a file is opened. The GetFD() function builds the virtual file descriptor for the path.

```
#include <errno.h>
#include <procid.h>
typedef char *POINTER;
#include "format.h"
#include "PathDesc.h"

GetFD(pd, regs, procd, SysGlobs, fdcode)
PD_TYPE pd;
REGS regs;
ulong fdcode;
{
   int RVal;

   if(pd→PD_FDHash == fdcode)
      return 0;
   else
      if((RVal = RawReadSector(pd, (ulong)(fdcode >> 4),        /* pg. 469 */
         (char *)pd→PD_FDBUF, regs,
         procd, SysGlobs)) != 0)
            return RVal;

   Dir2FD(&pd→PD_FD,                                            /* pg. 476 */
      ((MSDirE)pd→PD_FDBUF) + (fdcode & 0x0f));
   pd→PD_FDHash = fdcode;
   return 0;
}
```

C.4.3 TransDir

TransDir() converts PC-DOS directory entries into OS-9 directory entries, and merges OS-9 directory entries with virtual file descriptors to make PC-DOS directory entries.

```
#include <ctype.h>
#include <errno.h>
#include <procid.h>
#include <direct.h>
typedef char *POINTER;
#include "format.h"
#include "PathDesc.h"

void OS9DirE2MS();

SectorMs2os9(pd, buffer)
register PD_TYPE pd;
register MSDirE buffer;
{
    register int i;

    for(i=0; i< (SECTORSIZE/sizeof(struct dirent)); ++i, ++buffer){
        pd→PD_FDBUF[i] = *buffer;
        ms2os9(buffer, buffer, pd→PD_CSector, i);            /* pg. 478 */
    }
}


void Dir2FD(fd, msdir)     /* This can be done in place */
register VirFDPtr fd;
register MSDirE msdir;
{
    unsigned short DateNum, TimeNum;

    fd→vfd_att = AdjustAttributes(msdir→FileAttr);
    fd→vfd_own[0] = 0;
    fd→vfd_own[1] = 0;
    DateNum = (uchar)msdir→Date[0] + (256 * (uchar)msdir→Date[1]);
    TimeNum = (uchar)msdir→Time[0] + (256 * (uchar)msdir→Time[1]);
    fd→vfd_dcr[0] = fd→vfd_date[0] = (DateNum >> 9) + 80;
    fd→vfd_dcr[1] = fd→vfd_date[1] = (DateNum >> 5) & 0x0f;
    fd→vfd_dcr[2] = fd→vfd_date[2] = DateNum & 0x01f;
    fd→vfd_date[3] = TimeNum >> 11;
    fd→vfd_date[4] = (TimeNum >> 5) & 0x03f;
```

C.4. ARTIFACTS OF PC-DOS

```
        fd→vfd_link = 1;
        fd→vfd_fsize[0] = msdir→FileSize[3];
        fd→vfd_fsize[1] = msdir→FileSize[2];
        fd→vfd_fsize[2] = msdir→FileSize[1];
        fd→vfd_fsize[3] = msdir→FileSize[0];
        fd→vfd_cluster[0] = msdir→StartCluster[1];
        fd→vfd_cluster[1] = msdir→StartCluster[0];
        return;
}


UpdateDirEntFromPD(DirPtr, pd)
register PD_TYPE pd;
register MSDirE DirPtr;
{
    register uchar *from, *to;
    register int counter;

    /* Convert the file name from OS-9 format to PC-Dos format */
    for(from = pd→PD_Name, to = DirPtr→FileName, counter = 8;
            *from && (*from != '.'); counter--)
        *to++ = *from++;
    for(;counter > 0; counter--)
        *to++ = ' ';
    if(*from == '.')
        ++from;
    for(counter = 3, to = DirPtr→FileExtension; *from > ' '; counter--)
        *to++ = *from++;
    for(;counter > 0; counter--)
        *to++ = ' ';

    for(counter = 9; counter >= 0; counter--)
        DirPtr→Reserved[counter] = '\0';

    DirPtr→FileAttr = ReAdjustAttributes(pd→PD_FD.vfd_att);

    DirPtr→Date[1] = (pd→PD_FD.vfd_date[0] - 80) * 2 +
        (pd→PD_FD.vfd_date[1] >> 3);
    DirPtr→Date[0] = (pd→PD_FD.vfd_date[1] & 0x07) * 32 +
        pd→PD_FD.vfd_date[2];
    DirPtr→Time[1] = (pd→PD_FD.vfd_date[3] * 8) /*hour*/ +
        (pd→PD_FD.vfd_date[4] >> 3);
    DirPtr→Time[0] = (pd→PD_FD.vfd_date[4] & 0x07) << 5;
```

```c
        DirPtr→StartCluster[0] = pd→PD_FD.vfd_cluster[1];
        DirPtr→StartCluster[1] = pd→PD_FD.vfd_cluster[0];

        DirPtr→FileSize[0] = pd→PD_FD.vfd_fsize [3];
        DirPtr→FileSize[1] = pd→PD_FD.vfd_fsize [2];
        DirPtr→FileSize[2] = pd→PD_FD.vfd_fsize [1];
        DirPtr→FileSize[3] = pd→PD_FD.vfd_fsize [0];
        return 0;
}


static ms2os9(msdir, osdir, csector, coffset)
register MSDirE msdir;
register struct dirent *osdir;
ulong csector, coffset;
{
        register uchar *ptr1, *ptr2;
        register short i;
        struct dirent work;

        for(i=0; i<28; ++i)
            work.dir_name[i] = '\0';
        for(i=0, ptr1 = (uchar *)work.dir_name, ptr2 = msdir→FileName;
                (i < 8) && (*ptr2 > ' ') && (*ptr2 < 0x080); ++i)
            *ptr1++ = *ptr2++;
        if((msdir→FileExtension[0] > ' ') && (i > 0)){
            *ptr1++ = '.';
            for(i=0, ptr2 = msdir→FileExtension; (i<3) && (*ptr2 > ' '); ++i)
                *ptr1++ = *ptr2++;
        }

        if(msdir→FileName[0] == '\0')
            work.dir_addr = 0;
        else
            /*
                Make a fake fd sector address out of the sector # and position of the
                directory entry.
                Sector number is SSSSSSSS.
                CP is PPPPPPPP.
                Fake fd is SSSSSSSP,
                high-order 7 nybles of S and the bits from P that are picked out with
                ones in the following string:
                000 . . . 00000111100000
            */
            work.dir_addr = MAKE_FD_HASH(csector,coffset);
```

C.4. ARTIFACTS OF PC-DOS

```
        *osdir = work;
}


FakeRootDir(cp, Length, ptr)
register ulong cp;
register ushort *Length;
register char **ptr;
{
    for(;(cp < (2 * sizeof(MSDirEntry))) && (*Length > 0);
        ++cp, (*Length)--)
      if(cp == 0)
          *((*ptr)++) = '.';
      else if((cp == sizeof(MSDirEntry) -1) ||
              (cp == (2*sizeof(MSDirEntry)) -1))
          *((*ptr)++) = 1;
      else if(cp < sizeof(MSDirEntry))
          *((*ptr)++) = '\0';
      else if(cp < (sizeof(MSDirEntry) + 2))
          *((*ptr)++) = '.';
      else
          *((*ptr)++) = '\0';
    return cp;
}


WriteIntoDir(offset, length, to, from)
register long offset;
register long length;
register char *to, *from;
{
    short int diroffset;

    for(;length > 0; length -= sizeof(struct dirent),
         offset += sizeof(struct dirent)){
      diroffset = offset % sizeof(struct dirent);
      if(diroffset == 0){
         OS9DirE2MS((struct dirent *)from,          /* pg. 480 */
            (MSDirE)to,
            (MSDirE)to);
         from += sizeof(struct dirent);
         to += sizeof(MSDirEntry);
      } else if(offset < 12)
         return -1;   /*error */
```

```
        else return 0;    /*do nothing */
   }
   return 0;
}


void OS9DirE2MS(os9, ms, oldms)
register struct dirent *os9;
register MSDirE ms, oldms;
{
   register uchar *ptr1, *ptr2;
   register int i;

   *ms = *oldms;

   for(i=0, ptr2 = (uchar *)os9→dir_name, ptr1 = ms→FileName;i<8;++i)
      if(*ptr2 && (*ptr2 != '.'))
         *ptr1++ = *ptr2++ & 0x7f;
      else
         *ptr1++ = ' ';
   if(*ptr2 == '.') ++ptr2;
   for(i=0; i<3; ++i)
      if(*ptr2)
         *ptr1++ = *ptr2++;
      else
         *ptr1++ = ' ';
   return;
}
```

C.4.4 FATSupport

The File Allocation Table (FAT) stored on each PC-DOS disk is used to store links between sectors. Free sectors have a distinguished link number. Other link values indicate errors or point to other links. Each link corresponds to the equivalent of an OS-9 cluster.

```
#include <errno.h>
#include <procid.h>
typedef char *POINTER;
#include "format.h"
#include "PathDesc.h"

#define DIRTYFAT(DriveTable) (DriveTable)→V_FATDirty = TRUE
```

C.4. ARTIFACTS OF PC-DOS

```
#define CLEANFAT(DriveTable) (DriveTable)→V_FATDirty = FALSE
#define SECTORS_ON_DEVICE(pd) ((((pd→PD_DTB→DD_TOT[0]<<8)+\
        pd→PD_DTB→DD_TOT[1]<<8)+\
        pd→PD_DTB→DD_TOT[2])

Errno(FATCode)
ulong FATCode;
{
    switch(FATCode){
        case T_FAT_BADTRACK:
            return E_DAMAGE;
        case T_FAT_LASTSECTOR:
            return E_EOF;
        default:
            if(FATCode >= T_FAT_BADTRACK)
                return E_DAMAGE;
            else
                return 0;    /* no trouble */
    }
}
```

/*
   *Take the file relative location and convert it into a disk-relative sector
   number.*
*/

```
static ChaseFat(FATPtr, FCluster, ThisCluster)
register uchar *FATPtr;
register ulong FCluster;
register ulong ThisCluster;
{
    register ushort CNumber;

    if(FCluster == FAT_LASTSECTOR)
        return FCluster;

    for(CNumber = FCluster ; ThisCluster>0; ThisCluster--)
        switch(CNumber = FAT(CNumber, FATPtr)){                /* pg. 485 */
            case FAT_BADTRACK:
                return CNumber;
                break;
            case FAT_LASTSECTOR:
                return CNumber;
                break;
```

```
        default:
            break;
    }
    return CNumber;
}


/*
    Return the last cluster number for a file and the number of clusters in
    the file.
*/

static ChaseToEnd(FATPtr, FCluster, Count)
register uchar *FATPtr;
register ulong FCluster;
register ulong *Count;
{
    register ushort This;

    This = FCluster;
    *Count = 0;

    if((This == FAT_LASTSECTOR) || (This == 0))
        return FAT_LASTSECTOR;

    for(*Count = 1;
            (FCluster = FAT(This, FATPtr)) != FAT_LASTSECTOR;      /* pg. 485 */
            ++(*Count))
        This = FCluster;

    return This;
}


static FindFreeSector(FATPtr, HiFAT)
register uchar *FATPtr;
register short HiFAT;
{
    register ushort num;

    for(num = 2; num < HiFAT; ++num)
        if(FAT(num, FATPtr) == 0)                                   /* pg. 485 */
            break;
```

C.4. ARTIFACTS OF PC-DOS

```
        if(num < HiFAT)
            return num;
        else
            return FAT_LASTSECTOR;
    }


    static GetFreeSector(pd)
    register PD_TYPE pd;
    {
        register ushort num;

        DIRTYFAT(pd→PD_DTB);

        if((num = FindFreeSector((uchar *)pd→PD_DTB→V_FATPtr,         /* pg. 482 */
                (short)((SECTORS_ON_DEVICE(pd) − pd→PD_DTB→V_DataStart)
                / pd→PD_DTB→DD_SPC) + 1))) > 0)
            SetFAT((uchar *)pd→PD_DTB→V_FATPtr,                        /* pg. 485 */
                num, FAT_LASTSECTOR);

        return num;
    }


    static ExtendFile(pd, CCluster)
    register PD_TYPE pd;
    register ushort CCluster;
    {
        register ushort num;
        register ushort Last;
        boolean FirstCluster=FALSE;

        DIRTYFAT(pd→PD_DTB);
        Last = CCluster;

        if(Last == FAT_LASTSECTOR){/* an empty file */
            /*
                This will require an update to the directory as well as an update to the
                FAT.
            */
            FirstCluster = TRUE;
        } else if(FAT(CCluster, (uchar *)pd→PD_DTB→V_FATPtr)           /* pg. 485 */
            != FAT_LASTSECTOR)
            /* Can't extend from the middle of a file */
            return FAT_BADTRACK+1;
```

```
        if((num = GetFreeSector(pd)) < FAT_BADTRACK){                /* pg. 483 */
            if(FirstCluster){
                DirSetFCluster(pd, num);                              /* pg. 465 */
                pd→PD_FCluster = num;
                DIRTYFD(pd);
            } else
                SetFAT((uchar *)pd→PD_DTB→V_FATPtr, Last, num);       /* pg. 485 */
        }
    }


static void FreeFrom(FATPtr, Cluster)
register ushort *FATPtr;
register ushort Cluster;
{
    register ushort Next;

    while(Cluster < FAT_BADTRACK){
        Next = FAT(Cluster, (uchar *)FATPtr);                         /* pg. 485 */
        SetFAT((uchar *)FATPtr, Cluster, 0);  /*Free this cluster */  /* pg. 485 */
        Cluster = Next;
    }
}


/*
    This sets the file length in the FAT. This is sufficient for directory files.
    For other files the directory entry (FD part) for the file must also be
    updated.
*/
FATSetFileLength(pd, Length)
register PD_TYPE pd;
register ulong Length;
{
    ulong CurrentLength;
    register ushort CurrentEnd, Current;

    DIRTYFAT(pd→PD_DTB);
    Length = u_bound_div(Length, SECTORSIZE * pd→PD_DTB→DD_SPC);
    CurrentEnd = ChaseToEnd((uchar *)pd→PD_DTB→V_FATPtr,              /* pg. 482 */
        pd→PD_FCluster, &CurrentLength);

    if(CurrentLength < Length) {  /*Extend the file */
```

C.4. ARTIFACTS OF PC-DOS

```
            for(; CurrentLength < Length;
                CurrentLength += (pd→PD_DTB→DD_SPC * SECTORSIZE))
                if((CurrentEnd = ExtendFile(pd, CurrentEnd)) >=        /* pg. 483 */
                    FAT_BADTRACK)
                    return CurrentEnd;
        } else if(CurrentLength > Length){   /* Truncate the file */
            Current =ChaseFat((uchar *)pd→PD_DTB→V_FATPtr,             /* pg. 481 */
                pd→PD_FCluster, Length);
            FreeFrom((uchar *)pd→PD_DTB→V_FATPtr, Current);            /* pg. 484 */
            if(Length == 0)
                pd→PD_FCluster = FAT_LASTSECTOR;
        }

        return 0;
    }


static FAT(Num, FATPtr)
register ushort Num;
register uchar *FATPtr;
{
    register short x;

    if(FATPtr == NULL){
        SYSDEBUG(2, Num);
        CATASTROPHY;
    }
    x = FATPtr[(Num*3)/2] +( FATPtr[1 + (Num*3)/2] << 8);
    if(Num & 1)
        return((x >> 4) & 0x0fff);
    else
        return(x & 0x0fff);
}


static SetFAT(FATPtr, Num, NewVal)
register uchar *FATPtr;
register ushort Num, NewVal;
{
    if(FATPtr == NULL){
        SYSDEBUG(2, Num);
        CATASTROPHY;
    }
#ifndef WRITEBOOT
```

```
      if(Num < 2){
         SYSDEBUG(3, Num);
         CATASTROPHY;
      }
#endif
      if(Num & 1){    /* Odd cluster */
         FATPtr[1+(Num*3)/2] = (NewVal >> 4) & 0x0ff;   /* high order */
         FATPtr[(Num*3)/2] &= 0x0f;   /* Clear high-order nyble */
         FATPtr[(Num*3)/2] |= ((NewVal << 4) & 0x0f0);
      } else {    /* Even cluster */
         FATPtr[(Num*3)/2] = NewVal & 0x0ff;
         FATPtr[1 + (Num*3)/2] &= 0x0f0;
         FATPtr[1+ (Num*3)/2] |= ((NewVal >> 8) & 0x0f);
      }
}


SectorInFile(loc, mode)
register ulong loc;
register uchar mode;
{
   if((mode & PD_RDIR_MODE) && !(mode & PD_RAWMODE))
      if(loc > (2 * sizeof(MSDirEntry)))
         return((loc - (2 * sizeof(MSDirEntry))) >> 9);
      else
         return 0;
   else
      return (loc / SECTORSIZE);
}


CheckSector(pd)
register PD_TYPE pd;
{
   return SectorOnDisk(pd,                                    /* pg. 486 */
      SectorInFile(pd→PD_CP, pd→PD_SMF));                     /* pg. 486 */
}


SectorOnDisk(pd, x)
register PD_TYPE pd;
register int x;
{
   register ulong ClusterInFile, SectorInCluster, Cluster;
```

C.4. ARTIFACTS OF PC-DOS

```
            if(pd→PD_SMF & PD_RAWMODE)
                return x;
            if(pd→PD_SMF & PD_RDIR_MODE)
                if(x < (pd→PD_DTB→V_DirEntries / DIR_ENT_PER_SECTOR))
                    return(MS_SECTOR(pd→PD_DTB→DD_DIR + x));
                else
                    return T_FAT_LASTSECTOR;


            /* Cluster = sector divided by sectors per cluster */
            ClusterInFile = x / pd→PD_DTB→DD_SPC;
            SectorInCluster = x % pd→PD_DTB→DD_SPC;
            Cluster = ChaseFat((uchar *)pd→PD_DTB→V_FATPtr,              /* pg. 481 */
                pd→PD_FCluster, ClusterInFile);

            if(Cluster >= FAT_BADTRACK)
                return(Cluster | 0x0F000);
            else
                return MS_SECTOR((((Cluster * pd→PD_DTB→DD_SPC) +
                    SectorInCluster + pd→PD_DTB→V_DataStart));
        }




        ReadFAT(pd, regs, procd, SysGlobs)
        register PD_TYPE pd;
        {
            /*
                If the drive table entry for this drive already has a FAT buffer, ensure
                that it is accurate. If it doesn't have a FAT buffer, create and load one.
            */

            if(pd→PD_DTB→V_FATPtr == NULL){
                if((pd→PD_DTB→V_FATPtr =
                    (POINTER)_srqmem(                                    /* pg. 429 */
                        pd→PD_DTB→V_FATSz * SECTORSIZE)) == (char *)-1)
                    return E_MEMFUL;
            }
            pd→PD_DTB→V_FATLinks++;

            return(FillFAT(pd, regs, procd, SysGlobs));                  /* pg. 488 */
        }
```

```
static FillFAT(pd, regs, procd, SysGlobs)
register PD_TYPE pd;
{
    register DriveTableType *DriveTable;
    register int ReturnVal, FatSector;

    DriveTable = pd→PD_DTB;

    for(FatSector=0; FatSector < DriveTable→V_FATSz; FatSector++)
        if((ReturnVal = RawReadSector(pd,                                    /* pg. 469 */
                (ulong)(MS_SECTOR(DriveTable→DD_FirstFAT + FatSector)),
                ((char *)DriveTable→V_FATPtr) + FatSector * SECTORSIZE,
                regs, procd, SysGlobs)) != 0)
            return ReturnVal;

    CLEANFAT(DriveTable);
    return ReturnVal;
}


WriteFAT(pd, regs, procd, SysGlobs)
register PD_TYPE pd;
{
    register DTBPtrType DriveTable;
    register int ReturnVal, FatSector;

    DriveTable = pd→PD_DTB;
#ifndef WRITEBOOT
    if(*(uchar *)DriveTable→V_FATPtr < 0xf0){
        SYSDEBUG(4, DriveTable→V_FATPtr);
        CATASTROPHY;
    }
#endif

    for(FatSector = 0; FatSector < DriveTable→V_FATSz; FatSector++)
        if((ReturnVal = RawWriteSector(pd,                                   /* pg. 471 */
                (ulong)(MS_SECTOR(DriveTable→DD_FirstFAT + FatSector)),
                ((char *)DriveTable→V_FATPtr) + FatSector * SECTORSIZE,
                regs, procd, SysGlobs)) != 0){
            SYSDEBUG(6,pd);
            return ReturnVal;
        }

    if(DriveTable→V_FATSz > 1)
```

C.5. SPECIAL HEADER FILES

```
        if((ReturnVal = RawWriteSector(pd,                          /* pg. 471 */
            (ulong)(MS_SECTOR(DriveTable→DD_FirstFAT + 1)),
            (char *)DriveTable→V_FATPtr + SECTORSIZE,
            regs, procd, SysGlobs)) != 0)
            return ReturnVal;

    CLEANFAT(DriveTable);
    return ReturnVal;
}


FlushDevice(pd, procd, SysGlobs)
register PD_TYPE pd;
{
    REGISTERS regs;

    if((pd→PD_DTB→V_FATPtr != NULL) && pd→PD_DTB→V_FATDirty)
        WriteFAT(pd, &regs, procd, SysGlobs);                       /* pg. 488 */
}


FreeFAT(DriveTable)
register DriveTableType *DriveTable;
{
    if(--DriveTable→V_FATLinks != 0)
        return;
    if(DriveTable→V_FATPtr != NULL)
        DoSRtMem(DriveTable→V_FATPtr,
            DriveTable→V_FATSz*SECTORSIZE);                         /* pg. 430 */
    DriveTable→V_FATPtr = NULL;
}
```

C.5 Special Header Files

C.5.1 Format

The format.h header file contains definitions that are specific to the PC-DOS file structure.

```
#define BOOTSECTOR         0
#define FATSTART           1
#define FILERASED          '\345'
#define DEFAULT_DRIVES     2
```

```
#define SECTORSIZE          512
#define DIR_ENT_PER_SECTOR  16

#define SYSDEBUG(a1,a2)
#define CATASTROPHY         *(char*)0xFFFFFFFF=0

#define E_DAMAGE            0x0ab

/*Attributes*/
#define MS_READ_ONLY        0x1
#define MS_HIDDEN           0x2
#define MS_SYSTEM           0x4
#define MS_V_LABEL          0x8
#define MS_SUBDIR           0x10
#define MS_ARCHIVE          0x20

#define FAT_BADTRACK        0x0FF7
#define FAT_LASTSECTOR      0x0FFF
#define T_FAT_BADTRACK      0x0FFF7
#define T_FAT_LASTSECTOR    0x0FFFF

#define LengthenFile(pd,length) SetFileSize((pd),(length))
#define ShortenFile(pd,length)  SetFileSize((pd),(length))

#ifndef TRUE
#define TRUE                1
#define FALSE               0
#endif

#ifndef NULL
#define NULL                ((void *)0)
#endif

typedef unsigned char uchar;
typedef unsigned long ulong;
typedef unsigned char boolean;

typedef struct {
    char    Reserved1[3];       /*A branch instruction              */
    char    SystemID[8];
    uchar   SectorSize[2];      /*Bytes per sector                  */
    uchar   SectorsPerCluster;
```

C.5. SPECIAL HEADER FILES

```
    uchar    ReservedSectors[2];      /*Number of reserved sectors at start    */
    uchar    FATCopies;
    uchar    RootDirSize[2];          /*Number of entries in root directory    */
    uchar    TotSectors[2];           /*Sectors on the disk                    */
    uchar    FormatID;                /*F8..FF                                 */
    uchar    SectorsPerFAT[2];
    uchar    SectorsPerTrack[2];
    uchar    Sides[2];
    uchar    S_ReservedSectors[2];    /*Special reserved sectors               */
} *BootSectorType;

typedef struct {
    uchar    FileName[8];
    uchar    FileExtension[3];
    uchar    FileAttr;
    char     Reserved[10];
    uchar    Time[2];
    uchar    Date[2];
    uchar    StartCluster[2];
    uchar    FileSize[4];
} *MSDirE, MSDirEntry;

/*File attributes*/
#define VOL_LABEL        0x20
#define SUB_DIRECTORY    0x10
#define READ_ONLY        0x08
#define MODIFIED         0x04
#define HIDDEN           0x02
#define SYSTEM_FILE      0x01

typedef uchar SmallFAT_Entrys[3];

typedef struct {
    long     R_d0, R_d1, R_d2, R_d3, R_d4, R_d5, R_d6, R_d7;
    char     *R_a0, *R_a1, *R_a2, *R_a3, *R_a4, *R_a5, *R_a6, *R_a7;
    uchar    R_ssr;                   /*Status register—system part           */
    uchar    R_cc;                    /*Status register—condition code part   */
    short    *R_pc;                   /*Program counter register              */
    short    R_fmt;                   /*68010 exception format and vector     */
} *REGS, REGISTERS;

typedef struct {
    uchar    DD_TOT[3];               /*Total number of sectors on device     */
    uchar    DD_TKS;                  /*Track size in sectors                 */
```

```
    ushort   DD_FATSIZ;           /* Number of sectors in FAT              */
    ushort   DD_SPC;              /* Number of sectors per cluster         */
    ushort   DD_DIR;              /* Address of root directory             */
                                  /* The address is actually an lsn: 24 bits */
                                  /* but since this lsn is small, 16 bits suffice */
    ushort   DD_OWN;              /* Owner ID (meaningless)                */
    ushort   DD_DSK;              /* Disk ID (probably meaningless)        */
    ushort   DD_ATT;              /* Attributes                            */
    uchar    DD_FMT;              /* Disk format; density/sides            */
    uchar    DD_SPT[2];           /* Sectors per track                     */
    uchar    DD_FATCnt;           /* Copies of FAT                         */
    uchar    DD_FirstFAT;         /* First FAT Sector                      */
    uchar    DD_Reserved;
    ushort   V_TRAK;              /* Current track                         */
    ushort   V_Reserved2[3];
    ushort   V_FATSz;             /* FAT size                              */
    ushort   V_DataStart;         /* First cluster in the data space       */
    ushort   V_FATLinks;          /* FAT use counter                       */
    POINTER  V_ScZero;            /* Pointer to sector zero buffer         */
    boolean  V_FATDirty;          /* FAT buffer has been changed           */
    uchar    V_Init;              /* Drive initialized flag                */
    ushort   V_Reserved5;
    ulong    V_SoftEr;
    ulong    V_HardEr;
    POINTER  V_FATPtr;            /* Pointer to the drive's FAT            */
    ushort   V_DirEntries;
    ushort   V_Reserved[13];
} DriveTableType, *DTBPtrType;

typedef struct {
    /* I/O Device Static storage required by the kernel for all device types. */
    POINTER  V_PORT;  /* Device base port address */
    ushort   V_LPRC;              /* Last active process ID                */
    ushort   V_BUSY;              /* Current process ID (0=idle)           */
    ushort   V_WAKE;              /* Active process ID if driver must wakeup */
    POINTER  V_Paths;             /* Linked list of open paths on device   */
    ulong    V_Reserved[8];
    /* Static storage for RBF drivers */
    uchar    V_NDRV;              /* Number of drives                      */
    uchar    V_DReserved[7];
    DriveTableType V_DRIVES[DEFAULT_DRIVES]; /* This may be the wrong size,
                                                but that's ok */

    /* Followed by device driver static storage */
```

C.5. SPECIAL HEADER FILES

} *STATICSTORETYPE;

```
typedef struct {
    char    *I_DevTbl;          /* Pointer to Default device table    */
    ulong   DirCluster;         /* First cluster for directory        */
    ulong   Extra[2];           /* Unused space.                      */
} DefaultDescriptor;
```

C.5.2 PathDesc

This pathdesc.h file contains the path descriptor format used by the msfm file manager.

```
#define PATHDELIM '/'
#define ENTIRE_DELIM '@'

#define MS_SECTOR(n) ((n) - 1)      /* Convert pcdos sector # to OS-9sector #    */
#define FDOFFSET(x)          ((x)&0x0f)
#define FDSECTOR(x)          ((x)>>4)
#define MAKE_FD_HASH(sect,off) (((sect)<<4)|((off)&0x0f))

typedef struct {
    uchar vfd_att,
          vfd_own[2],
          vfd_date[5],
          vfd_link,
          vfd_fsize[4],
          vfd_dcr[3],
          vfd_cluster[2];
} VirFD, *VirFDPtr;

typedef struct PDTYPE {
    ushort  PD_PD;              /* Path number                     */
    uchar   PD_MOD;             /* Mode (read/write/update)        */
    uchar   PD_CNT;             /* Number of open images           */
    struct DEVTAB *PD_DEV;      /* Device table entry address      */
    ushort  PD_CPR;             /* Current process ID              */
    POINTER PD_RGS;             /* Caller's register stack pointer */
    char    *PD_BUF;            /* Buffer address                  */
    ulong   PD_USER;            /* User ID of path's creator       */
    struct PDTYPE *PD_Paths;    /* L-List of paths to this device  */
    ushort  PD_COUNT;           /* Actual number of open images    */
    ushort  PD_LProc;           /* Last active process ID          */
    short   PD_Reserved[6];
```

APPENDIX C. BUILDING A FILE MANAGER

```c
/*
    File manager storage
*/

    uchar       PD_SMF;             /* State flags                          */
    uchar       PD_Unused;
    ushort      PD_Parent;          /* FCluster of parent dir               */
    ulong       PD_CSector;         /* Number of sector in the buffer       */
    ulong       PD_CP;              /* Current logical byte position        */
    ulong       PD_SIZ;             /* File size                            */
    short       PD_CCluster;        /* Current cluster                      */
    MSDirE      PD_FDBUF;           /* Buffer for file descriptor info      */
    ulong       PD_FDSector;        /* Sector number for above FDs          */
    ulong       PD_FDOffset;        /* Offset in sector for FD below        */
    DTBPtrType  PD_DTB;             /* Drive table pointer                  */
    ulong       PD_FDHash;          /* Combined sector/offset               */
    uchar       PD_Accs;            /* Allowable file access permissions    */
    VirFD       PD_FD;              /* First part of virtual OS-9 FD        */

/*
    The fields so far add up to 35+18=53 bytes of file manager storage.
    86 bytes are required to bring us up to the option area.
*/

    char        PD_Unused2[29];     /* 86 - 35 - 22                         */

/*
    Path descriptor's options section
*/

    uchar       PD_DTP;             /* Device type                          */
    uchar       PD_DRV;             /* Drive number                         */
    uchar       PD_STP;             /* Step rate                            */
    uchar       PD_TYP;             /* Disk device type                     */
    uchar       PD_DNS;             /* Density capability                   */
    char        PD_NewLine;         /* New line character for Rd/Writ-Ln    */
    ushort      PD_CYL;             /* Number of cylinders                  */
    uchar       PD_SID;             /* Number of sides                      */
    uchar       PD_VFY;             /* 0=verify disk writes                 */
    ushort      PD_SCT;             /* Default sectors per track            */
    ushort      PD_TOS;             /* ""  "" (tr0, s0)                     */
    ushort      PD_SAS;             /* Segment allocation size              */
    uchar       PD_ILV;             /* Sector interleave offset             */
```

```
    uchar    PD_TFM;              /*DMA transfer mode                      */
    uchar    PD_TOffs;            /*Track base offset                      */
    uchar    PD_SOffs;            /*Sector base offset                     */
    ushort   PD_SSize;            /*Size of sector in bytes                */
    ushort   PD_Cntl;             /*Control word                           */
    uchar    PD_Trys;             /*Number of tries (1=no error corr)      */
    uchar    PD_LUN;              /*SCSI unit number of drive              */
    ushort   PD_WPC;              /*First cylinder using write precomp     */
    ushort   PD_RWC;              /*  ""  "" reduced write current         */
    ushort   PD_Park;             /*Park cylinder for hard disks           */
    ulong    PD_LSNOffs;          /*LSN offset for partition               */
    ushort   PD_TotCyls;          /*Total cylinders on device              */
    uchar    PD_CtrlrID;          /*SCSI controller ID                     */
    uchar    PD_reserved3[14];
    uchar    PD_ATT;              /*File attributes                        */
    ulong    PD_FCluster;         /*Starting cluster (was PD_FD)           */
    ulong    PD_DFD;              /*Directory FD psn                       */
    ulong    PD_DCP;              /*Directory entry pointer                */
    POINTER  PD_DVT;              /*Device table pointer (copy)            */
    uchar    PD_reserved4[26];
    uchar    PD_Name[12];         /*Filename                               */
    char     PD_NotName[20];      /*Leftover space                         */
} *PD_TYPE;

#define PD_RAWMODE      0x01
#define PD_DIR_MODE     0x02            /*Any directory              */
#define PD_RDIR_MODE    0x04            /*The ROOT directory         */
#define PD_DIRTYFD      0x08            /*The FD copy in the PD is dirty */
#define PD_GOODBUF      0x10            /*The data in FD_BUF is valid */
#define DIRTYFD(pd)     (pd)->PD_SMF|=PD_DIRTYFD
#define CLEANFD(pd)     (pd)->PD_SMF&=~PD_DIRTYFD

typedef struct DEVTAB {
    POINTER             V_DRIV;
    STATICSTORETYPE V_STAT;
    POINTER             V_DESC;
    POINTER             V_FMGR;
    short               V_USRS;
} *DEVTABTYPE;
```

C.6 The Device Descriptor

opt   −1

00000002	TrkDns	set	2		Double step
00000002	BitDns	set	2		Double density
00000006	Density	set	BitDns+(TrkDns<<1)		
00000020	DiskType	set	%00100000		Non-standard 5" floppy
00000f00	TypeLang	set	(Devic<<8)+0		
00008001	Attr_Rev	set	(ReEnt<<8)+1		
00000001	Edition	set	1		
		psect	MSFDesc,TypeLang,Attr_Rev,Edition,0,0		
00ff8000	Port	set	$00FF8000		
0000001d	Vector	set	29		
00000005	IRQLevel	set	5		
00000001	Priority	set	1		
000000a7	Mode	set	Dir_+ISize_+Exec_+Updat_		
00000000	DrvNum	set	0		
00000002	StepRate	set	2		
00000050	Cylinders	set	80		
00000002	Heads	set	2		
00000000	DevCon	set	0		
0000 00ff		dc.l	Port		Port address
0004 1d		dc.b	Vector		Auto-vector trap assignment
0005 05		dc.b	IRQLevel		IRQ hardware interrupt level
0006 01		dc.b	Priority		IRQ polling priority
0007 a7		dc.b	Mode		Device mode capabilities
0008 0038		dc.w	FileMgr		File manager name offset
000a 0031		dc.w	DevDrv		Device driver name offset
000c 0000		dc.w	DevCon		(Reserved)
000e 0000		dc.w	0,0,0,0		Reserved
0016 0019		dc.w	OptLen		

* Default Parameters
    OptTbl

0018= 00	dc.b	DT_RBF		Device type
0019 00	dc.b	DrvNum		Drive number
001a 02	dc.b	StepRate		Step rate
001b 20	dc.b	DiskType		Type of disk 8"/5"/Hard
001c 06	dc.b	Density		Bit Density and track density
001d 0d	dc.b	13		New Line character
001e 0050	dc.w	Cylinders		Number of cylinders
0020 02	dc.b	Heads		Sides (Floppy) Heads (Hard Disk)
0021 01	dc.b	1		Don't verify writes
0022 0009	dc.w	9		Sectors per track
0024 0009	dc.w	9		Sectors per track (0)
0026 0002	dc.w	2		Segment allocation size
0028 01	dc.b	1		Sector interleaving factor
0029 00	dc.b	0		No DMA
002a 00	dc.b	0		Track offset
002b 01	dc.b	1		Sector offset (sectors start at 1, not 0)

C.6. THE DEVICE DESCRIPTOR

```
002c 0200              dc.w    512           Sector size
002e 0000              dc.w    0             Control word
0030 01                dc.b    1             Number of tries
00000019  OptLen       equ     *-OptTbl
0031 7262 DevDrv       dc.b    "rb1772",0
0038 6d73 FileMgr      dc.b    "msfm",0
0000003e               ends
```

Appendix D

Sample RBF Device Driver

> *This chapter contains a complete device driver for the NEC 765 floppy disk controller. It contains many of the common features of RBF device drivers.*

The device driver in this chapter is Microware's standard NEC 765 FDC device driver for OS-9/68k version 2.1.[1] Subsequent releases of OS-9 may have slightly different requirements for the device driver. Microware supports most older device drivers with options and compatibility modes, but up-to-date drivers work best.

D.1 Module Header

A device driver should have a module type of Drvr and the ReEnt and SupStat attributes.

The stack size in the *psect* directive should be zero. The device driver uses the caller's system stack[2] except in its interrupt routine. The interrupt routine uses the master system stack.

The amount of stack space available to the driver depends on the size of the system stack in the process descriptor (about a kilobyte) and the stack requirements of the kernel, IOMan, and the file manager. The safest policy is to keep stack consumption below about 256 bytes.

```
        nam     NEC-765
        ttl     Driver Module
```

---

[1] This source code is the proprietary confidential property of Microware Systems Corporation, and is provided to licensee solely for documentation and educational purposes. Reproduction, publication, or distribution in any form to any party other than the licensee is strictly prohibited.

[2] A process' system stack is in its process descriptor

0000000a	Edition	equ	10	current edition number
00000e01	Typ_Lang	set	(Drivr<<8)+Objct Device Driver In Assembly Language	
0000a000	Attr_Rev	set	((ReEnt+SupStat)<<8)+0	
		psect	NEC765,Typ_Lang,Attr_Rev,Edition,0,DiskEnt	
		use	defsfile	

The defsfile includes oskdefs.d and systype.d.

D.2 Static Storage

The device static storage contains fields that are related to the device (as opposed to the path).

00000002	DriveCnt	equ	2	*** Must be linked with for two drives ***
00000000	True	equ	0	
00000001	False	equ	1	

```
******************************************************************
*
* This Controller Uses A Nec 765 FDC
*

***************
* Static Storage definitions
```

		vsect		
00000000	V_BUF	ds.l	64	addr of local buffer
00000100	V_LSN	ds.l	1	logical sector #
00000104	V_IMask	ds.w	1	interrupt Mask Value
00000106	V_Side	ds.b	1	side select value
00000107	V_Sector	ds.b	1	sector buffer
00000108	V_Track	ds.b	1	track buffer
00000109	V_TfrMod	ds.b	1	0=No Transfer 1=read 2=write
0000010a	V_CurDrv	ds.b	1	drive select bit
0000010b	V_Count	ds.b	1	count byte for moves
0000010c	V_Size	ds.b	1	current disk size 0:=5"
0000010d	V_DOSK	ds.b	1	force seek flag
0000010e	V_FREZ	ds.b	1	freeze dd. info flag
0000010f	V_IRQ	ds.b	1	1 = process command with IRQ's
00000110	V_CMDSIZ	ds.b	1	size of FDC command
00000111	V_SPCFY	ds.b	1	if 0 have not initialized NEC 765

D.3. DEFINITIONS

```
* Nec command buffers
00000112  Command1  ds.b  1
00000113  Command2  ds.b  1
00000114  Command3  ds.b  1
00000115  Command4  ds.b  1
00000116  Command5  ds.b  1
00000117  Command6  ds.b  1
00000118  Command7  ds.b  1
00000119  Command8  ds.b  1
0000011a  Command9  ds.b  1

* Nec result buffers
0000011b  Results   ds.b  9
00000000            ends
```

D.3 Definitions

```
***************
* VME8400 register layouts
*

00000000  MSR       equ  0      NEC765 main status register
00000002  DataReg   equ  2      NEC765 Data Register
00000004  TermCnt   equ  4      issue end of read or write
00000008  MotorCtl  equ  8      5 1/4 motor control 0= motor off
0000000c  IntEnabl  equ  $C     interrupt enable/disable 0=disable

***************
* Nec 765 Commands
*

00000003  F.Specfy  equ  $03    specify command
00000007  F.Rest    equ  $07    restore cmd
0000000f  F.Seek    equ  $0F    seek cmd
00000006  F.ReadSc  equ  $06    read sector
00000005  F.WrtSec  equ  $05    write sector
0000000d  F.WrtTrk  equ  $0D    write track
00000040  DDensity  equ  $40    double density bit in command byte
00000004  F.SnsDrv  equ  $04    sense drive status
00000008  F.SnsIRQ  equ  $08    sense interrupt status
00000001  N         equ  $01    256 bytes/sector
00000064  HLT       equ  100    head load time * 2 ms (100 × 2)
00000001  NonDMA    equ  1      non dma flag
000000e5  Filler    equ  $E5    sector fill byte
0000001e  GPL8SD    equ  30     gap length for format
```

```
00000032  GPL8DD    equ    50           gap length for format
0000000f  GPL5SD    equ    15
0000000a  GPL5DD    equ    10
0000000a  GPL       equ    $A           gap length for 5&8" drives
000000ff  DTL       equ    $FF          data length n/a for 256 byte sects
0000000f  EOTSD8    equ    $0F          last sect on track 8" sd
0000001a  EOTDD8    equ    $1A          last sect on track 8" dd

0000000a  DelayTim  equ    10           time to delay between commands
```

* Nec Status register bits

```
00000001  D0B       equ    $1           drive zero in seek mode
00000002  D1B       equ    $2           drive one in seek mode
00000004  D2B       equ    $4           drive two in seek mode
00000008  D3B       equ    $8           drive three in seek mode
00000010  CB        equ    $10          read or write in progress
00000020  NDM       equ    $20          FDC in non-DMA mode
00000040  DIO       equ    $40          0 = processor > FDC
00000080  RQM       equ    $80          data register ready

00000005  Busy_Bit  equ    5
00000005  Seek_Bit  equ    5
00000004  CB_Bit    equ    4
00000006  DIO_Bit   equ    6

00000000  PDDN_Bit  equ    0            density bit in path descriptor

00000080  Invalid   equ    $80          invalid command code
```

* Nec Error register bits

```
000000c0  IC        equ    $C0          command completion status
00000080  EN        equ    $80          end of cylinder
00000040  EC        equ    $40          fault or bad restore
00000020  DE        equ    $20          CRC error
00000008  NR        equ    $08          device not ready
00000004  ND        equ    $04          seek error
00000002  NW        equ    $02          write protect
00000001  MA        equ    $01          missing address (seek error)
```

* Command code bits

```
00000006  MF_Bit    equ    6            format bit 0=single density 1=double density
```

D.4. THE VECTOR TABLE

```
00000007  MT_Bit    equ   7           multi track bit
```

* Error code bits

```
00000000  MA_Bit    equ   0           missing address mark
00000001  NW_Bit    equ   1           disk write protected
00000002  ND_Bit    equ   2           no data
00000003  NR_Bit    equ   3           not ready
00000004  EC_Bit    equ   4           equipment check
00000005  DE_Bit    equ   5           data error (crc error)
```

* Bit numbers for DD_FMT

```
00000000  Side_Bit  equ   0           0=single 1=double
00000001  Dens_Bit  equ   1           0=single 1=double
00000002  Trks_Bit  equ   2           0=48 tpi 1=96 tpi
```

* Bit numbers for path descriptors

```
00000000  Size_Bit  equ   0           0=5 inch 1=8"
```

D.4 The Vector Table

A device driver offers several services, but it has only one entry point specified in its module header. The problem is resolved through indirection. The module entry point offset does not locate code, instead it points to the following table. The table contains a list of offsets, one for each standard entry point in an RBF device driver.[3]

```
*
* Branch Table
*
0000 000e  DiskEnt   dc.w   InitDisk    initialize I/O
0002 00e4            dc.w   ReadDisk    read sector
0004 0088            dc.w   WritDisk    write sector
0006 047e            dc.w   GetStat     get status
0008 046c            dc.w   PutStat     put status
000a 0570            dc.w   Term        terminate device
000c 0000            dc.w   0           exception handler (0=none)
```

---

[3]OS-9/68k does not use the same strategy for its vector table that OS-9/6809 used. The older OS-9 put actual branch instructions in the table. Now the table contains offsets. This gives a small savings in memory.

D.5 Device Initialization

The device initialization routine is called by IOMan when the device is attached (usually when it used for the first time).

The initialization routine is responsible for initializing data structures that have not been filled by IOMan and RBF, and putting its I/O hardware into the initial state defined in the path descriptor options section.

The drive table is maintained by the device driver. This table reflects the fact that IOMan treats all the drives attached to a controller as a single device. In particular, it assigns them one common device static storage. This has advantages in that the floppy disk controller (FDC) has a common set of control and status registers for all the disks, and only one of the disks can be in use at any time. The shared device static storage includes a drive table. The drive table is used to store the characteristics that may vary from drive to drive.[4]

The first thing the initialization routine does is fill the drive table with default values: current drive, size, and high track are all given impossible values. Useful data will be inserted in the drive table when the driver reads sector zero (the system sector).

```
* Initialize
*
* Input:
* (a1) = Device descriptor
* (a2) = Static Storage ptr
* (a6) = System global data pointer
*
         InitDisk:
000e=266a            movea.l  V_PORT(a2),a3   point to controller ports
0012 7002            moveq    #DriveCnt,d0
0014=1540            move.b   d0,V_NDRV(a2)   init # of drives

* initialize drive tables

0018 72ff            moveq    #$FF,d1           init fake media size
001a 1541            move.b   d1,V_CurDrv(a2)   init high drive #
001e=41ea            lea      DRVBEG+DD_TOT(a2),a0 point at first table
0022 1081 Init10     move.b   d1,(a0)           set up size
0024=1141            move.b   d1,V_TRAK(a0)     set high track #
0028=41e8            lea      DRVMEM(a0),a0     move to next table
002c 5300            subq.b   #1,d0             last drive?
002e 66f2            bne.s    Init10            branch if not
```

---

[4]The drive table is, for the most part, a copy of the system sector on the disk, but it also includes a set of reserved fields. These are for Microware's use.

D.5. DEVICE INITIALIZATION

The init routine configures the FDC by setting the stepping rate [5] and indicating that DMA will not be used. The stepping rate is stored in the device descriptor and copied into the path descriptor's option area when the path is opened. The following block of code fetches the stepping rate from the device descriptor (the init routine doesn't see the path descriptor), and converts it from the device-independent descriptor code into a value that has meaning to the controller. It adds a flag that causes the controller to use programmed I/O and forwards the command to the FDC using a routine that is shared among all the code that manipulates the controller.

```
0030 7e00          moveq    #0,d7                          clear transfer mode
0032 7000          moveq    #0,d0
0034=1029          move.b   PD_STP-PD_OPT+M$DTyp(a1),d0    step rate from desc
0038 41fa          lea      RateTabl(pcr),a0               point to baud rate table
003c 1570          move.b   (a0,d0.w),Command2(a2)         move step and head load vals
0042 157c          move.b   #HLT+NonDMA,Command3(a2)       head ld & no-dma flag
0048 157c          move.b   #F.Specfy,Command1(a2)         put last command in buffer
004e 7803          moveq    #3,d4                          load command count
0050 6100          bsr      DoComand                       process the command
0054 6524          bcs.s    BadUnit                        exit if error
```

The FDC will raise an interrupt when it completes certain operations. The *F$IRQ* SVC must be used to inform the kernel that these interrupts should be forwarded to the driver's interrupt handler.

```
* Set up for IRQ's
0056 7000          moveq    #0,d0
0058 1400          move.b   d0,d2
005a=1029          move.b   M$Vector(a1),d0    get irq vector number from descriptor
005e=1429          move.b   M$IRQLvl(a1),d2    get hardware irq level
0062 e14a          lsl.w    #8,d2              shift to irq mask
0064=08c2          bset     #SupvrBit+8,d2     set system state bit
0068 3542          move.w   d2,V_IMask(a2)     save for future use.
006c=1229          move.b   M$Prior(a1),d1
0070 41fa          lea      IRQSrvc(pcr),a0    point to IRQ routine
0074=4e40          os9      F$IRQ              get on the table
0078 4e75 Return   rts

            BadUnit
007a=323c          move.w   #E$Unit,d1
007e=003c          ori      #Carry,ccr         set carry
```

---
[5] Note that stepping rate is a characteristic of the NEC765 FDC, not a drive. This fixed stepping rate could cause trouble in a system with several different drives attached to one controller. The controller would be forced to a stepping rate low enough for the slowest drive on the controller. Most drivers do not set the stepping rate in INIT.

0082 4e75   rts   exit with error

This table is used to convert the stepping rate value in the device descriptor into values suitable for the NEC 765.

```
         RateTabl
0084 48           dc.b    $48        12 ms step rate
0085 98           dc.b    $98        9 ms step
0086 a8           dc.b    $A8        6 ms step
0087 d8           dc.b    $D8        3 ms step
```

D.6 Write Sector

This routine is called by the file manager to write a sector to the disk. It is responsible for converting a logical sector number into side/track/sector coordinates,[6] seeking to the required track, and transferring the data. If write-verify is enabled, the driver reads the sector into the verify buffer after writing it from the primary buffer, and compares the read buffer to the write buffer.

Since most of the details of reading and writing are common—start the motor, calculate the track, seek (maybe restore), calculate the side and issue a read or write command—they share a routine called XfrSec that performs the common tasks.

```
* Write Sector
*
* Input:
* (d0.l) = Number of contiguous sectors to write
* (d2.l) = logical sector #
* (a1) = path descriptor
* (a2) = Static Storage ptr
* (a4) = Process descriptor pointer
* (a5) = Caller's register stack pointer
* (a6) = System global data storage pointer
*
         WritDisk:
0088 2f02              move.l   d2,-(a7)                save sector #
008a 6608              bne.s    Write10                 branch if not writing sect 0
008c=0829              btst     #FmtDis_B,PD_Cntl+1(a1) ok to write sect 0
0092 6642              bne.s    Write99                 no goto error rpt routine
0094 7605 Write10      moveq    #F.WrtSec,d3            write a sector cmd
0096 7e02              moveq    #2,d7                   flag disk write
```

---

[6]Sometimes the conversion from LSN to side/track/sector is done by the controller or the drive.

[†]*XfrSec*: see page 509

D.7. READ SECTOR

```
0098=2a69          movea.l  PD_BUF(a1),a5    point to buffer
009c 6170          bsr.s    XfrSec           transfer sector
009e 4cdf          movem.l  (a7)+,d2         restore sector #
00a2 6530          bcs.s    WritErr          leave if error
00a4=4a29          tst.b    PD_VFY(a1)       verify ?
00a8 6628          bne.s    WritExit         no, leave
00aa 4bea          lea      V_BUF(a2),a5     point to verify buffer
00ae 6138          bsr.s    ReadDs10         re-read the written block
00b0 651a          bcs.s    VerifyEr         exit with error
00b2 4bea          lea      V_BUF(a2),a5
00b6=2069          movea.l  PD_BUF(a1),a0    point to original buffer
00ba 303c          move.w   #256/4,d0        get # of bytes to check
00be 6004          bra.s    Verify10
00c0 5340 VerifyLp subq.w   #1,d0
00c2 670e          beq.s    WritExit         branch if so
00c4 bb88 Verify10 cmpm.l   (a0)+,(a5)+      is data the same?
00c6 67f8          beq.s    VerifyLp         branch if so
00c8=323c          move.w   #E$Write,d1      flag write error
00cc=003c VerifyEr ori      #Carry,ccr       flag error
00d0 6002          bra.s    WritErr

00d2 7200 WritExit moveq    #0,d1            no errors
00d4 4e75 WritErr  rts
00d6 4fef Write99  lea      4(a7),a7         restore stack ptr
00da=323c          move.w   #E$Format,d1     flag write error
00de=003c          ori      #Carry,ccr
00e2 4e75          rts
```

D.7 Read Sector

Unless the driver is reading sector zero, the entire function of ReadDisk is performed by XfrSec. The driver simply sets up the parameters to read a sector and branches to XfrSec. The *rts* at the end of XfrSec will return to the file manager.

If the driver is reading sector zero, it must update the drive table from the system information in sector zero. The contents of the system sector are simply copied from the primary buffer into the drive table entry for this drive.

[†] *XfrSec*: see page 509

```
*
* Read Sector
*
* Input:
* (d0.l) = number of contiguous sectors to read
* (d2.l) = logical sector #
* (a1) = path descriptor
* (a2) = Static Storage ptr
* (a4) = Process descriptor pointer
* (a5) = Caller's register stack pointer
* (a6) = System global data storage pointer
*
              ReadDisk:
00e4=2a69              movea.l  PD_BUF(a1),a5
00e8 7606  ReadDs10    moveq    #F.ReadSc,d3    get NEC read command
00ea 7e01              moveq    #1,d7           flag disk read
00ec 4a82              tst.l    d2              reading sector 0
00ee 661e              bne.s    XfrSec          branch if not
00f0 611c              bsr.s    XfrSec          read sector 0
00f2 6518              bcs.s    ReadDs99        exit if error

* UpDate Drive Table
* a0 points to drive table

***
* Here If Sector 0 Being Read
*
              Read20
00f4=2069              movea.l  PD_DTB(a1),a0
00f8=2669              movea.l  PD_BUF(a1),a3   point to sector buffer
00fc=323c              move.w   #DD_SIZ−1,d1    copy this many+1
0100 11b3  Read30      move.b   (a3,d1.w),(a0,d1.w)
0106 51c9              dbra     d1,Read30       branch if not
010a 7200              moveq    #0,d1           clear carry
010c 4e75  ReadDs99    rts
```

D.8 Service Routines for Read and Write

The preceeding read and write routines were very short blocks of code. If that seems to indicate that reading and writing with the NEC 765 is absurdly easy, you have been deceived. There is plenty of support code shared between the two routines.

The transfer routine is the top-level routine of the support code. Read sector and write sector load up registers with parameters and *bsr* (or *bra*) to XfrSec.

The code in XfrSec is almost device independent. The more intelligent hard disk

D.8. SERVICE ROUTINES FOR READ AND WRITE

controllers will be simpler than this because they read and write sectors by sector number. This version of XfrSec calls for a seek and calculates the side. The controller scans the track and picks out the sector.

The outline of XfrSec is:

>Turn on the drive's motor.
>Set the retry pattern.
>Get a pointer to the drive table entry for this drive.
>If the LSN is not zero
>Retry_point:
>>If the LSN is out of range
>>>declare an error and return to the caller.
>>If the LSN < sectors on track 0
>>>track = 0
>>>Sector = LSN
>>Else
>>>Sector = LSN − sectors on track 0.
>>>If(Sector ≠ 0)
>>>>Track = 1 + (Sector / sectors per track).
>>>>If double sided disk
>>>>>Side = low bit of Track;
>>>>>Track = Track / 2.
>>>>Sector = Sector mod Sectors per track.
>>Seek to track.
>>Setup command buffer.
>>Do the transfer.
>>If there was a recoverable error anywhere
>>>Restore and retry then just retry 3 times.
>>>Then restore and do the sequence again.
>>>Then just keep restoring and retrying

The retry logic is a little different from the official specification. This driver only consults the number of retries specified in the device descriptor to determine whether it should retry at all, not to govern the number of retries.[7]

The retries are controlled by a bit of tricky assembly language. The retry pattern is initialized to $EE, or %11101110 in binary. Before each retry the driver shifts the retry pattern one bit to the right. If it shifts a zero out the right side, the driver restores the head to track zero before retrying. If it shifts a one out the right side, the driver just retries from the seek..

The XfrSec block calls Restore, Select, SetTrk, SetUp, and DoCommand.

---

[7] It appears that this driver will do an unlimited number of retries if neccessary.

```
*
* Transfer Sector
*
* Input:
* (d0.b) = Read or Write Command
* (d2.l) = logical sector #
* (a1) = path descriptor
* (a2) = Static Storage ptr
* (a5) = data buffer
          XfrSec:
010e 2542           move.l    d2,V_LSN(a2)         buffer LSN
0112=266a           movea.l   V_PORT(a2),a3
0116 177c           move.b    #1,MotorCtl(a3)      turn on motors (5")
011c 7cee           moveq     #$EE,d6              set retry pattern
011e 600c           bra.s     XfrSec20
0120 6100 XfrSec10  bsr       Restore              reset to track zero
0124 6500           bcs       SectEr10             branch if error
0128 242a XfrSec15  move.l    V_LSN(a2),d2         restore LSN
012c 6100 XfrSec20  bsr       Select               get drive table pointer
0130 4a82           tst.l     d2                   reading sector 0
0132 6740           beq.s     XfrSec40             branch if so
0134=2028           move.l    DD_TOT(a0),d0        get total # of sectors
0138 e088           lsr.l     #8,d0                adjust for 3 byte value
013a b082           cmp.l     d2,d0                sector out of range?
013c 6366           bls.s     SectErr              branch if so
013e 7000           moveq     #0,d0
0140 1540           move.b    d0,V_Track(a2)       clear track number
0144 7a00           moveq     #0,d5                clear all of d5
0146=3a29           move.w    PD_T0S(a1),d5        get # of sectors in Trk 0
014a 4a82           tst.l     d2                   are we reading sector 0?
014c 672c           beq.s     XfrSec50             branch if so
014e ba82           cmp.l     d2,d5                is sector in track 0
0150 6228           bhi.s     XfrSec50             branch if so
0152 9485           sub.l     d5,d2                subtract track 0 sectors
0154 670a           beq.s     XfrSec30             if not zero continue
0156=1a28           move.b    DD_TKS(a0),d5
015a 6700           beq       BadUnit              exit with error
015e 84c5           divu      d5,d2                find track #
0160 5242 XfrSec30  addq.w    #1,d2                count track
0162=0828           btst      #Side_Bit,DD_FMT(a0) is it double sided?
0168 670a           beq.s     XfrSec40             branch if not
016a e24a           lsr.w     #1,d2                adjust track number
016c 6406           bcc.s     XfrSec40             branch if side 0
016e 157c           move.b    #4,V_Side(a2)        set side flag
0174 1542 XfrSec40  move.b    d2,V_Track(a2)
0178 4842           swap      d2                   get sector # in lower word
017a 1542 XfrSec50  move.b    d2,V_Sector(a2)
```

D.8. SERVICE ROUTINES FOR READ AND WRITE

```
017e 6100              bsr     SetTrk              move to track
0182 650a              bcs.s   XfrSec60            branch if error
0184 612c              bsr.s   SetUp               set up command buffer
0186 6520              bcs.s   SectEr10            exit with error
0188 6100              bsr     DoComand            do transfer
018c 6410              bcc.s   XfrSec70            branch if no error
018e=0c29 XfrSec60     cmpi.b  #1,PD_Trys(a1)
0194 6716              beq.s   XfrSecEr
0196 e20e              lsr.b   #1,d6               shift retry
0198 6486              bcc.s   XfrSec10            branch if restore
019a 668c              bne.s   XfrSec15            branch if retry
019c 600a              bra.s   SectEr10

            XfrSec70
422b                   clr.b   MotorCtl(a3)        shut off motors
01a2 4e75              rts

            SectErr
01a4=323c              move.w  #E$Sect,d1          flag sector out of range
            SectEr10
01a8 422b              clr.b   MotorCtl(a3)        shut off motors
01ac=003c XfrSecEr     ori     #Carry,ccr
01b0 4e75              rts
```

Setup is called only from XfrSec. It fills in the command buffer for the read or write command as specified in D3. It turns out that the *only* difference between a read command buffer and a write command buffer for the same sector is the code in the Command1 position in the command buffer.

The outline of the code is:

```
Setup(CmdByte)
    If Side = 1
        If the drive doesn't support double sided
            declare an error
        The drive number is already in Command2
        Command2 = Command2 or Side
    Command4 = Side / 4
    Command3 = Track
    if Double Density Disk
        Set DD bit in CmdByte
    Command5 = Sector + SectorOffset
    Command6 = bytes per sector (* div 256 *)
    Command7 = Sector
    Command8 = physical format gap length
    Command9 = physical format data length
```

```
Command1 = CmdByte
return 9 (* Command size *)
```

There are a few non-obvious places in this code.

- The drive number is set in Command2 by the Select routine which must be called before Setup.

- The side number in PD_SID is set by the caller. It is zero for side zero or four for side one. Floppy disk controllers usually address up to four drives numbered zero through three. Or'ing a four with the drive number to indicate that it is side one of the drive has the effect of supporting eight single-sided drives: 0–3 are side zero , 4–7 are side one. The side number is divided by four to give the ordinary zero or one before it is stored in Command4 as the head number.

```
*
* Setup
* sets up command buffer for reads and writes
*
* Input:
* d3.b floppy command byte
* (a0.l) pointer to drive table
* (a1.l) path descriptor
* (a2.l) device static storage
* (a3.l) pointer to port
*
* Returns:
* d4.b command size
*
              SetUp:
01b2 48e7             movem.l d0–d1,–(a7)
01b6 122a             move.b  V_Side(a2),d1           is it side 0
01ba 670e             beq.s   SetUp20                 branch if so
01bc=0c29             cmpi.b  #2,PD_SID(a1)           can device do double sided disks?
01c2 654c             blo.s   SetUpErr                branch if not
01c4 832a             or.b    d1,Command2(a2)         merge with drive #
01c8 e409             lsr.b   #2,d1                   move again for side register
01ca 1541  SetUp20    move.b  d1,Command4(a2)         set head number
01ce 156a             move.b  V_Track(a2),Command3(a2) set up track #

01d4=0829             btst    #PDDN_Bit,PD_DNS(a1)    is device double density?
01da 6704             beq.s   SetUp60                 branch if not
01dc 08c3             bset    #MF_Bit,d3              set density bit in command
01e0 102a  SetUp60    move.b  V_Sector(a2),d0         get the sector number
01e4=d029             add.b   PD_SOffs(a1),d0         add in sector offset
01e8 1540             move.b  d0,Command5(a2)         set up sector #
```

D.8. SERVICE ROUTINES FOR READ AND WRITE

```
01ec 157c          move.b   #N,Command6(a2) set up bytes per sector
01f2 156a          move.b   V_Sector(a2),Command7(a2) say last sector on track
01f8 157c          move.b   #GPL,Command8(a2) set up gap length
01fe 157c          move.b   #DTL,Command9(a2)
0204 7809          moveq    #9,d4           set command size
0206 1543          move.b   d3,Command1(a2) set command
020a 4cdf          movem.l  (a7)+,d0–d1
020e 4e75          rts

          SetUpErr
0210 4cdf          movem.l  (a7)+,d0–d1
0214=323c          move.w   #E$BTyp,d1
0218=003c          ori      #Carry,ccr
021c 4e75          rts
```

Restore is called from XfrSec as part of error recovery and from the SS_Reset setstat. It selects a drive (which sets the Command2 byte) and attempts to seek to track five. Then it uses the controller's F.Rest command to restore the head to track zero.

The seek to track five gives the head a little motion if it is already on track zero before the restore. If restore is called to help recover from an error, this motion could be important. Seeking to track five is also important on some older drives that may move the head beyond track zero. By moving the head out a few tracks before restoring it, the driver gets the head out of this hole.

```
*
* Restore Drive to Track Zero
*
* Input: a1 = Path descriptor ptr
* a3 = Controller base address
* a2 = Static Storage ptr
*
* NOTE: This routine steps in several tracks before issuing
* the restore command.
*
          Restore:
021e 612e          bsr.s    Select              select drive
0220 652a          bcs.s    Restor20            branch if error
0222 157c          move.b   #5,V_Track(a2)      seek out five tracks
0228 6152          bsr.s    SetTrk
022a 6520          bcs.s    Restor20            exit with error
022c 157c          move.b   #F.Rest,Command1(a2)
0232 422a          clr.b    Command3(a2)        looking for track 0
0236 7802          moveq    #2,d4               set # of command bytes
0238 48a7          movem.w  d7,–(a7)            save transfer mode
023c 7e00          moveq    #0,d7
023e 617a          bsr.s    DoComand            issue seek command
```

```
0240 4c9f            movem.w (a7)+,d7
0244 6506            bcs.s    Restor20
0246=317c            move.w   #0,V_TRAK(a0)
024c 4e75 Restor20   rts
```

The Select routine uses the PD_DRV field from the path descriptor to set various fields that depend on the drive number:

- It sets the side to zero. This isn't strictly a drive number issue, but . . . .

- It sets A0 to point to the drive table entry for this drive. This pointer was pre-calculated by the file manager and saved in PD_DTB. The driver just moves it to A0.

- If the drive number is different from the driver number used for the driver's last operation, Select checks the drive number against the maximum permissible drive number and returns an error if the drive number is illegal.

- The drive number is stored in Command2.

To recapitulate:

V_Side	Is set to 0
A0	Is set to PD_DTB
V_CurDrv	Is set to PD_DRV
Command2	Is set to PD_Drv

```
*
* Select Drive
*
* Set up hardware to select proper drive.
* UpDate & Return drive table pointer.
* Clear V_Side,V_Seek
*
* Input:
* (a1) = path descriptor
* (a2) = Static Storage ptr
* (a3) = Device physical address
*
* Returns:
* (a0) = pointer to current drive table
            Select:
024e 157c            move.b   #0,V_Side(a2)     set side zero
0254=2069            movea.l  PD_DTB(a1),a0     point to drive table
```

D.8. SERVICE ROUTINES FOR READ AND WRITE

```
0258=1029              move.b   PD_DRV(a1),d0       Get Logical Unit Number
025c b02a              cmp.b    V_CurDrv(a2),d0     Same drive as before?
0260 670a              beq.s    Select30            branch if so
0262=b02a              cmp.b    V_NDRV(a2),d0       drive in range?
0266 640a              bhs.s    BadDrive            branch if so
0268 1540              move.b   d0,V_CurDrv(a2)     Update drive #
026c 1540  Select30    move.b   d0,Command2(a2)    Save drive #
0270 4e75              rts

0272=323c  BadDrive    move.w   #E$Unit,d1          flag bad unit
0276=003c              ori      #Carry,ccr
027a 4e75              rts
```

SetTrk compares V_Track, the target track, to V_TRAK, the current track. If V_TRAK equals V_Track, the head is already in the right place and SetTrk returns without changing anything.

If the head needs to be moved, SetTrk builds a command buffer:

- Command1 is set to F.Seek, the NEC765 op code for seeking.

- Command2 is already set to the drive number by a previous call to Select.

- Command3 is set to the target track, V_Track.

DoCommand is used to send the command to the controller.

```
*
* Step Head to New Track
*
* Input:
* (a0) = pointer to drive tables
* (a1) = path descriptor
* (a2) = Static Storage ptr
* (a3) = Device physical address
       SetTrk:
027c 102a              move.b   V_Track(a2),d0
0280=b028              cmp.b    V_TRAK(a0),d0       same track?
0284 6720              beq.s    SetTrk20            branch if so
0286 157c  SetTrk10    move.b   #F.Seek,Command1(a2)  set command buffer
028c 1540              move.b   d0,Command3(a2)     Buffer track #
0290 7803              moveq    #3,d4               set command count
0292 48a7              movem.w  d7,-(a7)            save
0296 7e00              moveq    #0,d7
0298 6120              bsr.s    DoComand            issue seek command
029a 4c9f              movem.w  (a7)+,d7
```

```
029e 6506              bcs.s    SetTrk20
02a0=116a              move.b   V_Track(a2),V_TRAK(a0)
02a6 4e75  SetTrk20    rts
```

The FDC can't receive commands at arbitrary intervals. It takes time to digest a command and more time to complete the command. The Wait routine delays 12 microseconds for the FDC's registers to become valid. Then it polls the FDC's main status register at full speed, looking for the flag that indicates that the data register is ready.

Delay returns after at least 12 microseconds have passed. This routine can be called between writing to the FDC and reading the FDC's main status register.

Wait returns when the RQM bit in the FDC's main status register is on.

```
* Wait for controller ready
*
* Input:
* (a0) = pointer to drive tables
* (a1) = path descriptor
* (a2) = Static Storage ptr
* (a3) = Device physical address
*
* Returns:
* (d1.b) = status of disk controller
*
* Destroys: d1
*
* Calls: Delay
*
02a8 6108  Wait:       bsr.s    Delay        wait for valid status
02aa 122b  Wait20      move.b   MSR(a3),d1   ready for command?
02ae 6afa              bpl.s    Wait20       branch if not
02b0 4e75              rts

* Delay 12 Micro Seconds for controller to give
* valid status
*
* Destroys d1
*
02b2 720a  Delay       moveq    #DelayTim,d1
02b4 5301  Delay10     subq.b   #1,d1
02b6 6afc              bpl.s    Delay10
02b8 4e75              rts
```

DoComand controls the submission of the command buffer to the FDC. The high-level outline of DoComand is:

D.8. SERVICE ROUTINES FOR READ AND WRITE

Wait for the FDC to become "ready."
Move all but the last byte in the command buffer into the FDC.
If this is a read
    Mask interrupts.
    Send the last byte in the command buffer.
    Disable interrupts from the FDC.
    Move data from the FDC to the data buffer.
    Unmask interrupts.
    Check for errors and return.
If this is a write
    Mask interrupts.
    Send the last byte from the command buffer.
    Disable interrupts from the FDC.
    Move data from the data buffer into the FDC.
    Unmask interrupts.
    Check for errors and return.
If this is not a read or a write
    If the command is *Specify*
        It came from init, don't wait for completion.
        Return.
    Mask interrupts.
    Set up for interrupts.
    Send the last byte from the command buffer.
    Enable FDC interrupts.
    Unmask interrupts.
    Sleep until the interrupt handler signals.
    Check for errors and return.

The first block in DoComand waits for the device to become ready for a command. First, it polls the DIO bit waiting for the device to be ready for commands. Then, it polls for the FDC to get out of execution mode. Finally, it polls for the FDC to indicate that none of its disks are in seek mode. If the drive door is open, or some similar problem, the driver could be stuck permanently in the polling loop. To prevent this, the loop is limited to 50 iterations. If the device isn't ready after 50 times around the polling loop, the driver gives up and declares that the device is not ready.

```
*
* Issue Transfer Commands
*
* Input:
* (a0) = pointer to drive tables
* (a1) = path descriptor
* (a2) = Static Storage pointer
* (a3) = Device physical address
* (a5) = buffer pointer
* (d4.b) = # of command bytes
* (d7.b) = transfer mode 0=IRQ 1=read 2=write
*
* Returns:
* (d1.w) = Error Code (if any)
* ccr = Carry set if error
*
* Destroys: d0,d1,d3,d4
*
* Calls: Wait, ReadRslt
*
          DoComand:
02ba 48e7            movem.l a0–a6/d7,–(a7)   savem all

* this code makes sure the controller is ready to accept commands

02be 7032            moveq   #50,d0               try fifty times
02c0 082b  DoCmnd10  btst    #DIO_Bit,MSR(a3)     device ready for commands?
02c6 6718            beq.s   DoCmnd40             branch if so
02c8 4a2b            tst.b   DataReg(a3)          ready byte of data
02cc 61e4            bsr.s   Delay                wait before testing again
02ce 51c8            dbra    d0,DoCmnd10          try again
02d2=323c  DoCmnd20  move.w  #E$NotRdy,d1         exit with error
02d6 4cdf            movem.l (a7)+,a0–a6/d7
02da=003c            ori     #Carry,ccr           set the carry
02de 4e75            rts                          exit with error

02e0 082b  DoCmnd40: btst    #CB_Bit,MSR(a3)      still execution mode?
02e6 66ea            bne.s   DoCmnd20             branch if so
02e8 102b            move.b  MSR(a3),d0           get controllor status
02ec 0200            andi.b  #(D0B!D1B!D2B!D3B),d0 any devices in seek mode
02f0 6718            beq.s   DoCmnd50             branch if not
02f2 177c            move.b  #F.SnsIRQ,DataReg(a3) sense irq status
02f8 61ae            bsr.s   Wait
02fa 4a2b            tst.b   DataReg(a3)          get first sense byte
02fe 61a8            bsr.s   Wait
0300 4a2b            tst.b   DataReg(a3)          get last sense byte
0304 0201            andi.b  #(D0B!D1B!D2B!D3B),d1 any devices in seek mode
```

D.8. SERVICE ROUTINES FOR READ AND WRITE 519

```
0308 66d6              bne.s      DoCmnd40        branch if so
```

The device is ready. Move all but the last byte of the command buffer into it.

```
030a 49ea  DoCmnd50 lea          Command1(a2),a4  point to command buffer
030e 5504             subq.b     #2,d4            adjust loop count
0310 6196  DoCmnd80 bsr.s        Wait             wait for valid status
0312 175c             move.b     (a4)+,DataReg(a3)
0316 51cc             dbra       d4,DoCmnd80      branch until one byte left
```

If this is not a data-transfer command, branch to IRQCmnd. If it is a data transfer command, prepare pointers to the data register and the data buffer and select read or write.

```
031a 618c             bsr.s      Wait             wait for valid data
031c 4a07             tst.b      d7               transfer data?
031e 6700             beq        IRQCmnd          branch if not
0322 4ded             lea        256(a5),a6       last byte to move
0326 41eb             lea        DataReg(a3),a0   point directly to data register
032a e20f             lsr.b      #1,d7            is it a read?
032c 6528             bcs.s      DoRead           branch if so
```

This block of code transfers data into the FDC for a write. Mask interrupts for speed and move the data buffer into the FDC's data register. When all the data is transferred into the FDC, touch the TermCnt register to signify the end of the write.

```
032e 40e7             move       sr,-(a7)         save IRQ status
0330=46fc             move       #Supervis+IntMask,sr  mask IRQs
0334 109c             move.b     (a4)+,(a0)       move last byte
0336 422b             clr.b      IntEnabl(a3)     disable IRQs
033a 7207             moveq      #DelayTim-3,d1   wait 12 us
033c 5301  DoCmnd90 subq.b       #1,d1
033e 6afc             bpl.s      DoCmnd90
0340 4a13  DoWrite    tst.b      (a3)             ready to move data
0342 6afc             bpl.s      DoWrite          branch if not
0344 0813             btst       #Busy_Bit,(a3)   in execution phase?
0348 6732             beq.s      TfrDone          branch if not
034a 109d             move.b     (a5)+,(a0)       move data to controller
034c bbce             cmpa.l     a6,a5            moved last byte?
034e 66f0             bne.s      DoWrite          branch if not
0350 4a2b             tst.b      TermCnt(a3)      flag last byte written
0354 6026             bra.s      TfrDone          all done get results
```

The following block of code transfers data from the FDC to the data buffer for a read. It is almost identical to the write code above.

```
0356 40e7  DoRead     move    sr,-(a7)              save IRQ status
0358=46fc             move    #Supervis+IntMask,sr  mask IRQs
035c 109c             move.b  (a4)+,(a0)            move last byte
035e 422b             clr.b   IntEnabl(a3)          disable IRQs
0362 7207             moveq   #DelayTim-3,d1        wait 12 us
0364 5301  DoRead10   subq.b  #1,d1
0366 6afc             bpl.s   DoRead10
0368 4a13  DoRead20   tst.b   (a3)                  ready to move data
036a 6afc             bpl.s   DoRead20              branch if not
036c 0813             btst    #Busy_Bit,(a3)        in execution phase?
0370 670a             beq.s   TfrDone               branch if not
0372 1ad0             move.b  (a0),(a5)+            move data from controller
0374 bbce             cmpa.l  a6,a5                 moved last byte?
0376 66f0             bne.s   DoRead20              branch if not
0378 4a2b             tst.b   TermCnt(a3)           flag last byte read
```

The read and write blocks of code rejoin here at TfrDone.

```
           TfrDone
037c 46df             move    (a7)+,sr              unmask irqs
037e 4cdf             movem.l (a7)+,a0-a6/d7
```

* fall through to read results

* Read Results
* Reads results bytes of command just executed.
*
* Input:
* (a1) = path descriptor
* (a2) = Static Storage ptr
* (a3) = Device physical address
*
* Returns:
* d1 = os9 error code
* ccr = carry set if error
*

```
0382 48e7  ReadRslt   movem.l d0/a0,-(a7)
0386 41ea             lea     Results(a2),a0        point to result buffer
038a 6004             bra.s   ReadRs40
038c 10eb  ReadRs10   move.b  DataReg(a3),(a0)+     move data to buffer
0390 6100  ReadRs40   bsr     Wait                  wait for controller ready
0394 082b             btst    #DIO_Bit,MSR(a3)      still reading data
039a 66f0             bne.s   ReadRs10              branch if so
```

D.8. SERVICE ROUTINES FOR READ AND WRITE

The following block of code converts the result code from the FDC into an OS-9 error code or a successful return.

```
            ErrorTst
039c 102a           move.b   Results(a2),d0
03a0 0200           andi.b   #(IC!EC!NR),d0      strip all but error bits
03a4 674a           beq.s    No_Error            exit with no errors
03a6=323c           move.w   #E$NotRdy,d1        flag not ready error
03aa e300           asl.b    #1,d0               valid command?
03ac 6538           bcs.s    Error_Ex            branch if not
03ae 0800           btst     #(EC_Bit+1),d0      bad equipment?
03b2 6632           bne.s    Error_Ex            branch if so
03b4 102a           move.b   Results+1(a2),d0    get next result byte
03b8 b07c           cmp.w    #EN,d0              any errors in this reg
03bc 6732           beq.s    No_Error            branch if not
03be=323c           move.w   #E$Seek,d1
03c2 e208           lsr.b    #1,d0               seek error?
03c4 6524           bcs.s    Err_Ex1             branch if so
03c6 0800           btst     #(ND_Bit−1),d0      seek error?
03ca 661a           bne.s    Error_Ex            branch if so
03cc=323c           move.w   #E$WP,d1
03d0 e208           lsr.b    #1,d0               write protect?
03d2 6516           bcs.s    Err_Ex1             branch if so
03d4=323c           move.w   #E$DevBsy,d1        flag device busy
03d8 e608           lsr.b    #3,d0
03da=323c           move.w   #E$CRC,d1           flag crc error
03de e208           lsr.b    #1,d0               crc error?
03e0 6508           bcs.s    Err_Ex1             branch if so
03e2=323c           move.w   #E$Unit,d1          catch all error
            Error_Ex
03e6=003c           ori      #Carry,ccr          set carry
03ea 4cdf   Err_Ex1 movem.l  (a7)+,a0/d0
03ee 4e75           rts

            No_Error
03f0 7200           moveq    #0,d1               clear carry
03f2 4cdf           movem.l  (a7)+,a0/d0
03f6 4e75           rts                          exit with no error
```

IRQCmd is used for commands that don't transfer data—seek commands and specify commands. The seek command can be particularly slow, so it is important not to tie up the processor for the duration of a seek.

This driver only sleeps during seeks, but drivers should, in general, try to sleep whenever they need to wait for an event that the device can signal with an interrupt.

The driver doesn't need to wait for results from the specify command. It comes to IRQCmd because the specify command isn't a data transfer command, but the command only sets the step rate and so forth, and it is only done at initialization time. IRQCmnd moves the specify command into the FDC and returns without even checking for a result code.

Other commands get to IRQCm10. Here the driver:

- Calls for interrupts from the FDC

- Stores the current process number (which is stored in V_BUSY)V_BUSY into V_WAKE

- Finishes the command by writing the last byte of the FDC command buffer into the FDC controller

- Sleeps

When the device raises an interrupt to indicate that the command has completed, the interrupt handler will get control and send a signal to the waiting process. IRQCmnd will resume after the sleep when it gets the signal.

The interrupt, and thus the signal, could mean that the seek completed successfully. They could also mean that the seek did not work. In SenseIRQ the driver asks the FDC for status information and verifies that the seek completed at the right track.

```
*
* Issue Last Command from command buffer
* using interrupts.
*
* Input:
* (a0) = pointer to drive tables
* (a1) = path descriptor
* (a2) = Static Storage ptr
* (a3) = Device physical address
*
              IRQCmnd
03f8 121c           move.b   (a4)+,d1              get last command
03fa 4cdf           movem.l  (a7)+,a0-a6/d7
03fe 0c2a           cmpi.b   #F.Specfy,Command1(a2) specify command?
0404 6608           bne.s    IRQCm10               branch if not
0406 1741           move.b   d1,DataReg(a3)        move last command
040a 7200           moveq    #0,d1                 no errors
040c 4e75           rts                            exit

040e 40e7  IRQCm10  move     sr,-(a7)              save IRQ status
0410 46ea           move     V_IMask(a2),sr        mask IRQs
0414=356a           move.w   V_BUSY(a2),V_WAKE(a2) set up for interrupt
041a 1741           move.b   d1,DataReg(a3)        move last command
041e 177c           move.b   #1,IntEnabl(a3)       enable FDC irqs
```

D.9. GETSTAT AND SETSTAT

```
0424 46df              move     (a7)+,sr              enable IRQs
0426 7000  IRQCm20     moveq    #0,d0                 sleep forever
0428=4e40              os9      F$Sleep
042c=4a6a              tst.w    V_WAKE(a2)            valid wakeup?
0430 66f4              bne.s    IRQCm20               branch if not
```

* fall through to sense what caused the IRQ

*
* Sense Irq
*

```
           SenseIRQ
0432 422b              clr.b    IntEnabl(a3)          disable IRQs
0436 177c              move.b   #F.SnsIRQ,DataReg(a3) give controller command
043c 6100              bsr      Wait
0440 182b              move.b   DataReg(a3),d4
0444 0c04              cmpi.b   #Invalid,d4
0448 67e8              beq.s    SenseIRQ
044a 6100              bsr      Wait
044e 142b              move.b   DataReg(a3),d2        read last byte
0452 0804              btst     #Seek_Bit,d4          was seek complete
0456 670a              beq.s    Sens_Err              branch if not
0458 b42a              cmp.b    Command3(a2),d2       seek to right track?
045c 6604              bne.s    Sens_Err              branch if not
045e 7200              moveq    #0,d1
0460 4e75              rts

           Sens_Err
0462=323c              move.w   #E$NotRdy,d1
0466=003c              ori      #Carry,ccr
046a 4e75              rts
```

D.9 Getstat and SetStat

This driver supports two setstats and no getstats. The *SS_Reset* setstat branches to the Restore routine, and the *SS_WTrk* setstat branches to a special routine.[8]

---

[8]The writetrack setstat is normally used to format disks.

```
**
* GetStat/PutStat
*
* Passed: (d0.w)=Status Code
* (a1)=Path Descriptor
* (a2)=Static Storage Address
* (a4) = Process descriptor pointer
* (a5) = Caller's register stack pointer
* (a6) = System global data storage pointer
* Returns: Depends on status code
*
            PutStat
046c=266a            movea.l  V_PORT(a2),a3
0470=0c40            cmpi.w   #SS_WTrk,d0      is it a Write Track call?
0474 6712            beq.s    WriteTrk         branch if so
0476=0c40            cmpi.w   #SS_Reset,d0     is it a restore call?
047a 6700            beq      Restore          branch if so
047e=323c  GetStat   move.w   #E$UnkSvc,d1     flag unknown service code
0482=003c            ori      #Carry,ccr       flag error
0486 4e75            rts
```

Since writing tracks bypasses all OS-9 disk security and could easily destroy the disk structure, it checks for format permission in the path descriptor. If the device descriptor didn't specify format permission, the driver won't permit the write track operation.

WriteTrk is very similar to TfrSec except that it concerns itself with sector numbers in an entirely different way from TfrSec.

WriteTrk builds the command buffer with information about the disk, the drive number, the side, the track number, and the write density. It also constructs an abreviated description of the track in the path's normal buffer. The buffer uses four bytes to describe each sector:

- Cylinder number
- Head number
- Record number
- Bytes per sector

The record number is taken from an interleave table supplied by the caller. The other values are from the path descriptor or calculated by the driver.

At four bytes per sector, a standard 256-byte buffer can describe a 64-sector track. If the controller requires an actual track image, the driver must either allocate a large

D.9. GETSTAT AND SETSTAT

buffer for the track image and build the image in the new buffer (and free it after it is written), or trust the calling program to construct a correct track image and use the track buffer pointed to by the caller's register A0.

```
*
* WriteTrk
*
* Write track buffer to disk
**
              WriteTrk
0488=0829                btst     #FmtDis_B,PD_Cntl+1(a1) enable for formatting
048e 670a                beq.s    WrtTrk10          branch if so
0490=323c                move.w   #E$Format,d1      flag bad mode
0494=003c                ori      #Carry,ccr        exit with flag
0498 4e75                rts
049a=266a WrtTrk10       movea.l  V_PORT(a2),a3
049e 177c                move.b   #1,MotorCtl(a3)   turn on drive motor

04a4 6100                bsr      Select            select proper drive
04a8 6500                bcs      WrtTrkEx          exit with error
04ac=2869                movea.l  PD_RGS(a1),a4     get register pointer
04b0=156c                move.b   R$d2+3(a4),V_Track(a2) save track # for seek
04b6 6100                bsr      SetTrk            seek to track
04ba 6500                bcs      WrtTrkEx
04be 157c                move.b   #F.WrtTrk+DDensity,Command1(a2) select command
04c4 157c                move.b   #N,Command3(a2)   Set up # bytes per sector
04ca=1569                move.b   PD_SCT+1(a1),Command4(a2) get sectors/track
04d0=362c                move.w   R$d3+2(a4),d3     get format byte
04d4 103c                move.b   #GPL5DD,d0        default to 5" drive
04d8=0829                btst     #Size_Bit,PD_TYP(a1) is it 5"
04de 6612                bne.s    WrtTrk15          branch if not
04e0 0803                btst     #Dens_Bit,d3      is it double density?
04e4 6620                bne.s    WrtTrk25          branch if so
04e6 103c                move.b   #GPL5SD,d0        set up 5" single density
04ea 08aa                bclr     #MF_Bit,Command1(a2) clear double density bit
04f0 6014                bra.s    WrtTrk25

04f2 103c WrtTrk15       move.b   #GPL8DD,d0        default to double density
04f6 0803                btst     #Dens_Bit,d3      is it double density?
04fa 660a                bne.s    WrtTrk25          branch if so
04fc 103c                move.b   #GPL8SD,d0        set gap to single density
0500 08aa                bclr     #MF_Bit,Command1(a2) clear double density bit

0506 1540 WrtTrk25       move.b   d0,Command5(a2) setup gap length
050a 157c                move.b   #Filler,Command6(a2) set filler byte
```

* Figure side

```
0510=1143            move.b   d3,DD_FMT(a0)
0514 0803            btst     #Side_Bit,d3      is it side 0?
0518 670c            beq.s    WrtTrk30          branch if so
051a 157c            move.b   #1,V_Side(a2)     set to side 1
0520 08ea            bset     #2,Command2(a2)   set to head 1
0526=102c WrtTrk30   move.b   R$d2+3(a4),d0     get track #
052a 122a            move.b   V_Side(a2),d1     get side #
052e 7601            moveq    #N,d3             get # bytes/sector
0530=3829            move.w   PD_SCT(a1),d4     get # of sectors/track
0534 5344            subq.w   #1,d4             adjust for loop count
0536 4bea            lea      V_BUF(a2),a5      build track buffer
053a=2c6c            movea.l  R$a1(a4),a6       get interleave table pointer

053e 1ac0 WrtTrk40   move.b   d0,(a5)+          set cylinder #
0540 1ac1            move.b   d1,(a5)+          set head #
0542 1ade            move.b   (a6)+,(a5)+       get record #
0544 1ac3            move.b   d3,(a5)+          set # of bytes/sector
0546 51cc            dbra     d4,WrtTrk40

054a 7806            moveq    #6,d4             get # of command bytes
054c 7e02            moveq    #2,d7             set transfer mode to write
054e 4bea            lea      V_BUF(a2),a5      point to track buffer
0552 6100            bsr      DoComand          execute the command
0556 650a            bcs.s    WTrkEr10
0558=266a            movea.l  V_PORT(a2),a3
055c 422b            clr.b    MotorCtl(a3)      turn off drive motor
0560 4e75 WrtTrkEx   rts

0562=266a WTrkEr10   movea.l  V_PORT(a2),a3
0566 422b            clr.b    MotorCtl(a3)      turn off drive motor
056a=003c            ori      #Carry,ccr
056e 4e75            rts
```

D.10 Terminate

The terminate routine is called by IOMan when the device is detached. It should reverse the effects of the init routine (except that it doesn't need to de-initialize static storage variables).

For this driver, the termination routine only has to disable interrupts from the device and remove it from the interupt polling table.

It is not likely that interrupts from the device would be enabled, but the termination routine should be extremely careful about interrupts. If OS-9 can't find a interrupt

D.11. INTERRUPT SEVICE ROUTINE

handler that will take responsibility for an interrupt, it will ignore that interrupt in the future. This is a desperate move.

If the driver may have outstanding operations, the termination routine should abort the operations gracefully or wait for them to terminate before returning. This would be an issue if, for instance, the driver maintained a write-behind cache. Recent writes might be stored in the driver's buffers but not yet written to disk. The termination routine would be obliged to flush the write cache to the disk before returning. If the driver allowed itself to terminate without flushing its buffers, the data in the buffered writes would be lost.

```
*
* Terminate use of device
*
* Passed:
* (a1) = device descriptor
* (a2) = device static storage
* (a6) = System global data storage pointer
*
* Returns: Nothing
*
         Term
0570=266a         movea.l  V_PORT(a2),a3    get port address
0574 177c         move.b   #0,IntEnabl(a3)  disable interrupts on device
057a=1029         move.b   M$Vector(a1),d0  get vector #
057e 91c8         suba.l   a0,a0            take device off table
0580=4e40         os9      F$IRQ
0584 4e75         rts
```

D.11 Interrupt Sevice Routine

This interrupt handler was connected to the OS-9 polling table by the initialization routine. The interrupt service routine is called with the device's interrupt masked each time an interrupt with its vector is raised.[9]

Any number of devices can share a common hardware interrupt priority and interrupt vector. The interrupt handler's first task is to query the device and find out whether this interrupt belongs to it.

Technically, a driver can't determine whether its device actually raised the interrupt, but it doesn't matter. If another device with the same interrupt vector raised the interrupt and this device completed a command and tried to raise the interrupt a moment later, two device drivers would be ready to claim the interrupt. The driver

---
[9]This driver assumes that the interrupt is intended for it. It must have an interrupt vector to itself.

earlier in the polling table would claim the interrupt and deal with its device; the device would respond by dropping the interrupt. When the IRQ routine returned to the kernel and the interrupt was unmasked, the other interrupt would still be asserted, this time by the other device, and the drivers would get another chance.

Action	Interrupt mask	Device 1	Device 2
Devices request service	0	Int	Int
Processor responds	mask	Int	Int
Driver 1 called	mask	Int	Int
Driver 1 completes	mask		Int
Kernel clears mask			Int
Process responds	mask		Int
Driver 1 called	mask		Int
Driver 1 isn't interested	mask		Int
Driver 2 called	mask		Int
Driver 2 returns	mask		
Kernel clears mask			

Theoretically, if many drivers shared a common interrupt/vector, a driver at the back of the queue might never be served. Practically, interrupt handlers are fast enough that it would take an astonishing burst of interrupts to keep the interrupt asserted for any length of time.

This interrupt handler considers three cases:

1. The driver is waiting for command completion. In this case the handler sends a wakeup signal to the sleeping process.

2. The driver is not waiting and the FDC is not ready for a command. The handler takes no action in this case.

3. The driver is not waiting and the FDC is ready for a command. The handler gives the FDC a command to sense interrupt status and reads the FDC's data register twice to throw out the result of the command.

D.11. INTERRUPT SEVICE ROUTINE

```
*
* Interrupt Service routine
*
* Handles irqs from Seek,Restore & NotReady
*
* Passed :
*
* (a2) static storage pointer
* (a3) pointer to device
* (a6) system global static storage
*
* Returns :
* carry set if device didn't generate irq
**
                  IRQSrvc
0586 422b         clr.b    IntEnabl(a3)       disable IRQs from controller
058a=302a         move.w   V_WAKE(a2),d0      was driver waiting?
058e 6620         bne.s    IRQSr20            branch if so
0590 082b         btst     #DIO_Bit,MSR(a3)   Ready for command
0596 6622         bne.s    IRQExit            branch if not
0598 177c         move.b   #F.SnsIRQ,DataReg(a3)
059e 6100         bsr      Delay              wait 12 us
05a2 4a2b         tst.b    DataReg(a3)        read first byte
05a6 6100         bsr      Delay              wait 12 more us
05aa 4a2b         tst.b    DataReg(a3)        read second byte
05ae 600a         bra.s    IRQExit

05b0=426a IRQSr20 clr.w    V_WAKE(a2)         flag IRQ occured
05b4=7200         moveq    #S$Wake,d1         get wake up signal
05b6=4e40         os9      F$Send             send driver signal
05ba 7200 IRQExit moveq    #0,d1
05bc 4e75         rts

000005be          ends
```

Index

.
.login, 418

/
/dd, 236

@
@, 193

A
active queue, 116–117, 119–121
address exceptions, 413
aging, 116
alarms, 87, 96, 99, 104, 345
alarms as timers, 96
alarms in system calls, 99
allocation map, 191
assertions, 379
async safety, 72, 74
atomic operations, 63–64, 72, 294, 297–298
attach, 25, 170, 236
auto linefeed, 161, 244
autosize, 358
autosize drives, 248
autovectored interrupts, 184

B
B_PARITY, 47
B_ROM, 47
B_USER, 47

background, 54
backspace, 244
backspace character, 243
bad sector (recovery), 211
baud rate, 297
best-fit allocation, 31
binding time, 11
bit density, 248
BIX, 68
boot, 5
    device descriptors, 237
boot file, 241
    pointer, 190
bootlist, 418
branch table, 152
broadcast signals, 75
buffered I/O, 200
bus errors, 413
bus locking, 186
busy waiting, 134

C
C static storage, 260
carriage return, 161
case translation, 243
CD–I, 49
checkpoint, 96
child process, 54, 162
cio, 143–144
classes of memory, 45
close, 452

INDEX

cluster, 190
CNTL_NOFMT, 337
coldstart
    user code, 232
colored memory, 45
colored memory definition, 46
colored memory descriptor list, 48
command
    backup, 199
    copy, 26
    dcheck, 191–192, 208
    debug, 10, 112, 239
    deiniz, 253
    devs, 196
    dir, 179
    dir of /pipe, 179
    dsave, 192
    dump, 192
    fixmod, 239
    format, 251
    ident, 10, 14
    iniz, 25, 36
    kill, 75, 141
    load, 241
    login, 59
    maps, 32
    mdir, 32
    mfree, 25, 32, 35
    moded, 240
    os9gen, 104, 241
    procs, 176
    qsort, 176
    rdump, 373
    save, 239
    sleep, 25, 34
    srcdbg, 112
    tmode, 160, 238
    unlink, 241
    xmode, 238

command line editing, 245
configuration commands, 339
contention, 135
contention (for a semaphore), 137
control-C, 53, 163
cost of trap call, 143
CRC, 10
    calculation, 7–9
    circumventing check, 10
create, 449
critical section, 186, 297, 303
cstart, 260–261, 264, 266, 373, 424
customization modules, 232
cyclic alarm, 99

D

D_BlkSiz, 39, 42–43, 45
D_MaxAge, 117–119, 121–122
D_MinBlk, 43, 45
D_MinPty, 64, 119, 122
damaged module header, 6
data module creation, 20
data rate, 253
data/stack allocation, 26
DD_BIT, 190
deadlock, 166
deadly embrace, 166
deadly signal, 88, 305–306
default device, 236
default directories, 273
default memory allocation, 42
defective memory, 5
deferred TLink, 146
defsfile, 288
delayed *F$TLink*, 145
delete, 453
delete key, 246
destructive backspace, 243
detach, 170–171

INDEX

determinism, 64
device address, 240
device attributes, 161
device configuration offset, 242
device control word, 251
device descriptor, 161, 235–237, 241, 293, 495
    /dd, 236
    common, 235, 241
    creation, 237, 241
    dd_tot, 330
    debug with, 239
    default device, 236
    device type, 247
    drive precompensation, 252
    format control word, 251
    interleaving, 249
    interrupt level, 242
    IRQ vector, 242
    logical unit number, 252
    media density, 248
    missing, 237
    mode byte, 242
    pd_ctrlrid, 348
    pd_drv, 348
    pd_dtb, 330, 337
    pd_lsnoffs, 252, 333, 359
    pd_scsiopt, 330
    pd_ssize, 347–349
    polling priority, 242
    port address, 241
    RBF fields, 246–253
    reduced write current, 252
    SCF fields, 243–246
    SCSI ID, 252
    sector base offset, 250
    segment allocation size, 249
    surplus, 237
    track base offset, 250
    verification, 248
device driver, 170, 235–236, 264, 283–285, 287
    abstraction, 283
    calling from file mgr, 276
    contention, 329
    cost, 283
    dd_tot, 333
    device static storage, 373, 383
    direct command, 339
    direct command interface, 370
    DMA, 326
    drive initialization, 348
    drive select, 514
    drive table, 330, 345, 504
    error handling, 365
    error retry, 509
    format, 341
    getstat entry, 376
    getstat routine, 308, 339
    Getstat/setstat routine, 523
    glue, 373
    init entry, 293, 374
    init routine, 329, 504
    interrupt handler, 316
    interrupt service routine, 303, 344, 382, 527
    pd_lsnoffs, 359
    pd_maxcnt, 336
    putstat entry, 377
    putstat routine, 339
    read routine, 303, 332
    read sector routine, 507
    restore routine, 513
    SC 68681, 287
    sector size, 352
    sector zero, 333, 345
    sector zero cache, 345
    setstat routine, 310, 339

INDEX 533

setstat/options processing,313
signal on data ready,322
sleep routine,305
SS_Break processing,314
SS_EnRTS,313
SS_Relea,312
SS_SSig,311
stack,287, 373
static storage,291, 500, 504
storage,291
terminate routine,315, 331, 526
termination entry,375, 377
v_busy,458
v_init,348
v_ndrv,330
v_sczero,336, 346
v_wake,344
v_zerord,337, 347
varsect,341
vector table,293
write entry,376
write routine,306, 336
write sector routine,506
write track routine,524
device drivers, 25
device initialization, 161
device static storage, 291, 294, 373, 383, 389, 500, 504
device table, 170, 273
direct command, 339
direct command interface, 370
direct I/O, 200, 203, 414
direct I/O—restriction, 200
directory entry, 191
disk access speed, 198
disk allocation map, 191
disk caching, 206, 416
disk cluster, 190
disk diameter, 247

disk fragmentation, 198
disk fragmentation (repair), 199
disk ID sector, 193
disk optimization, 206
disk recovery, 207
DMA, 325–326
DMA alignment, 200
drive step rate, 505
drive table, 268, 333, 473, 504, 507
drive timeout, 97
dummy file manager, 259
dup, 170
dup character, 245
duped I/O paths, 162
dynamic allocation, 40

E
E$MemFul, 41
echo, 246
emergency disk, 418
enable interrupts, 359
end-of-file lock, 166
events, 123
exceptions, 183

F
fast RTE, 80
fast semaphore, 137
FAT, 454
F$EvTick, 99
File Allocation Table, 480
file descriptor, 192, 198, 459, 475
file expansion, 165
file fragmentation, 165, 204
file length, 164
file manager, 236, 255, 259, 423–424
 chddir,272, 454
 chgdir code,455
 close,271, 452

close code,271
create,272, 449
delete,273, 453
fmmain,424
getstat,274, 454
getstat code,456
in C,259
makdir,272, 450
open,443
open code,269
open entry,268
read,433
read code,270
readln,274, 435
seek,454
seek code,270, 455
setstat,274, 454
setstat code,457
write,273, 437
writln,274, 441
file managers, 25
file overhead, 197
file size (changing), 197
file trimming, 165
first-fit allocation, 31–32, 34
fixed partition memory, 29
fixed-length messages, 179
floating point, 144
floppy disks, 247
flow control, 288, 322
flow-control characters, 161
fmmain, 424
foreign disks, 193
format, 341, 349
format inhibit, 251, 342
format-inhibit attribute, 413
formatted output, 244
fragment list, 43, 48
fragmentation, 44

fragmentation, memory, 34
fragmented memory, 35
free memory lists, 48
function
  _ev_creat,129
  _ev_delete,127
  _ev_info,126
  _ev_link,103, 127, 132–133, 138, 140
  _ev_set,141
  _ev_signal,131, 133, 140
  _ev_unlink,103, 127, 129, 132, 138, 141
  _ev_wait,103, 131, 133
  _getsys,118
  _gs_rdy,87
  _mallocmin,41
  _mkdata_module,138
  _setsys,118
  alm_cycle,94
  alm_delete,91, 94, 103, 107
  alm_set,91
  close,174, 177
  CyclicAlarm,107
  dup,174, 177
  ebrk,41
  exit,128, 132–133, 180–182
  fopen,180
  fwrite,175
  getuid,76
  ibrk,41
  intercept,92
  kill,76
  longjmp,71
  modlink,107, 138
  munlink,138
  open,174, 177, 181
  os9exec,107, 174, 177
  rand,181

read, 175
readln, 178, 181
setjmp, 90
setuid, 76
sigmask, 64, 93
wait, 107

G
general timeout mechanism, 92
generating polynomial, 8
generating polynomial (CRC), 20
getstat, 373
ghost module, 13, 27
ghost-fragmentation, 27
glue, 409
GMX Micro-20, 325

H
home security, 141

I
I/O buffer, 57, 185, 268, 288, 306, 316, 319
I/O buffering, 203
I/O hierarchy, 169
I/O interrupts, 185
I/O polling, 163
I/O port—new, 240
I/O queue, 267, 458
identification sector, 190
init module, 46, 231–232, 236, 418
initialization table, 235, 237, 242–243
input line editing, 162
intercept routine, 66
interleaving, 198, 249
interprocess communication, 120
interrupt, 316, 318–321, 505, 521–522, 527
interrupt handler, 505

interrupt latency, 410
interrupt level, 242
interrupt mask, 183, 186
interrupt masking, 410
interrupt priority, 296
interrupt service routine, 296, 303, 319, 321, 344, 410
interrupt vector, 183, 235, 242, 296, 316, 527
interrupt-driven, 241
interrupts, 183–186, 241
I/O Globals, 379
IOMan, 169, 236, 267–268, 274, 293, 370
IRQ vector, 242

K
keyboard abort, 59, 162, 305, 323
keyboard interrupt, 59, 162, 305, 323
kill signal, 84

L
limit on system memory, 40
line editing, 161
line feed, 161
linefeed—automatic, 244
link count, 27, 192
linker, 11, 40
linking a trap handler, 149
lockout, 166
longjmp on signal, 71
lowlevel RBF I/O, 359
LSN, 333
LSN offset, 252, 358

M
M$Mem, 42
M$Stack, 43
makdir, 450

makefile, 431
masking interrupts, 186, 297
masking signals, 63, 73
math trap handler, 144–145
Math2, 146
M$Compat, 13
memory
    allocation, 23
    allocation order, 47
    allocation table, 42
    allocator, 414
    conservation, 24, 143
    defective, 5
    fragmentation, 24, 34–37
    management, 29–32, 34, 36
    optional, 26
    priority, 47
    protection, 38
    RAM, 5
    ROM, 5
    type, 46
M$Excpt, 144
M$Extens, 231–232
Micro-20, 423
Microware Basic I-Code, 11
minimum directory allocation, 204
misdirected signal, 162
moded.fields, 241
modem hangup, 59
MODE_SELECT, 352
modular design, 11, 14, 24
module
    access permissions, 12
    attribute byte, 13
    attributes, 13
    CRC, 19
    damaged (detection of), 10
    data, 12, 20
    debugging symbol table, 15
    directory, 15
    edition number, 14
    generation, 16
    ghost, 13, 27
    group, 15
    header, 6
    header for trap handler, 149
    header parity calculation, 417
    header parity word, 6
    language, 10
    length, 6
    link count, 16, 19, 27
    name, 6
    protection, 6
    recognition, 6
    reentrancy, 13
    revision number, 6, 14
    security, 12
    sticky, 13
    subroutine, 11
    sych bytes, 6
    system, 12
    trap handler, 11
    TrapLib, 11
    types, 6, 10
    usage, 15
    validation, 7
Motorola 68681, 287
M$SysGo, 231
multi-sector I/O, 198, 200, 204, 251, 253, 414
multiple disk drives, 247
multiple links, 192
multiple processors, 120
multitasking, 165, 185
_mvector, 332

N

named pipes, 179, 413

INDEX

NEC 765 floppy disk controller, 499
new I/O devices, 255
new port, 240
new system call, 99
NFM, 255
non-contiguous boot files, 416
non-destructive backspace, 243
non-maskable interrupts, 186
non-standard disk format, 247
null count, 161
null padding, 244

O

OEM global area, 291, 297
open, 443
optimum sector size, 202
optional memory, 26

P

P$SigLvl, 64
P2 module, 99, 232
padding, 244
page pause, 161, 244
parent process, 54
parity, 297
parking analogy, 123
partition, 252
partitioned disks, 358
path descriptor, 160, 171, 236, 271–272, 443, 454
path descriptor initialization, 268
path options, 160
path use count, 170
paths, 160
pause character, 162
pause option, 161
PC-DOS, 423
PC-DOS FAT, 480
PC-DOS boot sector, 278

PC-DOS directory entry, 278
PD_ALF, 244
PD_BSE, 246
PD_BSO, 243
PD_BSP, 244
PD_BUF, 268, 270–271
PD_CNT, 268, 271
PD_Cntl, 248, 251, 334
PD_COUNT, 268, 271
PD_CP, 268, 270
PD_CPR, 267
PD_CSector, 270
PD_CtrlrID, 252, 348
PD_CYL, 248, 252
PD_D2P, 246
PD_DEV, 268
PD_DNS, 248
pd_drv, 348
pd_dtb, 268, 334, 337
PD_DUP, 245
PD_DVT, 268
PD_EKO, 243
PD_FD, 268
PD_ILV, 249
PD_INT, 245
PD_LProc, 267
PD_LSNOffs, 252, 334
PD_LUN, 252
PD_MaxCnt, 251, 253, 335–336
PD_MOD, 268
pd_ndrv, 348
PD_NUL, 244
PD_OVF, 246
PD_PAG, 244
PD_BAU, 246
PD_PAR, 246
PD_Park, 252
PD_Paths, 268
PD_PAU, 244

PD_PSC, 244
PD_QUT, 245
PD_Rate, 253
PD_SAS, 204, 249
PD_ScsiOpt, 253
PD_SCT, 249, 334
PD_SID, 248, 512
PD_SOffs, 250
pd_ssize, 250, 334, 347–349
PD_T0S, 249
PD_Tab, 246
PD_Tabs, 246
PD_TFM, 249
PD_TOffs, 250
PD_TotCyls, 252
PD_Trys, 251
PD_TYP, 247
PD_USER, 268
PD_VFY, 249
PD_WPC, 252
PD_XOFF, 246
PD_XON, 246
periodic execution, 104
physical disk format, 189
physical sector number, 250
Pipeman, 255
pipes, 173
    as a buffer, 178
    between siblings, 176
    communication through, 173
    named, 179
    operation, 173
    shared, 178
    unnamed, 173
polled timeouts, 88
polling, 184, 186, 331
polling list, 331
polling priority, 242
polling table, 185, 296, 527

port address, 294
preemption, 120
preemptive scheduling, 120
process
    active queue, 116
    aging, 116–118
    D_MaxAge, 117–119, 121
    D_MinPty, 119
    descriptor, 116, 273
    high-priority, 57, 117
    interactive, 57
    low-priority, 56, 117
    memory table, 41
    preemption, 120
    priority, 56–57
    queues, 115
    scheduling algorithm, 116
    synchronization, 129
processes, 53, 115
profiler, 105
program
    alias, 54
    analysis, 110
    attr, 389
    chown, 389
    Consult, 181
    deiniz, 332
    EvCreate, 128
    EvDel, 127
    EvDir, 126
    evtick, 100
    FDList, 211
    fixmod, 389
    forcecopy, 222
    FSemTst, 137
    InitTraps, 145–146
    J, 68
    killuser, 75
    Oracle, 180

INDEX

patchmod,389
pipes between siblings,176
profiler,105
quantumcache,390
recover,208
Selector,140
Semaphore,132
send,85
sigtrap,60
Silly,150
Sqrts,175
SyncWait,130
test silly,156
testtick,102
program data area, 38
program data memory, resize, 39
psect, 17, 145, 150, 156, 261, 287
psect examples, 18

Q
queued signal count, 62, 76

R
RAM disk, 253
raw device, 193
raw I/O, 193
RBF, 255, 373
read, 433
readln, 435
real-time systems, 285
record locking, 165–166, 193
recording density, 248
reentrancy, 13, 23–24
resource allocation, 56
retry, 509
ROM, 5
ROMbug, 379
root directory, 191
rotational speed, 253

RTE—fast, 80

S
S$Deadly, 306
saving a path descriptor, 170
SBF, 256
SCF, 162, 255, 274, 373
scheduler, 231
scheduling, 117
SCSI, 251
SCSI bus reset, 326, 365
SCSI commands, 385
SCSI direct command, 370
SCSI reset, 349
sector, 189
sector base offset, 194, 250, 358
sector size, 349, 352
sector size tradeoffs, 202
sector zero, 507
sector zero cache, 345
sectors on track zero, 249
sectors per cluster, 190, 203
security, 12
segment allocation size, 249
segment list full, 203
selector, 139–140
semaphore, 129–130, 135
servers, 180
servicing signals, 65, 68
sharable, 161
shared data, 72
shared variables, 125
shell, 10, 53, 162
    initiation,231
shortening a file, 165
siblings, 54
SIGDEADLY, 89
SIGHUP, 89
SIGINT, 89, 245

signal broadcast, 414
signal intercept, 59–60
signal mask, 63
signal mask count, 64
signal on data ready, 69, 163
signal performance, 78
signal queue priming, 79
signals, 59, 162–163, 312, 315, 320, 344
signals and priority, 77
SIGQUIT, 245
software handshaking, 161
spawn, 54
special signals, 82
SS_DSize, 251, 339
SSM, 38, 45
SS_VarSect, 339
stable id, 251
stack, 373
stack space, 373, 499
standard error path, 160
standard paths, 159
startup, 231, 421
starvation, 166
static storage, 264
static storage class, 373
stepping rate, 247
sticky modules, 13
subroutine module, 143
suicide attempt, 39
super user, 389
supervisor state, 13
SVC
    Ev$Creat,128–129
    Ev$Info,126
    Ev$Pulse,141
    Ev$Read,139
    Ev$Set,139, 141
    Ev$SetR,141

Ev$Signl,124, 129, 139
Ev$Wait,124, 129, 135, 139, 141
F$Alarm,98, 101, 108
F$CCtl,414
F$Chain,55
F$ChkMem,169, 370, 382
F$CRC,7, 19
F$DatMod,20, 46, 108
F$DFork,38
F$Event,101, 136–137, 380–381
F$EvTick,102
F$Exit,55–56, 157
F$FindPD,109
F$Fork,38, 55
F$Icpt,60–62, 68, 163
F$ID,118, 430
F$IOQu,266, 430
F$IRQ,186, 296, 382, 505, 527
F$Link,18–19, 24, 38
F$Load,18, 38, 46
F$Mem,38–39
F$Move,379, 431
F$Panic,415
F$PErr,60–61
F$RTE,60, 62, 69
F$Seek,164
F$Send,60, 320, 382
F$SetCRC,7, 20
F$SigMask,60, 64–65, 414
F$Sleep,60, 65, 69, 135, 381
F$SRqCMem,38, 40, 46
F$SRqMem,38, 40, 266, 378, 429
F$SRtMem,38, 40, 266, 378, 430
F$SSvc,100, 232
F$SUser,12
F$SysDbg,265, 379, 430
F$Time,151–152, 430
F$TLink,24, 144–146, 149, 156
F$Trans,46, 415

F$UnLink,16, 19
F$UnLoad,19
F$VModul,7, 20
F$Wait,55
I$Close,159
I$Create,159
I$Dup,160, 238
I$GetStt/SS_Opt processing,308
I$GetStt,69, 163, 523
I$GetStt/SS_Opt,237
I$Open,68, 159, 268
I$Read,159, 161–162
I$ReadLn,159, 161–162, 246
I$Seek,455
I$SetStt,69, 163, 523
I$SetStt/Relea processing,312
I$SetStt/SS_DCOff,164
I$SetStt/SS_DCOn,164
I$SetStt/SS_DsRTS,164
I$SetStt/SS_EnRTS,164
I$SetStt/SS_Lock,166
I$SetStt/SS_Reset,341
I$SetStt/SS_Size,165
I$SetStt/SS_Ticks,167
I$SetStt/SS_VarSect,341
I$SetStt/SS_WTrk,341
I$SetStt/SS_Break,314
I$SetStt/SS_EnRTS,313
I$SetStt/SS_Opt,237–238, 274
I$SetStt/SS_Reset,513
I$Write,159, 161–162
I$WritLn,146, 159, 161–162
sysdbg, 257, 379
sysgo, 53, 231
system abort signal, 59
system clock, 115
system global data, 116–117
system memory, 27, 38
system path number, 160

system polling table, 296
system sector, 507
system state, 119, 183, 232
system-state alarms, 96–97
system-state process, 104

T

tab character, 246
tab processing, 246
tas instruction, 134
tcall, 147, 156
termcap, 284
threads, 93
time stamp, 345
time-dependent activities, 87
time-dependent system code, 97
time-slicing, 117
timed computation, 92
timed events, 99
timed fgets(), 89
timed functions, 90
timed sleep, 104, 415
timeout—polled, 88
timeouts, 87
timer interrupt, 185
timing problems, 163
timing-dependent problems, 165
track, 189
track base offset, 250, 358
track density, 248
track zero, 249
track zero density, 247
trap call—cost, 143
trap exception routine, 145
trap handler, 143–144, 149
trap handler binding, 144
trap handler static storage, 144, 150
trap handler, writing, 149
traplib, 11

tuning for real-time, 120

U
undelete, 207–208, 210, 414
unified file system, 159
uninitialized trap, 148
universal disk format, 194, 416

V
V_BUSY, 458, 522
v_Bytes, 339
v_ddtot, 335
V_DEV2, 323
v_init, 341, 348
V_Paths, 268
v_port, 295, 332
v_sczero, 332, 336, 346–347
v_Sectors, 339
V_Track, 515
V_TRAK, 515
v_wake, 344, 522
v_zerord, 337, 341, 347
variable sector size, 250, 416
VarSect, 340
vector, 115, 186
vector table, 183, 503
vector table conventions, 260
vectored interrupts, 184, 242
verification, 248
vertical parity, 6

W
wakeup signal, 82
WD33C93A, 328
worst-fit allocation, 31
write, 437
write track, 341
writing a trap handler, 149
writln, 441

X
XOn/XOff, 161, 246, 303, 321